ORCE 883

DAB DIGITAL RADIO

CENTREFORCE

HOUSE MUSIC ALL NIGHT LONG

BY **MATT TROLLOPE**

MT Ink

MT-Ink.co.uk

A paperback edition published by MT Ink, 2021
ISBN: 978-1-8383883-1-7

Cover artwork: Neil Shand, Shandmedia.com
Interior photography: Jaxetta.com
Interior format and design: MT Ink

A catalogue record of this book is
available from the British Library.

Anecdotes and conversations in this book have been written and paraphrased based on the interviewees recollection of relevant events in their lives.

Printed and bound in Great Britain by Bell & Bain Ltd, Glasgow

DEDICATION

To the *Centreforce* family...

CONTENTS

INTRODUCTION

When *Centreforce* joined the pirate airwaves on a Sunday in May 1989, the management, DJs or those listening couldn't have imagined the far-reaching legacy it would have.

The pioneering 24-7 house music station was a short, sharp shock to the radio system, appearing five months after *Kiss FM* closed down in pursuit of a coveted legal licence.

When *Kiss* returned triumphantly in the autumn of 1990, *Centreforce* had been and gone.

Through the recollections of the key players involved, *Centreforce: House Music All Night Long* charts the station's initial roll-out, dramatic impact...and abrupt demise just eleven months later.

The backstories of some of the *Centreforce* DJs, past and present, reflect on the years before and after the station first came on air, focusing on the '90s and Noughties as the music and the scene exploded into different genres and movements.

We also talk in-depth to the producers behind some of the era's most-loved anthems — now all integral to the *Centreforce* soundtrack. And go behind the scenes as two attempts to bring back the station, either side of the law, had varying degrees of success before impromptu *Facebook Live* streams helped make an official reincarnation of *Centreforce* an unlikely reality.

In 2018, *Centreforce* was finally able to broadcast legally in its own right, without having to watch (or reinforce) the studio door.

The original *Centreforce* DJ who stood up in court and berated a judge three decades earlier was right...house music hadn't died.

Now the *Centreforce* family were ready to reminisce and, for some, to party with their grown-up children.

As the new all-singing, all-dancing version of the station evolved, a loyal listenership tuned in on their devices and in their cars to hear DJs trusted with a 'no-playlist' policy — unheard of at any major or mainstream legal radio station.

Connected by a relentless shout-out culture, that constant feedback meant the modern-day *Centreforce* DJ, like reading a dancefloor, knew what their listeners wanted — and which 'nugget' or 'weapon' to play next.

Six and a half million unique global listeners later, the official *Centreforce* story was ready to be told.

Back from the past...and into the future.

REINVENTING CENTREFORCE WAS THE BIGGEST RISK I COULD HAVE TAKEN. RELAUNCHING MY DAD'S RADIO STATION WAS A HUGE GAMBLE.

US?

Danny Swallow, the newly-named Master Pasha, was talking to Jonny C about recent *'Centreforce' Facebook Live* streams on the fire escape at the back of his father's pub in 2017.

Dad bowled over and said, 'Right, let's go for a DAB licence.'

I honestly thought he was on a wind-up.

'Can you get on it tomorrow please, Dan?'

Me and Jonny spent the next 20 minute pissing ourselves, laughing.

But Dad seemed deadly serious.

The streams had mainly been to raise awareness for good causes or in memory of family and friends, but applying for its own licence? *Centreforce*? The old man had to be joking.

I wasn't even born when the original *Centreforce* came on air. There hadn't been a station relaunched with the reputation and legacy we had. From what I knew and had been told, we could never hide the fact that we were a pirate radio station or where we had come from.

If I took this risk, and it didn't work out, I would have to be prepared to hold up my hand and say, 'I fucked up.'

I'd been obsessed about being a DJ as a kid, but didn't want to do the graft. I was given opportunities through our family connections. I warmed up at Garage Nation at The Scala when I was 15 years old and had a residency at Club 195 in Epping when I was 16, but I'd turn up and play a mix CD, usually pre-recorded for me by Artful Dodger.

Five years later I'd enjoyed the live streams and had done a few of my own shows, trying to mask my nerves by pretending to be somebody else...usually Bubbler.

When Dad named me Master Pasha, I didn't even question it because I didn't know or imagine what would happen. I could never have dreamed of being a radio presenter because I didn't even know how to be a DJ yet.

The next day I asked a friend to make a few enquiries, purely because I still thought it was a wind-up, and if I made the call, they'd tell me to do one.

But the DAB people were interested.

Really?

Us?

IN THE CITY

The mid-to-late-'70s and early-'80s was an unrivalled era for both West Ham United and British music. A 15-year-old Andy Swallow was about to live it all...and so much more.

We saw a lot of the greats in their early days. Thin Lizzy at The Kursaal in Southend. Queen, T-Rex and David Bowie up town... Rod Stewart at Olympia in 1976, his first solo gig in the UK after leaving the Faces. Everyone in tartan, scrapping on the train on the way home.

In 1978 my mum decided we were moving to Southend to keep me out of trouble. I realised I was closer to my best mate Grant Fleming. He'd moved to Benfleet, but none of us knew where it was.

One day he turned up for a match with a railman's Inner City bag he nicked out of a signal box, so we became the Inter City Firm and started using the logo. Recollections differ, but Grant and I were the founders of the ICF. Micky 'Ramsgate' Morgan was with us too.

Southend was full of Teddy Boys and I had 'Santa Is A Punk' written on my coat, so I found it a bit tough.

I was working as a bought ledger clerk for a shipping firm in Dagenham called Haye Pollock. Then as a junior wages clerk at the original Southend airport, which was a freight airport then.

We broke into the signal box again and found dozens of British Rail train ticket pads that inspectors used to write out tickets if you were traveling on a train without one. The day of an away game, we'd get to the mainline station and ask how much for four of us to travel to Liverpool or wherever and back that day. If they said five pound, we'd write four of us all on one ticket. We got away with that for about two and a half years. There weren't the systems in place back then for them to check.

I travelled the country from the age of 14 watching West Ham — all funded by jobs in and around Upton Park market on Waghorn Road where we lived.

Six years after I was born, West Ham stars Geoff Hurst, Bobby Moore and Martin Peters were immortalised as members of England's 1966 World Cup winning team.

As a child I'd walk across Green Street and look through the gates of The Boleyn Ground. My Dad left when I was eight when my sister was born. We were quite poor, so we all did what we had to do.

At 11, 12, I did my time going to watch Orient because I wasn't allowed to go to West Ham. On Friday nights, I'd go to Charlton.

We sat on the hill at the back of our school field listening intently to all the latest music on the Top 20 show. *Tie a Yellow Ribbon Round the Ole Oak Tree* was top of the charts for weeks in 1973. You wanted to throw your radio at someone.

There was a little gang of us, 14, 15-year-olds, going to away games on Lacy's Coaches. We called ourselves the EELF (the Essex and East London Firm). We made our name in the South Bank cage at Upton Park. It was all about who could get on the coach first and take the back seat. On the drive back home we'd be fighting with other little mobs. The Magic Roundabout Crew, run by a geezer called Zebedee; the Canning Town Snipers; the Chads, the Chadwell Heath lot; and the Hornchurch Mafia, who I always wanted to join. Before the ICF, we'd called ourselves the Inter City Jibbers, because of how we blagged it on the trains.

I was at Wembley when we won the 1975 and 1980 FA Cup Finals and at Heysel in Brussels in '76 when we lost to Anderlect in the Cup Winners Cup Final, so we were brought up on that unrivalled period of success for West Ham.

I didn't miss a game — home or away until — 1982 when we played at Newcastle. It broke my heart. My mates came for me at 5am but I was so ill I just couldn't get out of bed. I wouldn't see the others for a week, not until I'd been to another game, so the last game wasn't the one I missed.

Everyone in my year was West Ham, bar three kids. Russell Woods, Leeds...Gary Woods (no relation) Man Utd...and Victor Honest, QPR. I will never forget their names. Apart from those boys, I didn't know anybody who wasn't a West Ham fan. Growing up so close to the ground, it was a given.

We were at West Brom away in December 1977 and found out the Sex Pistols were playing a secret gig that night, just down the road in Coventry at a place called Mr George's. We'd gone up in cars that day, so a load of us drove to the gig after the match. Half of the lads got in and the rest of us ended up at an XTC gig nearby. Thankfully, I'd already seen the Pistols in London earlier that year.

We followed The Stranglers, The Clash and X-Ray Spex at venues like The Marquee, Ronnie Scotts in the West End and Electric Ballroom, The Roundhouse in Camden and The Hammersmith Palais. We went anywhere anyone like that was playing. The Marquee was probably the best one, because it had smaller and bigger bands on every night.

We became mods, which was a much smaller and closer-knit thing still. The bands and music were separate from the football and they did become different environments, but there was still a fighting theme because the punks used to go at it with the teddy boys.

There was that big skinhead revival, and different strands of the skins, but it seems more people talk about the political right now. There was a lot of fighting in-house between the skins, but we were in the middle anyway because we were mods. If anybody asked me I'd say I was West Ham, which kept me out of trouble most of the time, unless we were on a train full of Millwall, and then I was Orient.

The Bridgehouse in Upminster was a big mod pub in the mid-to-late-'70s, with a huge car park for all our scooters. We'd ride into Hornchurch town centre to The Bull where all the rockers shiny motorbikes were parked. If we kicked one at the end of the line the rest fell down like dominoes.

Grant became really good mates with Paul Weller, so we did quite a few of their gigs, out on tour with them, helping with their gear, and essentially becoming road crew. We'd go up to Walton and see Paul and the boys. Sham 69 were very close by in Hersham. Not many big stars came out of that mod scene, but Weller did.

We missed out on being extras in Quadrophenia in September 1978 when they were filming in Brighton because we had Sunderland away that weekend, which was disappointing, but at least we won 2-1.

A couple of months later at the end of 1978 The Jam released their third album, *All Mod Cons*, with the sleeve notes. 'Thanks to Nick, Alan, Dave and Roadies and Southend Kids for conversation'.

And that was us. We were the Southend kids at that time, even though we didn't live there that long.

We followed the band, Secret Affair, whose debut album was called Glory Boys. Some of our lot were big fans, so it manifested into its own little West Ham firm. Dave Lawrence, Crank, Seamus, Grant, Danny Harrison, Woolwich...all started saying they were Glory Boys. Some of the guys had it tattooed inside their lips. Even though I went to the gigs with them, I was never a Glory Boy. It had taken us two years to establish the Inter City Firm, for fuck's sake. I'd had an ICF tattoo when I was 16 so I wasn't suddenly going to become a Glory Boy instead. Me and Crank nearly had a fight over it. He was saying, 'We're the Glory Boys,' and I said, 'I don't give a fuck who you are, I'm West Ham.'

It's funny looking back, because we all still went to the games together. We also became good pals with The Chords and there was all the Oi stuff, the new punk movement at the time. We went from The

Jam to Sham 69, and got to know their lead singer Jimmy Pursey.

Garry Bushell was a good friend of mine, who wrote for the *NME* and Melody Maker during that time, and radio/TV presenter Gary Crowley was with us a lot as well.

Grant had started his own band called Kidz Next Door with Jimmy Pursey's younger brother Robbie on vocals and him on bass. They got signed on a single deal to Warner Records in 1979.

Later, Grant formed a band called Agent Orange, who were similar to The Alarm and Big Country, the way they dressed and jumped about.

Then we ended up being full road crew, full nuisances, full everything for The Cockney Rejects, who did their version of *I'm Forever Blowing Bubbles.*

I was more of an organiser of the ICF than Grant and Micky, but I didn't even have a mobile phone, let alone a mobile. It wasn't as if we were the toughest, but we probably caused the most trouble. We were well run, because you can't have a ruler of an unruly mob.

Jon O'Brien: I was a goalkeeper playing for the Arsenal under-17 team. We'd played on a Saturday morning, were due to watch the first team play at Highbury, but I said I was going to West Ham instead. I was stood on the south bank wearing a single-breasted jacket, stay-press trousers and Hush Puppy shoes with my kit bag and Andy came up and said, 'What you all about?'

Because I lived one stop away from him at Leigh-on-Sea, we started getting the train together to football. On a Friday night we'd go and meet Grant Fleming, Micky Moore (who I knew as Zomo then) and the Benfleet lot, or go and watch bands. We went on tour with The Cockney Rejects in the summer of 1980.

My first England game was v Scotland at Hamden Park, when 60 or 70 of us West Ham fans jibbed in. The next month we went to the World Cup in Spain. After that I concentrated on playing football, and played semi-pro for a few years.

Andy Swallow: I lived in Southend for a year and a half, then came back to east London. I got a job as an assistant loan manager at the Provident, aged 20. A few months later in March 1981, West Ham were playing Dinamo Tbilisi in the quarter finals of the Cup Winners Cup. I got a loan from the Provident for £500, fucked off to Russia and never went back to work.

Back in London I spent a lot of time in blues clubs because they were the only places open late. I also went to a lot of reggae and lovers rock house parties.

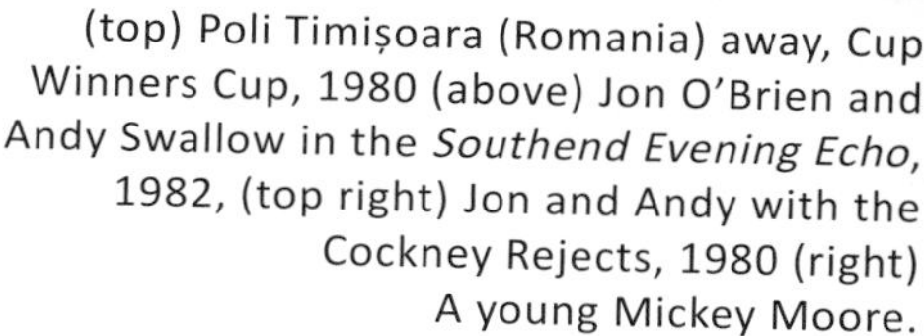

(top) Poli Timișoara (Romania) away, Cup Winners Cup, 1980 (above) Jon O'Brien and Andy Swallow in the *Southend Evening Echo*, 1982, (top right) Jon and Andy with the Cockney Rejects, 1980 (right) A young Mickey Moore.

As we entered the early-'80s, the youth were rebelling against the establishment. Riots in London, the miners' strike, mass unemployment, the Thatcher years. We came out of being punks and mods and were now casuals, travelling to all corners of Europe, with or without West Ham. I was in Spain for the '82 World Cup for most of the tournament.

When we got back, me and Jon O'Brien were asked to do a piece in the *Southend Evening Echo* about the heavy-handedness of the Spanish police, which is quite ironic, looking back now.

Ever the entrepreneur, Andy decided to set up shop, spending half of the week driving through Europe 'sourcing' the latest essential casual clobber.

I'd go on a Sunday night to Germany and Switzerland, bringing back the sports clothing that wasn't available at home in the UK. Adidas, Fila, Lacoste, we were there at the start of it all. The first casual trainers that blew up were the Adidas Trimm Trab, dark blue suede with sky blue trim. Then the Diadora Borg Elites, in kangaroo skin. Le Coq Sportif came out, but they were too Tottenham-y so we couldn't wear them.

Everyone was wearing Burberry macs, but we switched to Aquascutum. And at West Ham we also got into MacGregor. That's what happened. If everybody was wearing Pringle, we moved on to Lyle & Scott. Back then there was only red, navy and light blue Pringle jumpers. The yellow came out eventually, but with Lyle & Scott there was a lot more choice of colour-ways from the start. Later we got into Valentino and Georgio Armani.

Always trying to do something different and switching around. Constantly ducking and diving. It wasn't always an exact science, though. Our pal had some Georgio Armani car seat covers. We took a load, but they were obviously snides and we just couldn't shift them.

THE ACID HOUSE FIRM

With his notoriety in the east London area and among football terrace folklore already firmly established, Andy Swallow was about to embark on another eventful chapter in an already colourful life.

In the run-up to the start of the 1986/87 season, a dozen or so of us travelled on a Sealink Ferry to Holland with 150 Manchester United fans for exhibition matches that fell outside of the ban on English clubs playing in European club competitions at the time.

It kicked off and became a huge battle at one point.

The boat turned around and was met back in Harwich by a huge police presence. A few of our boys were jailed for piracy. It was the end of the ICF as we knew it. It was like we came off that boat and it took us out of football and into music full time.

When the Inter City Firm stuff was in full flow we hardly watched the games. I didn't realise how crap West Ham had become until the fighting stopped. I remember thinking, 'God, we're bad, aren't we?'

The music, the fashion and the rebellion of people wanting to go out and drink late all helped create what came next. We'd come through the whole soul-boy thing and then, bang, acid house. I remember someone giving me a small pill as I walked into Future in the back room at Heaven in Charing Cross at the end of 1987. That was it, I was all over it.

Ian D (Durridge) grew up in Bow and knew Andy from football.

I met Andy in 1987 when I was 15 and he was 17. Those two years at that age are huge, so I always looked up to him. Andy was always busy, getting things done and keeping us all together. We were all from different parts of east London but he managed to mould us into one group.

I started meeting Andy at warehouse parties and I knew once he got to see it, he'd want to be part of it, because that's Andy's way.

Andy Swallow: The summer of 1987 was the first year I went to Ibiza. Mates like 'Captain' Chrissy Harris had been going for a couple of years so I decided to check it out for myself.

I'll never forget the first time I walked into Pacha, how it went up in layers and tiers. It was so impressive. I hadn't seen anything like it before. Next level. There was this fella in the middle of the dancefloor, with white hair and beard, wearing denim dungarees. He must have been in his 70s. I later discovered his name was Lionel Melie and his nickname, Captain Birdseye. I couldn't imagine at the age of 60 I'd still be involved in the scene, thankfully without the white hair still...or the dungarees.

The tracks that stick out in my mind from that trip are *Driving Away From Home* by It's Immaterial and *City Lights* by William Pitt.

Since the mid-'80s on Sundays, we'd been going to a club in Hackney, right on Vicky Park, ran by the Goochi brothers, which had progressed from disco, soul and jazz-funk to some early house. Tony Wilson had his Balearic night Adrenalin there on a Friday.

At the end of '87, turn of '88 I remember all our lot off their nut on a Sunday waiting for an acid house track to come on. We were frightening the life out of the locals so we decided it was better to stick our own parties on.

Alan Bowers signed schoolboy terms with West Ham at the age of 14, but was released a few years later and quickly swapped the pitch for the terraces.

I had attitude problems and fell out of love with football. I became a member of the Under Fives, the younger faction of the ICF and, of course, knew who Andy was. We've been mates ever since. I was more interested in that side of football at that age so I ran with the boys for a few seasons. I was actually re-signed by West Ham and later released again after playing a few pre-season games in the first team,

In the summer of 1986 I was running illegal parties in Cactus Park in Tenerife with some pals, which we called Sunrise. For us, it was an obvious name to use when you're partying outside as the sun comes up.

We also did warehouse parties in the industrial area on the island. All events had an eclectic music policy, some pop, some early house. I had fake documentation made in case the authorities showed up. If they did, the Guardia Civil were easily buyable or fuckoffable.

'Here's our licence number, you'll need to check with the mayor in the morning' — who had been bought off anyway.

Back in London, Andy, Danny Harrison and I got talking about doing something together. For our first do in March 1988, I'd got an old glass factory, off Kingsland Road.

Andy Swallow: I called my half of the party 'Pasha', named after the best club I'd been to in Ibiza the summer before. People think my 'Pasha' had an 'S' so it wasn't the same as Pacha with a 'C', but the truth is I spelt it wrong. We didn't give a monkeys about copyrights back then. I'd come out of football violence and needed a new name. A rebrand they'd call it these days.

Alan Bowers: I said we could use the Sunrise name from my Tenerife parties, but I really wasn't that fussed what we called it.

Andy Swallow: We actually called it Pasha & Sunrise Presents The Lift Off, and it was a nice little line-up. Derek Boland, aka Derek B, who was about to have a Top 20 hit as a rapper with *Bad Young Brother,* topped the bill alongside Lennie Dee, who was actually Lennie De Ice, who a couple of years later produced the jungle anthem, *We Are I.E,* plus my mates Ian Durridge and Gary Dickel. Derek was out of Canning Town and someone we'd grown up with.

Alan Bowers: Then we did an underground car park at a warehouse in Docklands just off East India Dock Road. I had fake Channel 4 documentation, basically saying, 'This isn't a rave, this is a documentary about a rave.'

Andy Swallow: The car park party was part of what I began calling unofficially 'Pasha On Tour'. It was a week or so before our first legal nightclub party in May 1988 with Tony Wilson in Stepney Green at a place called Sorrells, a traditional dance round your handbag nightclub owned by a well-known East-End family, which had just been renamed Antics. A guy called Peanut helped us.

It was an all-dayer on a Sunday from 4pm which didn't even have a name or proper flyers. We just had 'Acid House Party' and the details printed on different coloured paper. We thought we'd cracked it. We went out the night before to a local warehouse party, telling everybody we were doing something the next day. As people were leaving we stood outside, saying 'Acid House Party at Antics this afternoon'.

I remember later that day, standing on the High Street outside Sorrells, as we still knew it, looking left and right, thinking nobody was coming, because everybody had been out all night. Then suddenly I saw people wearing multi-coloured outfits, smiley T-Shirts and bandanas approaching the venue, and then it just snowballed. It felt like the place filled up within ten minutes. The police came at about 10.30pm and shut us down, but it had been a decent party by that point, and it was probably the first full-blown acid house party in a nightclub in that part of east London.

We could get about four or five hundred people in Sorrells, which was a nice square room. The owners were happy for a bit of extra income on a Sunday but they were blown away by the crowd. They didn't know what had hit them. They'd gone from Sharon and Tracey in their white stilettos, boob tubes and lycra, to 'what the fuck is this?'.

You wouldn't know if it was a boy or a girl coming through the door. Big baggie T-Shirts, ripped jeans, dungarees, Converse. You look at how they portray it now, and think it wasn't really like that, and then you think back to what we wore, and you have to say, 'Yes it was.'

It's funny, we went all the way through the ICF wearing all this lovely casual clobber, amazing trainers and jumpers, and ended up wearing lilac Wallabees.

Steve Saucepan (which wasn't his real name, we just couldn't pronounce his actual surname, which was Sauzaman or something, I think...) had just done a big warehouse party in Curtain Road in Algate. We promoted our parties around events like that and among our friends and, bang, we were up and running.

With loads of companies going skint or folding and buildings becoming derelict in the late-1980s, the East End and Shoreditch area, which wasn't developed at all at that point, was perfect for the acid house scene.

It was a great time to seize opportunities. Our next event was what I would call our first proper full-scale warehouse party, for a lot more than the usual 500/600 punters. It was me, Danny Harrison and Peanut, with DJs Tony Wilson and Mervyn Victor, who also went by the name Jazzy M, and who we called Merv The Swerve.

Merv was manager at the Paul For Music record shop in Cambridge Heath Road, near the The Blind Beggar pub, and he'd tip us off the best records. We'd be stood there with our own little pile of records on the counter, everyone nodding. Most of them never sounded as good when you got them home. You'd be thinking, what the fuck are all these white labels, did they actually put the right records in my pile?

Mervyn Victor: I first met Andy when he walked in the shop one day. Paul For Music was quaint. It didn't look like we knew anything about house music, but we were really upfront, always pushing it. We opened at 9am, and when I arrived on a Saturday morning there would be a queue of people who had been out raving the night before wanting to buy the amazing music they'd heard for the first time a few hours earlier. And because we opened an hour before any other record shop in London, the distributor vans and any importers came to us first, so we got the cream of it.

The east London crowd were so faithful to the music, and I don't think there was another part of London who took it to heart so quickly and so passionately. And I had a great team there. Eamon Downes of Liquid - *Sweet Harmony* fame and DJ Billy Daniel Bunter worked for me.

Andy Swallow: For this large-scale warehouse party we found somewhere on Waterden Road, just off Bow Road, near the fly-over in Stratford, by the side of the railway. We broke in and found loads of industrial metal cages everywhere, so we turned one into a DJ booth on the night. Don't even ask me where the toilets were, because I couldn't tell you. My cousin gave us a load of Ribena, and fizzy orange drinks, which were about three years out of date and now flat. We charged £1 a carton. No alcohol. Five pounds to get in. We must have had three or four thousand people turn up.

Carl Cox had just started working for me. I first met him at a club Cass Pennant had called Breeze Inn out Sydenham way. Carl was playing that night and Cass asked me if we could get him DJ work. Carl had his own system so he became our sound and light guy and warm-up DJ, all for £300, for our next few warehouse parties. Tony Wilson wouldn't let Carl play any later because he said he couldn't mix. I only had one proper doorman, Gary Johnson, and he was taking the admission money as well. His mate, Mickey Fawcett, came down and helped out too.

About 200 West Ham turned up that night at Waterden Road, saying Danny Miller and the Arsenal lot were inside, and I said, 'I know, but I'm not letting you in. Do one.' It was a big call, but they weren't acid house people, and the Arsenal lot were. This little firm were a bit younger and it took them a bit longer to catch on to it. They were wearing acid smiley face T-Shirts and bandanas like everybody else a few weeks later.

The Old Bill turned up that night and we had an agreement that nobody else could come in and no re-entry for anybody that left. We went on until about midday the next day.

My mate's mum lived just round the corner, so I asked if we could put the takings through her front door in envelopes every hour, but he forgot to tell her. All through the night his mum could hear 'thud', 'thud', 'thud'. When she woke up she found fifteen grand in cash in her hallway, and thought somebody had put it through the wrong door, and was going to try and keep it.

Alan Bowers: Spectrum at Heaven on a Monday had become Land Of Oz. A group of us would meet there each week: like-minded people but from different walks of life. My own pals, plus Andy, Hans, the Pink Floyd sound guy, and the Dungeon boys. One night at Land Of Oz I spoke to Sex Pistols manager Malcolm McLaren and John Lydon. It was a fascinating insight into how they operated. It was also where I got to know Tony Colston-Hayter better. I liked him, he was a bright mind who was interested in what I'd done in Tenerife and said he'd like to start bringing his crowd over there for parties. I don't think he knew at the time that I'd been doing parties called Sunrise.

Carl Cox

Ian Durridge: I was always into music so, as we were drifting out of the ICF, I'd already been doing a few little DJ gigs here and there, playing soul in my local, The Lamb in Plaistow. I'd recently bought a few house records. There was a stag do at the pub so I chucked on *Big Fun* by Inner City and a couple of other bits, and the place went off — people were dancing on tables. The landlady was horrified, turned the music off and chucked me out. As I stood outside the boozer I remember thinking, this is much better than what I've been doing.

This new acid house movement was the opposite of what the football had been because this was all about love.

I think it was in the tunnels at Spectrum at Heaven where I really fell in love with house. It felt really good — the people were so welcoming.

Me and my pals started our own little do in a big old scaffolding yard off Poplar High Street. The turn-out was amazing. Everyone came from football one day and there were a load of Leeds fans partying with us, which would have been unheard of a few months earlier.

Andy Swallow: It seemed like we were doing warehouse parties every other week. There were always a few pubs midweek that catered for the same crowds. We were out five nights a week anyway, so it was easy to get the word around.

I remember for one party in Dagenham Dock. We had a load of posters made up to say it was affiliated with The Angela Rippon Trust, raising money for foreign aid, with her face all over the posters. She was a high-profile newsreader and TV personality at the time and about as wholesome as we could think. We got away with that for about two hours, before the police shut us down.

To supplement the warehouse parties we started doing more legit nights at The Camden's Head in Hackney Road.

At the start of 1989 we met Paul Dorsett and Jason Moody, who introduced us to their mate Johnny Eames and his pal Micky Carr.

They told us they were starting a Friday night at a new club at Bow Flyover called Echoes. Johnny and Paul had been doing something called Tranquility, and Tony Wilson was going to be their resident and bring in his Adrenalin thing, which he'd been doing at Guccis on a Friday. Of course, we said we'd support them.

Meanwhile, Peanut was mates with the Genesis boys.

And, by pure coincidence, I knew one of the Genesis personal security guards. When we worked it out, he was Wayne Anthony's stepdad, and he used to live across the road from my nan, so we used to play football in his garden when we were kids.

I actually got to know Wayne first at The Dungeons in Leyton, when Rob Acteson and Linden C played there, who I got to know well. I got to know all those guys well, jumping in the back of someone's car to go to a party or finding a warehouse and doing a party.

Wayne had a pal and partner in Genesis, Andy Pritchard, whose mum owned an off-licence in Hackney, so we'd go there late at night when it was closed and load up with booze, then in the morning return what wasn't used and settle up a cash payment. So Pritchard's initial involvement was as the booze man.

Genesis were using the same security firm we had at Echoes, so I was already involved with them when they started doing Sunset warehouse parties with Sunrise and Tony Colston-Hayter at Leaside Road over Christmas 1988 and NYE '88, '89 over three or four consecutive weeks.

I didn't pull any punches on a flyer invitation announcing my latest 'Pasha On Tour' party at the end of January 1989, which proclaimed...

Pasha started many months ago doing Warehouse Parties throughout the East End. People of all ages and colour dance the night away to the Acid Beat. Now the scene has taken new directions with Balearic, New Beat, Garage, Deep House and Alternative leading the way. So Pasha are back on tour, after two very successful parties under the name Genesis. Genesis took most of the credit but Pasha was the driving force behind both those venues.

Johnny Eames owned a boxing shop franchise with Title in Roman Road and also ran an electrical company.

Me and Micky Carr were three years older than Andy and had run with the Mile End. We knew Andy, but we weren't friends as such.

Just over a year before, I had 50 blokes working for me on the London Underground at Kings Cross installing better lighting for the cleaners under the wooden escalator that burned down. They were saying on the news it could be an electrical fault. I was sent there to isolate the electrics and had to step over dead bodies. The smell of burning human flesh was awful. I thought, oh my God, what have we done? But it was later proven to be started by a cigarette.

Our mates Jacko and Dougie, from south London, had the Downham Tavern. Only a couple of years before, we'd had loads of trouble with Jacko and Tiny, the big fella who was the main man at Millwall, but we'd moved on from that. Jacko and Andy still didn't get on so he wasn't exactly welcome, but we used to take a coach load down there when it was really hard to get in. Those parties gave us the idea to do something ourselves.

Andy Swallow: Jacko was the leader of Millwall youth and Dougie was one of the main boys in the Cockney Reds. When they came to Echoes we gave them a safe passage, but a lot of West Ham were complaining I was allowing them in.

The first time I went to Downham Tavern nobody said a word to me.

The next time I sensed they didn't really want me there. The third time Jacko was at the door looking like he'd seen a ghost.

'Andy, there's about 150 Millwall on their way because they know you're going to be here. Do you mind not coming in tonight?'

I laughed and said, 'Erm, no, not really,' but I did remind him that he was protected when he came to Echoes.

It was still that crossover period. A lot of our big guns were inside that night so there was a worry I could still instigate something.

It's true that acid house and ecstasy helped stop the fighting on the terraces, and in the clubs, but in those early stages we really had to manage the transition among ourselves very carefully. At the end of the day, none of us wanted it to kick off at one of our own parties. There were lots of other parties to go to, so it was okay.

Gary Dickel was also shocked that terrace rivalries had softened.

Coming from the ICF and going to parties in south London run by Millwall seemed strange at the time, but then it was a strange old scene, which took a lot of us by surprise.

My first DJ gig was in 1979 at the Queens Head in Pitfield Street in Hoxton, playing anything from Bowie to James Brown and Brass Construction. We were punks, then soul-boys, and like most of us, I met Andy at West Ham. I'd been going out up west to places like La Valbonne with The Captain for a good few years so I'd witnessed the whole thing gradually changing. Some of my mates weren't into the whole acid house thing and were drinkers, so they couldn't understand it.

Mervyn Victor: We did notice that people from east and south London were mixing better at parties, and it did seem to help stop the terrace violence, almost dead in its tracks. Suddenly people didn't want to risk getting involved in a fight after the football if it got in the way of them going out later.

In the years before, I remember black and white crowds didn't really mix together too much in east London. There was an inherent racism in the pubs and clubs at that time, from both sides, but raving changed all that. It brought people together, it was exactly like the song said...*'One Nation Under A Groove'*.

Johnny Eames: For our first party we rented a youth club in Poplar, telling the caretaker it was for someone's birthday. We called it Tranquility, had about 300 people in through to the next morning and made a few quid.

PASHA & SUNRISE
PRESENT
THE LIFT OFF
SAT 12th MARCH *BRAND NEW VENUE*
MEET AT LEASIDE ROAD
BETWEEN 12am & 6am
TOP DJ LINE UP
DEREK BOLAND GARY DICKLE
LENNIE DEE IAN.D
PLUS GUESTS

Pasha
invites you to Party 3
KEEP THIS INVITATION – ADMITS TWO PEOPLE
Saturday 28th January
TOUR SO FAR
First – Canning Town (East India Dock Road) – finished 10.00am
Second – Bow Flyover (Old Venue) – finished 12.00pm
Third – Saturday 28 January 1989 – Venue t.b.a
MEET
East India Dock Road/Bow Flyover (old venues)
Shanola/Hackney Dog Stadium/Mile End Station

LAND OF OZ
MEMBERSHIP

GENESIS
PASHA

NO SURRENDER
SATURDAY 15TH APRIL
MEETS: **WALTHAMSTOW DOGS**
BLACKHORSE STATION
GANTS HILL ODEON

INVITE ONLY
TOP DJ LINE UP
10K TURBO SOUND · LASERS
SPECIAL F/X AND DANCERS

OFFICIALS AT MEETS **11.00pm – 4.00am**
COACHES LEAVE ON THE HOUR FROM BLACKHORSE LANE STN
FROM 12 TIL 4

We heard about a new place at Bow Flyover that was struggling. The door was all wrong, with a couple of local herberts bullying people. Echoes was an amazing venue, but with a thousand capacity I thought it was too big for us.

Andy Swallow: Michael, the Turkish fella who owned Echoes, and his family had tried to open a smart disco at a time when discotheques, as such, were fading out.

They'd built a lovely main room in an old tyre warehouse. It had two floors, and the main room was just perfect for acid house or a rave. The stairs went up to the bar and a balcony, which looked down on to the main room. If you had it now, it would still be perfect.

Paul Dorsett remembers Echoes insisting on a strict dress code.

We approached Echoes because the sound system at Goochi's kept breaking down. Michael had recently opened as a smarter venue (no trainers, etc) but because of the new scene coming through, the place was empty. Benjis down the road in Bethnal Green had its own crowd and was busy.

So we struck a deal with Michael. We'll pay a small rent and keep the door, he takes the bar. 7pm - 2am, 800 capacity. We promised him his dress-code would be enforced but everyone was wearing trainers or Converse and baggy jeans.

Johnny Eames: Someone advised me to shut the doors halfway through the opening night. We had about three, four hundred in by 11.30 but didn't let anyone else in. The following week we had a queue down Bow Road by 9pm and 1200 in every week for months.

Paul Dorsett: I liked to do the early shift at Echoes. Get there about 6/6.30pm to help open up and then chip off to meet Chrissy Phillips and his lot up West at The Limelight.

We came into Echoes as Tranquility and Tony Wilson wanted to call it Adrenalin, which he brought over from Goochi's. We didn't care what it was called, we were making money and having a good time.

For me, Echoes was work. The best night out up until then had been the Downham Tavern, Bromley way. Everyone at Echoes was, 'Tony Wilson, Tony Wilson...' but I think Tony played his best stuff at the Tavern. James Mac played for us at Echoes too, he was great, so did his sister Lisa (Loud) and Andy Nicholls.

Michael was still moaning about the dress code and also the bar, because everyone was drinking soft drinks, but we believed there was still a great mark-up to be had.

Andy wanted to come in on the Fridays at Echoes, but we said, 'No, just take the Saturdays. Fine with us.' We were rammed anyway.

Andy Swallow: Pasha's House was slightly different to the Friday, musically. We were a bit more acid house and US house/garage, a bit more vocally, with Keith Mac, Ian D, Merv as residents. On Fridays they were a bit more Belgium Beat, a bit more Balearic. When Keith Mac first came to Echoes he was 16 but told us he was 18. He stood over Tony Wilson's shoulder, writing all the records down and then said to me, ' I can play that set for twenty quid.' I said, 'Go on then,' and he did. Tony would say, 'That little cunt, he's playing all my records.' But from that point Keith was in. Fridays was always really strong at Echoes, but we did well each week too, especially considering how many options there were on a Saturday.

By the age of 16, Keith Mac had managed to get a Wednesday night going at his local in Dagenham, the infamous Merry Fiddlers.

My first warehouse party was in 1987, aged 15, with Norman Jay and Judge Jules playing rare groove.

Then everything happened so fast. The music changed so quickly. The electro we'd been listening to got us into the Chicago house coming through and everybody jumped on that.

We listened to Steve Jackson on Kiss, when it was a pirate, and he started to play some house. And Dave Pearce on BBC Radio London, who was playing house on his Funk Fantasy show on a Thursday. It was the crossover point. It was like the rare groove swerved over to the right into the acid house which was running alongside it.

Suddenly everyone was going out to raves and it was like, 'Boom!' The next party I went to was house music. We were heading to a party in Algate East but that got cancelled, so we ended up at one in Farringdon, coming out at 8am, flying like kites. Late '87, early '88, aged 16.

My mate, Graham passed his driving test so we could get about now.

We started going to Future, Spectrum, Land Of Oz (when that changed) and buying records that we heard when we were out.

I left school early and did carpet-fitting for about a year, but going out every night of the week, apart from Wednesday, meant that the job was unsustainable, so I quit.

My local was The Merry Fiddlers in Dagenham. That was my little patch and where my mates from school went. That pub was like the Wild West. There were ten pool tables in there, one always covered with a large bit of ply, with a set of scales on. The Old Bill daren't go in there. It was one of those pubs where everybody stopped what they were doing to clock a stranger walking in.

There was a cheesy DJ on a Friday night, who wouldn't play any house. But everyone was going to the raves, so the locals were like, 'Get this geezer off, and get Keith on.'

The landlord reluctantly gave me a Wednesday night.

The pub's DJ set-up was belt-driven Citronic decks. You only had to look at them and the record jumped. The mixer was battered. I'd have six or seven one penny coins balanced on the cartridge needles.

But the Wednesday started getting as busy as the Friday nights.

A mate of mine mentioned the name Andy Swallow, that he was doing warehouse parties. I knew of him because of the football. Everybody did. And then they brought Andy down to the Fiddlers. He told me he was about to start Saturdays at Echoes and said I should come down with my records. I didn't even have a record box at that point, so I turned up with a rucksack of 12 inches.

My mates dropped me at Echoes on their way out somewhere else and Johnny Eames and his lot were in there.

Andy appeared and said, 'Right, I'm doing a party in Darnley Road, Hackney. You can come with me and play.' It was as blatant as that.

I didn't know where I was going, or anyone when I got there. I just got in Andy's car, but when you're a kid you don't care. You're just full of ego and you think, 'Let's do it,' because you're buzzing.

The venue was like a big hall, like one big room that might be used for reggae nights. It had a huge system and there were acid house banners all over the walls. It was rammed with lunatics. House heads. All off their rockers.

Andy took me up to the DJ stand and introduced me to Gary Dickel and DJ One, who was Ian Durridge then.

We were chatting and Ian said, 'Right, you can go on now.'

There was this big mixer and a club full of people, and I was like, 'What the fuck do all these knobs do?'

Ian was laughing as he told me what did what. I looked round and Dickel was going through all my records, asking me, 'Where did you get this? Where did you get that?'

I had the original *Your Love*, Frankie Knuckles on Trax Records, which was a B-side originally. And Dickel was saying, 'Are you going to play that?' and I said, 'Nah, I'm going to play the A-side, *Baby Wants To Ride*,' and he said, 'Can I play the other side, then?', and I said, 'Yeah, no worries,' because I just didn't know. *Your Love* just wasn't as big then.

So I realised this lot knew the records, they just didn't have them.

Andy Swallow: Echoes was thriving. The Friday boys had even opened up a cab firm, with a taxi rank outside to capitalise on how busy the club was. They also had Sparkles Car Wash.

Micky Carr was involved in the short-lived Echoes Cars.

We set up in a Portacabin on the corner next to the club. Me, Johnny Eames, Moody and Dorsett. We had a car each. Echo 1, 2, 3 and 4. I was a floor-layer by day, the only one of us who had a proper 9-5 job. It was a bit of a circus, really. Our controller Tony would randomly shut up and go over the bookies. We did get a few other drivers in, but we were all out partying so much and having fun so the cab firm flopped after a few months.

Andy Swallow: We'd still do the odd warehouse parties after Echoes, either on a Friday or a Saturday.

The Goochi brothers place was now called Twilights and had a 4am licence so I did Fridays there also, and everybody came after Echoes, which shut a couple of hours earlier.

In April 1989 we did a joint Genesis & Pasha No Surrender party at a big warehouse in Blackhorse Road.

Carl Cox was still involved, including warehouse parties in Canning Town and Walthamstow that didn't go ahead. Carl would sometimes play last set at our parties now too. He had some good sound, but his lights were quite a basic set-up. I remember a party Carl did for us in an old water tower in Lea Valley and another in Leabridge Road that I still owe him £50 for.

Alan Bowers: At this point one of the Genesis boys said to me, 'You've got to drop your Sunrise thing, Tony's doing Sunrise parties now. I said, 'Fine, but I know Tony, he's alright.'

Andy Swallow: It was only when we were looking at flyers for this book that I realised me and Alan Bowers did a 'Pasha & Sunrise' party six months before Tony's first Sunrise party. You wait until I see him. I'll be putting an invoice in, haha.

I guess you could say Genesis were the east London version of Sunrise, and it's true that there were so many decent warehouse parties in our side of town, so lots of promoters came looking.

But seriously, if you're talking about the pioneer, it was Sunrise all day long, so hats off to Tony, who was the governor when it came to putting on raves. We had an interesting start to our relationship at the

n, its just a craze, it wont last, the
ısted this as being an evil cult,
this style of music from T.V and
ıey disillusioned the media with
ıey read and heard, and so the
use music was condemned as
all evil, forcing the fun-loving
erground. With the government
ı their side warehouse after
d still is stopped wether it is
g these last two years we have
many other styles of music
aleric, New Beat, Garage and
ic, many of which have been
very talented undiscovered
l. To you we salute and to all
ple of this generation, we
ruggle will continue and the
have a good time and dance

rve the right to refuse entry

A MAY DAY
ALL DAYER
MONDAY 1ST MAY
1989
ENTERTIANMENT INCLUDES
2pm - 2am

DJ LINE UP	
ROG THE DODGE	10K SOUND
GROOVE RIDER	LASERS
LINDEN C	LIVE PA'S
DEREK BOLAND	SPECIAL F/X
IAN D	BOUNCY CASTLE
GARY DICKEL	STAGE PROPS
+ Guest DJ's	COMPETITONS
	MAGICAL LIGHT SHOW

FOR TICKET & COACH INFO AND TO RESERVE TICKETS
CONTACT: 0836336104
0836336103
01-517-9369
01-592-4131
840-7000 ask for 0717642

BASILDON FESTIVAL HALL
CRANES ROAD, BASILDON ESSEX
TEL- 0268/23456

DONATIONS TO THE CANCER RESEARCH FUND

Tickets are only available Genisis/Pasha club members with this invite

LONDONS TOP DJ'S
Genesis 89
UNIT 4
PASHA
Balera

The flyers on this page are courtesy of PhatMedia.co.uk

YOUNG MINDS
IN CONJUNCTION WITH
FOUR'S COMPANY

TRANQUILITY
EVERY WEDNESDAY
ECHOE'S EXCLUSIVE
NITE SPOT
BOW ROAD E3
ENTERTAINMENT INCLUDES:
MAGICAL LIGHT SHOW
SPECIAL F/X
LONDON'S TOP D.J'S
ROCK TO THE SOUNDS OF
ROG THE DODGE
(LAZER)
JOHN JOHN (TRAN)
INFORMATION HOTLINE 0836336104
THE STRUGGLE CONTINUES

PASHA
EVERY FRIDAY
10.00pm – 6.00am
295 VICTORIA PARK ROAD
HACKNEY
Raving
to the sounds of
DEREK BOLAND (PASHA)
LENNY DEE (UNIT 4)
GARY DICKLE (PASH/ADRENALIN)
IAN D (PASH/ADRENALIN)
KEITH MAC (PASHA)
IVAN CLARK (TWILIGHT)
DAN LEWIS (TWILIGHT)
Plus GENESIS at ECHOES every Wednesday
Bow Road, Stratford – 9 till 2

Sunset parties, but let's just say we got past any confusion and became friends. I've got a lot of time for Tony. He came along as this posh whizkid, who seemed on another level, and he was more clued-up than all of us. A clever fucker.

We took three or four coaches to the Sunrise rave at the aircraft hanger, near Brands Hatch. You can imagine the state of everyone as the coach drivers dropped us off at raves at three in the morning. I don't even know how we got home most nights. The coaches must have waited all night until 10am, 11am. Not everybody had phones back then so how we all managed to stay together, I'm not sure.

I remember some parties in a set of barns in Ockenden, one linked to another. With so much hay and everyone smoking and off their heads, it's a wonder they never went up.

The other Twilights, on the A127 near Brentwood, was like a little oasis in the middle of nowhere. And back in Hackney, The Four Aces became Labyrinth.

At three or four in the morning we'd bounce from one place to another.

It's strange, because even though the scene became huge, certainly at the start, there always seemed to be the same people knocking around at the end of each night.

A FORCE OF NATURE

Jim The Music Man learned about transmitters as part of Sunrise's initial CB Radio format.

When Bad Boy West told me in April 1988 that Sunrise was going on the FM dial, I said I'd sort the transmitter out for him, if I could do a '60s soul and ska show and he said, 'Okay, deal.' I took him up to the top of the 18 floor block on the De Beauvoir Estate, off Kingsland Road, near where I lived, and fitted a 60 foot aerial. By the time the sun came up we were off the roof and Sunrise was on air.

Martin Cee, Dave Reeves and Ruff Cut Paul were a little group of Kent boys involved in Sunrise and so I was asked to do the aerials at campsites at soul weekenders they played at for Brian Rix.

I got involved with a guy called Louie, who owned a black club called Oasis, behind The Four Aces venue in Dalston, which became Labyrinth. I played there a bit and helped him set up his own pirate station, *Lazer 94* in Edmonton. Louie paid me to look after things and gave me a Mercedes 500 Sport soft top to drive. Not even 20 yet, I tried to help whoever I could if it meant I could play music. I also used to DJ at Crowland Road in Tottenham. I'd been a carpenter and a scaffolder and also worked on the markets selling records.

Rodge The Dodge was like a brother to me growing up, always having dinner round at my parents house.

Rodge The Dodge: I'd been on *Lazer 94* for a while. I didn't think it was being run that well and I knew, between us, me and Jim, had the technical know-how to get our own station up and running. We just didn't have the cash to fund it.

I had a musician mate called George Norman, and when we went out we'd called ourselves 'The Force' for a laugh. We came out of The Astoria a few nights later, a bit worse for wear, and I looked up at the tall

Centrepoint building in front of me and said, 'That's it, I'm going to call the new radio station, *Centreforce*.

I got talking to Andy Swallow at Echoes one night and told him I played acid house and he put me on the decks there and then. Another night me and Jim told Johnny Eames about my idea for a new pirate station.

Andy Swallow: Johnny Eames called me into the office at Echoes and said, 'Have a listen to this. These two are asking if we want do a radio station.'

So I listened to the boys explain how they wanted to be the first 24-hour house music pirate.

They already had a studio location, had identified the frequency 88.3 and had a name, but they needed the initial outlay covered.

Johnny said to me: 'What do you know about radio?'

I said, 'Fuck all.'

'What do you reckon?'

'I dunno...shall we just do it?'

Johnny Eames: Rodge and Jim were already involved in the pirate radio business so they were perfect. As usual, we were just taking the opportunities put in front of us.

Rodge The Dodge: We'd broken into a squat on the ground floor of four-storey block in Kingsland Road and decided to put the transmitter on top of the 14 floor block over the road on De Beauvoir, so you could see the aerial from the studio.

A few days later we all sat round the desk in the Echoes office to firm everything up and Andy asked me how much we needed. I said a couple of grand and then, bosh, the cash was on the table.

'There you go boys, off you go.'

Andy Swallow: We went and had a look at the flat behind the fire station in Kingsland Road they had lined up and discussed the whole thing in more detail. We had an all-dayer at Echoes a couple of weeks later. We could do a test run about 6pm while the party was on, and as people were leaving tell them to tune in to 88.3.

A week before *Centreforce* muscled its way on the airwaves, Andy and 'Pasha' joined forces with Genesis for 'A May Day All-Dayer' called Free At Last from 2pm-2am at the Festival Hall...in Basildon. Featuring a line-up of Grooverider, Linden C, Derek Boland, Rog The

Dodge, Ian D (or Durridge) and Gary Dickel, the flyer explained...

A flash in the pan, it's just a craze, it won't last, the tabloid press blasted this as being an evil cult, as they tried to ban this style of music from TV and radio stations. They disillusioned the media with lies from what they read and heard, and so the birth of acid house music was condemned as being the root to all evil, forcing the fun-loving youth of today underground. With the government and the media on their side, warehouse after warehouse was and still is stopped, whether it is legal or not. During these last two years we have seen the arrival of many other styles of music including house, balearic, new beat, garage and other freestyle music, much of which has been made by young and very talented undiscovered musicians of all kinds. To you we salute and to all the fun-loving people of this generation, we promise to you the struggle will continue and the fight for the right to have a good time and dance all night long.

Ian Durridge: We'd got in with Wayne and Andy from Genesis and their Bethnal Green crowd. It was a nice little do in Basildon, but the doormen were bullies, and it kicked off towards the end of the night when they picked on the wrong people. There were 30 doormen in a line, but they were run out of the club, by what seemed like the whole of the ICF. That was it, the party was over and we needed to go. Before we left I made a speech from the stage apologising to the crowd for what they had witnessed and tried to explain that sometimes bullies just push too much.

Keith Mac: Andy mentioned to me one Saturday night that he was going to set up a radio station, and I said, 'Really?'

Andy Swallow: As usual, we seized an opportunity when it was given to us. And as usual, we weren't thinking much past the first day, the first party or the first transmission. The latest Echoes all-dayer — Sunday May 7th, 1989 — was at the forefront of our minds, and it was packed.

Jim The Music Man: We sorted out the transmitter on the top of De Beauvoir that morning and got *Centreforce* on quickly. I don't know why, but back then, I'd climb up anything and everything, no matter how high or dangerous. I don't know where it came from. I once abseiled from the top of a tower block, and swung on to the balcony of a flat three floors down to get a rig and then went back up to the top to install it.

Rodge The Dodge: On the day *Centreforce* launched, me and Jim were testing in the squat, and we'd already played a few records. The first was *Acid Thunder* by Fast Eddie, I'll never forget that, and *Big Fun* - Inner City was not long after. Andy and Keith Mac popped over in the afternoon, and Keith had a spin.

Keith Mac: I'd just done the warm-up at the all-dayer at Echoes and Andy said to me, 'C'mon, we're going down the radio.'

So me, Andy and Micky Carr went to the flat in Shoreditch where Rodge and Jim were testing the set-up. I had a quick go, played a few records.

Gary Dickel always says he played the first record, and I think he did play it when it went on officially later that night.

Technically, Rodge and Jim were really the first on there because they were doing the tests before any of us.

After the launch, Andy told me I was on the station and gave me a Tuesday afternoon show.

Gary Dickel: I remember that Bank Holiday Sunday when *Centreforce* came on well. One of the doormen from Echoes took us over to the flat where Jim The Music Man and Rodge The Dodge were setting up. There were no Technics. It was a cheap set-up, and I mean cheap.

There were some records up there, so I put a few on while Jim and Rodge were over the road putting the rig up.

Andy Swallow: We went back for the end of the all-dayer at around 10pm and made an announcement that our new radio station had just launched. By the time we got back to the studio, the pagers were going crazy. *Centreforce* was off and running. We had a great after-party in the studio that night, all the boys involved in Echoes came back for it.

Ian Durridge: I'm pretty sure I played the first record on that Sunday. I'd come home from a rave that morning and was sat with my bird at her house in East Ham and the phone went. It was Andy.

'Do you want to come and play on our new radio station?'

'Do what?'

I went down there with my records, Jim and Rodge were setting up, and I'm pretty sure I played the first record that day, *Big Fun*.

When I eventually got home, my girlfriend's aunt said, 'Ian, you sounded like you've been doing that all your life.'

I'd never done radio before but on *Centreforce* I relished being on air. In those days, you'd get so into your show, you'd just run into the next

DJ's show and play back to back with them. You couldn't do that now, it's much more scheduled.

Andy Swallow: I thought it was Keith or DJ One who played the first track. Gary Dickel was there too. If you're talking about the test transmission, that was Rodge and Jim. There's at least five people claiming to have put the first record on, and I've not thrown my hat in the ring yet.

Jim The Music Man: Sunrise management hated me for putting *Centreforce* on.

'How could you help that lot out, they're our rivals?'

I said 'What's the problem...why can't we all be mates?' I was happy to help anyone get their station up and running, because that's what I did. I was in with everybody, but I didn't know how well-known I was as Jim The Music Man, or sometimes just Music Man, when I DJd.

I had shows on both *Centreforce* and Sunrise at the same time, which Sunrise also didn't like. I was more about being able to play music on the radio, than getting paid for putting the aerials up. Sunrise was even run out of my parents house for a while. I used to say there's a few mates coming round to play music on the CB radio. They didn't understand what was going on or that their front door could have been kicked in at any moment.

Born and bred in Canning Town, Martin Cee's family had moved to the Kent area when he was four.

I can remember exactly where I was when *Centreforce* came on. A really hot day in May 1989. Loads of us hanging out in a big field in Bexley called Hall Place, listening to Sunrise 88.75, a station I had recently joined.

Somebody knocked the dial and it landed on a new station. My exact words were, 'Who the fuck are this mob?'

The DJs were mixing and saying '*Centreforce* 88.3' aggressively. It sounded like, if you didn't listen to them, they were going to come round and kick your door in.

Nobody had heard radio like this before. Raw, stripped back. All about the music and the shout-outs. The only people mixing live on *Sunrise* were Ratpack and Ellis Dee, but Sunrise was as much about soul and reggae as house and dance music. *Centreforce* gave people what they wanted, non-stop, 24-7 house music, whereas Sunrise were still playing Loose Ends or Atlantic Starr in the middle of the night.

Even though Jim and Rodge set-up Centreforce for Andy and the boys, none of us knew it was coming on. It was a surprise and blew all of us away.

Mervin Victor: It was great when Andy asked me to come on the station during the first week. There were very few DJs around the area who could actually mix, and the ones that could mostly ended up on *Centreforce*, because it was the first station that mixed house music through the night. It was such an exciting time. Echoes was *Centreforce*'s base and busy all weekend. There were loads of small illegal parties all over the place too. I must have done at least 50 or 60 of those in warehouses in Canary Wharf around '88, '89 for unscrupulous estate agents who came into Paul For Music and said, 'Wanna DJ at a party tonight?' ...at a property they had keys to. When you got there, they weren't in trousers and shoes now, they were in full rave gear, baggy jeans, Kickers, the lot.

Seeker learned to 'mix' on two belt-driven decks built into an old suitcase handed down to him by a neighbour. In May 1989, now the proud owner of not two, but three Technics 1200s, his mate Dave blagged them a trial show on *Centreforce.*

Dave had somehow managed to speak to Andy Swallow, who everybody knew of whether they were into football or not. Dave told Andy I was better than any DJ he had on the station. We were invited up to the studio at Dennison Point in Carpenter's Road.

The station had launched three days before my 20th birthday in the middle of May, and our trial show was a few weeks later. I was very shy back then, and still am really, so the whole thing was daunting. Johnny Eames, Micky Carr, Paul Dorsett and Juicy Jase (Jason Moody) were with Andy, who said, 'So, we've heard good things about you, son...'

'Yeah, I'm not too bad, but the only thing is, I can't do a show on those,' as I pointed to the Citronic decks in front of me.

I'm not sure they were even the same Citronic turntables. I don't know where I got the courage from, except there was no way I could play on those decks, especially for my big break on the radio.

So Andy said, 'You got better?'

'Yeah.'

'Well, go and get 'em, then.'

'Erm? Go and get 'em?

Now I had a real decision to make.

(right) Balfron Tower, Poplar.

BALFRON TOWER

'How often do you use them?'

'Well, all the time...they're my babies...'

'Look, anything happens, we'll replace them...the next day.'

I looked at Dave, who said, 'This is a big a call, mate...'

But I went home and got two of my turntables and walked back in. I could see the guys thinking, this boy is putting his money where his mouth is. It was a bittersweet moment, though, and a big call because pirate stations were getting raided and equipment seized all the time.

The guys gestured towards the decks and said, 'On you go...'

Then I said, 'Dave, Dave...I've got my mats, but I haven't got my plastic...'

So I got a pen and drew round the poly inner sleeves of two records, cut them out into 12 inch-sized circles and put them under each slip-mat. It gave me extra movement for scratching. I don't think Andy and the others had seen anything like that before, but they were all nodding their heads and we were asked to carry on for another couple of hours.

The pagers went nuts that first show and Andy said a load of his mates were listening in, bigging us up and asking who we were.

We'd killed it, but we needed to call ourselves something. We were driving through the City a few days later and saw a street sign saying The Corporation of London and that was it, we became The Corporation. Me, Dave, Hugs and MC Scottie.

Everything was moving so quickly.

Loads of people will remember Dave for his voice, but the beats and the mixing, that was mainly me. I always tried to be different, mixing French Kiss with the theme from Superman, stuff like that. If everyone is playing the A side, I'll play the B. Hugs, my old school pal, was probably a better DJ than Dave but he didn't buy enough records and he didn't like the spotlight on him.

After our second show, someone from another station tried to nick our transmitter. Ian Durridge suffered a nasty hand injury after one of their lot attacked him with a sword when he ran after them. We called him DJ One Thumb after that. I have very serious memories of that night. I'd gone from working as a trainee negotiator at an estate agents to thinking, what am I doing, what is happening to me?

Danielle Montana knew she had to be involved in a pirate station solely playing house music.

I met Andy at Echoes and told him I was a DJ. When I heard he was about to launch *Centreforce* and it was going to play purely house music 24-7, I knew I wanted to be involved.

I became obsessed with becoming a DJ when a friend let me play a record during his set at the Wag club when I was 16...and fell in love with house music soon after at a rave in a dingy place in London Bridge.

I was DJing at places like Crowland Road in Wood Green, but my only previous radio experience had been playing funk and soul on a female-only pirate in Harlesden called *Time FM.*

Sunrise played the odd house record, but not every station wanted to play this new daring and sometimes explicit form of music. There weren't radio edits of the acid house coming out.

When Andy asked me to be on *Centreforce*, I was stoked.

I was so nervous arriving for my first show, but everyone was so welcoming that those nerves turned into excitement. They just wanted to help me and I'd already been in lots of environments, which meant I would know if I was being received in a misogynistic way, but that was never the case at *Centreforce.* That said, as a female DJ on the station, we did get quite a few X-rated messages coming through from the listeners on the pagers.

I was living in Highbury & Islington, but moved to Plaistow, which was nearer to the various studios. My shows were usually early evening slots that crossed over with Seeker, The Corporation and Ian, DJ One, and also Keith Mac, who I remember doing a lot of shows.

Psychedelic Eric wasn't the biggest house fan, but he didn't want to miss out on being involved with *Centreforce*.

When acid house came along I hated it. I'd been into reggae music growing up in Custom House in the '70s. Then at the age of 15, 16, me and my good friend Smarty Cain started Psychedelic Soul Sound and took it all over east London. We would MC over the top of the music we played at house parties, pubs and clubs.

Smarty tragically died in a car accident when we were 18. I was lost. I didn't know what I wanted to do with music. My partner had gone.

I was living in a tower block in Plaistow and one day I heard a mate, Ian Durridge, DJ One, talking on the radio. When I realised people I knew were on *Centreforce*, I just had to try and be part of it.

I had a meeting with Andy, who my older brother knew from football, and he asked me to produce some of the advertising for the station, and to come up with some jingles. I had all the equipment to mess about with so I guess I was perfect to work on that sort of stuff back then. I'm the voice behind the booming 'CEN-TER-FORCE' jingle, which I made when I was 21 and is still one of the most used on the station.

Back in '89 I quickly became a regular MC on *Centreforce*. I'd been

Gary Dickel, pictured in *ID Magazine*, November 1989.

jumping on the mic since I was 12 so I was used to performing. I only lived half a mile from the studio at Dennison Point, so I'd pop in whenever I could and get involved. I later presented some soul shows on a Sunday as well. There were a few records like *White Horse* by Laid Back that dragged me into house music. But the whole thing was still strange to me. I went from listening to reggae to soul and then suddenly I was listening to acid house.

Ian Durridge: Eric's brother Roger was with us at West Ham, but Eric was always more into his music. He helped me do my first jingles, which was all new to me. I remember it took us several hours to do a couple of basic one-liners because we couldn't stop laughing.

When *Centreforce* came on it was set for us to move up to higher levels. Me and Andy weren't DJ's DJs. We could play music, but we weren't pros, but out of us lot, the residents and management, I think I was the most confident one back then. I probably did speak my mind on the mic a little bit too much. Advertisers would complain because I was having a pop at their promotions, but I was joking half the time.

A week after the *Centreforce* began I got a call from Andy saying the police were looking for the guy who was trying to incite a riot in Basildon, when I was actually trying to calm things down, so I decided to come up with a DJ name other than Ian Durridge of Ian D.

When I changed my name to DJ One, some people thought it was arrogant. But it was because loads of DJ names suddenly ended with B, C or D. It looked like the alphabet on the board at *Centreforce*. I said I'm going to be DJ One. I was waiting for DJ Two, but he never showed up.

Paul Dorsett: We had a nice afters thing going opposite Echoes, where the McDonalds is now, but the police shut it down on the second week. Then we did a legal *Centreforce* all-dayer at Shen-Olas, which was rammed. We sold out the second one but the police told the venue, specifically, they didn't want *Centreforce* in there because of our football links, and that it would affect the venue's licence renewal, so that was cancelled too.

Jon O'Brien: A few weeks after Andy started at Echoes, he invited me down. I walked in and saw all my old football herbert mates cuddling and kissing. It was mad, but I knew what was going on. I loved the music and that gave me the idea to do something myself.

My best mate, Russell Lee, was the resident DJ at The Pink Toothbrush for their alternative night on a Saturday, which we couldn't touch. There was a rockers night on a Friday that was quiet, so I said to the manager, 'Look, there's a big thing happening, can you give me and Russell a couple of weeks and see how we go?' Our first night was in May 1989. I booked Evil Eddie Richards, and we had about 450 people in. For the second week I approached Andy as the radio had just started, and he offered Seeker, Corporation Dave and himself as residents. That Friday we had 800 in and 200 outside. Every week after that for a year was amazing.

Seeker: Six weeks after I first played on *Centreforce*, my manager at the estate agents where I worked pulled me to one side. Somebody had grassed and told him I was working on a pirate radio station. He knew about my love of music but gave me an ultimatum.

'Wayne, we're an established company, we can't risk the station getting raided, it affecting our reputation, or you not being able to come to work. It's us or *Centreforce*.'

I told my manager that I had been given a huge opportunity and had to choose the radio.

My mum went doolally. But by now The Corporation had the residency at The Pink Toothbrush and regular spots at The Goldmine in Canvey, somewhere in Harlow and a place in Tunbridge Wells. There were so many events to play. We were scattered all over the place. The management also got me a set at the Downham Tavern.

I had an old Austin Metro, but was now able to afford a new Fiesta Ghia, which was the nuts. I popped up to see my old pals at the estate agents one day and they couldn't believe I was doing okay, despite losing my job, but I was now earning in one night what I used to in a week.

The management had to lay low and asked The Corporation to get more involved, so me and Dave took centre stage with the general running of *Centreforce*, looking after the transmitters and managing the schedule. I'd just my left my job so it was a no brainer for me. We had the music and the love of it running through our veins.

Connie Runtings was going with the flow...

Fabian and Fitzroy were mates who got me on the line-up of a Dungeons all-dayer with Paul Anderson and Grooverider. They formed The Runtings Crew and got the name from a lyric in a reggae song and a popular Jamaican phrase, 'We run tings, tings no run we.'

The three of us knocked around the same area in east London, went to the same cafes and played pool together. I was asked to join The Runtings Crew, as their first DJ. Rhythm Doctor, who had moved down from the Midlands and was living in Forest Gate, got involved, plus The

Babyface Ragga (RIP) and also Mr C, before he was part of The Shamen, and who would DJ and jump on the mic too.

When *Centreforce* came on and started to grow, Fabian introduced me to Ian Durridge who asked me up to the studio in Carpenters Road. I'll never forget walking into the studio in the front room of that flat for the first time, with the decks on milk crates, overlooking Stratford. White label records everywhere.

I was given a weekly show and The Babyface Ragga would come and play too. We were young and loved playing music. Everything grew from there. *Centreforce* and our own Runtings movement.

With *Centreforce* and Echoes working together hand-in-hand, Ibiza was calling Andy Swallow again.

This time, me and Paul Dorsett went to Ibiza specifically to set up a *Centreforce* tour later in the season. We spent two weeks telling the big clubs' owners and promoters we had a radio station in London and tried to do deals with them. I also managed to play at The Star Club and Summum, both smaller San Antonio clubs, while we were there.

Paul Dorsett: We hired a Suzuki Vitara at the airport, but didn't think we needed one with a roof on, because, surely, it wasn't going to rain. We were on our way out one night and it started to belt down, a proper storm. We got a blanket from the apartment to cover the car but it was little use. We pulled into the Space car park and saw a Vitara with a roof, so we ripped that off, and left them with the blanket. I bet the hire company were happy when we dropped our Vitara back with extras on the way home. Those were the good days: you'd come out of Pacha about 7.30am, go and get a coffee and get yourself straight and go into Space for another session.

Rodge The Dodge: Between us, me and Andy found DJs to fill the slots needed to keep *Centreforce* going 24-7, including my mate Kenny Ken. I started playing at more of Andy's events, including a massive warehouse party in Forest Gate with Paul Anderson.

Micky Carr: I'd go to Paul For Music on a Saturday with Pa Eames, a nickname given to him by Gary Dickel because he was the oldest among us, and he'd spend £200 on records. I loved the music, but I wasn't interested in buying any vinyl. I'd never even thought of being a DJ, but as management we had to jump on from time to time using Johnny's records. I'd play the graveyard shift, usually Sunday night through to

Monday morning. I mean, I was never going to tell you the weather, I'd just say, 'Ruthless Jack, 88.3' and that was about it. A geezer called Company B would come and help sometimes. Come Monday morning, when the first proper DJ came in at about 9, 10am, I'd sit and watch them start their show and say, 'Good morning, this is *Centreforce*...' blah, blah, chatting way, straight into the mix and I'd think, my God, what have I just been doing all night. I already had the nickname Jack, for some reason, and then one day at Echoes I wouldn't let someone in, and Jason called me, 'ruthless,' and then I became Ruthless Jack, when I wasn't ruthless at all.

We had so much energy, nobody wanted to go home in those days. I think Wednesday was the only night we didn't go out.

DJ One: When *Centreforce* came on, I was 26-years-old and coming out of a marriage with a couple of young children so I was in between things and places. The studio was like a refuge for me, really, and became a second home. Thankfully my kids were just old enough to listen to their daddy on the radio; I'd just left their mum so it was great to be able to tell them I loved them.

Gary Dickel: I probably spent as much time there as anybody — I just loved it. I had a regular show on a Monday and also some Saturdays. James Mac helped me to get on some mailing lists for records, and other companies would message the studio offering to send records to our DJs. I'd also spend four or five hours every Saturday at Paul For Music, City Sounds and Blackmarket. If I was still buzzing from the night before, I could buy some awful records, while many others turned into anthems. I liked my Sueno Latinos and Balearic stuff like that.

I loved Sunday mornings at *Centreforce* the most. Getting to the studio straight from a night out and helping out with the shows. They were really funny shifts. I was old compared to the others, 31, and married with kids, so my wife Lorraine, Mrs D came up to the station too. In fact, our two boys, Shaun and Lee, who were eight and six at the time, were at the studio when I.D magazine came to do a feature.

Keithy Mac used to come out with us older lot, but he was only a kid. I think the younger ones used to like hanging around with us because when we were out, we were out all night. There was always a rush to get in my car after Echoes.

Paul Dorsett: As part of the management we all had to do a night-shift from time to time to make sure there wasn't a break in the music. I'd sit with DJ One through the night, and if he went home after a long

LOADS OF DJ NAMES ENDED WITH ‘B’, ‘C’ OR ‘D’. I SAID I’M GOING TO BE DJ ONE. I WAS WAITING FOR DJ TWO, BUT HE NEVER SHOWED UP.

stint, around 7am maybe, he'd leave me some records I'd have to play for an hour or so, until the next DJ turned up. I couldn't mix, but being there through the night I picked up a few bits. They used to call me Trippy D 88.3, but that's another story.

Seeker was an absolute master. He could do three decks from a very early age. Us lot, the management, might have started *Centreforce*, but without the DJs it would have been nothing.

DJ One: People would message in and book us to DJ at their parties. I had my own show on a Monday, then Tuesday night was my nightshift with Eric and Paul Dorsett, who would sit back and keep an eye on things. I was doing an agony aunt type thing for a joke, and these guys paged in saying they were on a dodgy trip, so I said, 'Look lads, go and get yourself some orange juice...' and then I played another record. They paged back in, 'We've heard about the orange juice, that won't work' so I was back on the mic. 'Lads, you haven't let me finish, the orange juice has to be Mr Juicy, the one with the orange man on the carton. Put it on top of the telly and Mr Juicy will jump off and start dancing, and you'll be back in the room.' They messaged in all night, having a laugh with us. On the nightshift on a pirate...anything went back then.

The rest of the week I was at parties, either DJing or raving.

Andy Swallow: We very quickly exceeded the agreed limits on the four or five pager numbers we rented. Instead of costing £50 a month each in the first couple of weeks, we ran up a bill of about three grand. Worst still, the fella from the telecom company rang up to explain that the ladies who took the messages over the phone were either refusing to work or on the verge of breakdowns.

Seeker: Because I still had formal clothes from my old estate agent job and was quite well-spoken compared to the others, I was often sent suited and booted to deal with problems like the pagers. I drove down to the Southbank with a cheque for a fraction of the amount owed and managed to smooth it over. I did feel sorry for those ladies because those pagers were literally going all night - beep, beep, beep. And there were all sorts of weird messages coming through, especially in the middle of the night. We didn't always go straight home from a late-night stint on *Centreforce* because female listeners would proposition the DJs on the pagers and send their postcodes. Although, let's just say, with no camera-phones, social media or profile photos for reference, it was all a bit hit and miss.

Andy Swallow: At the start we were on and off for a while, so we moved about quite a bit, but then we had a decent seven month run at Dennison Point. Every now and then we'd get hit but we always had another transmitter fitted up on another block. We told the DJs to bring their records in sports holdalls or plastic shopping bags.

We'd moved from pagers to Nokias and big 0800 numbers. On air 24-7, we thought we were the bollocks, that we'd cracked it, but we were under surveillance all the time.

Bagz: I grew up on the Chatsworth Estate, but hung out on the nearby Carpenters Road estate. My mate Michael, aka Hermit, and a lot of our friends lived in the three tower blocks there, James Riley Point, Lund Point and Dennison Point.

We'd heard about *Centreforce* starting up, and that Andy Swallow was involved, and listened to the station. Then we noticed some comings and goings on Carpenters, and worked out that *Centreforce* was setting up a studio there. We gradually saw a lot of people we had heard of popping out on a first floor balcony, keeping a look-out, like Ian Durridge.

I used to sell Irons Kill Lions T-shirts outside Upton Park at the age of 15 for the older boys on my estate, not really realising what I was doing, and only found out later the T-Shirts came via Andy.

We were already aspiring DJs, but now we moved from being 16-year-olds playing rare groove and soul at blues parties in flats on those estates and in houses in Forest Gate...to 18-year-olds getting involved in acid house and *Centreforce*.

We were just nosey really, seeing what was going on. My good friend Michael Fraser was one of the older boys on our estate and a link between Ian and the likes of Andy and Gary Dickel, who were that bit older again. We'd started hanging out in Paul For Music. Mervyn was on *Centreforce* so we'd spend the afternoon there, maybe all day, getting tunes off him. Then Fraser said he'd been able to get Hermit a few slots on the radio. Because he still sounded like he was 10-years-old, I helped Hermit on the mic. Andy said we were good together so we kept it like that.

DJ One: When I heard a Hermit play I just knew he was class, and did what I could to help him get a regular show on the station. He and Bagz were a generation before us, but were proper people. With Danny Ward they went on to bigger things.

Andy Swallow: Micky Fraser was a useful link between us and the younger ones. He went on to become The Unknown DJ on *Centreforce*.

(top) Connie Runtings and The Babyface Ragga (above) Roger The Doctor, Keith Mac and Andy Swallow, 1990 (right) Psychedelic Eric, late-'80s.

I'm not sure if I'm meant to reveal that, but maybe it's time...

Rodge The Dodge: We were frequently moving transmitters and locations, due to DTI raids and fowl play from other stations. One time Jim had me in a lift shaft in a tower block in the early hours looking for somewhere to hide a transmitter. We were actually on top of the lift when someone got in and we went up and down the block for a few minutes. Jim said, 'Rodge, be quiet, don't laugh, they'll hear us,' but that just set me off. At least I forgot how dangerous this was.

When we were putting up aerials, Jim walked along the edge of those roofs without a care in the world.

When *Centreforce* had to move transmitters (again), Jim The Music Man identified 26-storey Balfron Tower near the Blackwall Tunnel, the work of architect Erno Goldfinger, twinned with Trellick Tower, just off Portobello Road in West London.

Me and Rodge went as far as we could in the lift and then climbed out of the fire escape on to the roof of the lift shaft, which juts out of the tower, connected to the main block by walkways...which was Goldfinger's iconic design.

Now I needed to scale the rest of the building, so I free-climbed it, using the clamps of the huge air ventilation ducts, with an aerial slung over my shoulder.

I was like a rat up a drainpipe. Rodge was petrified I'd fall and kept shouting, 'Where are you, what's happening?'

When I'd got the aerial up, for a laugh, I scaled down the other side to wind Rodge up. He was shouting out, 'Jim, where are you?' and I'd be saying, 'I'm here...' And he'd know that I sounded like I was a bit nearer but he just couldn't work out where I was.

For a few weeks we actually had the *Centreforce* transmitter and studio in Balfron Tower, and getting out as far as Tunbridge Wells and Southend on good days.

I'd open the control box — which ran the whole block, the electricity, the lights, etc — and I would connect to 'the live'. People were saying to me, are you mad? You could fry up there, but I had absolutely no fear when it came to heights or things like that.

We were only young lads at the time, so we were fascinated by it all and like, wow, wow, wow every day.

I was a resident DJ at The Dungeons in Lea Bridge Road, both inside and outside in the car park, the back area that was all fenced in, with DJs like Ellis Dee, The Swing Family and Richie Fingers. We'd start out there as the sun came up, 5/6am. One morning everything was going well, everyone buzzed up and happy, and then the police turned up and were giving it the heavy. One of the club's security, a huge black guy said to a copper in a squad car, 'I don't care if you are Old Bill, if you get out of the car, I'll batter you,' and they drove off. And I was thinking, what is going on?

I was in a club once in Victoria Park and all the windows got shot out. It seemed I was always there when the action kicked off but I always escape unharmed. I knew I couldn't ride that luck forever.

My family never knew who I was mixing with, working for or how they ran. They would have tied me up at home if they had known.

One night I was 'collected' from Sunrise studio on the De Beauvoir Estate in Hackney in a black Mercedes by the *Centreforce* management and taken to their studio in Stratford.

'Whose nicked our transmitter? You must know.'

Rival stations were stealing each other's rigs, but I didn't know who it was. I said to myself, I'll put them back on one last time, but then I'm going to leave them to it, this is not for me.

Andy Swallow: People wouldn't necessarily understand some of the grassroots stuff that happened at *Centreforce*, but to us it was normal, because we lived it as it happened.

Jim The Music Man: One night the *Centreforce* lot turned up at Balfron Tower mob-handed. There had been a power-cut and the radio went off. I was already down there, and was going up on the roof to try and sort it out.

Another time, me and Rodge were caught red-handed on the stairs as the Old Bill came up in the lift. In separate interviews at the local police station, we both said we met an old lady in Hoxton Market who needed help with her TV aerial. They obviously didn't believe us.

We appeared at Shoreditch Crown Court and told the judge we didn't know the aerial we'd been 'given' was a radio transmitter. Obviously the judge was having none of it either, gave us a fine and warned us we would be jailed if we were caught again.

A resident DJ from The Brewery Tap in Walthamstow was identified as someone who could bring something different to *Centreforce.* Roger Odle was approached at the pub one busy Friday night in the summer of 1989 by Gary Dickel.

I knew *Centreforce* as an acid station. Our little crowd didn't even call it house music at that point. So when Gary said they wanted me to come on *Centreforce* I said, 'But I don't play acid...'

'No, we want what you play in the pub...soul and dance music.'

Gary told me to wait outside the pub on Wednesday night, someone would come and pick me up. It went round the pub quickly. 'Wow, Roger's going to be on *Centreforce.*'

I'd never been on radio before. Over the past few years I'd listened to *Capital FM* mostly, guys like Froggy and Greg Edwards playing soul and jazz-funk, as well as David Rodigan's Roots Rockers show. I'd been listening to *Centreforce* on and off for a while too. Tunes like *Jibaro* by Electra, the more balearic stuff, I'd play in the pub, but they wouldn't get as big a cheer as, say, a Freddie Jackson track.

As I waited outside the pub that Wednesday night with a box of records, a car pulled up and a guy got out and ushered me into the car, where I was blindfolded, which was obviously very disconcerting at the time. The guys in the car apologised for the blindfold and I guess I felt safe because everybody at the pub knew I was going to *Centreforce.*

We drove for about 20 minutes. *Centreforce* was on the car stereo and we talked about how popular the Fridays at The Brewery Tap had become and about football and girls. I was Tottenham, they were obviously West Ham, but it was a friendly enough chat.

We arrived at our destination, which was in Bow, I later found out, then up a few floors in a lift. As we approached the flat where the studio was, the blindfold was taken off, the front door opened and we went in.

Inside? Well, if you've ever seen the TV show *People Doing Nothing,* it was exactly that set-up. The decks and mixer laid out on a door, on top of milk crates. Wires everywhere, cables going out of the windows, bed sheets instead of curtains.

I remember Seeker and Dave from The Corporation were on air, and Gary Dickel was there too. It was coming up to midnight and they asked me to go on. There were six or seven pagers on the side in front of the decks. I was told to pick them up and read the names and messages coming through if they started going off. I wondered if anybody was listening but those pagers were going 'beep, beep, beep' constantly. It was exciting because I recognised some of the names coming through because my mates were listening.

I must have done okay because I was asked back the following Wednesday and given the 10pm-midnight show weekly from then on. By the third week I wasn't blindfolded, I knew the score. I was part of *Centreforce* now, albeit my DJ name was causing some confusion.

Previously at The Brewery Tap I had just been known as Roger. I didn't play anywhere else, so if people asked who was DJing they'd say, 'It's Roger.' No need for a flyer, even. Simple.

But by the time I was on *Centreforce* I had started calling myself Rodge The Dodge. The other Rodge The Dodge, who helped set up *Centreforce*, had a show on a completely different day and time, playing acid house.

One day we were both in the studio when I was on air and the pagers were going mad, with listeners asking, 'Who is the real Rodge the Dodge?' Some listeners were joking that we should have a fight, and the other Rodge chuckled, 'He'll need a doctor by the end of it...'

Then someone paged in and said, 'Which one is Roger The Doctor?'. So I said, 'I'm the Roger The Doctor...' And that's how my name came about, live on *Centreforce*.

Like the 'Rogers', Keith Mac had a namesake too.

When James Mac came on *Centreforce*we, we stuck together. I was given the Friday afternoon show, and James would be on after me and then go and do the warm-up at Echoes.

I wasn't a good talker, though, that was a really big thing for me at my age. I was more than happy for Psychedelic Eric, Andy, Ian Durridge or Dickel to jump on the mic to do the shout-outs during any of my shows. I was much more interested in trying to mix properly, although not many people could. A set of decks, 1200s, were a lot of money. With a decent mixer, it was over a grand, even then. A lot of us learned to mix on *Centreforce.*

The first person who'd got me on a set of Technics was my mate Jason Cambridge, who went on to become the drum and bass DJ and producer, A-Sides. He went to my school, and I'd go round to Jason's house and practise on his decks when we were getting into hip-hop. I'd watch him scratching, thinking, how the fuck does he do all that?

Darren Emerson became another huge inspiration. We'd knocked about as kids in Romford town centre, hanging around the fountain, trying to breakdance. He and Ian Ellis did their parties at Twilights on the A127 near Brentwood, which were amazing. Darren became one of the leading house DJs in the UK, and globally, and had huge success as a producer with Underworld.

Kenny Ken grew up with Rodge The Dodge on the Holly Street Estate in Dalston.

We'd listen to reggae, hip-hop, R&B, disco and soul. Years later Rodge asked me on to *Centreforce*. I didn't start DJing until I was 28 years old, which was really late compared to all the other guys. I'd been a naughty boy most of my life.

One Friday night-Saturday morning I was on *Centreforce* and everyone else involved had disappeared to a rave. And I was actually locked in the flat, because that's what the management would do and that's how those *Centreforce* boys rolled back then. The next guy coming on had the key, but he hadn't appeared yet and I guessed he was probably at the rave too. I was fuming. Very fortunately, there was scaffolding on the outside of the tower block, and the studio wasn't many floors up, so I was able to climb out of the window and shimmy down the side of the building. I headed to the rave myself. When I got there the others were like, 'What are you doing here?' I told them, 'I've turned everything off.'

I remember the DTI trying to confiscate my records and I was like, 'You ain't taking my vinyl. We used to front the DTI and that's when they started bringing the police with them. But the Old Bill were usually all right. They'd say to the DTI guys, 'Just close it down and let them keep their gear.' The coppers didn't want all that paperwork.

I left *Centreforce* after a while to go on to *Dance FM*, but there was some beef between the two stations so I moved away from radio. I was getting work in clubs now, which, unlike the radio, was paid, so I was able to leave my job on the London Underground.

Andy Swallow: When we came on there was only really Sunrise as a competitor. They were playing a little bit of house, but we came on as full house. *Fantasy FM* were next and then *Dance FM*, who we had a lot of run-ins with. Dance kept trying to nick our transmitters so one day we sat on their roof waiting for them, chased them away, got their transmitter and sold it to *Fantasy*.

Bagz: One night we were on air and Hermit was in the mix...I don't know what possessed me, but I picked up a fire extinguisher and let Hermit have it, not realising the havoc it was going to cause. He jumped up and the whole set-up went on the floor. I was like, oh my God, what have I done? We were both scrambling around on the floor trying to get one deck working and on air so we could buy ourselves time to put everything else back together.

I think Hermit was more into the DJing than me; he was all about his music. I got involved in helping Michael Fraser and Tony Wellington sell tickets for *Centreforce* parties. We'd jump in a motor and go to London Bridge to meet listeners who had paged for tickets to Echoes and other events. It'd be chocablock with punters waiting in the street when we got there.

The one early *Centreforce* party that stands out for many is 'Woodstock 89 - 48 Hours Presents Music For Life 89', near Brands Hatch, held on August Bank Holiday Weekend.

Andy Swallow: Micky Woodward approached us: he had the field. It was literally 48 hours of madness with, I'm told, more than 30,000 people passing through over the two days.

DJ One: To keep that many people there for that long was fantastic. I went up there after Echoes on the Saturday night and stayed until the Monday. I played my set and then ran around causing mischief the rest of the time, riding round on a bike, wearing a poncho and a Mexican hat, none of which was mine.

Andy Swallow: Every time I went to the toilet I thought I saw monks in the bushes. Everybody said I was tripping, but it was reported later

that the festival had stopped the monks from praying, but they weren't allowed to come and talk to us about it.

Bagz: Hermit did a mammoth set that weekend. The build up and the hype in the run up to Woodstock was amazing, but then everybody disappeared. A few hours in, Hermit called me up and asked me bring him something to eat at the studio. He was saying he wanted to leave because he'd run out of record, and I said, 'You can't just turn the radio off, you nutter.'

So Hermit stayed 18 hours straight until someone else turned up. I'd like to say through love of the music, but it was actually pure fear.

Andy Swallow: Sometimes when everyone wanted to go to the same party we had extreme measures to make sure the radio kept going. We locked Roger The Doctor in the studio for two days one week-end, sticking Cornish pasties through the door for him.

Seeker: Woodstock was unbelievable. As well as playing, I helped out with ferrying the DJs from Stratford station to Brands Hatch and back again. For me, the other massive event was the huge rave, Karma Sutra, which was just amazing to be part of and play at. Paul Trouble Anderson came up to me after I played, gave me the thumbs up and said, keep doing what you're doing. Wow.

Danielle Montana: Once I was on *Centreforce* I picked up bookings quickly and got on a few promo lists too, but at my first big rave my hand was shaking so much I struggled to put the needle on the record.

I realised it was important not to play the same records on the radio all the time so I tried to be more selective, but that was difficult: I wanted everything, I was excitable. Some record shops would put tunes aside for me, others would try and sell me a load of crap. One guy, who became a good friend, would say, 'You need this one,' and pull a 12 inch from under the counter. I'd go in another shop and it would be in the normal racks. Import 12s were £12.99 even then (and I'd often buy two of each so I could do tricks) so I could spend a couple of hundred pounds on records each week in shops, including tracks I'd missed to build up my back catalogue.

Roger The Doctor: I listened to *Centreforce* as much as possible, and started incorporating the more soulful stuff I liked into my sets at the pub. I still hadn't played in a club yet so being on the station was a big jump because it brought me a lot of attention. Now when

I went into Record Village to see the guys there, Chris and Kai, other customers would ask for copies of records I was given or picked out, without listening to them. I took anything that came out on Strictly Rhythm, as standard, but I still kept buying my soul because that was my passion.

Randall, already quite a big DJ by now, came on my show and liked the soulful stuff I was playing. He introduced me to Players Kenny and we'd jump on each other's shows and became known as 3 Amigos.

We started to get bookings together, the first time I played outside of my regular pub. The guys were much more accomplished DJs and mixers than me: I was more the hype and promotion guy, really, taking bookings, etc. We had residencies in Portsmouth and Birmingham.

I got to know other *Centreforce* DJs like Danielle Montana, Keith Mac and Hermit and picked up warm-up or end of the night sets at station parties. For me, *Centreforce* was all about the service we were providing, where the parties were going to be at the weekend and getting that information out to the listeners.

***Centreforce* was about to hook up with the main clubs in Ibiza, for the station's pioneering trip to The White Isle.**

Andy Swallow: We took a nice little firm with us. Seeker and the Corporation boys dominated the line-up. Johnny Eames, Dickel and Paul Dorsett from the management came, plus Jonny O'Brien...and Tony Barker from the Tilbury Skins, who often helped out on *Centreforce* nightshifts.

I can't believe we managed to play at so many iconic clubs and so early in the scene developing there. I think we were some of the first British DJs to play at Space, which had just relaunched under new owner Pepe Rosello. I also played Es Paradis. Fuck knows how I personally got away with it. Well, I do, because mixing wasn't that technical back then. We called it slamming...slamming one track into another. As well as managing to get involved in nights at Pacha and Amnesia too, we also experienced Ku when it still didn't have a roof. At Space, it was the year before Alex P started the famous terrace there, so we were playing inside. I'd certainly gone up in the world since those smaller places on the recce trip.

Of course, we had a T-Shirt printed to commemorate the occasion.

Johnny Eames: The boys would be DJing from midnight, so we were out at whatever club they were booked in. When Space opened at 6am we'd be in there until about midday, then back to the villa and crack on (above) Andy Swallow, Jon O'Brien and Fabian Runtings, Amnesia, Ibiza, 1989 (right) Roger The Doctor on the same Ibiza trip (below) the back of that famous Ibiza tour T-Shirt.

round the pool all afternoon. Then try and get some kip before we were off out again. Each day, every day. It was madness. It would take me about four attempts to drive home from Space each day because we kept getting lost. I took my niece and her mate with us to look after our two toddlers, and they babysat for them two weeks.

We were in Es Paradis at the end of one night, and the sunken dancefloor they used for foam parties was being cleaned. My missus, off her canister, managed to switch the water back on again and got chased round the club by a cleaner with a broom. Corporation Dave took the poor geezer out.

Gary Dickel: I had been to Ibiza before a few times, but being woken up by my wife, Mrs D, at six in the morning to go to Space because it had just opened was a new one on me.

Seeker: It was our first time to Ibiza and our first boys holiday. An amazing ten days with hardly any sleep and some fantastic memories. The management had their own villa with a swimming pool, and us lot, the younger ones, were in apartments nearby.

The night we arrived, my set at Summum in San Antonio caught the attention of the manager of Amnesia, who was there socialising. He approached Andy and said, ‘Who’s the little guy, we want him to play for us?’ Micky Carr pulled me to one side and said, ‘I think you’re going to get some extra work here.’

I actually ended up with a black eye that night because we got into a scuffle with the resident DJs at Summum, who thought we were trying to take their jobs. Me, Hugs and Scottie are 5’4” guys and Corp Dave is 6’3” so he looked like our bodyguard, and certainly not the same age as us. A Scottish DJ started arguing with Dave and then a Spanish DJ clocked me from behind.

When I played at Amnesia, a couple of DJs known to the station back home, who were playing there too, actually tried to sabotage my set. They’d messed about with their monitor so when I put my headphones on it sounded like a heard of elephants stampeding towards me. There were so many speakers in Amnesia there were beats coming at me from everywhere. Thankfully, Andy had a word with them and it was sorted out. I had to brush any negativity off and try to understand that it all came with the territory. Fortunately, I always had such great back-up from the management.

It had been a whirlwind few months since first playing on *Centreforce*, and now I was playing in Amnesia. As well as a couple of sets at Es Paradis and The Star Club, I was the only *Centreforce* DJ to play at

Pacha and on the last night I got half an hour at Space. Unbelievable.

Roger The Doctor: I was lucky enough to get on the *Centreforce* trip to Ibiza. It was my first trip abroad at the age of 24. I'm not listed on the T-Shirt — I was too late for that, regrettably, but I played at Es Paradis, The Star Club and Nightlife in San Antonio, and went to all the other nights at those amazing clubs. An unforgettable experience.

Connie Runtings: Ibiza was brilliant, we were treated like family by the management and the West Ham mob. I played at Es Paradis and The Star Club, and going to Pacha, Space and Amnesia on the same trip was so memorable.

Keith Mac: I wasn't allowed to go to Ibiza. I was told I was needed to stay back and look after the station.

Paul Dorsett: All the local shops, Rumbelows, Dixons, were always paging in for shout-outs. Most of the listeners didn't have mobile phones yet, so they used the pagers and the shouts to arrange meeting up and all kinds of things. I remember one of my mates sat with me at *Centreforce*, paging in and getting a shout saying 'Has anybody seen Charlie from Tooting, I need him up the studio right now.'

Keith Mac: With Andy I was now doing The Camden's Head in Bethnal Green (Thursday, Friday, Saturday), Darnley Road on a Friday, Echoes on a Saturday, and Twilights in Hackney on a Friday and a Sunday. And whatever warehouse parties he'd would come up with. I remember one Saturday, we'd done a party on the Friday night, I'd been home about three hours, and Andy rung me.

'Keithy, I've found a warehouse in Harold Hill'.

The warehouse had big tongue and groove wooden doors. We spent all afternoon trying to cut the grooves out so the panels of the doors would pop open. You can imagine it, we'd both been out all night. Ruined. We got in there eventually, it was an old toy factory. It was about 5pm and we were going to team up with Genesis that night, but it was too late, so that place had to be held over for another time. Andy was always saying, 'I've got a warehouse'...and we'd go over there and kit it out, put up old parachutes in there for drapes.

Jon O'Brien: At The Toothbrush we had people like Cry Sciso! PAing *Afro Dizzi Act*. We booked Adamski for a one-off midweek night and he blew us out. He was touring his album at the time and his new single

N-R-G. So a couple of weeks later we heard he was at Hollywood in Romford. As he walked out of the venue towards his tour bus, we pulled him to one side and said, 'C'mon mate, sort us out another date...' And he did, a few Fridays later, which was a huge night for us.

One Pink Toothbrush flyer had 'MR' and the actual Pacha logo and cherries next to it...then 'Star Club, Ibiza' in brackets under his name, which is hilarious, looking back now.

Seeker: Just through The Pink Toothbrush I met amazing artists who had a huge influence on me at that time. Lisa M, aka Lisa Morrish, who performed her track, *Rock To The Beat,* at the club. I was well into my breakbeats so I was ecstatic when Frankie Bones from America played, but the biggest one for me was Adamski. Him playing live at the Toothbrush was huge for me.

When The Corporation were on the same bill as 3 Amigos (Randall, Players Kenny and Roger The Doctor) it was always a good laugh. Randall was just amazing. He'd smashed it at a party we'd all been at, and Andy said, 'Seek, get him on the station.' Me and Randall became great friends and a lot of people actually wanted us to get together and form a duo but we left it as we were both doing our thing.

There are also fond memories of Twilights in Hackney, adjacent to Vicky Park Road, another residency Andy set up for us.

And big up The Runtings Crew. Connie and The Babyface Ragga (RIP) were on *Centreforce*. They had those amazing parties in Cambridge Heath Road which were, especially when Rhythm Doctor came on. He always blew me away.

Danny Lines grew up in Plaistow and worked fitting car stereos when he first heard *Centreforce*.

Around '89, '90, aged 16, 17, we were always out raving. *Centreforce* was always on where I worked at A&F Security on a little plot at The Green Gate in Plaistow. It was next to The Village Inn pub where Andy used to drink, so I always looked up to that little lot. I was West Ham anyway, and a lot of the DJs and old faces from that era, came into get their stereos fitted.

When we were young we always listened to ska...The Specials, The Beat, Madness, Buster, all those people. I used to be around Jamaican sound systems, gambling houses and blues parties when I was younger, which led into reggae. Soul music and the rare groove influenced a lot of people we knew. Our mate, Psychedelic Eric had his system out of Canning Town. Then suddenly it was all about acid house, raving and being in and around *Centreforce*, meeting at Echoes and parties around

PINK TOOTHBRUSH

19-23 HIGH STREET, RAYLEIGH, ESSEX
TELEPHONE 0268 7700003

PRESENTS ON

FRIDAY 23RD FEBRUARY

LIVE ON STAGE

LISA M

"ROCK TO THE BEAT -
GOING BACK TO MY ROOTS"

+

DJ's TOUCHING DOWN
ON THE NIGHT

MR PACHA

(STAR CLUB, IBIZA — WOODSTOCK
BIOLOGY — CENTREFORCE 88.3)

D.J. SEEKER

(AMNESIA, IBIZA — WOODSTOCK
KARMA SUTRA — CENTREFORCE 88.3)

AND SUPPORTING

MATTY H + STEVE GEEZER

NO DRESS RESTRICTIONS

that area. Eric took me up to Dennison Point to hang out at the studio.

Jon O'Brien: At the start of 1990 a mate involved in the Clink Street venue, which had earned legendary status already for its RiP warehouse parties, offered it to me and Russell. It was the only the club in London at that time with a legal 6am licence, so I knew I had to get Andy involved because *Centreforce* was already huge. So Andy and Danny Harrison came in with us, and we had four or five great months down there, every Friday and Saturday, January to June, with parties like Step Back In Time. We paid rent and kept the bar. The first night was mobbo but the venue's membership policy meant we couldn't sell tickets on the door, so we sold them further down the road.

Andy Swallow: You have to laugh. Those Step Back In Time parties, well, at that point there were only a few years to step back to. It was a piss-take of the Back To The Future name Tony Colston-Hayter and Dave Roberts were using for some of their Sunrise parties. I had Seeker, Corp Dave, Hermit and Bagz as residents, and again we did really well.

Keith Mac: I'd do the West End record shop route in and around Soho. Trax on Greek Street and all those shops around Berwick Street Market. Locally, I was in JiFS (standing for Jazz, Funk and Soul) in Chadwell Heath every day. I got to know the owners, George and Lynn really well and I had a good relationship with the guys on the vans. George would overhear me asking for specific records and say, 'Get us another ten of those please.'

In early 1990 George put me forward for a residency at the Circus Tavern in Purfleet. He was friends with the Wheatley family that owned the venue and had heard they were starting a new 'rave' night. The Circus Tavern mainly did cabaret in the winter with comedians like Mike Reid, Michael Barrymore, Bernard Manning...the guys who did the big seaside summer seasons. Then in the summer the venue became Wheatley's Disco. They had booked Doug Lazy to PA *Let It Roll* the following weekend and asked if I could play too. I did it every week for the rest of 1990. It went from three or four hundred in there to at least three times that and another thousand people outside.

Long-serving Circus Tavern resident Steve Kite remembers the transformation.

Reacting to the change in the music, The Wheatleys started to book guest DJs. Tim Westwood played most weeks on a Saturday, and thankfully, we suddenly had some black faces in the crowd. Everyone at the venue began talking about this kid who was joining, who knew all the house tunes to play. And that's how I first met Keith Mac, who must have been 17 at the time. But acid house was also the downfall of Wheatley's Disco. When Keith came in on the Friday night it did really well, but *Centreforce* were doing such a good job of telling everybody where the acid house raves were, that word would suddenly get around the seven or eight hundred people inside the club and it would empty out. There would be lines of cars queuing to get out of the car park, about to set off around the M25. So the Circus Tavern changed tack again...the Chippendales era and darts.

Psychedelic Eric: We were always on the run and on the lookout for new studios. I was on with Seeker and a call came in from management saying the station was about to get raided. I was straight on the mic. 'London, we'll be off air for a bit, hold tight, we'll be back.' We had the equipment dismantled and in the back of the car in about ten minutes and were on our way to the next studio. But it wasn't suitable, so we were told, 'Don't worry, head to this place.' We got there, a little maisonette in Bow. We quickly had everything set up and the first record playing. I jumped on the mic, 'Welcome, London, we're back on air.'

We needed to get one more thing from the car so we could shut the door and crack on. When we ran downstairs a copper greeted us. 'So this is where the famous *Centreforce* is?' Thankfully he was just a bobby on the beat, who heard the music and stumbled upon us by mistake, and then walked off smiling. Me and Seeker looked at each other and knew we couldn't stay here either. So it was, 'Sorry, London, we've got to go again, we'll be back soon,' and we ripped everything out again and were off. That time we ended up in Micky Carr's house.

Micky Carr: I had just bought that house in Poplar in 1990 when they moved the studio in for a couple of weeks. I remember walking home one day and *Centreforce* was booming out of every other house window. Nobody knew the studio was a few hundred yards away in my kitchen. It was an amazing feeling.

Rodney White, who later adopted the DJ name Rooney, secured some nightshifts on the original *Centreforce* at the age of 17 when the studio was especially close to home.

My sister, Angie, was seeing a *Centreforce* DJ called Kirky D, aka Kirk Durridge, who was DJ One's brother.

They moved the studio to my sister's flat in Stockford Road in

Plaistow and I was lucky enough to do some back-to-back through-the-night shows with Scratchmaster Steve and Easy B. My mixing was very raw in those early days. I was nicknamed Hot Rod and always had a few tunes with me. During Seeker's shows I'd try and feed him records I thought he couldn't mix, but he always could.

DJ One: We were all so easy come easy go, rolling whichever way. It was like we had a power, but not the aggressive power that we had at football, a power that was positive and about love. It was nice to be appreciated for making people happy. We got a lot of stick back in the day but we were trying to turn ourselves around and show we had a different side. The radio was a chance for us to prove we weren't the psychopaths we were made out to be.

Danielle Montana: I loved those days at *Centreforce*. Taking it all in. The realisation that house music could become massive. It felt quite historic. Like we belonged to something special, a secret that nobody understood yet. A chance to educate others.

Psychedelic Eric: It was like being famous. We could walk up to any club and say, '*Centreforce* Radio' and we were in. People would be whispering, 'Look, it's the *Centreforce* boys.' It will never happen again like that: you could never recreate it. We were so lucky to experience it, all the wicked parties like Woodstock in 1989. Both amazing and sheer madness at the same time.

The convoys to the M25 raves were crazy. If you wanted to stop at a red light, then fine, but you probably wouldn't be getting to the party. On the way home, you'd see people walking back along the motorway, dripping in sweat still. Such dedication.

Andy Swallow: A lot of people mucked in when it came to running *Centreforce*. The station was all of ours, in my mind.

Martin Cee: As a station, *Centreforce* did have a fearsome reputation and I always thought it stole a bit of Sunrise's thunder, because it came on and was so dominant during the ten or eleven months it was on air. House music 24-7 was definitely a risk, but it worked and suddenly there were stations popping up where everybody mixed too. *Centreforce* had changed the dynamic of pirate radio.

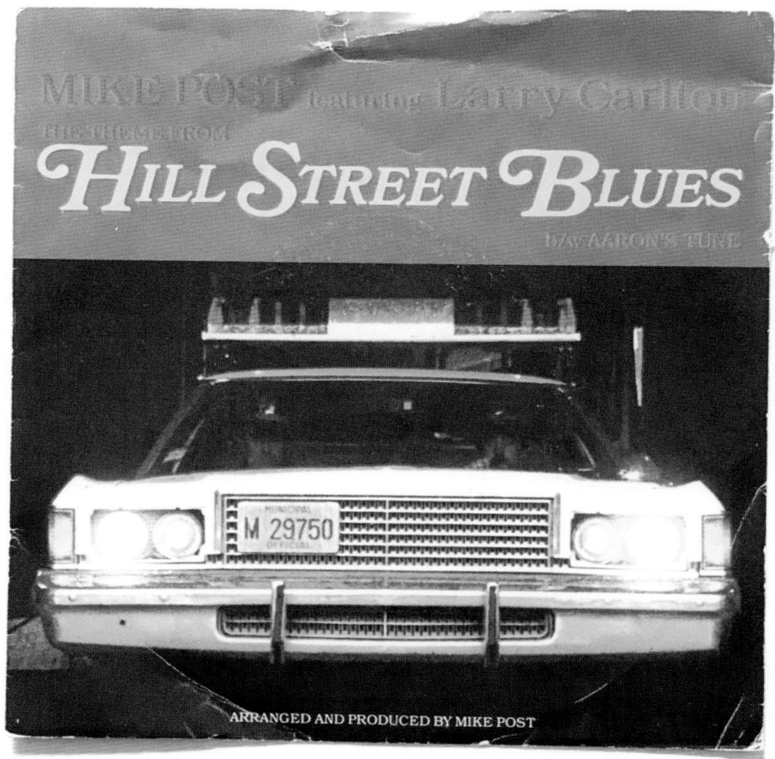

Andy Swallow received a tip-off. The DTI (Department of Trade and Industry) and the police were homing in on *Centreforce* and Echoes.

A friend phoned me in the Spring of 1990 and asked if he could come and see me. He explained he'd had a meeting with the police about his next event and one officer let slip that everything we were involved in would be raided at the weekend. I wasn't surprised. *Centreforce* had been getting so much attention. A week before *The Sun* reported that we had more listeners in London than *Radio 1*. They even claimed Richard Branson, who at that point still owned Heaven nightclub, was interested in buying *Centreforce.*

I called a meeting at Johnny Eames' house and said 'We're going to get nicked this Friday. Those who get arrested do, those who don't, don't, but let's make sure whatever happens, there are no statements.

I was due to DJ at The Pink Toothbrush that Friday so stuck to my usual routine, a Chinese first in the East End, then drove to

Rayleigh and parked up. As I walked into the venue I was grabbed from behind.

Jon O'Brien: I was at the front door of the club talking to one of the doormen as Andy walked towards the club. As he came into the foyer area I took his record bag and box off him and we said hello to each other. Then three or four fellas, one wearing dungarees, jumped him. Instinctively, I grabbed a bloke in a denim jacket with a ponytail, but he grabbed me by the throat, threw me against the wall and said, 'Fuck off, cunt, we're Old Bill.' And I said, 'Right, okay, mate,' and stepped away. I was shocked. In those days, you could half suss a copper out, but these guys looked like punters. Acid house guys.

Andy Swallow: I managed to get out of my coat and took off, and ran out of the club. I was chased down the road and up the hill, but I was unlucky. I ran into two more plod. If they hadn't have been there, I was gone. But they arrested me, and drove me back to east London.

'How's the raid on Echoes going?'

'Do what...how do you know?'

'Because your Superintendent's got a big mouth.'

It transpired the police followed me to Rayleigh because they couldn't arrest me until the Echoes raid had begun. They hit *Centreforce* at the same time, which was still at the maisonette in Stockford Road.

Mervyn Victor: I'd only just swapped my show from Saturday morning to Friday night because I wasn't doing so many pubs and working later at clubs on Fridays. I'd been to the toilet in between records and just walked past the reinforced steel front door of the flat when it came flying off its hinges, directly behind me and slammed against the wall on other side of the room. If I had been a second later the force of that door flying across the room could have killed me.

A dozen police officers piled in as I desperately tried to throw the link box out of the flat window. But it was still connected to the system and wouldn't come away from the leads, so it just bounced on the floor. As they cuffed me and my driver Nigel and read us our rights, one of the coppers actually played a seven inch vinyl copy of the theme from US police TV drama, *Hill Street Blues*, that they'd brought themselves. I was sat there in shock watching them play it. I think one of them said, 'That's all folks...this is the last record you'll ever hear on *Centreforce*.'

They confiscated my crate of records and started to dismantle the equipment, and took us to Bethnal Green police station for the night.

Bagz: Me and Hermit did the show before Merv. We hadn't left long when the raid happened, so we were very lucky.

Paul Dorsett: We had been tipped off by various sources that the club and the radio would be hit at the same time, so we were prepared.

About 10.30pm, me and Jason Moody were on the door, and suddenly 20, maybe 30 police came running towards the club, banging truncheons on their shields, and shouting, 'Ooh, ooh, ooh.' Me and Jason stepped forward, with our arms in the door, and said, 'Stop.'

And they all did.

I said, 'Sorry boys, you haven't paid your money, you not coming in.' And they just knocked us out the way. I turned to walk back in, and this acid house raver, with fluorescent face paint, long hair, baggy jeans and T-shirt, wearing Converse, said to me, 'Paul Dorsett?' And I said, 'Yes...' And then he held up his police badge and said, 'You're nicked.'

We soon realised loads of the acid heads in there were Old Bill. They held us back on the side while they searched everybody. They didn't find a lot. As our punters left the club the odd one would say in front of the police, 'Thanks, Paul, you were right, nice one...'

Micky Carr: I was out the back at Echoes when it was raided. I didn't get arrested, maybe because I was the only one without a brick mobile, and didn't look that involved in the photos outside Dennison Point.

Johnny Eames: We always assumed we were under surveillance and being photographed because Echoes was next door to a police storage pound. We'd heard whispers they were filming us from there. When the club was raided, punters we'd become friendly with over a number of week turned out to be undercover. Two police officers threw a girl up against the wall and a bag of a hundred pills, hidden by a dealer, fell out of the ceiling and landed by her feet, and they nicked her for them.

Andy Swallow: In total about 16 people were arrested, all lumped together. Charges ranged from piracy of the airwaves, racketeering, protection and drugs. Micky Woodward, because of Woodstock, got lumped in with us. Echoes owner Michael was also arrested and charged as part of the conspiracy, and the poor guy had to shut down his venue. He always 'no commented' and never gave up any names, to be fair.

Mervyn Victor: I was earning good money at the time, DJing six days a week so I could afford to take a solicitor to court with me for my individual trial.

I told the judge, 'You're trying to oppress us, like you have throughout the ages, with music in the '60s and the '70s and now you're trying to do it at the end of the '80s. House music will never die...'

The judge was trying to interrupt me, but I continued...

'It's the truth, though...I'm not sorry, I'd do it again...'

And the judge said, 'Mr Victor, I am imposing a fine of £2,000.'

I replied, 'How do you want it, cash or cheque?'

I was lucky I didn't get done for contempt of court, because I was still shouting 'house music will never die' as I was ushered off the stand.

My solicitor was able to argue that by confiscating my records they were taking my livelihood away, so it would impact me paying the fine, which I obviously negotiated down to a pound a week, once I'd left court. There was no way I was going to give them two grand in one hit.

I got my crate of records back a week and a half later.

Gary Dickel: They raided all our houses at the same time, got the missus and the kids out of bed.

I was led away from Echoes handcuffed and taken to Limehouse Police Station, but they couldn't find the key to my cuffs. So they took me to the station at Bow, and then Bethnal Green. No joy. The coppers thought it was so funny, and then they took me to Woolwich. Still no key. By the time I got to Bow fire station to have it cut off the fireman thought it was hilarious.

We went to court for weeks. They were trying to paint us out like The Krays and claimed we'd made millions. They had hours of tape of *Centreforce* but they fabricated so much. We used to wind up our mate, Slim, on air. He was a postman, but had made a point of telling us he had gone up in the world and was now delivering parcels. So we kept saying on air, 'Slim, drop us a parcel over,' and they said we were talking in code about drugs. I also got nicked during the raid at The Runtings party and my records were confiscated.

Andy Swallow: At our trial, they put us in sections and in order of importance — radio, club, owners, management and then the dealers they'd nicked at Echoes. Eight of us were at Snaresbrook court every day for two months. I began to think things were going well, then one day we were told the case was being aborted. The judge said, 'Everyone can leave apart from Andrew Swallow.' I was accused of jury nobbling. I didn't have a clue what they were talking about.

I was in Wormwood Scrubs for three days. The police visited me and I told them I knew nothing about it. All I could think was, fucking hell, I've got to get out, there's a big party at the weekend.

They came back on the Friday.

I WAS LUCKY I DIDN'T GET DONE FOR CONTEMPT OF COURT...I WAS STILL SHOUTING 'HOUSE MUSIC WILL NEVER DIE' AS THEY USHERED ME OFF THE STAND.

'Do you know John so and so?'

'No.'

'Well, he knows you.'

'He probably does.'

It turned out a kid waiting to be on the next jury recognised me from football and stupidly said to some of our jury in the canteen, 'If you're on Andy Swallow's trial and he gets off, I reckon there will be a few quid in it for you.'

When he realised the trial had collapsed he disappeared. They found him three days later and he explained himself so I was free to go. They then brought everyone back to court and said they were getting a new jury and were now adding 'half a million Es' to the charges.

However, there was a grass among us, so our barristers were able to argue that unless there was full disclosure, so revealing who the police informer was, the trial couldn't go ahead.

The police must have really cherished this informer because the trial collapsed and we walked. Charges on the other seven were dropped too.

We started up *Centreforce* again within two days, and I came back on playing the theme to *Dixon Of Dock Green*. That didn't last too long because the police and the radio authority were on us.

Centreforce was over...for now

Johnny Eames: The Old Bill had put a lot of work into the Echoes raid, but also a lot of lies as well. The case fell apart because, ultimately, the police tried to put too much on us.

After the trial we had a party at The Royal Navy in Limehouse, a pub I now owned. Our barrister came with us. I'll never forget it, he had an actual syrup under his wig. Let's just say, he got into the spirit of things. At one point, he was being pushed up and down Salmon Lane in a shopping trolley. He had the time of his life and stayed with us all night.

Seeker: After the raid, *Centreforce* was on and off for a few months. We couldn't really use the name, so we came back as *Space FM on the 100 frequency, but* it was hard going.

Mervyn Victor: I remember the week after the raid, some of our regular customers at Paul For Music had a whip-round and we bought one Technics deck, which we donated to Andy and *Centreforce* to help them get back on air.

Bagz: I helped The Babyface Ragga (Terry), a lovely guy and an amazing DJ, try and put the aerials up on the Cathall Estate in Leytonstone near where he lived, but they'd be taken down straightaway.

Andy Swallow: We also tried running Space 100 for a time from Terry's flat. But a couple of weeks later, sadly, he took his own life. It was so tragic.

Rodge The Dodge: I had already left the station to Andy when it was raided, and moved on to other things. We were cool. There was so much going on at that time. I started up *Deja Vu* with Laura and Jimmy, and we did that for about two or three years, alongside Sun City at Adrenalin Village in Battersea, a brilliant club. Then I moved away from the group and set up *Magic FM*. I later joined *Freek FM*.

Jim The Music Man: I started going out and DJing more, but kept doing my thing on Sunrise. But the scene got more aggressive when hardcore and drum and bass came in. The final straw for me was a Telepathy party in Marsh Gate Lane in Stratford I played at. After my set, a guy who had been stabbed inside staggered out into the street, fell over a barrier railing and died at my feet. Everybody was asking me who did it, and I said, 'I didn't see it happen, I haven't got a clue.'

Sunrise had just had its transmitter taken away again by the DTI. We told the police we could appeal to witnesses to come forward if we could go back on air. They approached the DTI but they weren't interested. Ellis Dee got me a regular gig DJing at the Metropolis on Cambridge Heath Road. While I was there, I developed arc-eye, an after-affect of too much welding, putting up transmitters and aerials. I went blind for five days.

Keith Mac: I had finished playing at The Camden's Head and I was heading to Echoes. I just got to the Bow Flyover, and that's when the police blocked all the roads off. It was like a military operation. I had *Centreforce* on in the car, and then I heard *Hill Street Blues* come on, and I was like, 'Who the hell is playing this?'

But that was it. Shut down. You're done. I guess, with the authorities on us so much, it was only going to last so long.

Centreforce was a group of mates, doing parties, having the best time in the world. 'Shall we do this?' 'Okay, let's do it.' We didn't even think about it. And then everybody slipped off and did their own thing for a year or so. In the early-'90s we weren't looking back, we were already moving on to the next party, looking for the next thing or coming up with new ideas.

With his time at Clink Street coming to an end, Andy was eying up another already legendary house music venue, as a decade of working in the music industry was about to unfold.

Andy Swallow: When they passed the Increased Penalties Bill in 1990, they pushed a lot of the big players in the illegal warehouse and rave scene inside nightclubs. We'd had a good run at Clink Street but it was becoming harder to manage, largely because their strict membership policy restricted walk-ups to the door. I'd heard via a south London contact that the Fitness Centre in Southwark, previously home to Shoom, was available. We launched our Step Back In Time weekly Saturday night there in July 1990 with Hermit, Bagz and Gary Dickel as residents.

Keith Mac: I hadn't seen Andy for about a year, but then I bumped into him. I'd been in the studio trying to do something but it wasn't happening.

Andy invited me down to the Fitness Centre and then I was back working with him again. Chaos and skullduggery had returned. I also had my eye on Fridays at Kings in Seven Kings, which used the same security firm as the Circus Tavern, so I asked them to put a word in. Me and Andy sorted out a deal with the venue and we started doing Fridays. We had a good run for about a year but when Hollywood down the road started Culture Shock, it was dead. I started to play there too, and also the Roma parties that Nicky Holloway did at Hollywood on Boxing Day and Bank Holidays.

Andy Swallow: I'd already asked Seeker, Corp Dave and Scottie if they fancied going into a studio and they found somewhere in Harlow. Me and Keith would do a track for one side of a release, and The Corporation boys the other. I watched our engineer for the day, Grant Bowden, laying some bits down for us. As usual I said to Keith, 'We can do this, can't we?'

Grant, who made his own music as Plastic Jam, had been working with Jimmy Low, aka MC Kann, and Dougie Bug on a track called *Made In Two Minutes*, together they became Bug Kann & The Plastic Jam. I got to know Jimmy and Dougie and invited them down to the Fitness Centre, and we became pals. Keith and I came up with the name New Class A and made a few housey-rave tracks...*Living Dream, You Can Do It* and *Feel The Rhythm* (featuring on vocals, Richelle, my wife at the time and Danny's mum). My West Ham mate, Grant Fleming, loved what we were doing and suggested me and him start our own label for those first few tracks, which we called Cupido Disque. Grant's mate Alan McGee, from Creation Records, helped us set the label up. We went to meet him in Hackney and he told us what we needed to do.

Then *Feel The Rhythm* and *Made In Two Minutes* were signed by Optimism Records in Tottenham — who originally signed Richie Malone's *Move Your Body* track. Suddenly Richelle was PAing as New Class A on the same bill as Prodigy, Shades Of Rhythm and Bug Kann & The Plastic Jam. When we signed for Optimism, it was in somebody's house, so again I looked at Keith and said, 'We can do this ourselves, can't we?'

Keith Mac: When Optimism went bust, we started pressing white labels ourselves. I'd drive round to record shops in London with boxes of vinyl, sale or return, and it did really well. Andy decided we should set up an official label. Grant Fleming came up with the name Labello Blanco, and Andy ran it out of his shed in his garden in Rainham.

Andy Swallow: We released 56 records on Labello Blanco in 12 months. I don't know of any other new label to put out one record a week in its first year.

Labello Blanco acts alongside New Class A included an album project by Nookie featuring Larry Heard, Shades Of Rhythm, Payback, another of Grant Plastic Jam's acts, plus mix CDs from Jose Padilla/Cafe Del Mar, Ray Keith and Aphrodite.

Keith Mac: Labello took off really quickly, but the label was mainly hardcore, which I didn't enjoy...or what New Class A had become. It came to a head, I could only take so much rave music, so in 1992 I left Andy again. I hooked up with Hornchurch producers Matt Clayden and Mark Williams, who were working as Acorn Arts. I started a side project with Matt...and then I bumped into Andy again. He was still running Labello from his house. Drum and bass was coming in now, but I played him the house track I made with Matt. Andy said, 'I'll put it out for you.' We came up with the idea of setting up Labello Dance, which would be much more house-orientated and much more up my street. I was the A&R Manager, and in control of it. I did another couple of tracks with Matt and then Labello Dance took off.

I had my own act and guises, Keith Mac Project and 88.3, and we went on to sign acts like 99th Floor Elevators, M&S - aka Ricky Morrison and Fran Sidoli - and Funkydory, who became Bodyrockers. And compilations, including a Clockwork Orange one for Danny and Andy, mixed by Brandon Block and Alex P.

Bagz: Andy was booked to play in the second room at AWOL (which in this case stood for A Way Of Life) at The Paradise Club in Islington, but couldn't make it one week, so asked me to cover for him. My set went well, but Andy did say I could have played a few more Labello records. I had to laugh...

Thankfully Jay Pender and Chris Leonard at World Dance, who ran AWOL, liked what I played, which was US house, early Masters At Work and Murk, all that stuff, and I became a resident. Me, Richie Fingers, Frankie Shag Bones, Tony Trax and Tommy Cockles in the garage room downstairs, and Randall, Micky Finn, Kenny Ken, Darren Jay and Gachet, playing mostly jungle upstairs, and we ran with that team for several years.

Jon O'Brien: It had gone a bit stale at The Fitness Centre, so in 1993 Andy moved to the Gass Club in Leicester Square with DJ Dominic and launched Spread Love on Sundays, a day that nobody would touch at that point. I began working on the door for Andy every week. Its strict Sunday licence back then only allowed Gass to sell alcohol until 10.30pm, but we still went through until 6am each Monday morning. Spread Love quickly became a popular meet up for footballers and the likes of Nigel Benn, Barbara Windsor and other soap stars, DJs, promoters, and bouncers, all clocking off after a busy weekend, underworld faces...and loads of ladies because in 1993 most hairdressers shut on a Monday. There was a smart dress code, no trainers allowed. Everybody made an effort. Somehow there was no agg, it policed itself. Our mate Matthew Thomas did the door, and knew a lot of people.

Andy Swallow: Again, I made Hermit and Bagz residents, alongside Darry B, Steve Flyte, and Dominic, with guests like Norris Da Boss, Matt Jam Lamont and Mikee B, later of Dreem Teem. With those guys on our line-up, as the music and their own DJ styles kept evolving, it meant our Sunday party at Gass was one of the places where UK garage was born, due to a vocal house and garage music policy that evolved into the 2-step stuff.

Keith Mac: We moved into an office in Rainham...and literally when the first Labello Dance single came out, Pete Waterman's PWL approached us, interested in signing *Made In Two Minutes* and a few other tracks, including my two new piano house tunes *De Dah Dah* and *Take Me To A Higher Life*, which were coming out on Labello Dance.

Bagz: I made a track with Grant (Plastic Jam) for Labello called *Good Feeling* by Mello Core, which sampled *Barefoot In The Head*, which was also one of the tracks PWL were first interested in. Andy spoke to Sally from A Man Called Adam to clear the sample, and not long after the guys did their deal with PWL.

Keith Mac: We relocated to beautiful offices PWL had in Borough, where their studios were also based. We were in heaven. Staff engineers on hand 24-7 for the various artists popping in and out of studios that would cost £1500 a day. I'd be out all night with my mates at a club or party in Central and then head straight to the PWL studios and make a track. You know us lot, if it's not being used, we'll use it. The problem was...our stuff was coming out too clean, not edgy enough. Then Pete cottoned on to it, and tried to charge us for the studio time.

Pete started investing in independent dance record shops and labels around the UK, like Eastern Bloc in Manchester, setting up a record label at each one. The theory being that locals always came in with cassettes of tracks they'd made, so the boys behind the ramp could sign the ones they liked, and also have their ears to the ground on any big tracks blowing up in their shops. As part of our deal I was now managing loads of different labels and we had huge club crossover hits with tracks like *I Believe* - Happy Clappers and *Waterfall* - Atlantic Ocean.

Jon O'Brien: When Andy moved into the PWL offices I worked there doing admin from Tuesday to Friday, then I'd play non-league football on a Saturday and run Sundays at Gass for him each week. Andy only came down for the big Bank Holiday Sunday parties, because each week he needed to be at the PWL offices first thing on a Monday morning. Gass ran for three years until 1996.

Andy Swallow: PWL had another proposal. They wanted us to start a subsidiary label for anything that looked like it would cross over to the charts, and then anything underground could be kept on the Labello labels, which PWL also signed. James Mac had come to me with an idea. He wanted to utilise the American connections he had through his sister Lisa (Loud) so it was perfect timing and together we set up Public Demand Records.

During the 1994/95 period, we were at PWL, we had full vocal tracks by established American garage producers like Danny Buddha Morales, Lenny Fontana and Benji Candelario. Victor Simonelli was involved too. Ramsey & Fen played for us at Gass and worked with Public Demand too, as well as M&S (Ricky Morrison and Fran Sidoli). We were also able to dip into the PWL catalogue so we re-released Mandy Smith's Balearic anthem *I Just Can't Wait* with mixes by Brandon Block and Alex P, Shades Of Rhythm and Keith.

David Morales did a mix of Robbie Craig's *Special* in 1995, while we were still at PWL, a track which was co-written by Fran, Ricky, Robbie and Richelle, who also sang backing vocals. Morales did us a great deal on that one, thanks David.

When UK garage started coming through, inspired by what we were doing on Sunday nights in Leicester Square, me, Keith and Richelle released a track called *Darkside* under the name Gass, with remixes by 2as1 (aka Hermit and Daniel Ward) and an emerging MJ Cole. We call it *Darkside* because that scene seemed so underground at that point.

In 1995, five years after his passing, we released *The Babyface Ragga Tribute Volume 1 EP*, in memory of our old mate and colleague Terry White, with jungle tracks from Bizzy Bee, Dr S Gachet and D Cruze.

Keith Mac: There were only a handful of Public Demand releases while we were with Pete Waterman, but then Warner bought out PWL and it wasn't going to work with us so we left and took Public Demand with us. We were able to get the leading UK garage DJs we knew to remix all the American vocal house stuff signed by James Mac, who moved on to do his own thing in artist management and now looks after Carl Craig and Steve Aoki.

Andy Swallow: After we left PWL, we regrouped for seven to eight months. Then Jimmy Low signed the Artful Dodger and Craig David track *Re-Rewind* in 1999...and the rest is history.

Public Demand became a leading UK garage label and *Re-Rewind (The Crowd Say Bo Selecta)* THE signature anthem of the scene, reaching No 2 in the UK charts. Artful Dodger's album *It's All About The Stragglers* featured singles *Moving Too Fast* (No 2) *Please Don't Turn Me On* (No 4*) and Woman Trouble* (No 6). There were also Top 20 hits for Tru Faith & Dub Conspiracy's *Freak Like Me* and *Booo!* by Sticky featuring Ms Dynamite, a successful DJ EZ had Pure Garage mix CD series, and releases from Dreem Teem and Wideboys.

Andy Swallow: I rarely say I was the first at anything, but If you talk to anybody who likes garage and you mention Public Demand, they know her. If you mention Labello Blanco to anyone who is into hardcore and drum and bass, they know her. Like acid house, we were always representing our area at the forefront of those scenes. We had more than 300 releases on Labello Blanco/Dance and Public Demand, so we were prolific in the music industry. The Labello labels, Public Demand and Public Demand USA became bigger than anything we'd done up until that point.

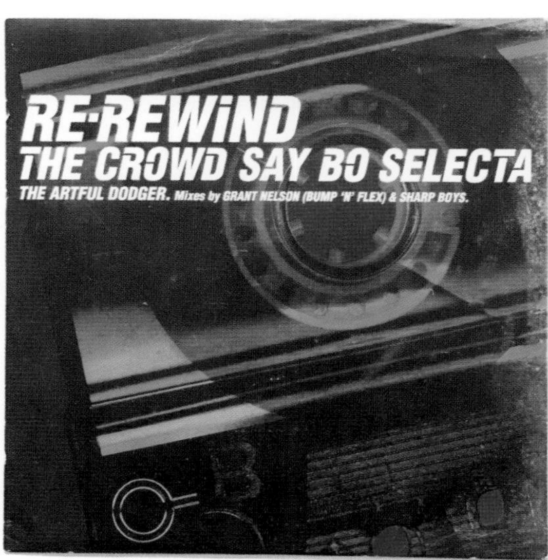

I LOOKED AT KEITH AND SAID, 'WE CAN DO THIS OURSELVES, CAN'T WE?'

EAST LONDON
BACKSTORIES

A nine-year-old Roger The Doctor was inspired by soul and reggae parties in his local park in Islington in the mid-'70s before his family relocated to Leyton.

My sisters sneaking me into early evening Saturdays parties in the community hall at Arundle Square was my first experience of hearing music outside of my house. I'll never forget the DJ, Leon Patterson. He was 19, maybe 20, and the coolest dude I knew. The first man I'd seen with ripped jeans.

Now I'd spend my pocket money on Trojan seven inches from a stall on Chapel Street Market, and still went back when we moved to Letyon when I started secondary school. I also went to Record Village in Walthamstow. I was told, 'Buy the album instead of the 12 inch, you'll get more tracks.'

By the age of 14, I was going to soul parties at The Thatched House in Leytonstone with mates from school. We'd get a drink and kept our heads down and our arses quiet. Then The Lion & Key in Leyton, where a big guy called Sylvester was the resident, playing tracks like *Dancing In Outer Space* by Atmosfear and Brit-funk bands like Light Of The World. An amazing era for music, I just loved it

My mate Lee Andrews kept saying to me, 'We've got to go to The Brewery Tap in Walthamstow.' Eventually we went one Friday, and I can honestly say that night was when my life changed. An Italian DJ called Mickey Fish played all the records I'd been buying, and there were more girls than we could ever imagine. My mind was blown. I'd play for regulars at their house parties after the pub. Still just playing on one deck at that point, but always a chatterbox on the mic. As I was putting the next record on I'd say, 'Happy Birthday to so and so...' 'Have you lot seen what so and so is wearing tonight...' or 'Look at Billy in the corner with Julie...' That was my apprenticeship for presenting.

When I was 16 Mickey Fish asked me to play at The Brewery Tap. They had a Citronic DJ console with a pitch slider and that was the first time

I played on two decks, stuff like *Turn The Music Up* by The Players Association, the faster side of dance and disco.

I also started venturing out to bigger parties, getting introduced to Chris Hill and Froggy. Going to Ilford Town Hall on Monday nights and The Goldmine in Canvey Island.

The Brewery Tap were persuaded by the guys at the Early Rise Disco Centre in Walthamstow to install Technics decks. My mixing was like windows smashing at first. I'd start at 8pm with a bit of Luther Vandross or some Teddy Pendergrass, then some of the better New Romantic stuff, or some credible pop, *Love & Pride* by King or *Living In A Box*, then the more uptempo disco and soul at the end of the night.

I wasn't even thinking about playing in a club yet. My day job was at Mister Byrite in Leyton: the pub was packed every Friday, I played for the pub football team, it was the mid-to-late-'80s, and life was good.

A group of girls at The Brewery Tap we called The Lovies were regulars. One of them, Sharon Dolphin told me about *Centreforce*. 'You've got to listen to the station, Roger, they play acid music.' I was like, 'What you talking about acid music for, I don't listen to that...'

But I did start listening to *Centreforce* and realised some of the house music on there had already been crossing over into my DJ sets. I was still surprised a few months later when I was approached by the station, and even more shocked when I was driven blindfolded to the studio.

Veteran east London DJ Peter P cut his teeth in 1981, aged 15 playing northern soul at The Regency Suite in Chadwell Heath, a venue with soul mafia stars Froggy and Pete Tong among its residents.

I grew up in Plaistow, then Manor Park and Ilford. My parents had managed the PLA (Port of London Authority) Recreation Ground in Ilford from the early-'70s. My mum also worked for Polydor, at the old Britannia building in Ilford, as a supervisor at the pressing plant so we always had plenty of vinyl at home, signed by bands like The Who and Status Quo when they visited Polydor.

I got into the mod thing, went to see The Jam, and that turned me on to Motown and then northern soul. My mate was doing a mod night with Eddie Pillar at The Regency Suite and was late one night so I stepped in. We were given every Tuesday and had it packed, loads of scooters outside, playing all the mod stuff and a bit of R & B. We eventually took the Friday off Eddie. It was my first residency and I'd always had one 40 years later...until Covid came along.

Other mod and northern soul pubs I played included the The Mild May in Dalston on Sundays, the Westmoreland Arms in Marylebone, aka

The Soul Shack. A lot of disco crossed over to northern soul, and I was much more into my '70s and '80s northern soul. I wasn't a connoisseur, like a lot of them, stuck in the '60s stuff still. The music changed again and we started to play stuff like Grandmaster Flash, *The Message* and *White Lines*, Paul Hardcastle and D-Train.

Before Paul For Music, Mervyn Victor had worked in his local video shop/gambling den, east London pubs and clubs playing upfront soul and jazz-funk, and on a record stall in Petticoat Lane run by Izzy, later the owner of Uptown Records in Soho.

In the early-'80s, my pal, Ray Lotharo, aka Jazzy Ray, and I DJd with the likes of Trevor Nelson, Karl Brown and Lee from Bomb The Bass. We didn't aspire to be that successful because we played urban music. We didn't see it as getting any bigger than playing in our local area.

After first playing under my actual name, I was Mr Magic until about 1982, then in 1983 Barry T, from Solar Radio, gave me the name Jazzy M, because of Ray's DJ name. We went to every record shop we could, up west on a Saturday morning and Camden in the afternoon, trying to get rare groove records each other didn't have.

Ray and I worked and played for a guy called Butchie Holland, who leased old pubs from breweries and then sold them on for a quick profit two months later. The following week that pub would have died a death, because we'd taken all our punters to Butchie's next place.

Then we started playing at Goochi's in Victoria Park around 1983.

We did The Camden's Head in Hackney in the mid-'80s, one of the first so-called fun pubs, with video screens everywhere. We had to play Tears For Fears and U2 videos, which we hated, otherwise it was soul, jazz-funk, a little bit of hip-hop and early electro. I think a lot of us played in pubs like that to earn money to buy the records we really wanted to play, so we could try and get gigs at better parties and clubs.

It was before the days of decent record boxes being readily available, so we'd used milk crates, cutting out the plastic middle of the crate which held the bottles with a hot knife, then sanding it down the best we could, and lining it with cardboard so the covers of the records wouldn't get scratched. Years later when I split up with a girlfriend she threw two of my crates from a fourth floor window. They both landed upright and were so well designed only two records broke.

In 1986 when I'd started working at Paul For Music, we had seen a lot of what I would describe 'electro-ish-house' coming through. It was a bit slower than the four floor 120 stuff.

When I became the first DJ and resident at The Labyrinth in Dalston

Lane for Joe Wieczorek, I opened my sets with *Al Naafiysh (The Soul)* by Hashim, which was originally out in 1983 but in the late-'80s was still a big crossover track.

Froggy had been a huge influence throughout that tim. He'd always been famous — as far I was concerned, like a God — and I was lucky to get to know him through Steve Walsh. I always missed his Saturday night Froggy Mix show on Capital because of work, so I bought a box, which you'd call a boom box today, that had a timer so you could record the radio whenever you wanted on cassette. When I finished work, a group of us would head to the bagel shop in Brick Lane and go back to mine and listen to Froggy's show.

Paul For Music wasn't the coolest looking shop, but it was one of the busiest. Each week a bike would come to collect a bag of records for Pete Tong when he moved to *Radio 1* in the early-'90s.

With *Centreforce* now, I worked on other pirates like Passion and Deja Vu as Jazzy M. I've had grief from the other Jazzy M (Michael Schiniou) over the years, but he did admit he was Jazzy Michaels up to a certain point, before he came on *LWR ((London Weekend Radio)* in the mid-'80s. One night we both turned up to an Energy event because 'Jazzy M' was on the bill. He'd played the last party but I knew I'd been booked for this one. In the early-'90s I went back to using the name Mervyn Victor when I started playing at clubs like Legends in the West End, because I wasn't playing the stuff I played as Jazzy M in the early-'80s. Gary Dickel first suggested we both have a play-off for the name and I also put up a challenge to Michael on *Facebook*. The offer still stands. Back then, I guess we didn't know our DJ names would matter 10, 20, 30 years later.

By the age of 17 (in 1986), Seeker had played a house party in Brixton and at the Notting Hill Carnival. Having moved from West Hampstead to East Ham three years earlier, the reserved turntable enthusiast had experienced all four corners of London already.

Moving from North West London to Upton Park and changing schools was a massive ask at the time for an Arsenal fan who mostly kept himself to himself. But I made some great new friends at St John's School, which was actually in the grounds of the Boleyn Ground.

A kid a few years older than me I used to body-pop and breakdance with, aka DJ Fingers, had just got a set of Technics. He gave me this old suitcase set-up he had, which had two belt-driven decks in it, and speakers in the lid that you could remove and place either side of the case. I lugged it up to the Jubilee Line at West Hampstead and struggled with it all the way back from Upton Park station to my house. Back in my room, I quickly realised there was zero chance of being able to scratch on these turntables like my old neighbour so I began doctoring the controller knob which acted as the mixer/volume part. By attaching a screw and tape around the knob, I was able to flick the screw and that would give me a fader effect. Nobody told me what to do; it was just a problem that I needed to solve. I practised through the night with the volume down, just by hearing the 'ttcchh, ttcchh, ttcchh' of the records. I learned to beat match by spinning the centre of the record, either speeding it up or slowing it down.

I was able to mix the records quite well this way, soul and early hip-hop, and then started going to breakdance battles with mates from school like Simon Hugs, who did actually have a resemblance to Huggy Bear out of *Starsky & Hutch*, which everyone called Car Keys & Clutch.

I hated the thought of talking on the mic, but I knew if you put me on a set of decks in front of a million people I'd smash it, no problem. I taught myself to breakdance and do robotics, and I didn't mind doing that in public either. I started to develop good contacts, because everybody knew I was all about becoming a DJ, but those contacts were only really like-minded school friends.

Some pals involved in Gremlins, a sound system playing soul and reggae, asked me to play at a house party in Brixton. I said I'd need to check with my parents, and I remember a guy from Gremlin actually came round to our house to discuss it with them. The party was great and I did a few more local gigs with them. I'd just passed my driving test after only 11 lessons, and a few days later Gremlins asked me to play for them at Notting Hill Carnival. It was all too much.

One of the Gremlins guys was seeing a woman who had a big house in Notting Hill, just off Ladbroke Grove, so we set up our decks on the balcony on the third floor, and put up six towers of speakers in the street, each with six bass bins and mids and some tops just for the treble. The bass bins were so big you could climb in them. They sounded phenomenal — it could probably be heard it in Shepherd's Bush.

I remember someone dropped a Technics 1200 in a flight case down a couple of flights of stairs and it still worked. So robust, that deck.

We weren't far from LWR's system but our street was packed. I was doing my thing, playing soul grooves and hip-hop and had it rocking. Then two DMC mixing champions, DJ Swift and DJ Pogo, aka Adam Montout, who is from Plaistow, arrived. I was so into turntablism, I didn't mind when I had to come off. I didn't even look at the street going off. I was so in awe, I just watched the decks the whole time.

Towards the end of the night it started to get a bit lively, and trouble started at the end of our street. Me and Hugs, the smallest and youngest guys, were thrown up on top of the speaker stacks to dismantle everything. Bottles of beer and Thunderbird were flying through the air, but we managed to get everything out of there okay.

Carnival was a massive experience for me. Gremlins went on to bigger things, and their sound system was used a few years later by Run DMC on one of their tours.

Connie Runtings: I grew up in a musical family in the Hackney side of Stoke Newington. My dad used to DJ in our church hall and my brother made sound-systems. A friend and I went to Tottenham Court Road and bought a pair of 1200s and a MK60 mixer when we were just 15. Some nights we'd be at one of our houses mixing the same two records for hours to get it as tight as possible.

I first got a flavour for house one night at Dingwalls at Camden Lock where Adeva performed *Respect* live. I thought, I like this music. The next party was a Genesis rave in Tottenham Hale, aged 19. I can get into to this, I thought. By the time I started buying house music at Record Village and City Sounds in Holborn I was able to mix really well.

Peter P: For soul music and more underground music, east London was hugely influential in the '80s. Not so much Essex, for me, because when you got any further out than Romford, things started to get much more commercial.

The bigger clubs in the area, like Ilford Palais, were also very commercial. It was the smaller clubs and the wine bars that were the backbone of the decent underground music being played.

One of my first early soul residencies around 1984 was a club called Simpsons in Forest Gate, which is now a MacDonalds, with Bobby & Steve, long before they started Garage City. We hired decks in one big unit from Newham Audio and carried the kit in the venue together.

The rare-groove and jazz-funk wine-bar circuit in Ilford and the surrounding area was heaving in the mid-to-late-'80s, and I lived and played most of it. Left out of Stop Outs, where I was later resident for three years, a hundred yards on the same side of the road was RBs and across the road and right was Pickwicks, next to Chinatown restaurant. In Cranbrook Road you had Corks at the town centre end near Valentines Park, Harts at the Gants Hill end, which became Hobnobs, and then Sidneys, and The Villa which later became Faces, and Flamingo Road opposite that.

There was Oscars at the old Green Gate in Newbury Park, and in Forest Gate, The Princess pub had an upstairs club, while The Lotus Club opposite was for an older crowd. Whispers, a basement wine bar in

Manor Park, was where I first met Danny Lines.

So many great little nights, and later everybody would end up either in Ilford town centre at The Room At The Top, where residents Snoopy and Larry Foster were amazing, or the Palais or Kings just down the road in Seven Kings, for iconic nights like Chris Hill's Lacy Lady.

There were some great little sweaty basements which shut their doors at 2am and carried on illegally. At Stop Outs, the guy who owned it had a wine bar at the back, his missus had a hairdressers at the front, and there was a knocking shop upstairs.

My first radio show was on a pirate called *Planet FM*, a small station set up by friends. I'd always chatted on the mic at our northern soul parties. You had to because the records were only two minutes long and a lot of clubs only had one deck. I was on pirates like *Unknown FM* and *House FM* for a couple of years in the late-'90s and also played on *Stomp FM* for Scott James.

Kenny Ken, real name Ken Delsol, secured a cleaning job on the London Underground when he was released from prison in 1986. Finally a straight-goer, acid house was about to change his life again.

A guy I met inside hooked me up with a firm contracted to clean certain underground stations. I was just grateful to get a regular job, but fortunately one of the managers put me forward a year later to take an exam at Baker Street to become a railman, and I got a job collecting tickets at Oxford Circus and Holborn.

A mate kept saying, 'Ken, you need to get to one of these acid house parties,' but the word 'acid' was putting me off. Eventually I went to a rave in Backchurch Lane in Whitechapel, some time in 1988, and was converted straight away. I thought, yeah, this is a bit of me, so I started to buy the records too.

I'd go to a rave with my uniform in the back of our car, then sometimes straight to work, which only made me want to be a DJ more, because I knew I couldn't sustain that for much longer. One Sunday morning I was collecting tickets by hand at Holborn and I'd fallen asleep in the box. Two old ladies, bless them, banged on the window and said, 'You better wake up, son, you'll lose your job.' I made sure I left before I was fired.

My first DJ booking was at The Lion Boxing Club in Pitfield Street in Hoxton for pals of mine, playing stuff like Queen's *Another One Bites The Dust* and Phil Collins' *In The Air Tonight* mixed in with house. I was awful so bought some 1200s and taught myself to mix, trying to pick up bookings where I could. But I was a punter as much as anything still. Rage at Heaven on a Thursday, The Astoria, all the M25 raves. Anything to do with the scene. I went to every Sunrise because I knew some guys who helped the promoter Tony Colston-Hayter and those connections really helped.

Some of the people I met raving could have got me back in trouble, but I wanted to go straight more than anything and I was fully focused on getting involved in music. As I became more recognised as a DJ, it helped to keep away from all that. My first regular club gig was at Labyrinth in Dalston Lane for Joe and Sue, who proper looked after me.

I'd be out raving after my set on Saturday night/Sunday morning and we'd go to Crazy Larry's in King's Road on a Sunday for Crazy Club, put on by Carl and Dave. I always tried to get amongst it and to know the promoters. One night I told Carl I could do better than the DJs he had, who were playing house, acid house and a bit of Belgium techno. Jumpin' Jack Frost and Ray Keith were both in Carl's ear too — we were all trying to come through the ranks. Carl explained he was getting Busby's in Charing Cross Road and told us all to bring our records there next Sunday afternoon. Whoever plays best will get a residency. The three of us rocked up the following week and we all smashed it, so Carl and Dave offered me Frostie and Ray all regular slots. I was so pleased, because alongside Labyrinth I now had work every week.

I had been on *Centreforce* by now, and Danielle Montana, another DJ from the station I knew, also played at Crazy Club. But I wasn't anything to do with Players Kenny, if I can just clear up that myth. Kenny was on *Centreforce*, but it's a completely different DJ, who was part of the 3 Amigos with Randall and Roger The Doctor, not me.

When budding TV executive Jonathon Ross spotted 18-year-old Bekir Remzi (aka DJ Ramsey) and his pals dancing at Gulliver's in Mayfair in 1986, it was a Willy Wonker moment for the lads from Hackney.

I was born in Stepney Green and brought up in a Turkish Cypriot family on soul and rare groove. I started going out aged 16/17 to places like Septembers on Hackney Road, the old Temple Street Tap pub... Shoreditch end. Me and my Turkish mate, and a couple of black kids we knew, fancied ourselves as dancers and called ourselves The Untouchables. We'd been listening to pirate stations like *Solar* and got into *Kiss*, which had just come on as a pirate. *Kiss* announced one day that the producers of the TV show *Soul Train* would be at Gulliver's. This was our chance to become studio dancers on the show.

Gulliver's was so urban when Jonathon Ross and his team walked in suited and booted, they looked like coppers. I said, 'Right, they're here, the *Channel 4* lot. Don't look at them, just go into the routine.' And it worked. When we finished Jonathan came over and said, 'Well done, boys. Here are your tickets.' We grabbed them and ran out.

Now what to wear for the big day? Fortunately having access to rolls of genuine Burberry fabric gave Bekir a head start.

I was working in a huge factory in Hoxton, where clothes were made for shops like Top Man. My department, though, just two of us, was exclusively for Burberry. Some nights we were asked to stay and help clean the factory. Our boss paid us in Burberry jackets and macs worth £300. We had them coming out of our ears, so were very popular.

Now we had tickets for *Soul Train,* I decided to make myself a pair of trousers and a poncho, all in the signature tan with red, black and white striped Burberry check. It was some get up, but it worked. When we arrived at *Soul Train,* Jonathan took one look and put me straight up on the stage, directly behind where the main artists performed, while my pals stayed on the main dancefloor. There's footage on *YouTube* somewhere of me dancing in that Burberry outfit, complete with permed hair.

Coincidently, one of our lot worked at Cecil Gee opposite Selfridges and Jonathon, who obviously went on to be a huge star, became a regular customer. He dropped off a dozen Soul Train/Solid Soul tickets each week with any spares we had selling for up to £50 a pop.

We started to take the dancing really seriously and took singing lessons to see if we could become a boy band or something. We were going for it big-time, but always got injured trying better moves.

I got more into DJing, started to play at local bars and house parties. One friend carried on the singing and another pal really got into the dancing. Years later I spotted some of our moves in a Take That routine, and then found out he was now a choreographer for them.

I was definitely going more urban, though. It was unavoidable. I was now part of a little crew called Force Of One. Me, now called Easy B, my mate Wallace, MC Cranks, and Mixmaster Max.

Rooney sold 'Super Smiley' T-Shirts outside Heaven on Monday nights before Spectrum.

We'd buy 100 tees for 50p each, spray them up using stencils and sell them for a tenner outside Heaven. When they's sold out we'd go inside, wearing our own limited edition T-Shirts that glowed in the dark. I had one made up that said, 'I'm not as think as you stoned I am.'

Spectrum was amazing. The way they dressed the club, always something different going on, special nights for Halloween or Guy Fawkes and the all-dayers when they opened Soundshaft next door. I loved the huge gyroscope, covered in lights with a geezer painted fluorescent spinning on a laser inside. I went all through '88 and when it became Land Of Oz.

Centreforce originals (left) Mervyn Victor (above) Jim The Music Man (below) Kenny Ken.

The best thing was coming out at 3.30am on a Tuesday morning, everybody from the club dotted around Trafalgar Square waiting for their night-bus home. I'd go from Charing Cross all the way to Canning Town with a bus full of ravers, having the most mental time. That was one of the pure joys of the scene then.

We witnessed come crazy things back then. I saw Jack Nicholson in the original Legends one night in 1989.

It was great to be able to grow up in two influential parts of London during my teens. Canning Town was a hard area, and south London, where my brother had moved to, was like being on a different planet. The girls were different, they had their own lingo. I'd come back from visits to Streatham in 1986/87 and playing my mates in east London acid house. They didn't know what it was and didn't like it. Ten months later they were on it, but I was like, 'You lot are long, you're late.'

My roots into music had been via my parents. My mum was a drummer in an all-girl band called The Queen Bees, taught by Keith Moon. She never moaned about me playing acid house at home — her favourite track was *White Horse*.

I learned the piano from the age of ten, and used to take a big synthesiser to school and play stuff like Alex F in the playground. My dad had a reel-to-reel in a nice set-up, separates and old wooden Wharfedale Glendale speakers, which were the nuts. At parties at home I mixed between the reel to reel and tape deck.

When I was 16, I got a job in a Hi-Fi shop in Bethnal Green. There was a gay fella who worked there who went to Heaven at the weekends so we had a talking point. I'd play a 12 inch vinyl copy of *Give It To Me* by Bam Bam to demo the stack systems...and sold loads.

Seeker: My next break was at Romford Ice Rink in 1987, where me and Hugs blagged a Friday night residency. We had it nice and busy, playing some early house, bought from Bluebird Records in Church Street, Paddington, plus soul beats still and stuff like Will Downing's *Love Supreme*.

In the winter of 1988, I got my first full-time job at an estate agents through a youth training scheme in Ilford. A friend's brother was manager of the local Tandy and did me a deal on two Citronic decks and a mixer, for £267. They were still belt driven but there was a pitch control rolling button at the front of each deck. I couldn't scratch on them, but mixing was obviously much easier.

A girl called Janet worked in the solicitors' office above Tandy's and walked past our shop front regularly, smiling at me. One day I was horrified to see her inside our doorway, speaking to my manager. He chuckled as she walked over and handed me a note with her home number on. It read 'Hey Seeker, give me a call if you want to meet up?'

Seekers was the name of the estate agents, and when I told my mates, well, that was it...I've been called Seeker ever since.

I knew I needed some Technics decks to progress as a DJ. I still didn't have enough money saved, though. Fortunately, my aunt offered to pay the rest and even drove me to a Hi-Fi shop near Romford market. Because I wanted to be a bit different, I took my aunt to one side in the shop and said, 'Everyone mixes on two decks, but I reckon I'd be able to mix on three.' I'd never even heard of three-deck mixing, I was just so confident by that point. My aunt, bless her, said to the store manager, 'Actually, can we have another one?' I was now the proud owner of three Technics 1210s, which back then cost £280 a piece. I cherished them so much, but five weeks later I was taking two of them up to *Centreforce*. It was hard to be without all of them at home, but the station's need was greater at that point. They survived all the raids but someone swapped one for an older 1210. I noticed when I did my next show, and true to his word, Andy later replaced it for me.

Connie Runtings: We used a beauty and sauna place on the Cambridge Heath Road across four levels for the Runtings parties. The main room, an outside yard, a chill-out area and a basement too. We always had the best sound, Turbosound and amazing DJs. The mixing, the music, the sound — it was all on point. DJ Ron, who I went to school with and is the godfather of my son, played regularly.

All kinds of people came from all over London. We only had one raid, and that was it...but there were maybe six or seven parties before that. We promoted them on *Centreforce*. Runtings was in full effect and Echoes was thriving too.

When we got raided, quite a few of us got taken to Bethnal Green police station, and two big boxes of my records were confiscated with all the alcohol we were selling, I remember being taken out of my cell to be interviewed, and as I walked down the corridor I could see the officers in a room, toasting their success, drinking our beer.

We were let out the next day, but without my records. It was horrible to leave the police station without them because I just didn't know if I'd ever get them back. Thankfully, I was able to collect them eventually.

Steve ESP grew up on the Chatsworth Estate in Stratford, a stone's throw from Dennison Point.

Centreforce was a massive influence at the time. We were the same age as some of the younger DJs on the station and mates with Bagz,

Seeker and Randall, who were a couple of years older and went to my school. Randall's mixing was seemless and, to this day, he would be in my Top 3 DJs ever.

I cobbled together my first set of decks in 1986, a belt-driven Citronic and a JVC turntable with a rotary pitch control, which was like cracking a safe, that I bought from Loot magazine for £2. My mixer was home-made by my dad. Thankfully, he helped me buy a pair of Technics and the Phonic MRT60 mixer with blue and yellow trim for my 16th birthday. I was walking on air and didn't leave my bedroom for weeks.

In 1989 I was an apprentice electrician, earning about £37 a week. I played the odd gig at Borderline in Soho and the Fitness Centre a couple of times, but back then I didn't consider DJing a job. We were part of a scene and a movement and just happy to be around it.

I work in project management now and, I don't know how, but it seems like I had more money then, even though we spent any spare cash on going out and records.

As the various sub-genres of house were forming, the music each night was so varied. I loved trying to hunt down the tunes you heard the night before. One Saturday morning I was trying to describe a track to Noodles in his record shop in the basement of Mash on Oxford Street.

'It goes, 'Omp, omp, omp, omp...ermf, ermf, ermf...' I only got that far and he said, 'Yeah, I've got it,' and pulled out a copy of Joey Beltram's *Energy Flash* from under the counter.

Roger The Doctor: Nightlife, the club at the bottom of the strip in San Antonio in Ibiza, offered me a residency so I quit my job at a camera shop in Walthamstow. In my mind, if I was being offered a residency in Ibiza, I was a DJ now.

Towards the end of the 1990 season, as I prepared to come home to London, the workers I'd been hanging around with explained that they usually island-hopped to Tenerife and spent the start of the winter there, so I went with them. Better than going back to rainy UK, they said.

And when I got to Tenerife I was pleasantly surprised. The strip, especially at that time of year, was like the Kings Road. Gents in slacks and loafers, women in jodhpurs and heels, compared to the football shirt-wearing stag parties at the strip in San-An, Ibiza. Tenerife, by comparison, was suave. I went to Bobby's, Tramps and Gigolos. Then went home for the winter to get some new tunes, clothes and some money together so I could go back out to Tenerife the following season.

I played the odd party in the West End in early 1991. Moonlights in Mayfair and Cincinnatis in Cavendish Square. Then I was offered a residency at D'riz (the old La Valbonne) in Kingley Street, off Carnaby Street, earning £250 a night. That was more like it.

I was back out to Tenerife in April, advised to get out there early and find a cheaper place to live before the season started. As I walked down the strip, struggling with two large record boxes, a guy shouted out, ''Oi, what you doing?'

So I shouted back, 'I'm painting and decorating, what do you think?'

'Oi, cheeky fucker, come up here...'

It was Tony Palmer, the owner of Roxy's Bar.

We got chatting and Tony said, 'You any good?'

'You heard of *Centreforce*, I used to be on there...'

He said, 'Yeah, Andy Swallow's thing...but I've never heard of you...'

'Tell you what, I'll come and DJ for two nights for free, and if I don't get your place busy, you can tell me where to go.'

By the end of the first night, I got the word round, 'Roger The Doctor from *Centreforce* is playing.' Roxy's Bar was rammed, so Tony offered me a residency.

Tony Palmer was an absolute character. We became good mates, but that residency didn't last long. Within weeks I was poached by Bobby's Bar, which was opposite Roxy's.

Bobby's owner Jo Quaranta was opening a new 1,000-capacity venue further down the strip. Resident Steve Foster, an amazing DJ, came to check me out, and advised Jo to get me involved.

It was another pivotal moment. I played at Bobby's Bar for the entire 1991, '92 and '93 seasons, and most of 1994. I came back to the UK for a holiday each year, saw my mum, but Tenerife became my home because Bobby's was open all year.

Paul 'Bubbler' Edwards had his record shop route mapped out from his early teens.

I'd get a one-day travel pass every Saturday morning from Manor Park and head to Romford first to start at Boogie Times, for anything I needed from Suburban Base.

Then on the way back through, head to Music Power in Ilford, and then work my way back up to Soho to Blackmarket and the basement at Mash on Oxford Street.

I also loved De Underground I'm Forest Gate, owned and run by Mike De Underground, Cool Hand Flex, Randall and Uncle 22...local boys making hardcore in the studio downstairs, tracks like Lenny De Ice's *We Are I.E*, so great for exclusive tunes.

Because I went on to play on lots of east London pirate stations, I liked to check out shops in north, west and south London to get tracks DJs local to me might not have.

I'd meet people in record shops, other DJs, producers...it was like a community...not like these days when you buy a download online with no interaction. And it was great for DJ bookings, because promoters I'd meet would have heard me on the radio. Great times.

Growing up, we were soul boys so the first pirate I listened to was *LWR*. They started to play a bit of house and the first track that grabbed me when I was ten was *Let's Get Brutal* - Nitro Deluxe. That was it, I was in.

A few years later, inspired by DJs on *Centreforce* when it came on, I began to learn how to mix. Twelve months later, I was on *Chillin' FM*, a hardcore station based in Stamford Hill, north London, run by Joey G. I moved to *Conflict FM* when I started playing jungle, and then *Risk FM* in Leyton when I got into garage.

Seeker: I was really gutted that *Centreforce* had come to an end. I'd given up my job and I thought it was going to be my future. It hit me quite hard, really, but there were still gigs to play, including a decent little one every third week in Plymouth.

Then the management started something called London Dance each week at a hotel in Cromer in Norfolk. I went up there to play the first weekend and stayed for eight months.

The promoter Royston just took to me and Andy said, 'Well, this can be your bread and butter for a while now, then.' As part of my deal I was given a room at the hotel. The club was in the basement, called The Pit, mainly open Friday and Saturday evenings and also for regular all-dayers. I also got gigs in Kings Lynn, Sherringham and Great Yarmouth off the back of it.

The club only held about 300-400 people, a little sweat box mobbed with queues round the block. A few people would come from London. Randall guested, and the locals started handing in mixtapes so we gave the best ones a go too.

When the hotel's owners Paul and Lynn sold up, I came back to east London and had major reconstruction surgery on a childhood knee injury. With *Centreforce* coming to an end and me being in Norfolk, The Corporation had fizzled out. When I was fit enough I started working as a plasterer's mate.

Connie Runtings: After the Cambridge Heath Road raid, there were a few more Runtings parties in other places, but we had to move into legal venues so the scene changed. We partnered up with someone for a Runtings festival in Cornwall, but we were arrested on the way out.

In 1990 I was playing in The Dungeon and in the West End and Limelights and Busby's. When *Centreforce* shut down, I didn't think it was the end of an era because I was busy doing other things. In 1991 while I was playing at The Astoria hardcore was coming in. I just liked playing music so I moved with the scene.

Steve ESP: During the early-'90s, I was lucky to have a couple of friends who worked for Mo's Music Machine, one of the biggest distributors of underground dance music at the time, so I was quite upfront with what I had. I think 1990 had been a defining year for the British sound. With their reggae sound system background and hip-hop influences, people like Shut Up & Dance and DJ Hype brought that breakbeat in and helped create hardcore. There was the Belgium stuff but predominantly the UK led that scene. It was exciting how new music month on month was getting faster and faster.

In '91 my aunt hooked me up with a guy she worked with at Barclays Bank in Stratford.

'He's into the same music as you and I've told him you've got decks.'

I gave her a mixtape to pass on, and then the guy rang me up and said, 'Where did you get that tune, the first one on the tape, it's not even out yet, how have you got that, can I come round and meet you?'

It was DJ Zinc. He and his mate Swift took me up to a pirate station they were on, *Impact 88.2*, and I watched them do their thing. They even got me a show on Impact. So good of them. It was crazy how things happened back then. Radio wasn't something I was desperate to do, but pre-*Centreforce* we listened to *Lazer* and *LWR*, especially Mike Allen's hip-hop show, plus early Westwood stuff on *Capital*, so I knew this was an amazing opportunity.

My hands were shaking so much before that first *Impact* show I could hardly put the needle on the record. By now I was playing hardcore and stayed in that scene until late '92, early '93.

My DJ name had always been SP, an abbreviation of my full name Stephen Pellicci, but after mumbling it to an MC one night he called me ESP on the mic for the rest of the night and it stuck. There is another guy in Kent called ESP. Our paths crossed eventually and we decided we'd both keep our DJ name if we'd put our first names at front.

I stopped Impact and was on a station called Format for a while. Then I got into the jungle, but that got too dark for me, and I went full circle and started playing broken beat and trip-hop. I moved into acid jazz and a mate was in the Brand New Heavies, so I did some album launches and after-parties for them. I was never really trying to infiltrate any one scene, but I ended up crossing over to quite a few different ones. It kept me interested.

Ramsey: By 1991 we had joined *Defection FM*, a pirate which started in the Leabridge Road end of Hackney, going into north London. We had a show as Force Of One, playing hardcore, then Jungle. Early days. Guys like Goldie would MC for us. Cranks worked in the Music Power record shop on Grand Parade in Harringey, owned by another Cypriot, Nick Power, who became a great friend of mine. I travelled to Cyprus regularly in the early-'90s to visit my young son, so Nick always booked me to play at The Kool Club in Ayia Napa, which he ran then. I played American stuff, years before Ayia Napa and the whole UK garage thing kicked off. The square was very different then but still really busy. Great times.

Back in the UK, we mainly played hardcore, but we were also moving into drum and bass too. Cranks got loads of records for free from Music Power and I bought what I could so between us we had everything we needed. But with the likes of Grooverider and Kenny Ken such a tight unit, it was very hard to get on the club circuit. We weren't getting anywhere so we split up. I was now using the name Ruthless B and *Defection* was taken over by *Rush FM*, which moved to 92.3FM.

My older brother Huss passed away after the onset of Multiple Sclerosis in his adult years. He had played for West Ham under-16s in the 1970s and had been such an influence on me growing up. Huss was always known as Ramsey, the cockney version of our surname Remzi. So I decided to take that name on, in honour of him, and went on *Rush FM* as Ramsey, playing more house now, on what was a predominantly a drum and bass station

I was shopped at City Sounds in Holborn and Pure Groove in Archway and every month I'd pop down to Bow to see Daniel Ward at Rhythm Division too.

I started getting a few bookings in the small rooms at drum and bass events playing house. It was me, Norris Da Boss, Matt Jam Lamont, Karl Brown, Dominic Spreadlove. Nights and places like Roast, Thunder & Joy and The Dungeons. Then I jumped on *Freek FM*, which was in Archway, so not far from where I was now living in Manor Park.

Someone introduced me to Fen (Aktan Fenman) in a local phone shop, so I brought him on to *Freek* with me, and we started doing a show called The Freek Zone, 8pm-10pm on a Saturday.

We liked tracks coming out of the US, especially the Todd Edwards stuff and from Nice N Ripe, George Power and Grant Nelson's label. We were buying a lot of that, but we were not playing the vocal mixes. Because of what we'd come from, we liked the dub mixes, with more of an underground flavour. We were young, we were loose cannons. We didn't want to play cheesy vocals, we wanted all the hyper stuff.

We left *Freek FM* and I decided to start up my own station. My mate said to me, 'What you going to call it?...' I was drinking a coffee out of a TFL mug and looked at it and said, *London Underground*.

I didn't have enough money to pay for the set-up of a station, and when that mate and his pal said they fancied a bit of it, I said great, 'You fund it, and me and Fen will manage it.' I brought in people like Hermit, Daniel Ward, Dominic, Richie Fingers and a lot of people came over from *Freek*. Texsta came on board too. *London Underground* was going really well. We were getting loads of work off it, at some of UK garage's founding clubs. Sun City, Lord Of The Underground, La Cosa Nostra, Numb Nums and The Breakfast Club. Three of the DJs on *London Underground*, Spoony, Mikey and Timmi Magic asked if they could do a show together and the Dreem Teem was born.

Like many house and rave DJs of his generation Kenny Ken's music policy had moved more towards hardcore, and then jungle.

The transition from house to jungle was gradual. It started around '91 and I'd say by the end of '92 jungle had come through fully. The more new music I was sent, the more I got into it.

I met Randall, another original *Centreforce* DJ, properly in 1991/92 when we were both residents at AWOL at the Paradise. We'd both play two-hour sets every Saturday. Initially, a lot of the jungle still had a 'douf douf' four to the floor house beat, but with hip-hop beats sped up, so they called it jungle-techno. Then the house beat got taken out and the fast breaks remained and then that's when it was pure jungle.

I was also playing at Roast and Sunday Roast parties at venues like The Astoria, SW1 Club in Victoria, Linford Film Studios in Battersea and Turnmills where we were every Sunday from midday to 8pm in 1991. I was a resident with Jumping Jack Frost and Mickey Finn, with Fabio and Grooverider often headlining. All these parties were jungle, jungle-techno, with a little bit of hardcore, but it was always heading to full-on jungle, which was where it was in 1993.

I never felt there was a 'them and us' thing between the house DJs and the jungle or drum and bass scenes. We knew all the house DJs previously, and even though I was a jungle DJ, I'd be raving at garage and house clubs and house parties after my sets, so I knew Creed and PSG and Masterstepz, all those guys. But I never crossed over into UK garage, that wasn't for me. Jungle was doing really well for me and helped pay for my house, so I stuck with it.

Laurence 'Bagz' Bagnall became part of the AWOL and World Dance management team, initially working on merchandise, and then in promotions, and DJing for both brands too.

AWOL ran and ran and was huge for the scene.

I went from Bagz to Laurence Bagnall because Jay and Chris said I had a shit name. Simple as that.

MUSIC POW R 2
RECORDS - TAPES - C.D's & ACCESSORIES

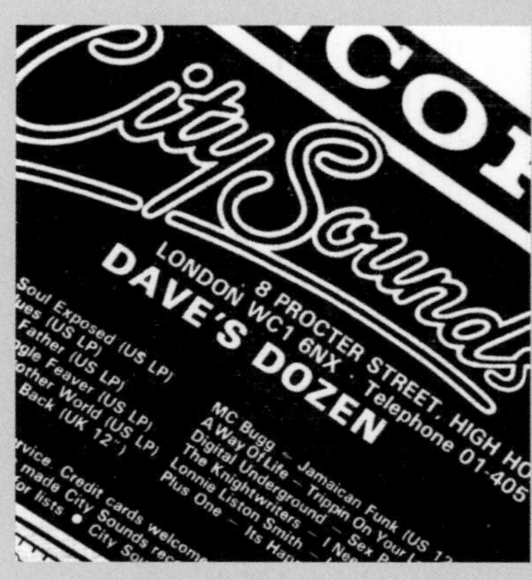
City Sounds
LONDON 8 PROCTER STREET, HIGH HO
WC1 6NX . Telephone 01-405
DAVE'S DOZEN
MC Bugg – Jamaican Funk (US 12
A Way Of Life – Trippin On Your
Digital Underground – Sex P
The Knightwriters – I Nee
Lonnie Liston Smith
Plus One – Its Ha
Soul Exposed (US LP)
ues (US LP)
Father (US LP)
ogie Feaver (US LP)
other World (US LP)
Back (UK 12")
rvice. Credit cards welcome
made City Sounds rec
or lists ● City So

BOOGIE TIMES
DANCE MUSIC SPECIALISTS: IMPORTS & DELETIONS: UK RELEASES
FEEDWELL

rhythmdivision
391

PAUL
for
MUSIC
LTD.
Head Office
11 CAMBRIDGE HEATH RD., LONDON, E.1
Phones: BIS 2004 & CRE 3778
67 LEATHER LANE, LONDON, E.C.1
Phone: HOL 1270
4 STATION PLACE. LONDON, N.4
Phone: ARC 0455
Stalls
FRIDAYS & SATURDAYS Outside WHITECHAPEL STATION
SUNDAY MORNINGS CYGNET STREET, CLUB ROW, E.2

Record
Village
The Dance Music Specialists
TEL 520 7331
256

BLACK
MARKET
RECORDS

For one World Dance event there was a DJ poll on the back of tickets asking for people to write down their Top 3 DJs who played at our events. I got my pals to sit in the office and add my name to as many as possible. When I came in on the Monday, Chris was beaming and said, 'You never guess what, you've only come in second in that DJ poll...', then added, 'Mate, they were all written in the same pen.'

I couldn't play at the next couple of World Dances as a punishment for trying that blag. World Dance absolutely smashed it with huge parties at Lydd Airport in Kent for 10,000 people and at London Arena in the mid-'90s. Working with Jay Pender was incredible — the guy just had no fear.

Connie Runtings: I had a hardcore track out with Bizzy B called *The Crowd Says Rewind* as C-Biz, and then I joined a four-piece jungle outfit called UK Tribe that got signed to BMG.

I'd started playing jungle. I was at The Wax Club in Hackney Wick, on the same line-up as Kenny Ken and Andy C, and at the end of the night was waiting for a car to collect me. I'd put down my two boxes of records as I chatted to someone. As I looked out for the driver, I heard a car screech off. My records were gone. All my best jungle tunes disappeared. I was heartbroken.

It was the end of me playing jungle because back then you couldn't replace those records easily, so I came away from DJing in 1993/94 and concentrated on the band over the next two years. We went to LA to produce music for Japan. We had pluggers, got really looked after, were paid retainers and given a pre-production studio. We recorded some good stuff, but found it difficult to chart and split up in 1996.

I started producing my own music again with the singer Hifer, and we PAd at places like the Country Club, Sexy Exit parties and at Cafe De Paris for Tangerine Dream.

Then I moved away from music and became a bus driver.

Kenny Ken was on *Kiss 100* for three years from 1994 and a year later became the first DJ to play jungle on *Radio 1*, when he was chosen for the one-off show One in The Jungle. Since 1997 he has run his own label Mix & Blen, but admits that a full week of DJing, producing, radio and raving was difficult to juggle at times.

I was 100% in the scene and loved to rave, always did. Sometimes I'd overload myself and have to back off for a week or so and go home straight from gigs, but it was hard because I loved the scene. I have a couple of days to recover from 'the weekend', then have to get my radio show sorted...then off I'd go, it was the weekend again. I managed to keep it all going for quite a while, but suddenly I was older.

We've had 25 or so releases on the label, including many of my own, but up until fairly recently I've never felt I was taking it that seriously. I only got a label because everybody else had one. DJ Mace has done everything and without him there would be no Mix & Blen.

Danny Lines: I really started going out hard in 1991 and around that summer I met Andy Swallow properly at a rave called Living Dream in Temple Mills Lane, one of the biggest marquees ever put up at that point — 13,000 people all packed into one tent.

I wasn't a straight-goer in those days and went on the run in 1993, spending a couple of years in Manchester. I had no option. I was wanted by some serious people and my life was in danger, but I got through it and that experience made me the man I am today.

At least I carried on raving up there at the Hacienda. I also started working the doors in Princess Street, which gave me a feel for security.

Rooney: In 1992 I started going to *Eruption FM* with my mate Leon, DJ Reflex. I hadn't had any pirate involvement since those nightshifts with *Centreforce,* but being involved with *Eruption* made me realise I wanted to become a DJ. My mum came up with the name Rooney on the spot and it stuck.

In 1998 I joined *Flava FM* and started playing out, in the house room at places like Just Jungle, a big gaff in Forest Gate. Nicky Blackmarket was busting a jungle tune one night and the speaker caught fire. I met Bubbler at *Flava*, but it took us a while to work out we knew each other from mixing at a mutual friend's house when we were younger. When Bubbler relaunched *Chillin' FM* in 2001, I jumped on board. I did online streaming for *Chillin'* using a Bang & Olufsen cassette radio I got when I was 15 because it had such a good acoustic sound to it.

Seeker: I hadn't DJd properly for a while, maybe the odd house party. I was labouring for a mate's brother on a site in Bow behind where Echoes was. We were working on an old snooker hall which local brothers, Alfie and Michael, were turning into a club called Alfa Centauri. My pal Alan said, 'The guys used to listen to *Centreforce* and are big fans of yours, they can't believe you're working here, doing up their club and wondered if you'd be their resident DJ.' I took up their offer. It was a wicked venue, really psychedelic in its concept, the DJ stand was inside a juggernaut, it was crazy. But for whatever reason the club didn't stay open long and closed in 1993.

So I came out of the scene because I just wasn't feeling it anymore. There were various complications, relationship and job issues. And after my latest operation my ankle still wasn't strong enough for me to carry heavy boxes of records around. When the jungle and garage scenes came in I stopped buying records. Too much talking on the mic killed the vibe, for me. I loved trying to make my set sound like one continuous record, but talking over the records instead, well, it just wasn't for me.

Mervyn Victor: In 1993/94 I started playing a mix of Gat Decor's *Passion* and Degrees Of Motion's *Do You Want It Right Now* in my sets, at places like Legends or Splash at Country Club. My mate Tony Wybrow paid for me to go into a studio for a birthday present to knock up a bootleg on vinyl. Every shop I went to turned it down. At City Sounds, a certain DJ said it was rubbish. Then Dave, the governor, came out the back and said, 'I love it, I'll have a couple of hundred.' He sent one down to Tongy who played it on *Radio 1* that Friday, and it just took off. I sold 500 in Paul For Music that week. Simon Slater, who produced the original Gat Decor track, rang me up and asked me to go to the studio with him and produce it officially, and we charted with it.

I left Paul For Music in 1996, pissed off the owner wouldn't consider selling the shop to me when he retired, but that only spurred me on to set up my own company Millennium Distribution with Tony Wybrow. We grew quickly and I rented a vault at the old City Hall in Mile End, where we became the first distribution company to have its own recording studio.

I heard The Architechs remix of Brandy & Monica's *The Boy Is Mine* in 1998 and loved it. We put it out as bootleg for towards the end of that year and distributed it for The Architechs. EastWest/Warner me rang up and threatened to send a cease and desist. But I was able to argue that since the bootleg the Brandy & Monica album had shot up the album charts in the UK, so they left us alone to carry on selling that album for them.

I even suggested they put the bootleg mix on the B-side of Brandy & Monica's next single, but they didn't understand what was happening with garage, that it was an urban movement that came from the streets. For the past couple of years lots of little shops like Paul For Music had been selling Grant Nelson's Nice 'N' Ripe tracks and the stuff Tuff Jam had been throwing out.

I had such good contacts by that point, and we did well because we pushed the music that we loved. We had come from the scene, we weren't distributors that had inherited the music.

We became the biggest national distributors for UK garage, and sold Andy's Labello and Public Demand stuff. Nobody embraced that scene as quickly as us. We founded Red Rose Recordings, which launched the careers of DJ Luck & MC Neat and *A Little Bit Of Luck*, on the back of a one minute jingle of that track that they played us.

We initially pressed up 500 on white label, and told my drivers to give one copy to every DJ working at every shop, and by the end of that weekend every garage pirate station in London was playing it. Then, we pushed it up another level and pressed up 5,000 copies on red vinyl, charging a couple of pounds more, and they all went within a day.

We bought a place in Camden where we had a warehouse, offices, studio and a record shop called Planet Phat. I later started another company called GB Tunes, and we were one of the first distributors for a lot of the French stuff, like Daft Punk in the UK and loads of US house imports. We'd even invested in our own pressing plant.

Those were the money-making days: we had accounts with HMV, and 700 shops in the UK and 300 shops abroad in total...and then it all went digital and the game completely changed.

Bubbler: I joined *Deja Vu FM* when it came on around 1995, and played house and garage on there for the next six years. During that time I lived in Lund Point, the 'smiley acid face' tower block on the front of this book. I changed my DJ name to Bubbler, an extension of childhood nickname Bubs. I just fancied a change, so I was the original DJ Majestic, between 1991 - 1995.

Deja Vu became pretty big very quickly. We picked up residencies like Sun City and La Cossa Nostra. We also had weekly things at The Rex and Powerhouse in Stratford, which was heaving in the mid-to-late-'90s. We could see the queue at The Rex going down the road from the studio. It was a great feeling. When we'd finished our shows it took us about five minutes to get over there. When The Rex was packed, with a couple of thousand people in there, condensation poured off the ceiling. The records were so wet I don't know how I was able to play them.

I was also on *Flava FM*, which was run by Chris Low, and where I met Rooney. When grime began to come through in 2000,2001, it wasn't my thing so I left *Deja Vu*. *Rinse FM* gets a lot of credit for grime, but a lot of those boys started on Deja Vu...I couldn't find a new station I liked so started my own. I learned the ropes, how to get a transmitter up on a roof. I'd got my station up but needed a name. I asked Joey G if I could use *Chillin' FM*, and he told me go for it. Rooney came on and we ran until 2009. I just wanted to be able to play the music I liked and hopefully the other Djs would make a bit of name for themselves on the station too.

Steve ESP: I'd taken a break from it all for a few years. I was always a big Paul Weller fan, coming from a mod-upbringing, and I got into the Ocean Colour Scene era, that kind of stuff, in the mid-to-late-'90s.

Then in 2000 I'd just had my first son and to wet the baby's head me

I WAS DESCRIBING A RECORD IN THE SHOP AT MASH. ‘OMP OMP OMP OMP, ...ERMF ERMF ERMF’, AND THE FELLA GAVE ME A COPY OF JOEY BELTRAM’S *ENERGY FLASH*.

and a few pals went to Camden. Towards the end of the night we wandered down to Camden Palace and there was a Back To 92 night on. As we walked in, Slipmatt was playing Satin Storm, *Think I'm Going Out Of My Head.* It was like we'd gone back in time.

I went up to the loft and dug out a load of tunes and put some mixes together. A lady I worked with in Dagenham heard I was trying to get back into it, and told me that her son ran a radio station. I went to meet him at The Ploch pub at Gallows Corner, and that was my introduction to *Force FM*, a pirate based in Harold Hill.

A week later at a station meeting I met Matt Emulsion and we just hit it off. Soon after, we did a mammoth Christmas Eve show together, playing everything from '80s pop, jazz-funk, hip-hop and house, ripping the piss out of each other for eight hours, like we'd known each other for ages.

Force FM was great. Monday was old school, Tuesday, drum and bass, Wednesday, R&B, Thursday, garage, Friday, house and the weekends were a mixture of house and garage. I became Monday night manager and I loved my time there.

A few years later, a DJ I met on *Force* called Flipside set up an internet station called *Remaniss Radio* in the garage of his house in Laindon, near Basildon, and that's where I met Jonny C.

Danny Lines returned from his enforced sabbatical in Manchester and began to carve out a career in security.

My grandfather was head of security at Philip Morris in Silvertown so was a big influence. I did a little bit of Territorial Army and it helped get me straight. I actually ended up a warranted officer on the Park's Police, which was mad considering where I'd come from. People looked at my past and thought, how the fuck has he done that, but you can do anything if you put your mind to it, get your qualifications and work hard. I got into body-guarding and back into the music that way, and worked for Tim Westwood for a while. I took a security course with a company called Roaming Concepts and then got into dog security in the early-Noughties.

Ramsey: As Ramsey & Fen, on the back of the success of *London Underground*, remix offers started to come in. Our first production work was with the guys behind A Homeboy A Hippie And A Funki Dredd, who had the big rave track *Total Confusion* but that stuff never came out.

Around 1996, '97, a friend said he wanted to introduce an up-and-coming producer to us. 'He's a drum and bass boy, he doesn't really know about garage, you're gonna have to clue him up.' And that was Matt 'MJ Cole' Coleman.

At the same time we were asked to remix two Kym Mazelle tracks — *Big Baby* and *Quality* — so we worked with Matt under the banner, Rafmatt Productions. Our love of US garage and also anything from hardcore to jungle combined with Matt's drum and bass influences to help create a 2-step sound that went on to be known as UK garage.

Matt certainly caught the UK garage bug, and both those Mazelle tracks were released as 'Ramsey & Fen + MJ Cole' remixes and really helped put me and Fen on the map, production-wise.

We went on to set up our own label, Bug Records, and had big crossover club hits as Ramsey & Fen with 2-step anthems like *Love Bug, Desire, Always* and *Style*, all with Matt involved in the production, programming or engineering. Our remixes of Fabulous Baker Boy's *Oh Boy*, The Heartists' *Belo Horizonti*, Lovestation's *Teardrop*s and Sandy B's *Make The World Go Round* were all highlights...plus a remix of *Special* by Robbie Craig for Andy and Jimmy at Public Demand. We also mixed some big garage compilations like *Garage Nation* and the 3rd volume of the popular *Locked On* series.

Darrell Privett cut his teeth on radio in the late-'90s as DJ Frenzie on *Rinse FM* alongside garage and grime stars like Wiley, Target and the station's co-owner and founder Geeneus.

But before he joined *Rinse*, Darrell's first experience of performing was as a singer when he PAd a garage track he written and produced at a Mother Funkers night at Epping Forest Country Club, booked by a certain Roger The Doctor.

I played saxophone and drums from an early age, and could sing a bit, but I was trying to be a DJ for years.

As a kid, every Friday lunchtime I'd get a bus from school in Bow to Rhythm Division Records in Roman Road and spend whatever dinner money I'd managed to save up that week, probably on one vinyl record, preferably with a decent A and B side. If I'd done all right at penny up the wall, I might be able to get two records. That was a good week.

I had a pair of bad Soundlab belt-driven decks at home. I'd only played at one pub in front of eight people and a dog that wouldn't stop barking and never at a club.

The first proper club night I went to was Lords Of The Underground in Camden, aged 16, wearing what I thought was a powerful look. A cheap Calvin Klein suit from TK Maxx and a Moschino T-Shirt underneath, plus some grey Patrick Cox shoes.

Before my first show on *Rinse,* I'd never used Technics or direct drive decks, so it was a shambles. I don't know how I got asked back.

I was playing semi-pro football for Barnet and also had studied for a degree in engineering. I had to choose what I wanted to do, but I was so wrapped up in music it always took priority.

The first *Rinse* studio was in someone's kitchen in Whitechapel. Then we were at The Crossways Estate in Bow, aka 'The Three Flats', on the 16th floor in a derelict flat. A soundproofed box had been built inside the flat, but the DTI busted us eventually. Still all vinyl then, I'd take as many of my best records possible, in my case squeezed into a Royal Mail bag, given to me by DJ Uncle Dugs, who was a postman.

Another *Rinse* studio was above a mechanics garage in Aberfeldy Poplar. My weekly show time was 1pm-3pm on a Sunday, before SPP (the other Rinse co-founder Slimzee, plus MC Plague and MC Paco), which eventually became the Pay As You Go show, also with Godsgift, Wiley, Maxwell D and the great Major Ace, who is sadly no longer with us. So we were all there from the beginning, hanging out in the same studios, growing up together through the radio, running across roofs being chased by DTI during raids.

Dugs managed the station during the early-Noughties when music policy evolved from garage to grime and dubstep.

I was playing garage predominantly, and there had always been this reference to 'house and garage'. There was always a huge American influence, which is obviously the house sound that always comes back round again. UK garage was our own take on it, and we made it our own, be it 2-step or four-four. That unmistakable garage sound never died. Music by Tuff Jam, Todd Edwards, Groove Chronicles, Steve Gurley, Ray Hurley, 2 As 1 (Hermit & Daniel Ward), The Dreem Teem...the list goes on. The raw UK element paved the way for the many sub genres of garage we hear today. And, for me, a lot of house sounds today derive from the old school garage scene, so it's all a natural progression.

It was intriguing being around the likes of Geeneus, Slimzee, Wiley, and Target, watching the grime tunes they were making build a scene from a sound they created in their bedrooms, which is just as relevant today.

By the end of the '90s, Laurence Bagnall, Hermit and Daniel Ward had formed production group United Grooves Collective, which also featured Mark Yardley, later of Stanton Warriors. But, like many promoters, Millennium Eve was a difficult time for World Dance.

Laurence Bagnall: Our event at 3 Mills Studios had not gone well. Jay put me forward for a job at the Ministry, but I was told by the management I was 'a round peg for their square hole'.

A few weeks later Jay picked me up and took me to the Millennium Dome, and told me it was the venue for our next New Year's Eve party. I couldn't see there was any way the Government, after spending millions upon millions on this place, would allow that. But Jay had already done a deal with the Ministry and together we put 25,000 people in there on NYE for the next three years.

Now Ministry wanted Jay and I to go back in and have look at their Fridays. That square hole was suddenly a round one. They had a night called Move which we renamed Smoove. Matt White and I booked some amazing UK garage and R&B talent, and it went on to be one of the most successful Fridays they'd had. I really enjoyed working with great industry people like Gareth Cooke, Amy Thompson, Phil Sales, who went on to run Three Six Zero, and Andy Blackett, who became Musical Director of Fabric. I met my wife, Kelly, working there as well, so that's probably got something to do with it.

I left in 2004 when going to work on a Friday wasn't enjoyable any more, largely because of the gang culture at that time.

Darrell Privett: In the early-Noughties I played a lot at Warehouse in Edmonton for Paul Gardner, as that funky house era came through. But I wasn't earning enough money from DJing to focus on doing that solely...not many DJs do. I'd done so many things by now. An apprentice engineer, graphic design for Credit Suisse bank and at Sky TV and manager at Purple E3 nightclub in Bow.

In 2006 a mate who was a teacher got me some supply work in the music department at the Bethnal Green Academy. Since renamed the Mulberry Academy, Shoreditch, and previously called Daneford School, former pupils include The Kray Twins, Mickey Flanagan...as well as the girls who left to join ISIS, who I taught during my time there.

With the Head of Music about to retire, the headmaster was looking to modernise the department and asked me to take a PGCE (Post Graduate Certificate in Education), which I did and then joined the teaching staff full-time. We built a recording studio and taught the kids how to produce music. Some went on to get record deals so it was very rewarding.

ESSEX
BACKSTORIES

As he entered his teens, growing up in the Upminster area, Dean Lambert was immersed in soul and jazz-funk.

I was a big fan of Tony Blackburn and Robbie Vincent on BBC Radio London in the early-'80s. I always listened to Tony's weekday shows when he began to champion soul music. I loved Arnold too, which was an audio clip of a barking dog. A bit of fun, and I like to have a laugh on my radio shows too. A lot of people have a pop at Tony, but he was a huge influence and his musical knowledge is phenomenal.

My first turntable was made by Garrard, just normal standard belt drive, no speed control, nothing. It had been built into a homemade console made out of chipboard, with a plastic veneer wood effect stuck on it. The volume controls were knobs, not sliders. It was bought for me second hand out of the *Recorder* newspaper.

I was the first kid in the queue with my pocket money every Saturday at JiFS in Chadwell Heath, run by the amazing George and Lynn.

I'd be up early to get the bus over from Rush Green and fuming each week when the shutters didn't go up at 11am. Usually, when they finally did, either Steve Davis or Frank Bruno or both of them would be sat behind the counter going through all the good bits first after being let in the back door early. And Steve bought all the obscure stuff. Lots of albums. His record collection must be something else. I was never an album man. I quickly worked out playing at the school disco, that recordings on LPs were low in quality. Too much information on that vinyl.

I started going to pubs and clubs as early as possible, whichever ones we could get into, mid-teens onwards. Flicks over in Dartford and my favourite, Ilford Town Hall on a Monday night with Froggy.

My first DJ gig in a club was at Daniels, a small club above the bus garage in Hornchurch, when I was 16, in 1982. It held about 200-300 people, a crazy little place.

The Bird Cage and Ben's above The Bitter End in Romford, Lords in Ilford and Oscars in Newbury Park were regular soul and jazz-funk haunts.

But Froggy at Ilford Town Hall was the one. I was like a kid in a sweet shop, stood at the front of the stage each week watching in awe. When David Joseph performed *You Can't Hide Your Love* he came out and did a standing somersault on the stage.

Froggy is my hero, without a doubt, and we became good friends later in life when he had his sound system at The Berwick Manor in Rainham. He had an amazing hexagon-shaped DJ consul, with one section that turned orange, which I believe Disco Supplies in Chadwell Heath made for him. I bought a black and white one in 1992...what a bit of kit.

Froggy's remix of Love Town by Booker Newbury III uses phasing — playing two copies of the same record, one two beats back — and is just amazing.

The first record Matt Nelson bought with his pocket money aged four was cheesy Eurovision entry *Jack In A Box*, but at least it had the word 'Jack' in it.

I was toddling around at 18 months putting records on my parents' turntable, which I later took to my fourth year juniors end of term disco and plugged it into the school amplifier so I could play my own tunes. I became a big lover of reggae music around 1980/81, aged 13/14, and also a big David Rodigan fan, listening to and recording his show every week on *Capital Radio*. My dad had a reel-to-reel so I taped Rodigan's show and cut the adverts out. I'm sure I was the only kid at my school in Loughton hanging out in reggae shops in Walthamstow. I also travelled west to Dub Vendor next to Ladbroke Grove station, which had its own label Fashion Records.

The music taste of one of Matt's classmates, John Fernandez, would combine perfectly after they left school.

We both got into electro but John was into his Depeche Mode too. We met in the middle with soul, reggae and electronic music and began talking about becoming DJs. At the age of 14 we blagged it into Oscars, and in Tottenham, the Ritzy and Elton's behind the police station.

From the age of 16, 17 we really started taking notice of DJs mixing. Simon Harris, who hit with Bass (How Low Can You Go), was resident at Billy Jean's in Epping, just off the High Road. The mid-'80s, a fight every week, but it's where we saw Simon mixing a capellas over the top of soul tunes on Technics 1200 decks. After all those years of messing around with records, I just had to find a way to DJ myself.

I'd left school at 16, marching straight down to the jewellers on my way home to get my ear pierced, because that had not been allowed.

jock on his box

dean parties hard and plays out with the likes of fellow caner Brandon Block. here are his top 10 tunes

dean lambert

steamin'

tips for the week

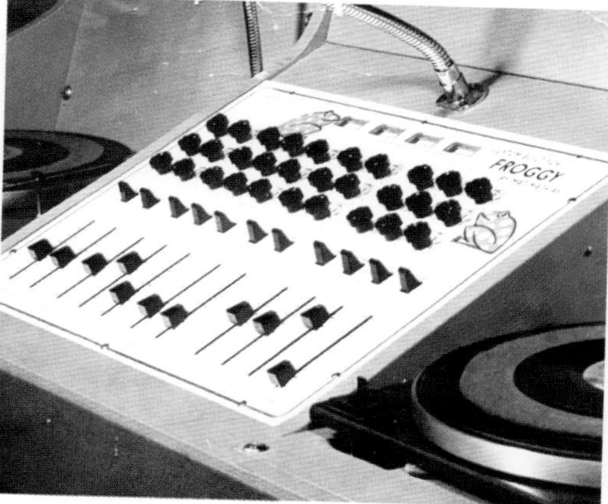

(Top) Froggy at a *Radio 1* Roadshow in the '80s and (above right) one of his DJ consoles. (Above left) A *Music Week* feature on Dean Lambert from the '90s.

I got a little Suzuki ER50 motorbike and worked for my brother Paul's courier business, then began a three-year electrical apprenticeship.

John and I met a couple of rappers at the Tottenham Ritzy — really nice fellas — and made a track with them at my parents' house which we got played at the Ritzy the following weekend, which is mad, thinking back, because it must have been such a shit production. We weren't mad ravers, out every week, but we did Camden Palace some Fridays and got to a few of the big raves like Biology.

In early '89 six of us started our own pirate station, *Raw FM*, 104.4. Me, John, DJ Crews, Freestyle, DJ R and Mash. Two of the guys were locksmiths and welders who worked for Hackney and Tower Hamlets Councils and knew empty properties. They found us an old squat in a tower block on the edge of Hackney Marshes, broke in and secured it by welding up big metal gates. Shame it was on the 18th floor. Crews, our mate Graham, knew a geeky geezer over Chingford way who was making up rigs for £60 a pop.

I gave the station my old pair of Citronic because I'd now bought a set of 1200s and a Phonic MRT60 mixer from a shop in Dalston called Hi-Tech. I designed a coffin flight case for the gear to sit in, and asked the guys at Hi-Tech to make it for me. They ended up selling loads.

The rig was in the flat with an aerial on the balcony. We were up there every weekend, but within a couple of months we got done, and everything was taken. So we moved up to the 20th floor and this time we did it properly. Loads of soundproofing on the floor and egg boxes on the walls. We placed a dummy rig on the top of the lift shaft and fed power cables through the soil pipe that went up to the actual rig we were using on the roof. The theory was that if anybody cut the power at the dummy rig, they'd think they'd taken the station down, but the actual rig could be powered up again easily. And we did lose the dummy rig a few times, but never the real rig again.

Jonny C remembers growing up in a busy community full of musical inspiration. Setting up a pirate station with his mates was a no-brainer.

As a ten-year-old in 1982/83, our street in Grays was buzzing with kids playing out after school each night. You could in those days. Because of my cerebral palsy I didn't spend as much time at junior school as the other kids. I had to go through a lot of physiotherapy for my disability so I lived for those evenings, knocking around at the front of the house with my mates. The local skinheads would hang out at the end of our road, blasting out soul tunes from a boom box. We got into the music, because it was the next progression.

My dad was big into Motown, and then he got me and my brother into Pink Floyd and took us to see them whenever they toured.

Around the age of 11, I had a couple of electro-funk albums on cassette. My introduction was breakdancing at the end of the street with my mates on a piece of lino to Kraftwerk. The body-popping films that all came out around 1984/85 and their soundtracks were really influential. *Beat Street* and *Breakdance* and tracks like *Street Dance* by Break Machine and Ollie & Jerry's *Breakin'...There's No Stopping Us.*

I was bought a stereo stack system for one of my birthdays, the one we all had then, with the double cassette, a radio tuner, with your aerial wire stuck all up your bedroom wall with blue tack. I became fascinated by radio. The usual, taping the Top 40 until the DJ spoke.

My first decks were made by Memorex and had a little green light at the front. The Gemini mixer was made out of wood, really early stuff, just an up and down fader and no mic socket. All the music that came out now seemed to be electronic. Paul Hardcastle's *19* was a big one that stood out when it went to No 1.

When I was 13 I met Tony Moule and Robin Edwards, aka Robin EE, three or four years old than me older. They had decks and early electro and house mix-tapes from American radio stations.

Then in the summer of 1986, Morgan Khan's Street Sounds and *Capital Radio* put on the huge event at Wembley Arena, *UK Fresh*. The line-up was crazy, bringing so many of the American hip-hop stars we'd heard about, to London. Afrika Bambaataa, Grandmaster Flash, Roxanne Shante, Mantronix and Just Ice.

And then the music just got better and better. We all liked sitting round having a puff and, let's face it, the music just went well with it. I didn't even know what a rave was but I started putting on parties in the woods, with a radio player blasting out *Stomp FM*. Early event planning. None of us drank, though, until our late 20s. No need. It was a different buzz we were all on. It was all starting to bubble up nicely now.

We could get *Centreforce* when it came on in 1989. It had a crackle, but you didn't mind that. We could pick up most stations so we knew what was going on. I started to tape *Centreforce*, obviously not minding if the DJs spoke over the records now. I found a tape of a Keithy Mac show recently and played it to him and he couldn't believe it. You wouldn't recognise him, his voice hadn't broken yet.

I was now training to be a civil engineer on a two-year placement with Balfour Beattie in Norfolk but I came back at the weekends.

The natural progression for us, even at that young age, was to try and start our own pirate station. With my training, I evolved into the radio set-up side of things. Our first station was *Dancezone* at the end of 1990.

We broadcast from my mate' dad's house at the end of the road. Colin went under the name Flying Doctor C and had made a few tracks. He had all the equipment up there, keyboards and mixing desks. We used army technology, coming straight off the chimney stack.

We went to the pictures one Friday night to watch *Star Wars*, everyone involved in the station. When we came back, the loft was being raided by the DTI. There were 16 of us in the dock at court, hilarious.

Our next pirate, *Cyndicut, 100.4*, was with a group of pals including our mate Daz, aka Undercover Agent, who later had huge success with his label Juice Records. Some of the biggest names in drum and bass started on *Cyndicut*. I met Andy C and Shimmon before they'd even picked up a record. Red One and Lifted Spirits were on *Cyndicut* too, as was Tony Moule. By now I was all about keeping a pirate radio station and the music going. We did parties in a little school which had closed, but never made much money out of events in the '90s. We were happy if we got our coats back at the end of the night.

Dean Lambert: I've always been a tech-head and had equipment. It always surprised me how many DJs didn't have decks. At one point I had four sets of 1210s, one pair set up at home, and the others always out on hire.

When we started DJing in the '80s we had to use the microphone. And you can't get anywhere near a man holding a microphone.

I signed up with Juliana's, an international events and management agency, and worked for two months at a time in Denmark, Norway and Sweden. I had my 21st birthday in Egypt as part of a six-month contract at The Sheraton Hotel and DJd all over the Middle East.

The bemused residents of leafy Havering suburb Harold Park must have wondered about the 13-year-old boy strutting the streets with a huge clock around his neck, but then they probably hadn't just bought a copy of *It Takes A Nation Of Millions To Hold Us Back* and weren't aware of Public Enemy and its colourful frontman Flava Flav.

In 1987 Matt 'Emulsion' Smith was already a self-appointed 'hype man, MC and dancer' for a duo he formed with childhood pal Stuart J. More than 30 years later the pair still DJ together as The Acid Brothers.

Our families are close friends so Stu and I have known each other since we were six months old. As kids, we started off with one turntable, one tape deck and two amplifiers, turn downing one amp and the other one up to bring in each record from our limited vinyl collection.

My older brother blasting out Kraftwerk's *The Model* at full volume kickstarted my love of electronic music. We saw some breakdancers on *Pebble Mill At One* and it blew our minds. When E.T, BMXs and the break-dancing movies came out they were the coolest things we had ever seen.

We lived hip-hop as much as we could growing up where we were.

The music, the fashion, the sportswear. We were really into graffiti, but too scared to do any. It would have stuck out like a sore thumb in our suburban surroundings. We did a little bit under a subway once, and were shit-scared for weeks. I bought my first 12 inch record by accident in 1986. I was walking through Romford market and my mum pointed at a record stall and said. 'That's where your cousin Vincent works.' We went over and I thought it was so cool. They were playing *The Magnificent Jazzy Jeff* by DJ Jazzy Jeff & The Fresh Prince. I was massively into electro by this point, so bought it with my pocket money there and then.

The next year I bought Public Enemy's debut album *Yo Bum Rush The Show* from Vincent's stall and I learned all the lyrics, which were so powerful for me.

On the face of it, I'm a fat white bald guy, but because my father is South African, I'm actually mixed race. So I experienced a lot of racism growing up. When Public Enemy came out with those two albums in quick succession, 1987, '88, I was getting picked on a lot and it was starting to get quite physical. My dad sent me to judo so I could stick up for myself.

Then I heard *Don't Believe The Hype* and Chuck D say, 'I'm not a hooligan, I rock the party and, Clear all the madness, I'm not a racist, Preach to teach to all.' And it really resonated with me at the time, and I just felt this strong affiliation to the music. It really helped.

Vincent went on to form Drizabone and had huge success with tracks like *Real Love* and their radio mix of Shanice's *I Love Your Smile,* which was a No 2 hit in both the UK and America.

Growing up, we just dreamed of going to a gig, maybe getting a bar or club booking or. We watched *Top Of The Pops* religiously. I remember seeing D-Mob, Cathy Dennis and Adeva in the same episode. Doing radio would have been even more of a dream. We had started listening to pirate stations on Stu's brother's Kenwood stack system, like *Stomp FM, Sunrise*...and then when *Centreforce* came on, we were blown away again. Later *Fantasy FM.* Brilliant times. Stu bought some belt drives and a Realistic mixer and we started doing birthdays and weddings when we were still at school, but we relied on Stu's mum to drop us off and pick us up in her car. I always wondered why somebody would book a kid to DJ at their special occasion.

(Above) Matt Emulsion and Steve ESP (below) Jonny C.

When my older sister told us there was this new thing out called acid house when we were about 14, we didn't know we'd already been buying some early house music. We had created a hip-hop crew at school called The Beatjammers and were getting into hip-house and bands like De La Soul...but now we were running round the playground shouting 'acccciiiieeeed', because we had heard older kids in the streets saying it. I even bought some dungarees with my pocket money.

One day Stu said he was going to a rave, and I said, 'You're joking.' His sister was dating someone who knew someone who knew a guy called DJ Melon, who was putting on a rave in Hackney and, as Stu's mum worked a lot of nights at a care home, he was able to sneak out. Of course, he came back with all this amazing information and knowledge.

The next week we started going up to Music Power in Ilford. Roland from *Grange Hill*, Erkan Mustafa, used to work there. We also used to go to Trumps in Hornchurch, which was another great record shop.

Jonny C: My mate Robin EE, and his brother Spencer started *Twilight 105.4 FM*, based around the small club of the same name, set back off the A127 at West Horndon, next to a petrol garage. We had N-Joi on the station, who were Southend-based and big with their bleeps before their hit Anthem. Robin and Spencer had a label called EE-FFICACY Recordings and did well with some house tracks like *So Sweet* and *Keep On.* They were also part of a production team, Temple Of Life with Tony Moule. We were all making acidy-techy-house at the time.

The postman woke me up delivering 12 inch promos, which I'd flick through and then head to the radio to play some of them. I feel blessed to have grown up when I did. It felt like there was this big lull when Maggie was in, which just seemed to give people a kick up the arse because the rave scene exploded after that.

Matt Smith: My first DJ gig at 16 in 1990 was for my brother at one of his karaoke gigs at a pub in Epping called The Entertainer. I began playing loads of Strictly Rhythm stuff, right up my street...real house music, with all the elements of disco and soul you need.

We never stopped buying house. It's always been the bedrock of everything. That and hip-hop, that's why hip-house was perfect for me, my two favourite things in the world. I particularly loved all the piano stuff, like Beatmasters featuring Merlin - *Who's In The House*. For me, hip-house didn't go on to be the genre that it could have been.

After acid house, we also got into hardcore and breakbeat. Renegade Soundwave, Shut Up And Dance, the '91, '92 rave scene. Production House, Acen - *Trip To The Moon*. When it started moving towards happy hardcore, that's when I lost interest. And I wasn't into jungle or drum and bass. Then house got a bit tougher, more progressive. I've spent a lot of time in local record shops over the years, including Izit Dance in Romford in the mid-'90s, then Millennium Dance in Hornchurch and Hard House in Romford, which became Trackmasters.

Dean Lambert: I loved Hermit on *Centreforce*...and his partner Bagz, who I got to know through A.W.O.L/World Dance, playing at huge events with him like Lydd Airport.

I leased an old road rig from a company in Maidstone and split it up to hire out to clubs. The Astoria had 20k off of me, Lazerdrome another 10k. I ended up with a seven and half tonne lorry, owning the system and putting it in and out of clubs all over London, including from 5am at the Breakfast Club at Busby's for Orange, then playing there all morning. Grafting.

I already knew Andy from football, and when he had Gass on a Sunday, we had it on Saturdays for a while with the Happy Days crew, Timmi Ram Jam and Paul Nelson, a night we also took to the Elephant & Castle pub and The Frog & Nightgown. The early-'90s, that period, 1993,'94 was amazing for me, DJ-wise. My old mate Chris Paul's Orange Bank Holiday and Halloween parties at Hippodrome, and at The Astoria, where I also played for Wonderland and Living Dream, plus Bagleys and Club UK. Then there was that huge Sunday scene, Sunday Mass at The Arches in Southwark Street and things like Sunnyside Up.

Closer to home, I had great success at Berwick Manor in Rainham with my own Underground Connection parties, where Hermit was a regular guest for me. One Bank Holiday, I put two and half thousand people in the Berwick, with Graham Gold in the marquee at the back. I hold the record. I'd put all the traffic light boards up and hand 5,000 flyers out myself. If you gave them to someone else, they'd end up in the bin. I insisted I used Froggy's sound-system at Underground Connection.

I was one of the first British DJs to play in Russia when I went out there with World Dance. Times were good. I'd had the first Jeep Wrangler in the UK in the early-'90s. One time I played at The Yacht Club at Embankment, I dropped my speed boat in the river at Woolwich and rode along The Thames with good pal Dave Courtney and my records on board. What an entrance! I got pulled by the police when I was wearing the staple outfit of white shirt, black leather trousers and cowboy boots. As I stepped out of the Jeep and put my boot on the footplate, the copper said, 'Fuck me, it's John Wayne.'

Slipmatt: I picked up more DJ work, as Slipmatt, including at our local pub in Loughton, The Golden Lion, where Rob Acteson was resident.

With *Raw FM* stabilising, John and I booked a studio in New Cross owned by Michael Menson (RIP) from Double Trouble & Rebel MC. We'd planned a tune out and identified our samples. We made *Do That Dance/ It Ain't Nothing* in a day. Michael loved the track and the label he was with,B-Ware Records, took it straight away. With John now known as Lime, we took the initials of our stage names and came up with SL2, as simple as that. That first release did okay, but the label knocked us. There was no particular fall-out: we took it on the chin. We were just were chuffed to get our first record out and decided instead to set up our own label, Awesome Records, and get the tracks cut ourselves.

Step forward Matt's Nelson's brother, an entrepreneur who loved seizing an opportunity.

Paul left school, like me, at 16, and got a job at our local NatWest in Loughton. However, he left his cushty job at the bank at 18 to start a courier business and had now also bought our local cab firm, Sadlers. His mate, Ray Spence was the manager of the HQ venue in Camden, now called Lockside, and managed to get me a booking playing alongside Coldcut, which was a big deal for me at the time. Next door to Sadlers was a cafe run by a guy called Lou, who also managed an industrial site in Barking.

My brother was never really a raver, but he saw his little brother become a DJ, playing this new music coming through. His mate managed a cool club in Camden, loads of illegal dos were popping up, and the geezer in the cafe had access to land. He introduced Lou to Ray and they came up with the idea of Raindance. Obviously I was right in there as resident of the huge raves that followed, but I went from playing in small bars and clubs to 10,000 people, so I was shitting it.

The first Raindance was on a Saturday in September in 1989 at the Jenkins lane site that Lou managed. It says 'Totally Legal' on the flyer, but it was anything but. My brother and the guys used legal loopholes to get away with it, and the party went right through until 2am on the Monday morning. The event was actually paused for a few hours on the Sunday afternoon so a car boot sale could go ahead, although most people carried on raving in the car park.

SL2 was the first name on the flyer, alongside the likes of Linden C, Paul Trouble Anderson (still Paul Anderson at that point), Trevor Fung, Colin Dale, Cleveland Anderson and Fabio & Grooverider. The second Raindance a couple of months later, also at Jenkins Lane, was also illegal, but under the guise of a Children In Need fundraiser. I was on the decks with Lime when the police came and closed it down at around 1.30am when it was just getting going.

After that, all the parties were legal, including the next one at Jenkins Lane and a huge one in a circus tent in Cambridge on the August Bank Holiday Sunday in 1990. Future guests included Kevin Saunderson from Inner City. My brother was actually the first person to get a licence for a legal rave of that size, which then paved the way for the likes of Perception and Fantazia.

As the '80s ended, everything was happening at once. It was crazy juggling DJing, running *Raw FM*, Raindance events and studio time with our day jobs. Because I'd only been on £40 a week for the first year of my apprenticeship I'd also been doing a bit of cabbing for my brother.

Studio-wise, John and I were working on our next SL2 release, *The Noise/Bassquake*, during 1990, which we released on Awesome Records on white label in early 1991. We got all our ideas together for our next release, *DJs Take Control*, and made it in a day with an engineer at a studio in Whetstone, North London. We knew exactly what we wanted to do with the record, which sampled Nightwriter's *Let The Music Use You*. We did the flip side, *Way In My Brain,* at John's house. We got 250 white labels pressed and they were all snapped up that day. It went down well at Raindance the next week, and even better at the Raindance six weeks later.

Virtually at the same time, the summer of 1991, I passed my apprenticeship as an electrician with flying colours, but had to give it all up when we were offered a record deal by XL Recordings. I felt sorry for my governor, who had supported me all through college, but what could I do, with everything happening around me? The phone hadn't stopped ringing and we turned down loads of other labels including Warp and Orbital, but being Essex boys and now on the same label as Prodigy, was a no brainer.

We waited for what felt like ages for the release to come out, which it did finally in October, and then it charted in its first week, in at No 24. Crazy. We got the call to go on *Top Of The Pops*, which was unbelievable. As a kid I used to watch every Thursday night with a cup a tea and a biscuit...so to be on the show was mental and nerve-wracking. We jumped to No 11 the next week. The Prodigy never did *Top Of The Pop*s, but we were of a different mindset. We weren't rebels, we were just in it for the music and the rave and to have fun. Any money that came through was a bonus.

Our follow-up *On A Ragga Tip* did even better and reached No 2. We appeared twice on *Top Of The Pops* during the nine weeks it was in the Top Ten. One time we had lunch in the BBC cafe with Dot Cotton and Pete Beale and also I got a kiss on the cheek from Kylie Minogue, so I can't complain.

PRESENTS

RAINDANCE

SATURDAY
16th SEPTEMBER

10,000 STRONG – DANCE 'TIL DAWN
For coaches and meeting points
Listen to: SUNRISE, LASER, CENTREFORCE

SLII Beware Records	**LINDEN C.** Hypnosis	**PAUL ANDERSON** Love
TREVOR FUNG Land of Oz	**JC** Twilight Zone	**COLIN DALE** Legends
EVIL EDDIE Dungeons	**GEORGE KELLY** Centreforce	**MAD AXE** Sunrise
FABIO Fun City	**CLEVELAND ANDERSON** Tom Tom Club	**GROOVE RIDER** Rage

Tickets Available *NOW*

HIT AND RUN RECORDS – Walthamstow – 521 7422

RED RECORDS Beak Street & Peckham 734 2746	**G & M RECORDS** Elephant & Castle 708 0988	**JUST FOR THE BEAT** Tottenham 885 2775
SUMMIT RECORDS Birmingham 021 643 7895	**MUSIC POWER** Ilford & Haringey 478 2080	**WIRED FOR SOUND** Mare Street 985 7531
BLACK MARKET Soho 437 0478	**POUR HOMME** Welwyn 301 1625	**SOUL SENSE** Luton 0582 20423
IN THE MIX Leytonstone	**BLUE BIRD RECORDS** Edgeware Rd & Streatham 723 9090	**BOXER** Loughton 508 4103

ADVANCE £12.00

LOCATION GUIDE
0831 487 505

SAME DAY £15.00

My parents were really happy, but probably weren't that surprised given my love of music from such an early age, but I've never ever been a showman or ever wanted to be a performer. The success of the two big SL2 tunes and Raindance meant I was getting DJ gigs throughout the UK and John and I were doing SL2 PAs all over the place too.

Raw FM was exciting at the time. We'd all go up there and get stoned, but we didn't want anyone else knowing where it was so nobody else got involved. I was too busy after a while and it fizzled out at the end of 1991.

That New Year's Eve Raindance in Leicestershire for 10,000 was headlined by Carl Cox with a PA from Prodigy, but it was the end of my brother's involvement. He was on a different path from a business point of view to Ray and Lou, so they parted company. Paul went on to open The Aquarium nightclub in Shoreditch. I played for Raindance over the next few years, and at most of the reunion parties since.

Alan Bowers: I got a call from Ray Spence from Raindance because they needed to expand. My dad owned the land next door to Jenkins Lane, the Norwegian Playing Fields, where West Ham reserves trained. Raindance was becoming more and more legit, with paramedics on-site, far removed from what we ever did. Pasha and Genesis shared the same security, the older lot from football, Matthew, Johnny Butler, Carlton Leach, Cooky and Sid, so I hooked Raindance up.

I worked on the next few Raindance events and then went back into football. I signed for Norwich City in 1992 and later to Fulham, but putting on a rave and potentially earning thousands of pounds definitely excited me more than playing football in the third division in those days. I eventually moved to Spain and launched a successful property development business and also became director of a leading car dealership group in the UK.

In 1989, a nine-year-old Carly Denham wasn't exactly sure what acid house music was, or what happened at a rave, even…but she was obsessed with the music and chat she had discovered on pirate radio and vowed one day to try to become a DJ.

I was listening to *Kiss* when it was still a pirate and suddenly *Top Of The Pops* wasn't good enough. Tracks like *Big Fun* and *Good Life* by Inner City seemed really cool. At that age I didn't quite appreciate the whole thing was about to explode, but the music felt different from the seven inch pop records I'd been buying at Our Price in Romford town centre.

I got my mates involved and for us, pre-mobile phones, ringing a pager number and leaving a message with a lady and then talking to each other over the radio was magical.

I was bought a boom box with a double tape deck and I'd record any pirate station I could and listened to cassettes on repeat. When I was 12, I got my hands on my grandad's Sony separates in a glass cabinet.

I feel like a rave baby, because in my early teens house became hardcore and then jungle and drum and bass. When I was 15, my friend's step-dad worked on the door at the Soundshaft, next door to Heaven, so we blagged our way into a party called Rapture. It was the Grant Nelson-type house and garage I was getting into so I was mesmerized. When it evolved into UK garage I focused on house.

Now I'd been to an actual club, and in central London, I was even more hooked on the thought of maybe becoming a DJ, but it was definitely still a dream, at most.

My friends would be like, 'Yeah, okay, right...for a start, you're a girl...' And they were right, because the DJ world seemed so male-dominated and unaccessible. My mates were so dismissive I promised myself I'd have a go one day. I've always had a rebellious nature, so for me it was bait.

By 1992, Steve Kite was in Faliraki opening his own bar. His decade-long stint as resident at the Circus Tavern and work in and around the Essex pub and club circuit had set him up nicely for his time on the Greek party island.

My first pub gig was from a 'DJ required' advert in the *Romford Recorder* in the early-'80s...for The Dover Castle in Shadwell, near Wapping. Then I got regular work at The Top House in Aveley and South Ockendon pubs Henry Gernett and The Prince Of Wales, which was a proper soul-boy place.

My first stint on radio was for SEHB (South East Hospital Broadcasting) out of Basildon Hospital, still in my late teens. I was useless, I sounded like a Tilbury docker.

Loads of people were out five or six nights a week. The Goldmine in Canvey Island, TOTS (Talk Of The South) in Southend, Wheatleys at the Tavern, Epping Forest Country Club and later Hollywood in Romford and Zero 6 in Chelmsford...all busy clubs throughout the week.

Before beat mixing, as a DJ you were really only as good as your record collection. Influenced by Robbie Vincent on *Radio London* and Greg Edwards on *Capital*, I ordered imports from a little record shop in South Ockendon called Route 66, run by a guy called Dave Potter.

I had several auditions for the Circus Tavern, but eventually became cover for resident Steve Merrill and stayed for ten years. Keith Mac did really well when he came in during the summer of 1989, but the venue changed tack again the year after — the Chippendales era and things like darts.

New Circus Owner Aaron Stone and his son Aaron Stone introduced lap-dancing upstairs and opened a new club in Rochford called The Casino, with me as resident.

Then a phone call out of the blue...from a guy I met on holiday two summers before. We'd decided to jet-ski the 20 miles from our resort in Marmais to Rhodes and, of course, ran out of petrol. As we bobbed around waiting to be rescued, we made plans to open our own bar abroad.

Iggy was phoning to tell me he'd found a great location in Faliraki.

After a decade of fun and games DJing in Essex, it was just the opportunity I was looking for. A few weeks later, I flew out with a couple of bags and some records and sound equipment.

Our place, Jazz Bo's on Bar Street, attracted couples and families with its karaoke, pub quizzes and the odd Mr or Miss Faliraki competition, and shut at midnight. That was my bread and butter, but I quickly secured a residency at Set on Club Street, alongside Jamie T and Mark Howlett, Froggy's son. I began mixing with CDs on a Denon deck I'd brought over from the UK, earning me the nickname of DJ Gadget.

I rented a flat in the village and once a week, walked to the phone box to call my girlfriend to tell her how I was getting on.

There was always a revolver on the desk when we queued up in the office to get paid at Set. The local mafia who ran the club were strong on people selling drugs. If they caught anyone, it would be a gun to the head, time to leave the island.

I'd spend the winter in the UK playing at some of my old haunts, and I got a new residency at a club in Woolwich called Flamingo's, which was an old theatre with the DJ booth in the royal box.

The 1995 and '96 seasons were the golden years of Faliraki. Alongside running the bar, I played at new clubs like Q or Dune four or five nights a week, buzzing around on my scooter, loving life. I helped set up *UK Radio*, which piggy-backed on a station in the village where I lived. We broadcast during the day and sold advertising to bars and clubs. My one regret with Faliraki was working too much. Any spare hours at the bar, DJing or at the radio. Business was great, but in 1996 we decided to let the lease on Jas Bo's run out its final couple of years. It was getting so busy that on Bar Street you couldn't distinguish one bar from the other. The tour operators sold people a dream which didn't exist.

Roger The Doctor: I came home from Tenerife before the end of the 1994 season when my girlfriend Joanne fell pregnant (with my son Conna).

Through connections at Epping Forest Country Club, I landed a residency there. It was the start of an amazing two years at the Country Club, playing in the sports hall dressed each Friday as The Jungle to

1200 people, and double that at Splash Bank Holiday Sunday specials by the outdoor pool behind the original nightclub, all alongside other residents Paul Crawley, Jon Jules, El Tel and Normski. Cars parked all over the grounds, and traffic backed up on Aveley Road.

Now owner Peter Pomfrett wanted ideas for a Saturday night. A sculptor I knew had already approached me about dressing the sports hall in an underwater theme, with blue and white drapes as the sea, thousands of bubbles hanging down from the ceiling, huge life-size sharks everywhere and a boat in the middle of the room for the DJ booth. I presented the idea and said I needed a promotions manager role and a car to promote the new party and Peter agreed. A few months later we blitzed the area with 150,000 circular 'bubble' flyers and launched H20, which was packed every Saturday for the whole of 1995.

I played at Charlie Chans every Sunday for DJ Marie and at Steering Wheel in Birmingham with Jeremy Healy and Smokin Jo. We stayed at the best hotels and were treated like superstars up there.

It was time for Matt Smith to become Matt Emulsion and to take to the local airwaves.

I was crapping myself. With my East End accent, stutter and lisp I had never felt confident about public speaking, but I just thought, sod it. I quickly found I loved interacting with listeners when they paged in.

My first show was on *Quest FM* in Rainham in 1994, a station that helped me finally decide on my DJ name. I was always looking for something catchier than my real name. MC E, when I still believed I could be a rapper or dancer, sounded too druggy, when that's never been my thing. The Kemist, after my middle name Kem, or Matty Mash-Up both still sounded like I was popping pills or serving up. Then one day, aged 18, 19, I went to the shops with my dad wearing a pair of chunky white, red and black SPX high-tops and a baseball cap. We were chatting in *B&Q* and I walked slap bang into a display of tins of paint, which came crashing down on me. I picked one up and the words 'Matt Emulsion' were staring back at me. It was a gift.

In the late-90s, Stuart and I moved to *Force FM* with our friend Trevor King, aka producer Electronic Youth / Leisure Grove. *Force* had moved from Thurrock to Harold Hill and was run like a military organisation, and never raided, some achievement over a decade or so. My main show was 7.30pm on a Friday, but living so close I did loads of covers, which really helped establish me as a local name in the Essex area. Through *Force FM*, me, Stu, Wayne Anderson, Alex Arnout and ESP were given a residency at The Opium Lounge in Romford. It was great all being from (above) The infamous Hollywood nightclub on Atlanta Boulevard in Romford, pictured during the mid-'90s. (left) Roger The Doctor joining Faces in Gants Hill in 1998, and (below) at Epping Forest Country Club in 1995.

the same area, on a local station, playing at the club most weeks.

I also played in Ibiza in 1998 for the first time, as part of a BT -sponsored competition at Savannah in San Antonio, with Jonathan Ulysses on the judging panel. I won my heats, but couldn't afford to fly back out for the final later in the season. I had better luck a few years later when I was asked to play at a bodypainting festival in a remote village in Austria, fitting considering the DJ name I'd eventually settled on. The event is now set in the city, attracts up to 30,000 people each year, and I've been playing each year since. I'm also booked to play in Austria and Germany every couple of months on the back of it too.

I did have a seven-month period of being a DJ full-time around 2006 when I was made redundant, but it was too up and down. I was lucky to get a job back in IT with the NHS and I've been there ever since.

Promoting parties to his student friends and becoming a full-time DJ soon became Tony Nicholls' focus.

I arrived at college with 12 GCSEs, all top grades, and left the least qualified...but I had a great record collection, an amazing social life and a job at the biggest nightclub in the area.

I started putting on my own parties at The Cellar Bar in Romford, called S.H.A.G (which stood for Sexual House And Garage), with college friend, Steve Humphries, selling out the capacity of 200 in advance. Secrets just around the corner gave me a Wednesday night residency, then Gareth Cooke at Hollywood asked me work for him at Culture Shock so I moved over. Secrets weren't happy — the owners of those clubs didn't get on — but Hollywood was more about dance music. I was now earning £300 a week as resident at Culture Shock, and I hadn't even finished college yet. My job was to put flyers in local shops during the week and then do warm-up sets for the big guest DJs booked every Friday.

When Gareth moved to The Ministry Of Sound, I remember an excited convoy of cars from Romford to Elephant & Castle when he booked S.H.A.G to host the Baby Box room.

I started to do pirate radio on a Sunday morning at a filthy flat in an imposing tower block in Barking, and then I joined *Indulgence FM*, a small station in a block in Collier Row.

Roger's success at the Country Club saw him offered a £2m budget to relaunch The Ilford Palais, which was now called 5th Avenue. It was an offer he couldn't refuse. Just weeks after he left, a competition Roger had organized in conjunction with my *Club Mix* page in the *Recorder*

Newspaper Group to find a new resident DJ, with myself, Dean Savonne and DJ Fellatio as judges, saw newcomer George D win the first prize, a residency at the Country Club.

I'd never been headhunted before. Better money, a nicer car and health care. They wanted me to recreate what we'd done at the Country Club, which was an independent venue breaking the monopolies of the Rank Leisures, and those bad clubs that sprung up with two names.

I renamed the club The Venue and I did get that place going, but it was hard. There was so much red tape involved it was impossible to get anything signed off.

Then I got a call from Tony Hurrell, the general manager at Faces in Gants Hill. I knew Tony H from Charlie Chans, where he was bar manager at the same time as Faces owner Tony B was a DJ there. *Centreforce* DJ Max Fernandez's mum was also a manager at Chans at the time. Small world.

I took a big pay cut to move to Faces, but I became a Wednesday and Friday night resident still able to play where I wanted on other nights. I really wanted to go over to Faces, a smart club, with a good crowd, always a great vibe and hard to get in.

Faces in 1998 was at its peak. I remember coming outside one night with Tony H, Colin, the bars manager, and resident DJ Stevie O, and looking down the road. The queue was a couple of hundred yards all the way past Kwik Fit.

I retired from DJing at Faces in 2000, when I was 35, or at least I thought I did, and became assistant manager to Tony H, working on promotions and running the bar staff.

A couple of years later George D and Yankee, on the back of the success of their West End promotion Posh Funk, launched Sunday Sessions at Faces, which was a huge night for us for several years. One of the biggest and another Essex and East London institution.

Tony Nicholls: In 1997, Hollywood was being refurbished and 2000 people were looking for somewhere to go. I was asked to be resident at Berwick Manor, which was suddenly the place to be.

My musical inspiration came from American house labels like Nervous Records and Strictly Rhythm and producers like Masters At Work.

I was now playing regularly for Clockwork Orange too, their parties at The Cross and Camden palace in central London, but also in Ibiza for them at Es Paradis on Wednesdays, and getting regular work in Dubai, Marbella and Amsterdam.

When Hollywood reopened I got my residency back, but I could see that era was coming to an end. Bradley and Mickey from the Berwick had gone over to Ayia Napa to set up Club Mythology so I took up a full-time residency for a summer season.

Carly Denham: I listened to *Unity FM*, 88.4 for years. DJs like Scooby, Barnowl and Chipmonk, and *Shakedown FM*, I think, on the same frequency, plus *Pulse* 90.6 and *Energy FM*...and Steve Jackson on Kiss 100. At 16 I was going to Hollywood, Ritzy and Secrets in Romford and Oscars in Clacton and, when we were a bit older, the Country Club, Powerhouse in Stratford, Bagleys and World Dance events.

Then at the age of 17 I had my son. A lot of my aspirations had to be put on the back-burner. I still went out clubbing when I could, but Taylor was obviously my priority. I went back to college and retrained and when he started schoo,l I worked as a legal secretary.

It already seemed liked I'd been a punter for so many years, but now aged 22 I bought myself my first set of 1210s, on finance at Mix Direct in Chadwell Heath. Looking after a young son meant I wasn't able to go out much but all that time spent at home helped me practise my mixing. Up early most mornings with my headphones on for an hour before getting Taylor up for school. A friend helped me got a show on *Force FM* in 2008. I hadn't even played out anywhere yet, but I couldn't turn down the opportunity.

My first show on a Thursday night was after Matt Emulsion. I was so nervous. Every time I went to speak nothing came out, but Matt, bless him, put me at ease by staying back and cracking jokes to calm my nerves. We were all playing vinyl still and had a Nokia 3310 for text messages coming in. I started to get local gigs at places like City Limits in Collier Row and Pacific Edge in Romford market.

Jonny C: In the mid-'90s our family friend Tony Moule formed a 'jump-up style' drum and bass collective Prisoners Of Technology (POT) and set up Fresh Kutt Records to release his pioneering material and I got involved, working at the label. Tony, aka TMS 1, went on to remix Beastie Boys' *Intergalactic* and *Got's Like Come On Thru* for Buddha Monk from Wu-Tang Clan. When POT were asked to tour America at the end of 2000, Tony took me as a tour DJ. It was crazy, I was in the States for New Year's Eve and hung out in a hotel room with Afrika Bambaataa and the bloody Zulu Nation. It's mad, us lot from Grays, working with the Beastie Boys and their label Grand Royale.

Jon O'Brien: I started my own garage Saturday night at Zero 6 in Southend in 1997 called Cultural Vibes and had an amazing three years there. Andy bought Craig David down to do a live PA for me just as the

UK garage scene was exploding. Spoony, Timmy and Mikee had formed Dreem Team and later joined *Radio 1*. We had 1500 people through an 800-capacity club the first time they played as a trio.

During our last six months, the scene was turning and we started getting agg. That never happened with the house scene. I got offered Ayia Napa, but I wouldn't touch it with a barge-pole. I kept Cultural Vibes going until the end of 2000, but the scene was getting darker and, for me, there was too much jibber jabber from the MCs, who started charging as much as the DJs, so it was doubling the cost of your line-up. I preferred Kie and Creed. For me, it was always about the music and those guys weren't on the mic all night.

Dean Lambert: In the late-'90s I had an opportunity to play in Thailand. Russell Cleaver from The Flying Squad and Chris Leonard from World Dance, both old connections, booked me to play on an island just off Koh Samui for a DJ battle with Judge Jules. I like to think I won.

Then Brandon Block, probably one of the first of us lot to play out there, booked me to do a Christmas/New Year in Thailand with him. In the early-2000s I went out for a season and decided to stay out there. I rented my flat out in London and didn't come back for 17 years. I worked in Bangkok first for about nine months. A fantastic city, but not a great place to live. It's just too much. Down on the islands is just so much better. The sea, the air, and a simpler way of life.

I had various DJ residencies, and got on the F1 after-party circuit too. With Koh Samui being the No 1 wedding destination in South East Asia, I also started my own wedding planning company. Most couples wanted house music so had some amazing parties on the beach. One February I did 17 weddings in that month alone. I had a ridiculously big set-up. Four sub bases, four tops, moving heads, a really nice system. I was loving life in Thailand and married a beautiful girl called Amy.

After his foray in Faliraki, Steve Kite was back in Essex in the early -Noughties, setting up an internet company with his old business partners called Mouse To House.

In 2007 I was asked do a 40th at The Squire pub in Romford, specifically a 'Caister Soul Weekender' set. It went down so well the landlady offered me a weekly Friday, which was packed for four years. Ironically, on the back of that success I was asked to play at Caister itself, which I have done every year since.

IT WAS MAD...
US LOT FROM GRAYS
WORKING WITH THE
BEASTIE BOYS AND
HANGING OUT IN
NEW YORK WITH
AFRIKA BAMBAATAA
AND THE BLOODY
ZULU NATION.

CITY & ANGEL

BACKSTORIES

Sunrise Radio DJ Mark Jones remembers a novel way of settling his station's rivalry with *Centreforce.*

Edwin, who ran *Sunrise,* was really chilled, but also very well connected. He brought in guys like Ellis Dee, Seduction, Ratpack, Richie Fingers and Tony Trax, all great DJs, playing house at the time. It was great to be involved with DJs of that calibre. Edwin's dad, Judge Jimmy, did a reggae show on a Sunday. *Sunrise* had already made its mark, but was much more laid back than *Centreforce*, which seemed to be more organised.

An early DJ name of mine was Ginger Jones, but on Sunrise I was Funky G, part of The Swing Family, which also included Mr Magoo, Johnny Jacks and Ray Givens.

We had a residency at The Dungeons. I remember coming out of there after we'd played Saturday nights, and all heading to a nearby gym. The apparatus would be cleared out on the top floor and decks set up on either side of the room. One Sunday morning, Ellis Dee and Seduction battled for Sunrise against two *Centreforce* DJs. They turned into good little parties, those mornings.

I was originally out of Angel, Islington, and I also played at The Cotton Club in Stoke Newington, run by a relative of singer Eddie Grant. It was crazy in there, like Notting Hill Carnival every night.

I worked in record shops in the late-'80s and early-'90s, including Wired For Sound in Mare Street and Time Is Right in Chapel Street Market, which was run by the two Daves. A lot of faces passed through those shops and I made some great contacts.

When an 18-year-old Wayne O'Connell missed out on 22-strong 'first lads holiday abroad' to Magaluf in the summer of 1988 because of a clerical error, he thought his world was over. When someone on his building site suggested 'Ibiza' instead he was suspicious.

All our crowd were paid weekly, but me and my mate Julian had monthly salaries. The lady at the travel agents said she would hold our seats on the flight but when we went back to pay they had been given away. We were inconsolable.

A cool geezer in his mid-20s I was working with saw me moping around and said, 'You should go to Ibiza instead, mate.' I wasn't a cool kid — I'd never even heard of Ibiza. I thought he was making it up. There were so many wind-ups on the building site - 'Go and get me some skirting board ladders,' — all the kind of stuff they said to the younger sparkies like me. So we sheepishly sat in the travel agents again, expecting them to laugh at us when we said we wanted to go to a place called Ibiza. We were so relieved when they didn't.

We were on a late flight and booked to stay in San Antonio for a fortnight. Back home then all the pubs shut at 11pm, and the clubs 1, 2am latest...so we assumed we'd arrive in Ibiza, everything would be shut, we'd do a quick reccy and then bed. We were so shocked to find everything about to get going.

We lived in The Star Club on that 14-day trip, but went to Pacha, Amnesia and Ku, with the roof off. Some people we met were talking about warehouse parties in Curtain Road. I was like, 'What do you mean, I live two minutes from Curtain Road...and, anyway, what's a warehouse party?' All the way to Ibiza to discover there were amazing illegal parties right on my doorstep. We met so many interesting people on that holiday. It was some experience for an 18-year-old.

When we got back to London, our entire wardrobe changed from a ripped C17 jeans and white T-Shirt Nick Kamen-look to Timberland boots, baggy tracksuit bottoms, Aran jumpers and longer hair.

We were recommended Trip at The Astoria so we got the 55 bus down to Tottenham Court Road. When we walked in we were amazed to see people dancing on the tables. If you tried to get on a table at our local club, RaRas, you'd get lobbed out.

Ginger Jones (Mark) and his mate Mr Magoo were also early inspirations — DJs who played at house parties we went to aged 15/16.

I'd been a fan of Pete Tong on *Capital* for the last couple of years but the music he was playing at The Astoria for Nicky Holloway was so different. When Nicky opened The Milk Bar opposite, we followed him over there and were big fans of Dave Dorrell, Danny Rampling and Steve Lee, who became a friend. Steve was great at Raid at Limelight too.

We went to Echoes, but not every week because there was so much going on. We'd listen to *Centreforce* round one of our houses getting ready or in the car, on our way out. *Sunrise* was big for us too, because at one point it came out of Milner Square, on Liverpool Road and we knew DJs like Ginger on there.

We were in the thick of it in the Old Street/City Road area. Buses took us anywhere we wanted. Or the Northern Line from Angel straight up to Tottenham Court Road and into the West End. Camden Palace was the club Mecca for us. I think I tried getting in that place every week for a year. When we finally got in, we were like, 'Wow.' The resident DJ played all the music I liked, including some electro, so I asked who he was. I was told his name was Chris Paul. I was so happy when he got a show on *Centreforce*. Chris was such a huge inspiration, but he seemed to disappear off the scene.

I had Citronic decks and a shitty mixer at home that I hadn't mastered, so I wasn't dreaming of being a DJ because I was having so much fun going out. I played at a birthday, then someone booked me for another party and it went from there. Local promoters started booking me because I had a good following. Ginger and I decided we'd do our own club night, Stone The Crows at Oceans in Goswell Road, mainly because a mate's dad knew the owner.

Ginger went off to do The Dove Club and Dolly Rockers, and I started a night at RaRas called Bash with Gary Ingram, who I met with some Essex boys I met in Faliraki in 1991. When the owner of RaRas opened Iceni in Mayfair, he asked us to do the opening night, which we called Dirty, with Smokin' Jo headlining. Dirty ran bi-weekly for five years at Legends in Old Burlington Street and at most top venues in central London. I became resident DJ at my own party, and there was a period when we did every Saturday somewhere for three years.

Mark Jones: My first promotion was The Dove Club at Paddocks in Holborn in 1991 with Jason Edwards. It was still a snooker hall when we put our first night on, but one room was hired out for parties. There was clearly more money to be made from parties so they got rid of 50 snooker tables and turned the whole place into a club, which later became The Leisure Lounge. We hand-picked the DJs we liked and knew would work for our crowd and our sound. Now just 'Ginger', myself and Mark Felton were residents with guests like Gerry (Legends), Nancy Noise, Darren Roach and Magoo. We did 'Party in The Woods' with Craig Jenson from Puscha and Craig from Trax Records in Soho.

I played at Naked Lunch at D'riz in Kingley Street and parties at other central London clubs like Maximus in Leicester Square, Villa Stefano in Holborn and The Windmill Theatre in Soho.

And then I was chosen to be resident at Phillip Sallon's Mud Club when it moved to Bagleys in King's Cross. I'd be half asleep on a Sunday afternoon and my Mum would shout up, 'It's Philip on the phone…' He'd ask me how I thought the night had gone. He was so eccentric and

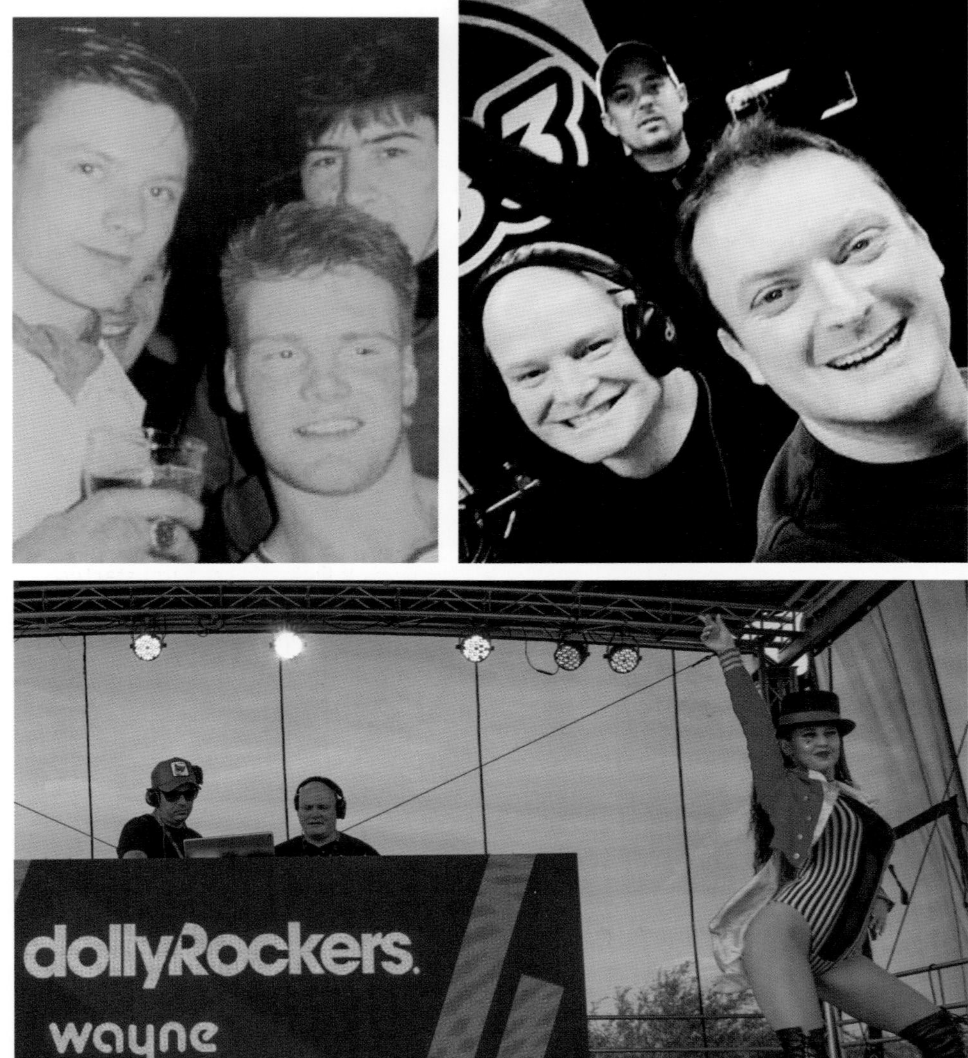

(top left) Wayne O'Connell and Mark 'Ginger' Jones pictured in the late-'80s and (top right) at the *Centreforce* studio in 2021 with production partner Paul Gullefer. (Above) Dolly Rockers duo Paul and Mark at *Centreforce's* Party In The Park, September, 2020.

artistic, my mum couldn't understand why a guy like that was ringing me up. Philip got me a gig playing at Boy George's book launch at Adrenalin Village, where he'd installed a bungee jump. Some of Philip's Halloween parties were like being on the set of a horror film. Funfairs, swimming pools, Vivienne Westwood hosting a room. Nobody could touch Philip for decor and his amazing mixed gay community.

We started the Dolly Rockers Ball in 1994; me, Mark and Jason collaborating with promoters we knew called Orgasm, starting to put on warehouse parties and dry-hire club nights in obscure venues in and around the north London area. Boats, ballrooms, art galleries, castles. We'd get the places as shells, the usual, say it was a film shoot or music video. We had the huge lips that The Rolling Stones used on tour, which we put our DJ booth in, which was a great wow factor. Guests like Farley & Heller and Fat Tony and Shovell on bongos. After parties in Kings Cross. We were one of the biggest promotions in Islington, because we all came out of there.

The Dolly Rockers Balls ran for a total of 18 years, up until 2012, when Mark parted company with his original partners and teamed up with Paul Gullefer, a Dolly Rockers punter turned resident DJ.

Paul Gullefer: I missed the *Centreforce* thing, I was just too young, but growing up in the Stepney, Limehouse, Wapping area in my early teens I'd hear the older lot talk about the Dolly Rockers Ball all the time. I'd see flyers in all the hairdressers at The Angel. Once I hit the right age I had to go. Before the internet, word of mouth was so strong. If people you knew said you should go to a party, you went. The ratio of girls being 60/40 was also a big selling point. I remember Dolly Rockers tickets selling on the black market for £100.

I was on pirate radio from the age of 17, starting on South London station *Supreme FM, 96.1* in 1997 as DJ Gee. I'd go to The Gass Club on a Sunday, the garage crossover from US to UK, which literally kicked off the whole scene, but I fell out of love with it when it got too dark. Then it was all about funky house. I'd always collected US garage as a kid so it was perfect for me.

Later, becoming a resident DJ for Dolly Rockers was a dream come true for me, and that ran up until 2012 when Mark and I decided to do our own thing. We sat in Mark's kitchen after the last party and decided over a few beers that we'd DJ and make music as Dolly Rockers. Later we got notebooks and wrote down our targets, the places we wanted to play and who for, and what we wanted to achieve with production. Gradually we were able to tick off those goals as achievements. We didn't have any management — we did it all ourselves.

Mark Jones: Meeting Paul was a breath of fresh air. He reminded me of myself when I started. The other guys wanted to do things differently so went our separate ways. They let us keep the name and actually said, 'Go and see what you can do with it,' and I'd like to think we did quite well. We did five Ibiza tours as DJs, playing at Pacha, Space, Bora Bora and in the main room and on the terrace at Amnesia. At the same time, we started to work in the studio together, the first few years very much a learning process. I doubt any of the stuff we made then we'd play out now.

Wayne Soul Avengerz: Paul Gardner and I knew each other from growing up in north London. Paul had done his own Just Can't Get Enough parties and played for Puscha so I booked him for Dirty.

Around 1999, coming out of that analog stage and into the digital era, we went into the studio together and Soul Avengerz was born.

Things really took off for us, both as producers and as a DJ duo. We remixed some huge artists, including Beyonce...and our Epic Club Mix of Marshall Jefferson's *Move Your Body*...well, I know, I'm biased...but, other than the original, I think it's the best mix out there. To be asked to do that was frightening. A lot of tracks are referred to as anthems, but *Move Your Body* really is an anthem.

We got signed to EMI exclusively, at a time when they only had four dance acts, Shapeshifters, Paul Van Dyk, Deep Dish and us. EMI saw something in us and we were taken back by that.

We had sampled *The Smurf* by Tyrone Brunson for a Soul Avengerz track and, an EMI A&R scout heard it out one night and the DJ showed him the white label and it said 'Soul Avengerz', so we got signed that way.

We became our management company, D&D's, first artist, and we were lucky to have strong guys like Dean Wilson, looking after us and negotiating our deal. He went on to set up the pioneering agency Three Six Zero, with artists like Calvin Harris and Deadmaus, and revolutionised how DJs and producers are managed and the deals they have, encapsulating all the components of DJing, production and touring.

We were flying around the world DJing too. Not earning the vast amounts the Calvins and the Tiestos of this world do, but there aren't many clubs in the world that I wanted to play and haven't.

We moved Dirty to Pacha London where I had become promotions manager, which led to Dirty nights and main room prime-time Soul Avengerz sets at Pacha in Ibiza

Paul wasn't travelling as much as me, so I did most of the gigs abroad: a regular in Russia, Slovenia, Moldova, Lithuania, Spain, anywhere and everywhere.

But then the economic crash happened and we lost our record deal with EMI. Paul and I wanted to go in different directions musically, him harder and me funkier and more soulful. I woke up one day hating being a DJ and all the international travel. I'd somehow fallen out of love with music. It was just sad — I was getting paid a lot of money to do such a privileged job, but I detested it.

I was approaching 40 and I could have worked as a DJ off the back of the Soul Avengerz name for a long time. I actually had a full calendar of bookings.

To sign the EMI contract I'd given up a really good day-job, managing electrical teams in a niche market in business critical environments. I started looking to get back in employment and within a week I'd had about five job offers. I rang my DJ agents MN2S and said, 'I quit, I'm not DJing anymore.'

They were like, 'You're mad, you've got some really good relationships. People would give anything to be in your position.'

But I said, 'I'm sorry but I don't need to do this to earn money.'

I couldn't stand the electro and EDM that was becoming popular. There was no way I was going to play it or make it. I couldn't sell my soul like that. Gary and I stopped Dirty around the same time, which we'd had a great run with, and I left Paul to do his own thing, so Soul Avengerz fizzled out. We nearly made it big, but I'm not bitter...I was big in my own little world.

NORTH LONDON
BACKSTORIES

Texsta was 'the only Turk in village', growing up in Edmonton and Tottenham in the 1970s.

All my neighbours and friends were Jamaican. I'd be at my mate's house on a Saturday morning waiting for him to get ready for football, sitting with his dad and his turntable, homemade speakers and Studio One and Motown seven inches. I hated leaving.

Musically, my main influence growing up was my own Dad. He had the voice of an angel, God rest his soul. He was pulled up to sing at every family wedding. I'd sit at the side of the stage at the age of seven, thinking, 'Wow, look at this guy, he's amazing, everybody loves what he's doing.'

Because my name Aytach sounds like 'I touch', my nickname evolved into 'I-Tech', then just 'Tech' and then 'Texsta'. I've had the name for years so it was inevitable when I started playing at house parties and on pirate stations I would become DJ Texsta.

I started DJing in the mid-'80s, always from a jazz-funk, reggae, rare groove and then a hip-hop background. We started hearing this new thing called house and got into the rave scene in the late-'80s.

In 1989 I played in the north of Cyprus a lot, before the Ayia Napa thing happened, at The Tunnel Club, anything from R&B to *French Kiss.* That switch-over period. I actually supplied sound equipment to the venue from London and sent new music over to them too.

In 1991, I opened a rare groove record shop in Market Hall, Seven Sisters called Destiny Records. I flew out to New York to source records from run-down radio stations. It was fascinating. I'd also stock up on old releases for 50 cents or a dollar at record shops. I'd come back and they'd all be gems, many sealed or unopened. Even original Elvis Presley records.

Jamie F joined forces with a pal to kick-start his DJ career.

We bought one Hi-Fi turntable each and went halves on a mixer from Tandy. Not quite the right age yet, we watched our brothers and older friends go to see Chris Hill and Froggy down the road at The Royalty in

Southgate. Thankfully, the older guys bought proper decks and the music they heard, and that influenced us.

We started putting on our own nights at The Crown & Anchor in Barnet High Street in 1987, playing soul mixed into early Chicago house, spending most of our wages on vinyl on a Saturday morning.

When *Centreforce* came on in 1989 we listened whenever we could. I began a residency at The Dandelion pub in Barnet, as Jamie F because my surname Farquharson is a bit of mouthful, and played there for 18 years. I went on to have residencies at Samanatha's and Hombres in the West End.

Hertfordshire born-and-bred Aston Evans was based in north-east London when he inadvertently became a DJ and spent three seasons working in Tenerife.

I'd been back and forth to Tenerife during the summer of 1991, trying to stay out there after being laid-off at work. My mates had gone home, skint, and I was sleeping in a studio apartment on airbeds with five other blokes I didn't even know, down to my last £150 and lined up for a glass collectors job.

I had a cassette player by the pool banging out some soul tunes one day and a guy came over and asked if I was a DJ. I told him I wasn't and he said, 'Would you like to be?'

I somehow blagged myself an early spot at Rah Rahs, but this guy hadn't been DJing long either so it was the blind leading the blind. I was due back in the UK for my grandad's funeral and came back with my records. I was warming up with SOS Band, Change, George Benson, Mtume, Roy Ayres, Brass Construction, all that gear I'd grown up on, and getting into house. *Are You Going To Be There* by Shay Jones and Extortion's *How Do You See Me Now*, were probably two of the first house records I bought.

Rah Rahs was run by the one and only Tony Palmer, who frightened the life out of me. We had guests flying over from the UK who probably thought, what the fuck's this kid doing? It was intimidating at the time, but I was at one of the best club venues on the island and gradually started to pick it up. I was back home for the winter of 1991, and then back to Tenerife for summer 1992, really getting the knack of it then... flying back to do Splash at Epping Forest Country Club, round the swimming pool, three thousand people on a Bank Holiday Sunday afternoon, playing the last hour and a half...and also getting gigs at The Hippodrome.

Every couple of months, I'd come back to London for a week just to get my head back together, because Tenerife gave Ibiza a run for its money back then, especially the parties at Cactus Park.

I became friends with Roger The Doctor, when Bobby's moved to the new place, and he was with Alfie and Stevie Foster.

At one point I left Rah Rahs and went to play for a Spanish guy at The Hacienda, just down the strip. Tony Palmer would throw ice cubes at me as I walked past on my way to work, and if I walked into Rah Rahs at the end of the night, he'd turn the music off, get on the mic and tell me to get out.

For the 1993 season I went back out to Tenerife and back to Rah Rahs. I really thought I'd reached a good standard of mixing by that point, and I knew I had the hottest tracks with me. I had Steve Foster and some of the other boys coming round to borrow *Feels So Right* by Solution/Victor Simonelli, because I was the first one on the island with it. They'd take it away and play it, and then bring it back so I could play it later that night. That's how exciting the music was back then.

An episode of TV show *London's Burning* about a blaze at an illegal warehouse rave intrigued a seven-year-old Sam Supplier.

I was literally transfixed. *Everybody In The Place* by The Prodigy was playing as the firefighters arrived on the scene. I remember thinking, wow, I want to go to something like that. Minus the fire, of course.

It took me a while to find the music, then I came across The Prodigy's *Experience* album. I was obsessed with it. I bought an old album called Rave 92 on tape cassette and listened to it repeatedly on my Sony Walkman. My step-mum's friend said I should listen to a pirate station. I didn't know what one was. Luckily my Walkman had a radio on it, so she tuned in *Unity 88.4* for me. I couldn't believe it. I'd listened to that Rave 92 tape a thousand times, now I had access to non-stop new music all the time.

When I found out pirates put up their own aerials and were illegal, well, as an eight-year-old it just felt so naughty. I was in my element, scrolling around the FM dial. Growing up in between Wood Green and Tottenham in north London in the '90s meant I found stations like *Pulse*, *Kool*, *Rude*, *Girls* and *Eruption*.

I was into anything rave. My school bag was a record bag. I loved buying live recordings on cassette from events like Dreamscape, Helter Skelter, Elevation. In my early teens the older kids I hung around with nicknamed me 'Supplier' so I began messaging into pirates as 'Supplier' and getting shout-outs.

Aged 13 I sent tapes into various stations. What was I thinking, with my squeaky little voice and with no real means to record anything properly, playing music in the background with myself MCing over the top? The people at those stations must have laughed their heads off.

By 1994/95 we were all into garage at school. I liked to jump on the mic and MC over jungle music at house parties and I got good at it, and that gave me a status boost.

When I was 15 my mate Fodis had an older cousin, DJ K, who started a pirate locally called *Selection FM*, and gave me a break, without hearing me. I was more used to MCing over jungle and Selection were playing garage, but I had to seize this opportunity. It went really well and I received a hero's welcome at school the next day. I've never wanted to do anything other than music since.

I started to model myself on a guy on *Unity* called MC Paranoia. I thought he was the best thing since wrestling. Selection only lasted three weeks but DJ K said to Fodis, 'Yeah, there's just something about Supplier. I think he's going to make it,' and that one line really inspired me and gave me so much confidence. I'm forever grateful to both DJ K and Fodis for that opportunity.

Aston: After the 1993 summer season in Tenerife I came back to London and took it up another level again, with three gigs every Saturday, early doors at bars like Browns in Enfield or The Den in Barnet, then head to the West End for residencies at Limelight and Legends. Then Fridays and Sundays at places like Busby's, The Milk Bar, Ealing Broadway, Smokin' Beats at The Warehouse, or The Scarehouse, as we used to call it. Not working the rest of the week, having the time of my life. Also playing at the UCLA club underneath Centrepoint for a Masters At Work party is a great memory. I've always loved the American producers and DJs. I was always the guy at shops like Catch A Groove in Soho, Record Village and City Sounds waiting for the stuff that came in from the States, and knew which day each shop got its new orders in.

Texsta: I have always been a big follower of UK music and had a taste of every little scene, whether it was Brit-funk, house, jungle or drum and bass. Then in the early-'90s when UK garage stepped in, I loved that too, but kept collecting house.

When I got involved in *London Underground* in 1995, my first pirate, I was monosyllabic. I brought my brother, MC H along with me because he liked toasting. He helped me breathe, play my first record, say my first few words and get in the zone.

UKG was massive on *London Undergroun*d at that time, and Ramsey and Fen, also being Cypriots, got me on the station and were always so supportive.

(right) DJ Texsta (below) Tony Perry, both at the *Centreforce* studio, 2021.

Sam Supplier: In 1997 an older mate suggested we go to the United Dance rave at the Stevenage Arts & Leisure Centre near where he lived.

I was 15, so it needed the age-old trick of telling our parents we were staying at each other's house to create the opportunity.

However, just after midnight, with the last train gone, we were stood at the side of the leisure centre after being knocked back at the door, the vibrations of the bass rumbling from inside.

As we skulked around dejectedly, the fire escape doors suddenly popped open and two St John's Ambulance ladies helped a worse-for-wear raver out to get some fresh air. As they tended to the guy, my mate and I looked at each other...and ran inside.

We couldn't believe we were in.

Then my mate spotted a friend of his backstage helping out with the sound for the event. He ran over, and lifted us over the barriers. Madness. A few minutes ago we weren't even in the building, now we were at the side of the stage in the main room, literally fast-tracked.

I was focused on the DJ booth, trying to take it all in, absorbing as much of what was going on as possible, in case we got chucked out.

The MC said, 'This is the last one from Force & Styles...' I don't know what came over me. Maybe it was the sheer opportunism of how we'd got in and were now backstage, but I walked over to the MC and said, 'Yeah, I'm on next.'

The MC looked at me, as if to say, this kid is a bit young, but he must be someone, because how is he even here? So he handed me the mic. At that exact point the music stopped. I looked at the huge crowd out there, five thousand in total in the whole place, and it's the first and last time my legs have turned to jelly. I'd heard of the phrase before, but this was it. Fuck.

A new DJ was coming on, but just before the internet, with no social media, DJs weren't as recognisable then. Who even is this, I thought? He was a tall black guy, wearing loads of gold, and I was like, shit, I think it's Grooverider, but I'm not certain. I turned round to the crowd and shouted into the mic, 'Who's ready for some jungle? Every single one of them blew their whistles and horns back at me like I was being hit by a soundwave.

And so I went for it...and screamed, 'GROOVERIDER!'

The whole place erupted, the DJ played a tune...and I was like, fucking hell...touch...it is Grooverider.

I MCd my lungs out and the whole place went mental. Such a buzz. I lasted about three or four records and then the actual MC turned up and said, 'Ah, thanks for covering for me, mate...' He said his name was Charlie B, and I said, 'Yeah, I'm Supplier, resident at Labyrinth club,' which wasn't true. 'Big up the Supplier,' he said as he went on, and I was like,

'Oh my gosh...' When I walked off stage everyone was high-fiving me. 'Yeah, Supplier...' 'Nice one, Supplier.' An unbelievable feeling.

After pulling off that little stunt, we decided to head to arena two, which was still a huge room. There are nightclubs smaller than that arena two. Brimming with confidence and bravado, this time I jumped over the barrier, and walked towards the decks. Andy C was playing, still up and coming at the time. I bowled up to him and said something like, 'They've just sent me from the main room,' He gave me the mic and I did about half an hour more MCing in there. Unbelievable. I was even name-checked in *Eternity Magazine*. *'A newcomer called Supplier had the whole place on fire alongside Andy C.'* When the tape pack came out two weeks later I was on it...and living the dream.

I think I get my confidence from my dad. He was the drummer in The Mark Williamson Band, a group that headlined Christian festivals for 25,000 people, so I grew up around that.

Now I convinced myself I had to get a residency at Labyrinth, to keep up with my blag to Charlie B. So I did exactly the same thing. We bought some tickets and headed to the club in Dalston. I went up to the DJ in the jungle room downstairs and asked if there was a mic. He shook his head but said, 'If you can find one, you can come on.' I hunted around. There wasn't a spare mic in the hardcore room, but I found one not being used in the house room, which compared to the others was a chill-out room, really. I went back to the jungle room, waved the mic at the DJ and he rolled his eyes, as if to say, 'shit...' I plugged in and MCd my heart out for four hours.

Then I went and found the owner of Labyrinth, Joe, and said, 'I've just been in the jungle room for four hours, is there any chance of a booking?' He said that a few people had asked who I was, and then he gave me 1am-2am the next Saturday. I was like, 'Great, sick.' I didn't even ask him how much money. The first night went so well I was offered a weekly residency at £25 a week. I thought I was rich. A lot of my mates had Saturday jobs, earning £20 for a full day's work. I was getting a fiver more for one hour's work. The Labyrinth residency opened so many doors. My name 'Supplier' was on a weekly flyer, which was awesome for a kid who had spent the last few years religiously collecting flyers from record shops and covering his bedroom wall with them.

It had been a crazy week or so. I dunno if it was some kind of kinetic thing. You know, say your vision out loud, which is not the kind of stuff I was into then, but I definitely am now.

Texsta: A track I produced with my friend, Persian, *Dangerous*, became a big track on the scene under the guise, Same People. We were signed by Locked On and it blew up when it was released in 1998.

For a while everybody wanted a piece of us.

I've been in and out of lots of jobs over the years, usually just to facilitate my DJing, which is my passion. When my recognition as a DJ and a producer stepped up in the mid-'90s, DJing did take over and it was earning me very good money. But as the scene changed, everything changed. Vinyl disappeared, and I'd been doing well from vinyl, distributing my own stuff.

When lots of DJs left *London Underground* for bigger stations, I was about to come off the scene when *Passion FM*, one of the biggest pirates then, offered a peak-time Friday night show. So I took it, and everything just blew up even more for me.

Health issues made me step back from music in 2001.

Sam Supplier: I left school with no GCSEs and dabbled in a few jobs. Working in a post room, an archive warehouse and labouring. All I wanted to do was work in music but my Labyrinth wages didn't go far.

Then a relative got me a sick job working as a barrister's clerk, running in and out of court. I moved up the ladder quite quickly and at 18 I was earning almost £30k a year. Then one day I quit. There were clerks aged in their 50s and 60s who had nothing else. I thought, if I don't leave now, I'll be one of those guys.

I had friends on *Freek FM* so I got involved, managing the nightshift and keeping an eye on the rigs with a couple of other lads. It was great for meeting girls who listened to the station, who we arranged to meet most nights. The DJs would pay us £5 subs each, which we'd share. It helped put petrol in the Fiat Punto I'd bought while working at the court.

I was existing like that. Labyrinth at the weekend, getting other bookings here and there. My mate Wesley was getting decent garage gigs so I'd hang with him and jump on the mic if there wasn't an MC. One of those promoters, Mickey Zoo, who ran Lords Of The Underground, Zoo Experience and Garage City, asked about booking me in Ayia Napa.

Mickey said he wanted me to go to Ayia Napa for the whole of the summer, to be resident at both The Spot Club, the No 1 club on the island and the pre-bar Marinella...and even I knew that was THE meeting place every night out there.

Bearing in mind Mickey is a black guy, he explained that the Greek people who owned the club had specifically asked for a white MC. Mickey was laughing his head off. 'I can't believe they've asked me this. I don't know any white MCs.'

But there was a catch. Mickey needed me to go to Cyprus the next Monday. Like, five days time. The following weekend was the last Bank Holiday Weekend in May 2000. As well as my usual gig at Labyrinth I had also been booked for Bagleys and a couple of other places. A total of four gigs, and a big deal for me at 18-years-old. My busiest weekend yet.

'Mickey, can't I go the weekend after?'

'No, you have to go on Monday, or I'll have to find someone else.'

And it wasn't the best deal either. Flights and accommodation paid, but then just £15 per venue per night. Three hours on the mic in each place. But I took the gamble and literally had the most amazing summer. Everybody in the garage scene at that time passed through Spot Club or Marinella. I met everyone from EZ to Norris The Boss Windross, Pied Piper and Matt Jam Lamont. My Ayia Napa experience had taken me out of the jungle and drum and bass scene, and it kickstarted everything for me.

I came back in the last week of October. I had missed my mum's wedding to her new husband. It was a tough decision, but I didn't want to come back and be replaced by someone else while I was away. I even had a grand in cash saved, because I rarely paid for anything out there. I also met my son's mum out in Ayia Napa at the end of that season, so deciding to gamble and take that residency really was life-changing in so many ways. I have to give a massive shout to Mickey Zoo, who took a huge gamble on me.

I had a really good winter, getting booked by all the people I'd met out there. I could now go on any radio station I wanted and now got up to a £100 a gig. I went back to Ayia Napa the next summer, but flew myself out there and was able to pick and choose where I worked. I did really well that summer, 2001. I was resident at all of the big events, seven nights a week.

I came back in the winter but I wasn't progressing the way I wanted too. Bookings were sporadic, and it just felt like I was waiting for the summer to come around again. My son, Sam, had now been born so I had an extra mouth to feed. The pressure was on.

By 2003 garage had really gone downhill. Grime music had come through, and for me, it was a bit crap, really. I was still on various pirate stations every week, but I was struggling to find my identity.

I decided to put on my own events. I had no option. I came up with the name Pure Temptation but I needed a venue. I was getting so many knock-backs and then I found this shitty little place in New Southgate called Castle Club, a place nobody went to. I had less than £150 to my name. I got a load of posters printed for £80, a bucket and some wall-paper paste and put them up all over north London. I was completely skint. Any spare money went on paste. People were saying to me, 'Sam, that club is really shit, are you sure?' I went on any radio station possible, saying, 'Don't forget, the big one, Castle Club...' I hyped the event up so much. I told everybody the club was getting extra security because it was going to be so busy...but really I was shitting myself. When I turned up on the night there was a queue down the road. The party was

I LOVE THE
‘OI, LET’S
FUCKING
HAVE IT,
BIG UP MY
MISSUS’
OLD SCHOOL
VIBE.

mobbed, 400 capacity, fivers to get in.

My next party was at Rudolphs outside Tottenham's football ground, a 'Sharon and Tracey club', with a bad rep. Everyone told me the owner was hard work and he eventually gave me Christmas Eve. I was like, yeah, sick, but it's obviously a really bad night to do. I had about £800 left over from what I'd made at the Castle Club party, and I thought I was Richard Branson. This time I bought flyers, posters and traffic light boards. I was able to buy my son some stuff, but about two weeks before the event I was skint again. Everything I had, pumped into the event.

I was really worried because I'd booked a couple of names now. Martin Liberty Larner, who was a few quid at the time, and MC DT of *We're loving it, loving it, loving it* fame. I hadn't bought any Christmas presents and I asked my younger sister, who doing the till, if she'd lend me £10 so I could put some fuel in the car. On the way to the party we ran out of that petrol, a couple of miles from the club, and had to walk the rest of the way. The owner was ringing me up, asking me where I was. We arrived half an hour after the doors were meant to open. As we turned the corner there was a queue as far as I could see down the road.

'What the fuck!'

And, 'Thank fuck.'

It was the busiest the club had ever been so the owner offered me every Friday, which I started from the last week of January, 2004. I called it Karess, the little sister of Pure Temptation, which I would keep for one-offs. It changed my life, financially, and professionally. I was putting 500-700 people in Rudolphs every Friday. It was a garage night, and there was hardly anyone else doing garage anymore. I was booking all my contacts from Ayia Napa for mates rates. I had a different headliner every week, and all my pals on local pirate stations on the rest of the line-up.

Twelve months later Purple E3 in Bow, next to Mile End Station, approached me. We've seen what you're doing in that shit-hole in north London, just think what you could do here.' So I took every Saturday, and called it Nookie. The exact same formula. All of the local guys from the pirates in east London, *Rinse* or *Shine*, and then one big headliner each week...rammed from the start, 800+ people every week.

So my life had changed again. I had no partners. Just me. I was a complete and utter workaholic, doing all the promo myself. I was putting my name on the flyer for each night, the last on the list, but I kind of forgot about myself as an artist. I realised I could earn huge amounts and not even have to perform. I started Pure Temptation once a month at Eros in Enfield, a 2,500 capacity venue. I was chasing the money, I guess, which was probably natural given my finances before the weekly nights started. Without quoting figures, it felt like footballer wages.

But I was paying so much for adverts on various pirate stations, when

I did the math I realised it made much more financial sense to set up my own station. So I found a partner and launched *True FM 100.2* and told all the DJs I liked other pirate station, 'If you join *True FM*, I'll book you for my events.' It wasn't all plain-sailing. It had its downsides. I got shot at a few times, and was borderline kidnapped at one point, but those stories are maybe for another day and another book.

True FM became massive overnight. I put the station's logo on the corner of every flyer. I was OCD with collecting people's mobile numbers. I had a computer system which sent texts from the *True FM* number, until I had so many numbers it wasn't cost effective to use.

Most pirates were using 300 watt transmitters, but I found a guy doing a 500 watt one. They were really expensive. Other stations wouldn't spend that much in case their transmitter got robbed or raided, but I was making so much money I didn't care. I had the most expensive everything. Our transmitter was based east on tower blocks, but it was so powerful it would shoot over north, cover the whole of London, and reach as far as Brighton, all the way up to Watford and down past Gatwick to Crawley. I now know that was a mistake, and just taking the piss.

Tony Perry caught the DJ bug from his dad, an events planner and his second cousin, a DJ and mash-up pioneer, and became Junior DMC mixing champion in 2003.

My dad's family lived above a banqueting suite called Mozart House in Albion Road, Stoke Newington, N16. Specialists in Mediterranean weddings, those usually took place on Saturdays and Sundays so my dad, Errol Perry, persuaded my grandad to let him host a party night every Friday for the local community.

Half-Greek, half-Turkish, my dad is a soul-boy and true selector with a playlist for any occasion, who shopped for imports in Soho in the '80s.

That rubbed off on his cousin, Eren Abdullah, aka Dr Eren, who was part of The Source's version of Candi Staton's *You Got The Love*, which was a Top 3 chart hit in 1991. It was 'Eren's Bootleg Mix' that put that classic vocal over Frankie Knuckles *Tears* and became a club anthem.

My parents are both from Stokey, but I was born and raised in Southgate. Years later we realised that the previous owner of our family home were the Winehouses, and that me and my sister's bedroom had been Amy's until she was six or seven-years-old. My grandmother still lives there and fans often knock at her front door.

The middle bedroom was dad's record decks and record room. He always had the latest Pioneer mixer and recorded tapes for family in Cyprus with me announcing the tracks in between.

I was born with an Arsenal scarf round my neck. My mum, who's English, had her season ticket at Highbury before my dad. Her name is Sue, and she is such a mad football fan we call her Sue-ligan.

In the late-'90s at the age of 12, I followed in my dad's footsteps and was hanging around underground record shops so I feel really lucky at my age to have caught the tail end of vinyl culture. As a child I was obsessed with Fatboy Slim and his sound. I'll never forget hearing his album *You've Come A Long Way, Baby* in 1998, and all its samples. *Right Here, Right Now* was the track for me. I got more into the housey stuff, so getting my own turntables was a natural progression. In 2003 at the age of 17, I entered the Junior DMC Championship. I didn't think I was the best at scratching, juggling or tricks, and not what I considered to be a DMC DJ, but I won. There's some footage of me on *YouTube* when I was interviewed and mixed live on CBBCs.

I had always wanted to be a full-time DJ, but I went to Uni in Leeds in the mid-2000s and studied marketing. I'd been madly in love with UK garage but that had crashed hard. When I came back to London in 2009 I interned at Kiss 100 and Warner Music, helped out with the family events business and thought I'd have another crack at DJing.

Jamie F: I'm also involved in a family event called Summer Soulstice. A friend of ours, Andy Weekes, sadly passed away from cancer in 2006 and a group of his friends decided to put on a soul event in his honour. The first one for 500 people, which has now organically grown to around 5,000 people each year at Old Elizabethans Memorial Playing Fields in Barnet. We've raised more than £400k. Nicky Holloway always plays, a Barnet boy and friend of Andy's, and Incognito and Light of The World live.

Texsta: In 2007, after I had thankfully got over my health issues and my daughter had been born, I started to look at the scene again. For me, garage and now grime, had changed the scene so drastically ...in fact, the MC was now THE scene. No disrespect to MCs, because I love that they got their own identity and style of music, but I thought, nah, I'm not a part of this. My love and feeling for the music had completely disappeared. So I sat back and thought, right, where is my heart? It took me back to my roots, which is house music.

Sam Supplier: By 2007 all my nights were still getting bigger. I also had the club at 02 on a Saturday...and started getting offers from the Greek islands so I took Pure Temptation out there. My mate Kenny ran Cos on a Monday, and got the boat over to Faliraki on the Tuesday with the headline act. Another friend Charlie ran Malia and my sister ran Zante on a Thursday. By this point I had at least one event on every day of the week. I was killing it.

On *True FM,* I had a show every Wednesday and Friday afternoon, but I was going away every other week to Greece to pick up money, check everything was okay and obviously enjoy it all as well. The week I was away I might miss my Wednesday show, but I always made sure I was back for the Friday, otherwise the numbers would drop at the clubs on the weekend in London — that's how powerful the station had become.

But pirate radio is obviously a world which is un-policed. Lots of beefs and no laws, that's why everybody nicks each other's transmitters. Nothing gets reported because you just don't do that.

The *True FM* studio was in Cable Street near the Limehouse Link, which was soundproofed and had cameras outside. A secret location, where nobody was allowed to bring their mates or girlfriends.

One Friday I was on air on my own. I could see about 20 people outside. All at the door. Shit, I'm about to get battered, stabbed, robbed. I knew the re-enforced gate I'd spent money on would hold for a bit so I played a record and then ran around the room looking for something to use as a weapon. When I saw the guys all had police hats on I was like, ah, it's Old Bill, thank God!'

But then my attitude changed again. I knew there was a rule that if you're not actually on air when they catch you there might be a loophole. So I grabbed the link box, the bit of kit that turns you on and off air, and launched it out of the window.

BANG, BANG, BANG, still on the door, still not able to get through.

'Fuck, what else can I do?'

So I grabbed both my phones. Delete all, delete all. Just as the second phone finished deleting, loads of police and Ofcom piled in. I was put in cuffs and as they started bagging everything up, I said, 'Woah, 20 of you for a pirate station, really.' And then gave it the old, 'Haven't you got anything better to do?'

One of the officers said, 'This is the third time we've come to get you, but you keep buggering off to Faliraki or somewhere, don't you? We were all listening to you in the van just now. Don't worry, son, we'll go and get some real criminals later.'

The police were all right, trying to have a crack. But Ofcom were the people prosecuting and they take it a lot more seriously. They searched my car and found some 'microwave horns', which link the aerial on the tower block to the studio by shooting an invisible laser. I was taken to Bethnal Green Station and held for 48 hours, the maximum amount of time. They questioned me and I 'No-Commented' all of it, but the amount of stuff they knew? Wow, they'd been following me for six months. Fortunately, there was a lot of stuff they didn't get or understand, so they were

Sam Supplier

putting two and two together and getting five. They told me *Kiss* paid £500k a year for their licence and had complained more than 50 times about *True FM's* infringement, just 0.2 away from them on the dial...as well, I'm sure, about nicking lots of their listeners, haha.

I was put on bail, but the case ran for two years. They froze my bank accounts. I couldn't leave the country the whole time so I had to end the parties on the Greek islands at the end of that summer.

When it finally got to court there were three charges. Being on the radio at the time, but that's a slap on the wrist. Then the day-to-day running of a pirate station, which has a maximum two years inside. And they also put in money laundering, because if the profit earned was promoted through an illegal entity then I'm technically cleaning money. Fortunately, I had formed a limited company and was declaring everything.

And someone was looking down on me, because my dad had remarried recently...to a leading barrister, so my new step-mum represented me. I definitely wouldn't have been able to afford her otherwise. My case was the smallest she's ever handled. The fact she came in with a different surname also helped. But I was worried that the judge might think I'd made even more money if I could afford her.

There were concerns I might be looking at doing some time, but I was only convicted of the first two charges. My 'legal team' shut down the money laundering charges, by presenting annual receipts for text messaging (£87k) and printing (£35k). 'Does this look like a man who relies on a pirate radio station to get people through the door?'

I was hit with an £8k fine and a two year suspended sentence, and banned from running a pirate radio station, or even going on one again. Or a two year custodial sentence would be actioned.

Fortunately, the week after my trial, *Rinse FM* became legal so when I was offered a Friday night show on there I jumped at the opportunity.

And then my life changed again.

While I was waiting for the trial I had moved Friday nights from Rudolphs to The Opera House in Tottenham because it had double the capacity. I got on really well with the owners, Steve and his brother-in-law Ken. When the case was over, the guys approached me and said they were thinking of retiring, and offered me a really good deal to buy the club, as long as I kept on the family members who worked there. I thought about it for a week, and then I said, 'Fuck it, let's give it a go.' I was 27 and now owned a thousand capacity nightclub. The day I got the big bunch of keys to the club I drove straight there. It took me ages to let myself in and about an hour to turn the lights on. I had this sinking feeling of what I had taken on.

Being dropped off to his grandad each weekend so his parents could work at local club, Charlie Chans is one of Max Fernandez' earliest memories. Mum, Helen, was a bar manager at the legendary venue on the site of the Walthamstow dog track and Dad, Tony, one of the resident DJs.

I wasn't even born when the first *Centreforce* happened but I've been around music as long as I can remember. I'm lucky that my dad played soul, jazz-funk and rare groove because that gave me a great education in the roots of dance music. And because my mum is a house and garage girl she also schooled me in that stuff too. It's mad to think Mum worked with Roger The Doctor when he was a resident at Chans and now me and Roger are on *Centreforce* together. My mum loves that. My Godfather Richie Malone, another Chans resident, was also a big influence when I was younger.

It helped that I was so tall as a kid. When I started Year 7 I was six foot with facial hair. From the age of 13 I sometimes managed to blag it into clubs with my dad and stand in the booth watching him. I first went to a Caister Weekender when I was 14 because Dad was playing there. My first concert was Cameo at The Jazz Cafe soon after.

After I'd been out once, that was it, I was hooked. But at that point I had no ambitions to be a DJ. I just loved the music and being at the parties. I wasn't like your average teenager getting bladdered on their first nights out, I was all about the music right from the start.

At my first few Caisters, I'd mingle in the middle of the dancefloor in case any door staff smoked me out. But the more I went the more the security would say, 'Ah, you're Tony's son' and they'd look after me and sort drinks out for me all night.

I feel so lucky that I started going out at that age, and meeting Caister DJs like Chris Hill, Tom Holland and Steve Kite, who helped me grow and get into the scene so easily. I was in awe of these guys, closely watching them play to thousands of people.

My first break actually came about by chance. In 2015, when I was 17, I went to a weekender in Reading my dad was playing at called Licks. At an afternoon set DJ Fab Freddie from the Rumshop Crew said: 'It's about time you started DJing, isn't it? You've been coming to these events for a while now.' Dad was on *Stomp FM* at the time, and he had been DJing so long we didn't even have decks at home, so I had never tried to mix, but Fab Freddie persuaded me to have a go in that second room. There was only about two people in there, at that time, and I was shaking as if I was about to play the main stage at Glastonbury. Flicking through Freddie's CDs, if I saw a tune I recognised I'd put it on.

Slowly the room was getting busier, people were starting to dance and I began to enjoy myself. I got bigged up for the rest of the event, I'm sure mainly because I was 'Tony's son', but I admit I did feel like the bollocks. I thought I was the man, haha.

I bought myself a cheap controller so I could practise the art of mixing. My dad ran an event called Soulful Union at Cheshunt Country Club, the old Tesco Country Club, so he'd blag me warm-up sets there. As I got more into soulful house, which was a natural progression for me, I started to get house bookings in the alternative rooms at soul weekenders.

Boys At Work: Master Pasha (left) and Max Fernandez at Party In The Park, 2020. © Sharpscape Photograp

CENTRAL LONDON
BACKSTORIES

Chris Paul's Orange nights are firmly established in late-'80s, early-'90s Central London clubbing folklore, but it had already been an eventful decade for the DJ/producer/promoter...and policeman!

There was always a piano in my house growing up, so I taught myself to play as a child. My first DJ gig was at Barbarellas in Southall at the age of 17. Then I became a Tuesday night resident alongside Gary Crowley at Bogart's in South Harrow, a night attended by the likes of George Michael, Paul Weller and Bananarama.

I was mates with George and got to know Paul when I started working at his studio, Solid Bond, in Marble Arch. Back then everything led to something else. Lots of DJ work in central London at clubs like the Hippodrome and I also played regularly at the Middlesex and Herts Country Club. I was part of the jazz-funk Caister/Prestatyn-weekender scene too, with the likes of Froggy, Chris Hill and Sean French.

In 1986 I produced a version of Lonnie Liston Smith's *Expansions*, with David Joseph from Hi-Tension on vocals, which came out 4th & Broadway. Loads of remix work came in and when I got signed to EMI I had access to Abbey Road Studios.

In the background I had also been in the Met for nine years, and was caught up in the Southall Riots in 1979. I kept that completely separate for as long as I could...but when I was booked to appear on the TV show *Solid Soul* I knew I couldn't do both, so I left the force in late '88.

During a residency at Broadway Boulevard in Ealing in 1987 the manager of Camden Palace came down and, 'We want you to do this at our venue.' A big ask. I went down to a Friday there, they had about 400 in and it was dodgy, so we cleared that out and started again.

I was playing hip-hop and a bit of house and was back and forth to New York, Newark and New Jersey, working with Movin' Records and people like Adeva, Turntable Orchestra and Vicky Martin, and bringing back all those influences. And I think my musical background did help me as a DJ, certainly with mixing, counting and understanding key changes.

Back in London the timing for Camden Palace was perfect, because we were already in place at a huge venue that had a warehouse feel to it and two huge speaker stacks either side of the decks. Acid house came along, pirate stations like *Centreforce* popped up, and we jumped all over it. The Fridays in Camden became legendary, but it might not have worked at some of the other clubs I was involved in. We became embroiled in the rave scene and had amazing success over the next few years...queues from 6pm for a 9pm opening at a 3,000-capacity venue which shut at 2.30am. We didn't realise how big the scene was becoming or how important it would be, because we were all just raving.

People were doing lines of coke all over the DJ booth during the jazz -funk scene, but ecstasy was a completely different thing. Drugs were never my thing; I used to drinks cup of tea. Witnessing the music progression and the different reactions of the punters from the dancefloor back to the DJ booth was fascinating.

The Orange concept was developed at Camden Palace, but it really kicked on at The Rocket in Holloway Road, which was the adjoining venue to the polytechnic run by a pal of mine, Ross. I took on Saturdays and brought my resident DJs like Grooverider, Randall and Hype with me. The Rocket was special...amazing people attending, a wonderful atmosphere and great security. It just worked. We had both venues rammed every weekend.

For me, it was always about the sound and the production, and always a top line-up of DJs every week. I liked to keep the curtains closed behind the decks and do a countdown at midnight. So we opened, but then we'd open properly. Videos, lights, lasers — all so important I put an extra 28k sound into The Rocket, which I think they could hear in Kentish Town, and 20k more of Martin Audio F2 sound into the Hippodrome...way too much, really.

Danielle Montana's father, a Westminster-based Italian restaurateur, and legendary *Radio 1* DJ John Peel were both huge childhood influences.

At the age of four I really thought there were little people in the transistor radio at home. I told my dad a couple of records I liked, *Uptown Ranking* by Althea & Donna and Earth, Wind & Fire's *September*, and he bought me them both on seven inch, which I played on the one record deck we had at home, where the vinyls stacked up and dropped one by one.

Dad loved jazz and classical music, and was always playing the piano in our house. I was good on sax and clarinet and found music an escape. I got into alternative music listening to John Peel, which paved my interest in everything Balearic because he played anything from reggae through to punk, the hard sounds of which I think aren't too far removed from acid house.

When I was 15 I met an older girl, Alison, who fronted a Siouxsie and the Banshees tribute band. I hung around, taking money on the door at their gigs, but was always into my rare groove, funk and disco too. Some friends from that scene were DJs so I'd badger them to let me play a couple of records during their sets at the Wag club. One day they gave in. I was hooked.

After living in a shared house with friends in Brixton, I moved to Highbury & Islington in the mid-'80s when I studied sports management at a polytechnic there.

I first experienced house music at a small place in London Bridge and fell in love with it. I started building a small collection, patiently waiting for a record that I recognised to be played in shops like Uptown Records in Soho.

I was good friends with Bryan Gee. We were 17-year-old kids: him playing reggae, and me rare groove and soul. We both realised we liked the acid house coming through, then hip-house too. I loved tracks by Marshall Jefferson and Juan Atkins, and then early Todd Terry stuff. Due to the sheer demand we were literally relying on these producers to make more music as quickly as possible.

While at college, I got a nightshift job at an information retrieval company called Media Scan in the City. It was two weeks on, two weeks off, cutting out articles about the Royals, the Government and celebrities, so they could be biked over to press officers and management before their clients woke up.

Everyone who worked there was getting into house music. We'd all try and finish a few hours early so we could find a club that stayed open until 6/7am. Invariably at that time of the night you wouldn't even be charged to get in. It was usually quiet enough for me to find the promoter and try and blag a DJ booking. I always had some records with me so they'd sometimes say, 'Jump on now, let's see what you can do.'

I had also been working as a beauty counter girl, anything to help fund my vinyl purchases of at least £100 a week. A friend introduced me to drag queens at The Vauxhall Tavern, so I started helping with their make-up. One artist, Talula, showed me tricks most women wouldn't know for years yet.

On the last day of a Media Scan fortnight we'd all turn up to work with a suitcase and fly off to Ibiza or Amsterdam at the end of our shift. In between all the partying and working, I managed to blag a few club bookings, always standing on the pay phone at the family restaurant

Chris Paul then and now (top and middle) and (below) his Camden Palace Orange crew.

during any shifts there, with a big bag of 10 pence pieces phoning any promoter numbers I'd got hold of.

At any house parties with decks I'd spend as much time practising, all the time learning on the job, like a lot of people back then, because I didn't have my own set of Technics until many years later.

Fortunately, because of my musical background I found mixing relatively easy, although I'm sure if you listened back to some of my early radio shows it would sound like a herd of elephants. When Andy gave me a weekly show on *Centreforce* I felt so honoured. Things seemed to happen so fast back then, and I loved every minute working with those guys. *Centreforce* helped kickstart my DJ career, but the station was over so quickly.

When the Ulysses family relocated from Catford to an estate in Paddington, aspiring DJ Jonathan could hardly have imagined one of his musical heroes would call by...to say he loved him.

I was 16 and working in Safeway on Edgware Road pushing trolleys. I'd been going to The National in Kilburn for Tony Blackburn and Steve Walsh's *BBC Radio London* Soul Nights Out. During one show in 1984 Stevie Wonder appeared as a special live guest. An amazing night.

The next day, a rumour swept the Mozart Estate where we lived that a special presentation was happening on the basketball court. A crowd of about 150 residents gathered, a small stage and sound-system was set up, and a table of sandwiches was laid out. Then two big black cars pulled up and Stevie Wonder got out. It was surreal. We all rushed forward — it was like touching a God. Stevie's security were really cool and he was enjoying interacting with the locals. Apparently, he did it a lot...visited deprived areas at the end of a tour.

Then Stevie got up and sang his huge hit at the time, *I Just Called To Say I Love You,* and *The Woman In Red*, and then said his goodbyes.

It was massive thing for me. I'd grown up watching my older brother Hayden and his pals with their sound-system, then me and my pals Nicky and Mikey built up our own one called Soul Plus. One of us had speakers, another the record deck, and someone else a microphone. Then you'd have your equalizers and your sound effects. It was all very black, one of us playing reggae, one playing dub and another a bit more modern, Loose Ends, Alexander O'Neil, etc. I'd play rare groove...Barry White, Bobby Womack, The Jones Girls. We'd mix and mingle all those sounds throughout the night, at birthday parties and Christenings. What we were paid just about covered the cost of hiring a van, but that didn't matter. It was all about playing music to people. When I started working for Club 18-30, none of the other reps understood basic sound equipment so I played party music at our events, when needed...in Greece, Andorra, Italy, Austria and then Ibiza.

Danielle Montana: Post-*Centreforce*, a gritty British sound gradually evolved from house to breakbeat into jungle. It was subtle, but I was moving into that direction too. There were so many hardcore and jungle gigs out there during that 1990-93 period, so I did really well. World Dance was my favourite.

I was still buying house, especially the American soulful stuff, and, as usual, it wasn't cheap. However, all the vinyl from the UK, the home-grown stuff, was £5-£6 for a 12", especially jungle. I really made sure I cherry-picked any imports I bought.

I was playing at Busbys/LA2 in 1991 when a tall dude walked up to the booth and handed me a dub-plate. It sounded amazing in my headphones. I would never normally play a record off the cuff like that, but I did this time, and blew the speakers because the recording was so raw and I hadn't re-set the mixer. The track was *Some Justice* - Urban Shakedown featuring Micky Finn and the producer standing there with a big smile on his face was Gavin King, aka Aphrodite, one half of Urban Shakedown. We became great friends.

It was another hugely exciting period in dance music during which I had residencies at Fairground Attraction, The Astoria with Grooverider and Top Buzz and Club UK in Wandsworth.

I was mates with Lenny De Ice and watched him create *We Are I.E* on his four track mixing desk. That inspired me to do my own thing in the studio. I became one half of Bass Construction, and had success with a breakbeat-hardcore EP and tracks like *Dance With Power* and *Check How We Jam*, which we PAd for a good year.

In 1992 I toured Europe with another female DJ called Tasha, who had organised dates in France, Spain, Germany, Austria, Italy, Finland, Denmark, Sweden, Poland and Czechoslovakia. We drove the whole way and back in her BMW. An amazing few weeks. Billed as Danielle & Tasha (London, UK), we played mainly house, and some jungle, because that was really fresh in those places, and were treated so well wherever we went, always appearing on national radio in each country.

I was also Aphrodite's tour DJ for eight gigs in Mexico, and later worked for Gavin and Micky's Urban Takeover DJ Agency and with Nikki Trax at Phuture Trax PR.

Chris Paul: With Fridays and Saturdays both flying at Camden Palace and The Rocket in the early-'90s I took on some Bank Holiday all-dayers

(above) Stevie Wonder pays a surprise visit to the Mozart Estate in Paddington in 1984.

(above) Danielle Montana at Centreforce HQ in 2021 and (right) with friend and long-time collaborator MC Jenny Bean.

at The Hippodrome, an extension of what I was used to in the jazz-funk scene, which had been just as musically-driven. Sometimes we'd do extra Hippodrome events on Sunday morning from 4am - midday. Everything would be in place and covered over during normal Saturday night opening hours. Then when the club closed at 3am we'd have an hour to get ready. When we opened the doors there were a thousand people queuing up. In those days there was such a captive audience and even years before the internet and social media people could be mobilised quite quickly.

I was offered Astoria on a Saturday so moved Orange there, changed The Rocket to Aquarius and launched Breakfast Club at Busbys (Astoria 2) on Sunday mornings, later doing that at the Wag so I now had four or five parties every weekend.

It was a case of putting 10,000 flyers in envelopes, and posting them out to your mailing list, so it was horrible at times, but it worked.

I was always producing too, spending a lot of time in studios. In 1992 I had a couple of Top 25 hits as Isotonik with rave tracks *Different Strokes* and *Everywhere I Go.* Again it was all about timing. Isotonik sampled Ten City's *Whatever Makes You Happy* and *Salsa House* by Richie Rich and became an anthem firmly rooted in the rave scene. It reached No 12 and we ended up on *Top Of The Pops.*

I kept the Orange parties running at Camden Palace until 1995, which were now licensed until 6am, but then the music, the drugs and the attitude changed. I had a great run, already putting on something like 800 events. I decided to get out while I could, and moved to Hollywood, where I became a big name on the club circuit. I played everywhere and tore that up for about ten years.

Danielle Montana: I was a jungle DJ who loved house and was now hearing tunes with edgy baselines, but still quite soulful and housey even. It was the beginning of what was referenced as 'speed garage' or 'UK garage'. I was like, wow, I love this. I knew it was going to be massive and my experience with acid house told me to get in on it, at the beginning.

Garage now had its own identity in the UK, after previously being lumped in as 'house and garage' in the late-'80s and early-'90s or even 'garage house', although that was mainly in America. I became one of the first female DJs on the UK garage scene, and all the others that followed represented the scene correctly and were a credit to it. There was a great camaraderie among us. Like acid house and jungle before it, UK garage was mostly turned away from the bigger and more established venues so we had to begin in places like The Satellite Club and The Gass Club.

In 1996 I teamed up with Gavin King to form Aphradan, for some UKG and 'breakbeat-house' releases on Ruff City Recordings, including *Strutt* a year later. We were always able to meet in the middle of our own individual tastes to create something nice and edgy. In 2001 we had success with a UKG mix of *Uptown Ranking*, featuring MC Jenny Bean, who I became a great friend I continued to work with.

Chris Paul: People ask how I managed to play so many clubs in LA and I say, 'Because I was a good DJ and I was from England.' The guys out there are not worldly when it comes to dance music so it wasn't difficult to go and tear up their clubs and be different...and I was doing a lot of work with Ice T, so when he's on your guest list, everybody is like, who is this geezer?

Danielle Montana: When the garage scene slowed down in the early -Noughties, I had to reinvent myself again and went into tech and minimal house, playing to a new younger crowd at clubs like Pacha London, Egg and Ministry.

I had stepped away from radio full-time, but worked with stations with Restricted Service Licences (RSLs), trying to gain legal licences and had a couple of spots on the panel of the Judge & The Jury on *Kiss 100,* when it went legit.

In 2004 I was involved in the launch of a community station called *SW1 Radio*, which invested a lot into teaching local kids how to script, present and record a radio show.

And then I retired as a DJ/producer when I was 40. I was the mother of two teenage boys and I wanted to keep more of an eye on their studies, and them growing into young men, which was impossible when I was in the studio for days on end and then DJing in the evenings. A far cry from back in the day when I had residencies at places like the Boulevard and Haven Stables in Ealing, up until seven months pregnant.

I concentrated on my beauty business...and stopped listening to house music for about a year. We had some house shows on *SW1 Radio,* but I didn't listen to them in case I got sucked in again.

SOUTH EAST LONDON & KENT

BACKSTORIES

Mete's introduction to the music business was as a background 'dancer' in a Musical Youth video in 1982.

Me and my mates, aged 12, 13 at the time, were hanging out by a film studio near where we lived in Bermondsey. Musical Youth arrived and we recognised them from *Top Of The Pops* instantly. We shouted 'Mister, mister,' through the fence and they said, 'If you lot keep quiet, and dress up a bit smarter, we'll see if we can get you involved.' I went home and put on my best soul jacket...so that's us in the *The Youth Of Today* video.

I come from a family of musicians. My uncle owned one of the biggest record companies in Turkey, Eleanor, and my dad played 18 different instruments and could sing in seven different languages. His band was huge on the Turkish wedding circuit and released music back home. I learned to play the drums and by the age of 16 was filling in for the drummer if he couldn't make it.

I'd got into soul music in wine bars in Streatham when I was 15, hanging around my older brother and his DJ mates. I started going to hip-hop clubs like The Venue in New Cross, which was previously called Flim Flam, and then the Wag up town, although it was impossible to get a black cab back home. 'Sorry, don't go south of the river.'

And I get it. If I told my mates back then someone from east London was coming to see me, they'd say, 'Are you fucking joking?' I've always found it hilarious, people from east doing a cross sign with their fingers if I say I'm born and bred in Bermondsey. My parents came to the UK in the late-'60s, so as far as I'm concerned we're foreigners anyway, so east Londoners hating on south Londoners, and vice versa, does amuse me.

The hip-hop scene slowly phased out as the acid house thing gradually came in. My mate Wayne Eldridge started DJing but was finding it hard to get his wages, so he suggested I come out and DJ with him. He thought there was a better chance of getting paid if there were two of us. I wanted to try anyway, and if we weren't DJing we were out anyway.

Playing drums in my dad's band was an easy way to grab £200 and, yes, I'd often go straight from a night out because if anyone can remember the good old days when we were young, we were definitely burning the candles at both ends.

Martin Cee was born in Canning Town, in prime *Centreforce* territory, but his family moved south four years later.

We moved to Crayford. It was Kent then, but it's South London now.

BBC Radio London in the mid-'80s as I approached my teens was a big influence. Robbie Vincent, Steve Walsh and, mid-mornings, Tony Blackburn playing soul and jazz-funk.

I wanted to be Walshy. He played at The Drayman in Bexley Heath and drove around our local area in a Rolls Royce. He was literally the don and taken far too soon in a car accident in Ibiza a few years later. Walshy famously did his version of Fatback Band's *I've Found Loving* and people still sing his one over the top if you play the original. The Radio London Soul Night Out, hosted by Tony and Steve, were fantastic, broadcast straight into my bedroom, at an age when I wasn't allowed to go to anything like that.

There was also a guy on *Radio Kent* called Rod Lucas, who had a talk show. He would play soul music in between and that showed me that you could have a nice bit of chat about you and play decent music too.

My first pirate influences were *LWR* and *Horizon*. I didn't sleep well as a kid, so I'd be up all night, with a coat-hanger attached to the aerial of my radio, trying to pick up whatever I could.

When I was 13 I met a bloke called Barney through CB Radio who made transmitters. My first one was only ten watts, whereas most pirates had at least 200. He showed me how to set up my own basic pirate radio station, which I ran off my old brother's Kenwood stack Hi-Fi, and let me pay down £5 a week for the kit.

Ice 92.3FM, launched in 1987 with all my mates packed in my bedroom. It was probably the worst station ever. I only had one deck and about 20 listeners, but I loved the sound of my own voice and the music I played: stuff like The Funky Worm's *Hustle! (To The Music)*, which sampled another Fatback Band track *Spanish Hustle* and *Big Fun* and *Stakker Humanoid* by Humanoid when they came out a bit later.

After few months I got hold of an old Farminger disco system with two decks so I could now blend records in and out. I must have thought *Ice FM* needed a rebrand, but I wouldn't have used that term back then, because after a few months I changed the station's name to *Hotwire FM*. I got better decks with pitch controls.

I wasn't even 14 yet and a guy called Steve Collins, in his 20s, would come round and present a show from my bedroom. It seems strange now, but these were people I met through what I was doing. I had some jingles made and gave my parents' home phone number out as a request line. Even my teachers were listening at this point.

My mum, bless her, said she didn't mind me doing the radio, as long as I played her favourite Cliff Richard record, *Wired For Sound* or Sheena Easton's *9 to 5 (Morning Train)* every now and then. I think my parents were just glad I was at home a lot and not out 'robbing grannies'.

Alex Little was six years old when his rock star dad picked him up for the day in a limo full of groupies. When Hawkwind lead vocalist Robert Calvert finally returned his son to his home in Kent two weeks later he was arrested for kidnap and access was stopped. It was just another colourful chapter in a rock and roll childhood that a young Alex thought was the norm.

It wasn't the most conventional upbringing, I guess, but it's all I knew. Marc Bolan and other hairy men congregated in the front room of the huge squat in Notting Hill where we lived under a cloud of smoke.

A struggling actress called Helen Mirren, a family friend, was my babysitter. I can still picture myself with Helen on the big steps outside the house, years before she became a household name, let alone a Dame. The squat was actually a clean and respectable house, somewhere off Ladbroke Grove, I think.

My parents separated when I was four and my mum, an old hippy at heart, continued to live a bohemian life. She got with another guy whose surname was Little. She told my dad we were moving to Leicester because he'd threatened to take me to America, but we moved to Ramsgate instead, where I now live again.

When I was 11 or 12 (in the late-'70s), I remember my mother, my step-father and a group of their friends in our house clubbing together some cash to buy cocaine. It was quite a mission because one of them had to go on the train to London and bring it back, while the others cooked a huge curry. I can still remember the anticipation as they waited for the guy to return.

When I was 14 I reached out to my dad and we reconnected. I toured with Hawkwind two years later in 1981. Amazing times for a young man at that age. I remember Roger Walters from Pink Floyd being around when dad was working on a solo project. Their bands were intrinsically linked and both electronic music pioneers, Pink Floyd having actually supported Hawkwind on tour initially. Some of Dad's outfits certainly wouldn't have looked out of place at an acid house rave.

It was a disorganised Hawkwind concert in Brighton for 5,000 people that inspired Alex to carve out a career in events security and personal body-guarding.

I couldn't understand how badly managed the whole event was. There was no backstage entrance and a Hells Angel confiscated Dad's Walkman at the entrance so I had to explain he was the frontman of the headline band that night. Situations like that gave me the confidence to put my ideas forward so I got involved with Hawkwind's live shows and the security of the band.

Getting to know the guys as an adult was great too, because they all remembered me as a kid. I was lucky enough to go to some wild parties with my dad and have some special times together in my late teens. Dad died of a heart attack in 1988 when I was 23. Yes, he achieved fame and stardom, but it didn't last long. I'll never forget him telling me, 'If you want to go for something, you've got to reach for it.'

I missed the acid house revolution in 1989 because I joined the army to work in hostile environments in Afghanistan, Iraq, Somalia and India. When I left the military six years later I discovered house music and club-land. It was an epiphany. I was just mad for the music and the scene and got involved in a promotion some friends were doing called Juicy Tunes.

Dad had shown me the process of writing a song, and had me doing a bit of percussion with him in the studio, banging the odd drum, so I began playing bongoes at our events under the name A-Jax. Other bookings followed at the Ministry, Bagleys, Turnmills and in Ibiza for Fierce Angel. But I got frustrated with the DJs I worked with. I didn't like a lot of the music they played so around 1998 I decided to have a go behind the decks myself.

I was also able to carve out a career in events security and body-guarding. Having such intimate knowledge of the events industry in my teens was invaluable. I've toured with many bands and pop acts since, including Faith Evans and the Spice Girls. My last job was working for Microsoft co-founder Paul Allen, who was also a musician and a massive Hawkwind fan. We had some great chats in Paul's helicopter about what Dad told me he got up to.

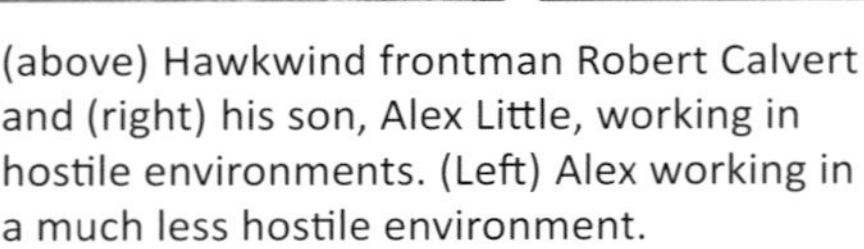

(above) Hawkwind frontman Robert Calvert and (right) his son, Alex Little, working in hostile environments. (Left) Alex working in a much less hostile environment.

(Above, from left to right) Bad Boy West, Jim The Music Man and Andy Swallow at the Centreforce studio in 2018.

Like the time in Paris when he was tripping off his head on acid as Hawkwind checked out of their hotel. As he staggered outside in his trademark full-length leather Luftwaffe trench coat, Dad thought his bandmates, instead of getting into a taxi, were actually being eaten by a dragon. So he pulled a double-handed broad sword from his coat, ran into the traffic and jumped on top of the taxi, determined to slay the dragon. Instead, he ruptured the roof of the cab and nearly killed saxophonist Nik Turner. Or at Reading Rock when performing *Urban Guerrilla* he fired off a round of blanks from a sub machine gun and thousands of people hit the floor. He received a police caution for that. He also had a dummy hand grenade, which he'd take out at after-parties and juggle in his hands. He'd say, 'Don't worry the pin is still in,' and then take the pin out and put it on the table. Yeah, my father did nutty things, but I didn't particularly see him like that.

I was body-guarding for a client at Stringfellows and I could see ex-Hawkwind member Lemmy, better known since as Motorhead's front-man, at the bar staring back at me. Peter Stringfellow, who we were having dinner with, said, 'I think he fancies you.' I said, 'It's okay, he's a friend of my father's,' ...and asked to be excused. When I told Lemmy who my dad was he nearly fell over. He was like, 'Wow, man, thanks for telling me, you guys are so similar, it's great to meet you,' and I guess I was at the age my dad was when Lemmy last saw him.

Martin Cee: In late 1988 I was introduced to a guy who built the rigs for most of the big London pirate stations. He went under the alias of Steve May and was renowned for having a full-sized Dalek in his house in a village just outside Bexley Heath.

Steve was able to make my rig stronger and also introduced me to the guys starting up a pirate called *Prophecy 99.9FM*. They took me on and gave me the 6am - 9am breakfast show, which was certainly a grave-yard shift in those days, but also a massive step up for me from *Hotwire FM.* I rode my bike to the council estate in Woolwich where the studio was. I had to pretend I was doing a newspaper round, which wasn't difficult at my age and at that time of the morning, or with my records in an actual paperboy bag.

After four or five months I left to join *LWR*, which was a big deal for me as I had been an avid listener for the last few years. The *LWR* studios were in a squat in a block in Daubeney Road in Hackney opposite Homerton Hospital. It was an ambition fulfilled to be on *LWR* with Fuzzy D and all those boys. I was still running *Hotwire FM* too, and then went back to *Prophecy*. Being involved in these bigger pirate stations was great, but it brought me a lot of unwanted attention also. *Prophecy* was one of the first stations to use a microwave signal which was much more precise, and freaked the DTI out for a while.

I was certainly an easy target broadcasting out of my parents' house. They were watching Coronation Street when the DTI and the police bust through their front door using a hydraulic ram. Colin Woof was the lead DTI Inspector — I'll never forget his name. He came in with a search warrant, but didn't have to look far. They could have taken all the records in my room, including my brother's collection, which would have been disastrous, but they thankfully only took the two records on the decks at the time, and all the equipment.

At Bexley Heath Magistrates Court just before my 15th birthday I became the youngest person in the UK to be convicted of running a pirate radio station. My parents weren't rich, but my dad paid the fine for me. He was more annoyed about the state of his front door than what I'd got involved in. I also received a five year ban on legal radio, but I wasn't planning on being on *Radio 1* any day soon so I didn't care.

It was reported on the *BBC* and *Capital Radio,* and as a kid back then that sort of thing puts you on a pedestal. We weren't hurting anyone, we were playing music and entertaining people. It actually gave me hero status at school. I was a ginger kid, but even the bullies liked me.

It couldn't have gone any better because all the publicity brought me to the attention of other pirate stations. And then *Sunrise* poached me. Peter Stapleton called me and I thought it was a wind-up. *Sunrise* hadn't been on FM long. It had been set up originally on CB Radio by Edwin 'Bad Boy' West, Tony 'Crucial' White and Judge Jimmy, Edwin's dad, whose house in Dalston the station came out of. On my way to my first show I listened to *Sunrise* on the train, and walking up Kingsland Road to the studio at Lancresse Court, off Downham Road, it was hard to believe I was going to be on this station in half an hour. It was a proper trek for me with a record bag full of records. I worked out after a while that I could do a two hour show with just 24-25 records so that lightened the load.

The main record shops I used back then were TW Records in Bexley Heath and Cruisin' Records in Welling. And if your shop had that bullet you wanted for your show or your gig, you were the man, literally. Your chest puffed out as you left that shop. I'd wait all night for the right time to play that nugget.

When I joined Sunrise, being able to give my record shops plugs really helped when I needed to have certain records saved for me. That extra kudos was essential.

Dave Tenacious reckons the Kent wedding and birthday party circuit at the age of 14 on a pair of Citronic decks was a tough paper round, but it wasn't the only 'round' he had.

I actually did a milk round too, because I needed as much cash as possible to spend on records at shops like Disco Jeans in Swanley and Challenger & Hicks in Dartford.

When I was old enough I went to T's Nightclub in Erith. I got to know the DJ there, Stuart Vant, who said he'd introduce me to the guy who ran the Kent Soul Festival at The Winter Gardens in Margate. I'd seen the posters all over the area for those events, so meeting the promoter Brian Rix was great for me. He gave me a warm-up spot at the festival and also the Camber Soul Weekender at Pontins in Camber Sands.

Then around 1987,88 as the rave scene began to unfold, Brian stopped the Kent Soul Festival, which was now at The Lido in Margate, and changed the name to Seduction and the music policy to house and hardcore.

Like a lot of people, and Seduction itself, I'd gone from playing soul and jazz-funk to playing house. As the rave and happy hardcore stuff came through guests like Slipmatt, Ellis Dee, Ratpack and DJ Rap were booked alongside myself, Dave Reeves, as resident.

Then the Seduction Weekenders moved to Great Yarmouth and I got into stuff like *Playing With Knives* - Bizarre Inc and *Searching For My Rizla* - Ratpack, and anything on Suburban Base.

My first experience with pirate radio was when Seduction gave Sunrise the second room to host at events, and in return myself and Stuart Vant were given shows on the station, along with Martin Cee. From that point on I fell in love with radio. I'm sure I was a bit flat on the mic and I'd hate to hear back the tapes now.

Martin Cee: *Centreforce* had been and gone, but even then you sensed the station's impact would never be forgotten. The authorities really had it in for them, and while *Sunrise* carried on, it got raided more and more too. If you heard the station go off and you were on your way in, you still went in so you could look the DTI in the face and smile at them, as if to say, we know what you know. We were cocky back then. Edwin's dad Jimmy was amazing. He believed we were doing absolutely no wrong at all, so it was him against the government. I arrived at the studio one day and it had just been raided. Jimmy was laying on the bonnet of a Leyland Sherpa police van.

Eric Gotts, he was the main DTI man in east London and he made it personal. He didn't like the music and what we stood for. Gotts, in his brown flared suit and tie made it his absolute mission to take pirates off air. He was horrible. It was a game and it was what it was.

I remained involved with *Sunrise* until it eventually came off air in 1994. *Hardcore FM* took over the 88.75 frequency with lots of the same DJs involved.

Martin's view of Eric Gotts is backed up by skyportradio.com.

'Eric Gotts and Brian Holder in particular were fond of their work and took almost sadistic pleasure in prosecuting pirates. They were so dedicated they even tracked down pirates on Christmas Day, which was an unofficial amnesty (day for pirates) in London.

Martin Cee: By 1994 I was a full-time DJ who had managed to turn his passion into a full-time job, playing out five times a week at residencies including The Kings Arms in Woolwich.

I hooked up with Dean Alexander and we set up a pirate called *Juice FM*, on 94.0.

In 1995 I started playing at The Bon Bonne in Herne Hill, which was the south London equivalent of The Epping Forest Country Club, with a similar clientele, as much as people from Essex and South London can be similar...haha. I was there until 2004, almost 20 years. Incredible times. I also had a residency at Benjis in Mile End, and a DJ agency with a mate.

In 2005,'06 I owned a couple of boozers, Blacksmiths in Orpington and Liquorice in Gravesend, but I was the worst landlord in the world, and went bankrupt. I carried on managing a place in Gravesend called Bar 24 and then was really ill with recurring pneumonia, which came back a total of five times.

Dave Tenacious: When Brian Rix revamped and brought back the legendary Caister Soul Weekender, which had started in the late-'70s, I did about eight weekenders between 1994 - 1998, one of Brian's newer and younger residents alongside legends Chris Hill, Froggy, Robbie Vincent, Greg Edwards and Chris Brown. One of the reasons I pulled away was because you can't compete with those guys, who had played The Goldmine in Canvey Island or The Royalty Southgate.

And while I love my old soul music, I wanted to play new music. I was doing both for a while, playing all the local nightclubs week to week, alongside the Seduction Weekender...then every six months I'd go off and play soul at Caister. All my clubbing mates wanted to go to Seduction Weekenders, and it's with some of those guys that I got into production in what I call the Kevin and Perry era. With my brother Steve Reeves and our friend Lewis Bellis, I made a trance record called *The Answer*, under the name Aptness. Judge Jules supported and wanted to sign *The Answer* to Manifesto Records where he was head of A&R, but we signed it to Good As, which was Graham Gold's label, who was at Kiss at the time. It did really well for us and naturally took us straight into the trance scene.

Mete

Mete: By 25 I'd had a bit of a rave and a bit of marriage, and was working in sales alongside any DJ work.

I went into pirate radio, starting on *Upfront FM* for Dagan and Chico and in the early-Noughties launched my own station, *Entice FM*. We had great rig-makers and engineers and went out to a 30 mile radius. *Entice* evolved into a digital company called Clubsound UK, which in 2004 was something new. Live cameras on a set of decks, with a chat box at the bottom of the screen so you could speak to the DJ.

In 2006 Mete and Wayne were on *Shine FM* and pulled a prank during a show changeover that would change the pair's lives and direction for the next decade or so.

A good friend of mine, Chris Doulou, a present-day *Centreforce* DJ, was on the show before us. Because his arms are so hairy we were winding him up, asking if we could wax them with some gaffer tape we'd found in the studio. The phone lines went crazy when Chris screeched in pain across the airwaves as we performed the act live on air. So we said, 'Chris, you've got a lovely hairy back, why don't we wax that in a club and raise some money for a good cause?'

'You'd have to raise at least five grand.'

'Deal.'

A week later we'd come up with the name Dance Aid and had planned our first event at The Scala in Kings Cross, with DJs like EZ headlining. Laying on a massage table on the stage, and with MCs CKP, Sparks & Kie hosting, Chris Doulou had his back waxed in front of 2,000 people and we raised £10k for Cancer Research.

We went on to have an amazing run with Dance Aid, raising £700,000 in four or five years through various parties and events, and built a treatment room at Great Ormond Street Hospital for Children. One Saturday we were doing an event at SE1 Club for the British Heart Foundation, working with a lovely guy from the charity who came to collect the money we raised. He was sitting on the till with me that night, helping out. I asked him if, like me, he did this for the love of people and he said, 'No, son, I'm on a wage.' I asked him how much, thinking he was going to say something like a £100 a week, for expenses, etc and he said, '£36k a year.' And then it hit me. We actually raised forty grand that night so that basically covered his salary. Where was the charity?'

So Wayne and I started our own one, Onelife UK, which we ran voluntarily, and only for expenses. Our modules were endorsed by various government bodies and we appointed a board of useful people above us including local MPs, headed by our chairwoman Lisa Street from respected think tank Lexis Nexis, who became our rock and arranged an audience with the Duke Of Edinburgh.

We won a Barclays 'Let's Do It' competition and used the prize money to buy DJ equipment so we could visit primary and secondary schools and children's hospices to teach communication skills through learning to DJ and writing lyrics.

With Onelife UK we weren't only teaching kids, we also had Silver Surfer classes. We bought ten Apple Mac laptops and taught over 55s how to use the internet, how to pay their bills online, some basic music production and how to mix.

SUPERSTAR DJS

HERE WE GO

Jeremy Healy's introduction to acid house nearly didn't happen, the doormen at Shoom adamant he and pal Boy George were 'not coming in tonight'.

Paul Rutherford from Frankie Goes To Hollywood said to me: "You've got to go to this club, it's amazing." And I said: "Why?" And he said: "Well, they've got all these strobes and smoke. You can't see anything, you don't know who anybody is and they play this amazing music."

Up until then, we'd gone to clubs to be seen and to show off. I thought, God, what's the point of that? But I was fascinated all the same, just because it sounded like such a weird idea.

Boy George at that point was very famous. We got to the door and if you are very famous you can get in anywhere, right? But the bouncers said: 'No, you can't come in."

'Why not?'

'There's lots of people from the East End of London in there and they might beat you up. We won't be able to protect you because we won't be able to see you.'

'We really don't care, we'll take the risk.'

But we didn't get in.

The pair had been mates since they met on a south London bus at the age of 15. Jeremy went on to national chart success in 1982 as a member of quirky pop act Haysi Fantayzee, with the No 11 hit *John Wayne Is Big Leggy*, while in September of the same year Boy George and Culture Club hit the tops of the charts with *Do You Really Want To Hurt Me*.

With Culture Club going on to enjoy global success over the next five years and Haysi Fantayzee splitting a year later, the pair drifted apart. Jeremy spent much of his time in the mid-'80s clubbing in New York at Paradise Garage and Danceteria, where he remembers Madonna was 'the lift girl'.

Their friendship rekindled, Jeremy and George were determined to give Shoom another try.

I told Paul Rutherford what happened and he said, 'Look, I'll fix it.' So George and I dutifully went down there the next week, the doormen apologised, and we were in. I met Shoom promoters Danny and Jenny Rampling, and everybody loved George, of course. There was no chance they were going to beat him up anyway because they were all on ecstasy. We had a whole new crowd of friends instantly. There were probably 150 people in that club and straight away I knew this new thing was going to be massive. I'd seen it before with hip-hop and the New Romantics, and all that stuff. Something very small and very special and the people so into it.

Shoom would have a profound and life-changing impression on the duo. Jeremy, then a jobbing hip-hop and funk DJ, decided to change tack. Boy George, meanwhile, launched his clubland alter-ego, Jesus Loves You, going on to enjoy underground dance hits with tracks like *Generations Of Love* and *Bow Down Mister,* and performing live in his new Hare Krishna-inspired guise at Shoom within a year. The Culture Club frontman would also cultivate a new vocation as a hugely successful club DJ, following encouragement from Jeremy, who would also record as E-Zee Possee on George's More Protein label.

What Danny Rampling and people like Paul Oakenfold did with house music and their Shoom and Future nights inspired me, because up until then I'd been a scratch DJ. I thought, I can do that. It made me get up off my arse and do it too. It was the first time that the DJ had been elevated to rock star level, and I really liked that. Danny even had a crew who would go around and chant his name and they wouldn't dance to any other DJs until he came on. So it was like a football supporter kind of thing, really. I was watching some Glastonbury coverage on the TV and the presenter was saying how amazing the reaction to Faithless was, everyone with their arms in the air, and I remember thinking it used to be like that every night, certainly every Saturday, at least. It was like the people were mad for this thing. I persuaded George to take up DJing full-time because I knew he would really enjoy it. I even took him out to get all the equipment so he could practise.

Suddenly there was one decent club in every major city. Venus, Renaissance, Golden, Progress, and all those great clubs. And you certainly had to be into it, because it was like 120 degrees in a lot of those places. You had to go through the pain barrier, much like you do at Glastonbury with the mud. The Gardening Club in Covent Garden was another club where you'd come out thinking you'd been in a hot shower for four hours. They could have filled that club three times over in those days, it was so busy, with queues three times round the block.

As the whole thing took off, I remember thinking how good it was that everybody could join in, and that anybody who wasn't involved was wasting their lives and missing out. But at the same time some Americans were developing the internet, and they must have been equally as excited.

But Jeremy would have missed a large chunk of the superclub era if he had accepted an offer from The Rolling Stones.

Oakey had done that marvellous remix of *Lemon* for U2 and then went on a world tour with them. The Stones decided they need a tour DJ too. I'd got to know Mick Jagger when I was booked to play at his 50th birthday party in Richmond in 1993, alongside The Chieftains, who I call The Irish Kraftwerk. I also knew Jade Jagger because our daughters went to the same school in Ibiza. However, the offer from the Stones was £500 a week...for two years. I was like, no fucking way. I didn't think twice. By that point I was already booked out for months, travelling 1500 miles a week on the road in the UK on the superclub circuit.

In May 1997 a call came in from 10 Downing Street.

I'd been DJing five nights a week for seven years and, being in the middle of it all, I didn't realise just how big it had got. Tony Blair and New Labour won the General Election and I was asked to DJ at a reception for the new Prime Minister. They also asked Carl Cox and I said: 'Why the hell are you asking me?'

And they said: 'Everyone under 25 knows who you are.' I remember thinking that was mad, because it wasn't like we were on TV loads or on *Top Of The Pops*... at least I hadn't been on *Top Of The Pops* for 16 years.

I thought about going to see the PM, but then remembered that when my friend John Galliano won a designer of the year award in the '80s, he had been invited to meet Margaret Thatcher, and because he was thinking about it, I'd called him a wanker, and he decided not to go. So I thought there was no way I could either. For a few years I regretted it, and then the Iraq war happened and I felt vindicated. Generally I've mellowed over the years and I have a softer opinion on things like politics. Back in the '90s I was still very punk rock in my outlook. I don't think Carl Cox went to Downing Street either, they got Noel Gallagher in the end and he never lived it down.

Jeremy cut down his DJ bookings in the Noughties due to his increasing commitments in the fashion world.

I've been working with my dear friend John Galliano for the last 40 years. Although, my first introduction to fashion was hanging around Vivienne Westwood and Malcolm McLaren's shop Sex in the King's Road when I was still at school in the '70s. John was very much influenced by Vivienne, who was an icon to us. When John started his own label it seemed like our thing.

Being involved with a leading fashion brand and their events and shows can be as punishing as DJing full-time in the '90s, and mean being in four countries in one week. When John became head designer of Christian Dior I moved with him, putting on two shows a year, then six, then put the music together for their TV commercials, until I was doing more fashion than DJing and working most of the year for Dior. At the turn of the Millennium I also started to work for Victoria's Secret, and became their musical director until 2017, after bringing in people like Rhianna at the start of her career, which was exciting.

John suffered quite a well-publicised meltdown in 2011 and was sacked by Dior, along with his team, including me. There's so much pressure on top designers in Paris, they're like megastars. He'd been awarded the French Legion Of Honour, which is like being knighted, so that was withdrawn. Thankfully John has turned his life around and is working with Maison Margiela, and is back in Paris, so I am too. We do a couple of shows a year and we've been able to license stuff from Bowie, which is cool.

After studying TV and video production, Lisa Nash became the face of *ITV*'s dance music show *Clubavision*.

My job from college was working as a receptionist at club promotions company, The Flying Squad. When my boss Russell Cleaver suggested launching a magazine, I said, 'No, we'll do it all on video, and I'll present it.'

I had created a role for myself and Clubavision was born, which we initially sold on VHS tapes to stores like HMV. The early episodes featured a cameo from up-and-coming comedian Matt Lucas.

ITV approached us and a deal was done for Clubavision to appear on an 'after-the pubs shut' late-night Friday slot. I convinced Russell it was my job to party every night…so I could get into work a bit later every day. We visited every superclub and I must have interviewed every superstar DJ during that era. We were also the first British TV crew to go to Ibiza, before Sky and their *Ibiza Uncovered* series. We had to visit the island first for meetings with the owners of the big clubs to sell them the concept before we were given permission to film.

In the UK we visited a different club on a Friday and Saturday – loads of motorway miles every weekend. I'd religiously do hundreds of sit-ups in my hotel room before I put on whatever scantily clad outfit I was wearing, often just a bra top, but that's what we wore in those days.

I had high-end fashion designers wanting to dress me. I wore a beautiful Etro dress to the Underground Garage Awards, and Issey Miyake made me a paper dress for another event.

The amazing Chuff Chuff parties held by Miss Moneypennys at various hotels and stately homes around the country were personal favourites of mine. In my mind I had the best job ever, aged between 19 and 23, getting paid to dress up, interview people and party afterwards. I was learning so much on the job. It was so exciting.

I'd been a weekend student at Sylvia Young Theatre School as a kid, and a guy I'd been doing some voiceover work with was Prince's drummer. He invited me backstage to his next concert at Wembley Arena. I was mesmerised by Prince, his performance, the costumes, the stage show and the whole glamour of it all. For me, it wasn't about fame, I was just intrigued about people...I wanted to be an interviewer rather than an actress.

In the week, Russell and I went through all the footage and used an edit suite in Shepherd's Bush to make the shows. After four years it was time to go off and do other things, so other presenters came in, like Sam Mann.

Allister Whitehead remembers a distinct difference between 1989 and the previous summer.

We'd regularly make the pilgrimage from my hometown of Nottingham to Manchester to the Hacienda because that was the big noise. And, of course, we went to London as much as we could too, because that's where the big raves were. I did go down a few times in 1988, but it felt a lot different in '89. *Centreforce* was a major part of that, and definitely a buzz word that summer.

I remember specifically the music on *Centreforce* being really bleepy, a bit like the stuff that came out later in Sheffield and on Warp Records. They were playing a lot of the underground US house, stuff like Steve Poindexter *Work That Mutha Fucker* and *Computer Madness.*

I have vivid memories of being in the back of a car on a mission down to London and, when we could begin to pick it up, listening to *Centreforce*, not just for the music, but to find out where to go that night. We went to the very hot and sweaty Labyrinth on one visit and ended up at someone's house afterwards.

Centreforce was well known up north. Every clubber who passed through London around that time knew about the station and many

(main photo) Jeremy Healy at work in the mid-90s and (above) being interviewed by Lisa Nash for *Clubavision* TV show on *ITV.* (right) Lisa Nash on the cover of *M8 Magazine* in the late-'90s.

others all over the UK had listened to a cassette tape recording of *Centreforce* doing the rounds. Listening to cassettes of other stations, whether it was from a different area of the UK to you, or stations from New York, became a huge network. I worked in clothes shops and those tapes had a very high value, not necessarily in monetary terms but just from a kudos point of view.

Growing up, the idea of being a DJ just sounded really naff. The only ones we knew were on *Radio 1*, like the Harry Enfield and Paul Whitehouse's Smashy and Nicey characters. In New York, they had block party DJs, but we had cheesy mobile DJs at weddings or family parties.

But Allister would go on to make his name as resident DJ at The Garage in Nottingham, replacing Graeme Park, who had moved to the Hacienda in Manchester. Allister would also step up to 'The Hac' and cover for Park as the '90s superstar DJ era unfolded. Managed by James Baillie, the man behind Nottingham's iconic Venus nightclub, Allister became a leading DJ on the UK's superclub circuit, boasting dozens of packed weekly nights and a fanatical fanbase. In the spring of 1992, Golden in Stoke opened, with Allister as resident, a week before Renaissance in Mansfield.

I heard that Geoff Oakes, who I knew from the Hacienda, was planning a new night just down the road from me in Mansfield, based around Sasha, who was at the peak of his powers at the time.

All the clubs in our part of the country up until 1992, including the Hac, shut at 2am, but Renaissance would finish at 6am, so this new weekly in Mansfield, the concept behind it all, the artwork, etc, created a lot of excitement. The big surprise, I guess, was that they were able to pull it all off.

I was lucky to play Renaissance on a number of occasions. The main room at Venue 44 was basically a take on the Paradise Garage, with the DJ box in the Gods a little bit, overlooking the crowd. There was this distance, and it sounds like it would be intimidating, but actually it wasn't, because for some strange reason, it was as if you were connecting with every single person there. People weren't coming up and asking for this or for that. They were there to go mad, and you were there to give them what they wanted. And as a DJ you can take all the risks you want with a crowd like that. This was clubbing of the highest order and just what every DJ wants. And with the records around at that time, you knew exactly what to do. It was like being a kid in a sweet shop really.

I think one of my favourite memories of Renaissance was after Mansfield had been running for a while, when there was a queue all the way around the block, and you knew it was going to be an amazing night — the sheer sense of anticipation, that's a memory in itself. And then for the last hour of my set, with the dancefloor in the palm of my hands, I'd realise I still had all my best tunes to come, bullets that were going to take the lid off the place. It was like an hour-long orgasm, really.

There was a period of time in 1997 when each club in the UK was playing the same ten records every night. I think so-called super-clubbing reached its peak with hard house and trance, another phenomenon, and then burned itself out. Also, the bars could now open later.

It's hard to imagine the origins of Ibiza's legendary Space Terrace, one of THE world's most iconic club arenas, can be traced back to Don's Disco in a small Hertfordshire village in the mid-'70s.

Alex P: Don had record decks set up in his front room. A few of us from the village would go and practise on them. Don got a bad rep from locals saying he shouldn't have us lot over but he was totally cool, a lovely fella. At weekends he'd do the local mobile circuit and take me with him. When he went for a fag I'd jump on play a couple of records, usually Norman Greenbaum's *Spirit In The Sky* and *Kung Fu Fighting* by Carl Douglas, which I knew would always get the dancefloor going.

My Cypriot-born Dad had made a few quid from a sheet metal air conditioning unit he designed, so set up a factory in St Albans and moved our family from Leytonstone when I was ten to the rural haven of Codicote. My younger brother, Andreas had left urban decay behind for a new life in the country and felt so free.

I was intrigued how music came out of a stylus on a turntable and when my mum bought the Queen album, *A Night At The Opera,* I was fascinated that it was seamless, with no gaps between the tracks. I got a taste for what I thought were good records. I was devastated when my seven inch copies of *5705* by City Boy and *Substitute* by Clout melted during a heatwave in the summer of 1978.

I was always busy, really into skateboarding, but good at football too. I'd signed as an apprentice to Tottenham when I was 13.

A kid called Troy Harewood, a huge fan of Jeffrey Daniels from Shalamar, who dressed like him, and had the same hair, moved into the village. Troy showed me and my brother the breakdancing and body-popping he learned studying his hero, like gliding down to the floor and back up again. It was like magic to us. We began to plagiarise some dance moves from music videos and the three of us became The UK Warriors. If our parents went out we rolled back the carpet so we could practise our head-spins on the marble floor underneath. We went up town rollerskating and to battles in Covent Garden, which we usually won, because we were so good at gymnastics.

I was released by Spurs at 16 and signed for non-league St Albans, who were offering me more than a hundred pounds a week, decent money in 1981. But I was spending as much time dancing, Troy and I both confident enough to hang around clubs like Bootleggers in Marylebone, with all the early-'80s glitterati crowd at the time.

As The UK Warriors, we were taken on by an agent who got us adverts for Loreal Studioline and a Carling Black Label spoof of Singing In The Rain. We were given clothes by sponsors and went on tour in Germany, where we performed alongside a DJ called Bamboo, who taught me how to mix and scratch. My dad had to go to court so my brother, who was 15 at the time, could miss school.

We were featured in a pictorial book about breakdancing and booked to perform at the premiers of films like *Beatstreet* and *Breakdance*. In 1985 we entered and won an ITV talent show called *The Fame Game*, presented by Tim Brooke-Taylor from *The Goodies* and Stan Boardman, and was the *Britain's Got Talen*t of its time.

I was living the dream, earning money playing football and decent wages through dancing which meant I could afford a set of Technics 1200s. But my schedule was hectic, playing football three or four times a week, dancing the rest of the time and going out whenever I could. Something had to give. I was now leaning more and more towards DJing, while my brother went on to become one of the most successful stuntmen in the UK, working with the *Star Wars* franchise.

I'd become good friends with a DJ called Colin Hudd, so jumped on his coattails, at soul weekenders, which became house weekenders, and he got me warm-up spots. I started playing at MFI at Legends for Spike and Neville and warehouse parties for Dave Mahoney. Ecstasy had filtered on to the scene — a growing movement that just escalated.

I worked for Tony Colston-Hayter and Dave Roberts at Sunrise, driving round the M25 collecting money from ticket agents on the night of the rave. Dave told me if I got a really lairy car I'd never get pulled by the police, so I bought a gold Ford Granada Scorpio. I'd drive to meet Tony in a flat in north London, sometimes with two hundred grand in cash in the boot. I also met James Mitchell through Sunrise. He was their spokesman, Dave the muscle and Tony the genius.

Next, my own night at a venue in an underground club in Hertford called Stags with Rob Playford, later of Moving Shadow. I got in with Tommy Mack and Alan Warman and went to Ibiza on holiday with them in 1987. I loved it. I came back and had this calling, to sell up and go back for the summer in 1988, but I just had too much going on.

I had a residency at Haven Stables in Ealing, where I met Brandon Block, the same night Grooverider was playing. He and Fabio were my favourite house DJs at the time...they were THE dudes. I'd go up to Rage and Clink Street and try and clock the names of the records they played.

In 1988 I went back to Ibiza with Paul Anderson, Matthew B and the Crazy Club boys, who I was now playing for at Astoria and Limelight. It was mainly a holiday but we DJd at Amnesia, which was an amazing opportunity. As I was finishing my set I noticed the residents had messed about with the graphic equaliser. I told Paul who was about to come on and he was furious and wanted to fight everyone, but I calmed him down and we sorted out the levels.

The next spring, 1989, I sold my flat and drove my new BMW 323i to Ibiza with my mate Martin Dodds. But we'd got there too early — nothing was open. We got painting jobs whitewashing a bar for a few weeks.

I'd given up loads of bookings but I didn't care. I could almost taste that things were about to happen. It was a slog trying to get DJ work, because all the clubs had Spanish residents in place, so I did a deal with a new bar-owner in San Antonio Bay. If he let me DJ he could pay me what he could at the end of each night. I just needed a base. I called it I-BEER-IA, for a laugh, because I thought we could attract Brits from the other side of San An. We got in with holiday reps and had a queue round the block. I was playing British warehouse music as opposed to more balearic, trancey underground stuff being played elsewhere in Ibiza. *La Prensa*, the local newspaper did a piece on me, which was great PR.

Tommy Mack came over to do Mad Mondays at Ku and asked me to be resident. Then I got a call from the owner of Amnesia, Juan, who was friendly with James Mitchell, and on the back of my set the year before, I was asked to be resident for the rest of the season. I played five days a week at Amnesia and Ku on a Monday, which was pretty unheard of then, a DJ playing two big clubs like that, and still did a few nights at the bar in San An. I remember Joey Beltram giving me *Energy Flash* on an acetate in Amnesia one night.

It was a brilliant year — I had the time of my life. Oakey came over and played at Mad Mondays, so did 808 State. Big line-ups at a massive beautiful club. Partying with promoters and club owners most nights. Andy and the *Centreforce* boys came out in the September, and Fat Tony and I played at something they did. James Mitchell was out in Ibiza and had hooked up *Centreforce* at Amnesia. And I remember Andy playing at Space too, although it was a very different club then: the same building but a lot smaller inside, with an oval-shaped sunken dancefloor.

I went back to London at the end of the season to a colossal amount of work, because I'd been away for six months. Everybody wanted a bit (top) Alex P (right) and Brandon Block at an Aqualandia water park party, Ibiza, and (right and below) at Space Terrace in 1993. Photos by Matt Trollope. 'At least some of the bottles are almost in focus in the shot below!'

EVERY SUNDAY
AT THE TERRACE

ALEX P.
&
BRANDON BLOCK

CADA DOMINGO
EN LA TERRAZA

of me, especially because promoters could put Amnesia and Ku next to my name. It had been an amazing couple of years already.

I returned to Ibiza ahead of the 1990 season and straight out for dinner with Juan, the owner of Amnesia, excited to hear his plans for the summer and to confirm my residency. Instead, he told me he had just sold the club.

I was like, 'You're kidding me?'

I had my whole summer planned out, but he said, 'I'm sorry, it was a deal we couldn't turn down.'

Juan introduced me to the new owner, Senor Martine, but we were like chalk and cheese. He came from the glamour of Barcelona, whereas the Amnesia I knew was hedonistic, with no roof.

Juan said to me, 'What about Space?'

Space was just an inside room at that point, opening at 6am, full of the craziest people, not surprisingly for that time of the morning. It was known as a techno club, but the residents would also drop things like *Another Brick In The Wall* in the middle of their banging sets.

Juan introduced me to Pepe, who had relaunched the venue the year before, and had done quite a lot of building work over the winter of '89, including an outdoor area for people to go and sit. Pepe and I got on like a house on fire, and over dinner with me and James, he asked me to be a Space resident.

I tried to persuade James Mitchell to stay out with me for the summer and rent out one of the bars inside Space, a practice that was common place at the clubs out there. I asked Pepe, but they had all been taken. We went back and sat outside and I looked around and said to James, 'Why don't we try and do something here?'

We put an idea to Pepe, that we'd build a bar and set up decks, and open in the evenings to passers-by. He laughed at first, said we were mad, but we could have a go. We plumbed everything in, fitted it out and painted the whole place ourselves. We opened what we now call The Full Moon Terrace from 10pm, but we were only allowed music until 2am and from 9am, so that's what we did.

I was like a front of house landlord, trying to capitalise on tourists milling around Playa D'en Bossa. There wasn't much going on, no Bora Bora, no Ushuaia, just Murphy's Bar and a fish and chip shop, really. When I opened in the evening, the Germans and Dutch staying in the Hotel Garbi side of Bossa came in their dodgy suits and shirts, spending good money, mixing with Brits staying at the Jet Apartments along the beach.

When we closed the terrace bar, I'd go inside and crash out on the cushions at the back of the club, and then play a banging set for a few hours when the club opened inside at 6am…at which point my head barman Graham Dennis would open up our bar for drinks.

The first year was a real struggle so I agreed to buy James out, who wanted to get back to everything he had on in London. I had sacrificed all that, but was convinced our new bar terrace area at Space could work. I wanted to give something back to the island too. I thought I could add to what was happening.

Slowly but surely I noticed the party crowd, who had been out dancing all night at other clubs, would turn up and sit and chat while they waited for the music to start. I arranged for The Croissant Show in Ibiza Town to bring boxes of fresh croissants and coffee over. Watching all that lot chewing on those pastries was hilarious.

When the people heard the click of the amp over the speakers a huge grin came over their faces. When I started to play they'd clap and cheer as they got up to dance.

The funkier music I played outside on the terrace started to get a bit of notoriety on the gay scene. We also attracted a lot of transgender folk, such amazing and colourful characters. Word was getting around. It was the lull before the storm. Looking back, we thought we were so worldly, but we were undertaking so much at such a young age.

Back in the UK, during the winter I had a packed diary, including a residency at the Hacienda in Manchester on a Friday night with Mike Pickering and Tom Wainwright.

As the 1991 season unfolded again, the terrace was getting busier and busier. I had a great deal with Pepe, but all day, every day was too much to handle on my own. I was losing weight and friends were worried about me. I knew there was only one man for the job.

Brandon Block had conveniently just arrived in Ibiza for the summer with his mate, Baggy.

'Brand, you got to come and help me. It's pretty mad in there, but you're gonna love it.'

He was with me in a heartbeat and Blocko was such a good fit for the terrace. After his first full session at Space, I found him and Johnny Mac lying in a pool of chocolate rum at my apartment, which was definitely a sign of things to come.

After one season as an 18-30 rep in Ibiza in 1991, Jonathan Ulysses went back the next year determined to become a DJ on the island.

I blagged a job MCing in Play 2 on the strip in San An, and was then offered DJ job at Exstasis, a bigger club on the roundabout and nearer to Es Paradis. I thought my bollocks were bigger than they were, because I wasn't really a DJ...and I couldn't mix. Within weeks I was found out — I sounded like a train crash and they said, 'You're rubbish, goodbye.'

Luckily, my old 18-30 line manager was now running a small party bar opposite Play 2 called Simples. Now I could do my apprenticeship, learn about house music and my craft, to a point where I was mixing on four decks, it just clicked. I did the first two years all night from 8pm-4am on my own, anything from drum and bass to house, hip-hop or soul. It was overwhelming, but Simples became one of the most successful bars on the strip.

I went to Space terrace every Sunday to hear Alex and Brandon. I loved their charisma and energy, the way they captivated the crowd, lots of eye contact, pointing people out, always smiling, so infectious. They were so good on the terrace. I started taking my mixes down to Fritz, the manager at Space. 'Let me have a set, let me have a set,' like a yapping dog. I'd try anything to play at Space, including one night, pretending to be resident Biko, when he didn't turn up. The security were having none of it.

One Sunday afternoon Alex P was chatting with DJ partner Brandon Block. 'Shall we turn this music off and put the telly on?' asked Blocko.

Alex P: I was just coming round to the idea that we were in Brandon's front room when I realised we were in fact huddled under the decks at Space Terrace, off our heads. I realised the long intro to George Benson's *Off Broadway* was playing, and as I got up on my knees the usual wonderful and hectic mix of the glam Euro party-set, havin-it Brit clubbers and vogueing trannies was in full flow. Crazy, hedonistic times.

Sundays at Space quickly became an exciting alternative to everything going on in Ibiza. A lot of people also stopped going out on Saturday night. They'd go for something to eat or chill in their rooms, then have a decent breakfast on Sunday before the fun and games began.

We did a mix CD with Polydor and at the start I say, 'Wakey, wakey,' and Brandon says, 'What time is it Peasy?', and I reply, 'It's 6am Blocko, it's time to get down to Space.'

A lot of industry people from the UK would fly over for the weekend or even on a Sunday morning after working on Friday and Saturday nights, and so for them it was all about Sundays at Space.

Music-wise, Ibiza had not been about the British warehouse sound, but we'd introduced 'phat' baselines with breakbeats, tracks like *Break Of Dawn* - Rhythm On The Loose and *Lock Up* - Zero B.

In 1993, me and Brandon had our own carry-on party each Sunday evening at Tahiti Bar on Bossa beach with the Italians, Roberto and Ernesto, who went on to do Zenith at Pacha and Music On at Amnesia. I was working with the Germans - Sven Vath, Mark Spoon, DJ Dag. They'd come and play on the terrace for me, and then I'd go and play techno at their clubs in Germany. I was always wearing two caps, a mad techno one, booked to play all over world. Then I'd come back to the UK and it'd be a happier, funkier housier vibe.

Later promoters like Manumission approached me to host 'carry-on' sessions at Space on a Tuesday after their own parties on Mondays at Privilege.

After a few seasons, Turbosound came in and decked out the whole club, which revolutionised the terrace again.

By then we had inspired notorious day-time sessions at a new club called DC10, and especially Circo Loco parties on a Monday, where people would carry on after Space. Towards the end of the '90s Space Terrace was taken over by Home, and then We Love, for what eventually became 24-hour sessions on a Sunday, which we weren't involved in. It was time to move on. Mine and Blocko's careers were flying by that point anyway. We had introduced Clockwork Orange to Es Paradis, so we became residents for Danny and Andy every Wednesday. We were asked back to play at the closing party in 2016 when Space closed its doors for the final time, which was a nice touch.

Jon Ulysses: One Tuesday night in 1996 the waiters at the restaurant across the road to Simples came running in while I was on the decks. 'Jonathan, Jonathan, Pepe from Space...he wants you to DJ for him on the terrace at 10am.'

I was shocked to say the least, but Pepe knew the guys who owned the restaurant, so late at night I guess that was the best way to get hold of me. This was the opportunity I'd been waiting for. So I finished work at 6am, and with no sleep, headed to Space. Awake more than 24 hours by this point, I played a six hour set and kept everybody on the terrace until late afternoon.

And then I heard nothing from Space.

I got another break when I was picked to be on Sky TV's *Ibiza Uncovered* series in 1997, usually filmed talking about wanting to play at Space. Haha.

I left Simples during the 1997 season and struggled a bit. I'd made connections over my time there, picked up the odd booking at Amnesia and for Miss Moneypennys at El Divino...and had also been advising Twice As Nice, who were launching a UK garage night at Summum. I played at Clockwork Orange at Es Paradis, and at some of their Camden Palace parties back in London, too. But at the end of the 1997 season I went back to England, and lived in Willesden and had nothing concrete sorted for the following season in Ibiza. I'd trod on a lot of toes being successful at Simples, so it wasn't easy getting work in other bars.

Then in the January of 1998 I got a call at home from Fritz, explaining that his regular DJ Daniel Klein would not be able to play the whole of the 1998 season. Would I like to be a Space resident?

'Woah!' I was speechless.

I went out to the island early in April and Fritz told me to keep it to myself. Everyone was asking me what I was doing that year and I was like, 'I dunno, I dunno,' when I already had one of the biggest gigs on the island. It was an amazing feeling.

Pepe and Fritz set out some ground rules. If you are caught doing drugs in the club, you're gone. It was such a big business now, things were changing from the early days of the terrace. I almost had to re-train how to be a DJ. Pepe explained I had to play music that lets people go to the bar to get a drink, or to the toilet, and makes them dance again when they come back. Let the guest DJs play all the big tunes. Keep an eye on the bar-staff, make sure they're dancing and the security staff are tapping their feet too. I had to step-up and know my role in the team, now a small fish in a big pond.

Because the club inside opened at 6am, I'd have to be there at 5am, even if I wasn't playing until 11am, in case a DJ didn't show up. And inside was tribal, with residents like Recce, so I had to have those records too, and learn how to play to the largely Spanish crowd inside most of the time.

I played every room at Space, including the Sunset Terrace, when that opened, which I really tried to put my own stamp on.

As the Noughties played out my summer schedule as a Space resident was relentless. Tour nights all over Europe on Friday and Saturday, then a flight back in on a Sunday morning to play the 10am terrace set to open Home. Monday was a 'day off', whatever that was, because we'd all go to DC10, then Cocoon at Amnesia in the evening. Then I'd play at Space throughout the week at the Manumission Carry On, Matinee and La Troya. And repeat.

The winter was packed with Space-affiliated events all over the world. Brazil numerous times, Indonesia, Columbia, Russia. I was fulfilling my dream and went on to be a resident at Space for 16 years.

In the second half of the '90s Alex and Brandon earned acclaim and notoriety for their radio shows on *Kiss FM.*

Alex P: We did a pilot for *Capital*, but I think we were too unruly for them. Gordan Mac at *Kiss* got wind of it, and approached us. He said we could have a free rein, and that was music to our ears. We were given a trial 2am slot Wednesday night/Thursday morning which was literally (above) Jon Ulysses at Space closing, 2016 and (below) in action on the terrace.

an overnight success. A few weeks later we were offered Friday drive-time and Saturday early evening too. All completely live.

It was full-on; we worked so hard back then. After the Friday show we'd do our gigs that night, anywhere in the country, come back, do the Saturday show and then off on the road again.

It was that whole superclub superstar DJ era of excess. Blocko and I both had Ferraris, and we'd lord it up on the Holloway Road on our way to the studios. Often the start of the show would be one of us on the phone, apologising we were late. The producer would put the call live on air. *Kiss* were brave back then.

The most popular segment of the show was 'In The Carsey' where listeners could vote if an awful record we'd chosen would 'flush or float'. They all got flushed. Never any floaters.

The *Kiss* show led to work with *MTV*, and I set up Piggy In the Middle Productions (P.I.M.P) with my pal Chris Brown and sold content to Sky channels like *Men & Motors.* We made a show in Ibiza which included interviewing clubbers for the Early Morning Gurning Club and aerobic classes with Ibiza legend Spiderman, a lovely guy, who is actually a lecturer from Portugal and who carried that fine tradition of wonderful, eccentric characters on the island like Pippi Sol and Captain Birdseye.

The rest of the '90s were so busy, playing at the big club nights every city in the UK now had. Multiple bookings throughout every weekend, plus loads of university gigs in the week. We couldn't walk into an airport without getting mobbed.

CLOCKED ON

Clockwork Orange duo Danny 'Clockwork' Gould and Andy 'Manky' Manston were both huge *Centreforce* fans first time around, but typically Danny took his fandom to extreme levels.

Andy Manston: I really got into Dave Pearce's hip-hop show on Radio London on a Monday night, the Fresh Start To The Week. I loved that 1986-87 hip-hop era — JVC Force, Biz Markie, Big Daddy Kane. I locked into that kind of music. I was messing about with an old belt-drive deck and a tape deck and almost by accident discovered I could mix Nitro Deluxe - *This Brutal House* into Derek B's *Bad Young Brother*. And that's how I got into mixing at the age of 15/16 and thinking about what a DJ could possibly do. Then the rave thing happened.

I was sitting in my bedroom listening to *Centreforce* and the first DJ I heard was Pasha, playing *French Kiss* by Lil Louis. With all its groans I was like, what the hell is this? We listened to Sunrise a bit, but *Centreforce* was just so fresh and exciting. We couldn't go back.

Danny Clockwork: I had *Centreforce* tapes I knew word for word. Me and my pals wore those cassettes out, years after *Centreforce* came off air, driving to clubs and parties. I can still remember one line. A guy paged in and asked Hermit for a request, and a voice on the mic said, 'I'm afraid Hermit can't play your request, he's a bit young for that one.'

The first pirate I listened to at 16 in 1988 was Sunrise, on the radio of my Sony Walkman. It was Ratpack playing house and hip-house and I fell in love with it. Tracks like Adonis, *No Way Back*, *Acid Over* by Tyree Cooper, Roxanne Shante, *Sharp As A Knife*. I wrote them all down, plus artists like Richie Rich, Phase II and Soul II Soul. I kept that bit of paper and sent a photo of it to Lipmaster Mark recently, 30 years later.

Then my mate Sean Coney said there's a new pirate on called *Centreforce*. It quickly became our station. We called it Centy.

I loved that you could tell those East End boys weren't mainstream, and all part of the same underground network. The connection to West Ham, the way they spoke.

And so I started going to Echoes. I was at the tea hut outside one night, and a geezer came bowling through with his hand up and said, 'That's why they call me DJ One Thumb.' I was like, oh my God, it's DJ One.

Seeker, Corporation Dave...Danielle & Rochelle...Hermit, Bags...I loved them all. I idolised Keith Mac, because we were both 17-years-old, and he was on *Centreforce*, and then I got to know him.

Sean and I went to Ibiza in 1990 when we were 18 and pretended we were *Centreforce* DJs to pull girls. One night a girl called us out and said, 'No, you're not, I know all the *Centreforce* boys.' We made our excuses and left.

I even remember the raid at Echoes. The police tried to say they found hundreds of the ecstasy wrappers on the floor, when everybody knew pills didn't come in wrappers, so they made a lot of stuff up.

One night a few months after *Centreforce* had come off air, we were on our way up town, and we actually drove via Carpenters Road to try and see where the studio had been. We were lurking in our car and a resident came out and gave us such evils, we sped off.

We were literally *Centreforce* super-fans.

Andy Manston: I'd put on a few small parties with my mates in the early-90s around the Walthamstow area, with me as the resident DJ.

A friend introduced me to Danny at Hollywood in Romford. He asked me if I wanted a drink, and when I said yes, Danny leant across the bar, grabbed a bottle of whiskey and swigged from it. The security ran over and threw us both out. And that's how me and Danny first met properly, standing outside on Atlanta Boulevard, turfed out of Hollywood.

The first party I put on in April 1992 was at Paddocks in Holborn, called The Strawberry Club, with Simon Hanson and Lawrence Nelson from Naked Lunch as the guest DJs alongside me. It was the night an IRA bomb exploded at The Baltic Exchange in the City. We actually heard it go off as we arrived. There was a ring of steel around the immediate vicinity for the next 48 hours so we had about 12 people in. It was a first reality check with promoting and how things don't always go to plan.

We needed someone involved that knew people, so we approached Danny. He said, 'Yeah, alright, I'll have a go.' We all spent a day in Soho and Covent Garden at cinematic shops, looking at old movie stills. I pulled out the iconic picture of the glass with the teeth in it, and we all said, 'Fucking hell, 'Clockwork Orange', that's a great name.'

Our first Clockwork party was at Paddocks in January 1993 with Lisa Loud. Then my two mates came out of it. One wanted to do his own parties and the other one was training to be a solicitor.

Danny Clockwork: I was ducking and diving in clubs in and around Essex and London. That's the way it was. I'd already been that young kid, knocking his pipe out, grafting four jobs from the age of 14. Then you discover you can earn a week's money in one night.

But then I bumped into Andy, and when we launched Clockwork I stopped all that. It was a new chapter for me and a chance to express myself in a completely different way. What became evident very quickly was that I loved Clockwork. I had such a passion for it.

Andy Manston: When we did our first birthday at The Paddocks with John Digweed, we'd only had one party in between.

I was working at NatWest in Piccadilly, and I spoke to Alex P and Brandon Block in the run up to the 1994 season and asked if they could hook us up with anyone in Ibiza. They suggested Claire (Miss Bisto) at Es Paradis, so I took a week's holiday. Danny and I flew out there to meet her and the club's owner, Pepe. We explained that we wanted to bring over guest DJs from the UK every week and Pepe said, 'Okay, you can have every Wednesday from July.' We were like, 'Oh, wow...'

I went home and handed in my notice at the bank. My parents gave me a hard time, said I was throwing my life down the pan. Years later, my dad actually apologised and said I'd proved him wrong, which he didn't need to do, because it was clearly a gamble at the time.

I was at Bagleys a few weeks later with Danny, and as we walked back out at the end of the night towards Kings Cross, we stumbled upon The Cross, which had recently opened. We looked at each other and said, 'What's this gaff?' It was emptying out so we walked in and got chatting to the owner Billy Riley. I remember we said something basic like, 'We do parties, can we do a party?' Amazingly, Billy gave us the Bank Holiday Sunday the week before we left for Ibiza. We booked Digweed again and gave The Cross their best bar spend yet.

That first season in Ibiza went well, but we weren't really busy. Maybe about five or six hundred in each week — just enough to fill in and around the dancefloor at Es Paradis — but the extra reach that it gave us when we returned to the UK was huge. We were the first UK promoters to take big line-ups out to Ibiza, and it became a springboard for us.

We came back to London at the end of that summer in 94 and did a party at Maximus. I remember looking outside the door at 10pm and seeing a queue stretching all the way through Leicester Square.

We started monthly at The Cross, parties at Camden Palace, club tours, student gigs and loads of parties for First Continental at Hollywood in Romford, and their other venues, UK Midlands, Club UK in Wandsworth and Club Art in Southend. Now people were travelling from Liverpool, Manchester, Nottingham or wherever to party with our traditional Essex and Kent fanbase.

After our second summer in Ibiza in 1995, our old mate Keith Mac got in contact and invited us to a meeting with Andy Swallow at the PWL

(top) Andy Manston at Space Terrace (above) the Clockwork van and (right) Danny hosting in Ibiza, in the '90s.

office in Borough. Andy was interested in putting out a Clockwork Orange mix CD on their Labello Dance label. I gave him a long wishlist of tracks we wanted on there, and to be fair to Andy, he got pretty much all of them, including *Yeke Yeke* - Mory Kante, *I Believe* - Happy Clappers and *Hooked* - 99th Floor Elevators. Being such fans of *Centreforce* it was great to work with Andy and we stayed in touch over the years.

Danny Clockwork: You had do a mix CD and as many parties as possible just to try and keep up with your competitors. All those nights and the miles and hours we put in back then was the equivalent of social media now. You had to be everywhere.

Over the next few summers, Clockwork Orange became synonymous with Wednesdays in Ibiza. Each May Danny drove there in the Clockwork van, loaded up with flyers, decor and props, stopping off at the Recorder office in Ilford on the way for an interview in my Club Mix column about the season ahead.

Danny Clockwork: We were just 22, 23 when we started at Es Paradis. I loved that buzz when I knew I was about to go to Ibiza for the summer. I'd get out there every year and do all my money immediately, then get a couple of grand on tick from Es Paradis....always, 'Don't tell Andy,' haha...and blow it all at Space on the first Sunday..

Sundays at Space was like our church each week, and we all went religiously. I actually heard a mate, Aaron, on his mobile one Sunday say, 'I've got to go, I'm with the family.' Then straight through to Manumission on a Monday night. The lives we led in Ibiza — so full-on all the time. Booze, chisel, bumbles. The '90s were so wonky, but we had the elasticity of youth. We also did carry-on parties at Space some Thursday mornings.

The head of security at Es Paradis, Paco, was always trying to keep me in line, as I buzzed in and around as Clockwork's front of house host. He'd use his stun gun to give me a click on the neck or ask one of his guys to clip me on the leg with a truncheon, just to slow me down.

After a few years, other holiday destinations wanted a piece of Clockwork. After Es Paradis we'd fly to Majorca on a Thursday with no sleep to do BCM. Proper twanged up at the airport, unable to speak. The things we got away with. We'd be up all night there, fly back to Ibiza, a couple of hours in the sun, into Ibiza Town, Dolce & Gabbana. Bosh. A nice meal, and then to Ministry at Pacha, my personal favourite ...always in the funky room. We'd have to leave by about six to go and sort out the flyer teams for our next party on a Wednesday. Somehow Andy used to go off and do Tenerife and Ayia Napa sometimes in between.

Andy Manston: Being involved in the Ibiza Uncovered TV series in 1997 took us to another level. They filmed it around July time and before it aired we were averaging 1500 people through the door each Wednesday. The week after the first show on Sky we had 2,500. It just shot up overnight and stayed like that for the next couple of years.

In 1998, with my production partner Julian Napolitano, I got to No 12 in the UK charts with *Keep on Dancing* as Perpetual Motion, which pushed my DJ bookings through the roof.

Danny Clockwork: At the start of the 1999 season, in the depths of my madness, I passed out at the wheel of the Clockwork van, and woken up by a large crunching sound. The dashboard was in my lap and my hands had gone through the windscreen. Smashed teeth and concussion. I'd driven into a stationary van on the wrong side of the road. Because my lips were split when they breathalised me I blew raspberries instead. A police officer slapped me round the face with his big hand.

I was arrested and locked up, but fortunately through some connections was out the next day...and straight to Space.

Later that day at Manumission's pre-party at Bora Bora for their opening Monday the next day, I wound up their host Johnny The Dwarf so much that he jumped on a chair, then jumped on a table, then jumped on a speaker and then jumped on my head and started punching me. We fell to the ground and rolled around on the beach. Apparently it was some spectacle. A week later my mobile rang. It was my mother.

'Have I forgotten your birthday again, Mum?'

'No...had a little crash did we?'

'How did you find out about that?'

'It's all over the fucking *Ilford Recorder*.'

Thanks Matt...

As the '90s drew to a close, Danny was happy to be recognised for his services to the 'caner' genre that a decade of debauchery had inspired. And another *Centreforce* DJ would find that there would be no let-up from Danny as the Noughties began.

Danny Clockwork: I actually aspired to emulate people like Brandon and Alex, who had unwittingly invented the 'caner' category years before those sorts of awards were created. In the Ministry Magazine Top Ten Caners Of The Nineties Blocko and Peasy were No 1, and I was No 3, which I was okay with, but I was also really happy to be voted Caner Of The Summer and No 1 Craziest Guy In Ibiza in other magazine polls at the end of 1999. I felt I'd achieved what I set out to do.

Andy Manston: In 2000, Danny completely lost the plot, and the music was unpredictable too. UK Garage and prog house were coming in and we didn't have our eye on the ball. We were so stuck in our own mad drugged-up world that we thought we were invincible, and just couldn't see it coming. Then there was the big fuck up in 2001 when we lost our trademark in Ibiza. We rocked up for the season and a guy in Benidorm had copyrighted the use of the Clockwork name and logo on the island. He did it to Moneypennys, Gatecrasher, Godskitchen too, and wanted us to pay him large sums of money just be able to trade in our own name. We went to court and the judge said, 'Sorry, I can't help you.' We carried on under the name Orange Summer Of Love, but struggled.

Danny Clockwork: The Ibiza parties were going downhill quickly and I was spiralling out of control too. Alister Whitehead was guesting for us and staying at our villa. Me and my mate Flumpy were sitting up getting proper wonky, dressed in women's clothes with cushion covers on our heads, the usual drill. Ali had given me specific instructions that he needed to be woken up by 8.30am so he could catch his flight home. Just before half eight I went to the door of his room, and lit a Spanish banger, which was like a fire-bomb, and threw it in and shut the door. I looked inside ten seconds later and loads of smoke poured out of the room, but Ali was still asleep. I thought, I'm not having that, so I poured some BBQ lighter fluid over a cardboard box, lit it and chucked that in. That did the trick, and Ali staggered out through four foot flames, shouting the odds, telling me I was sick in the head. He left the villa as quickly, but at least he caught his flight. Alister stopped playing for Clockwork after that. Judge Jules had already refused to play because of my behaviour.

Andy Manston: After the 2001 season, Danny wanted out. He was trying to get his shit together and I bought him out for just a couple of grand. At that time the brand wasn't worth much more than that, to be fair. My DJ career was still going really well, so I had that to fall back on. I tried to keep Clockwork Orange going for a couple of years, but it was never going to be the same without Danny involved.

Danny Clockwork: It had been such a rollercoaster. In 1996 we came back from Ibiza £2,000 down, and in 1998 returned £250k up. I spunked my share over that winter and at the end of 2001 I was skint. I was fortunate to be given a job on a building site by a pal, who paid me £90 a day, which was well over the odds. I was still deep in the depths of drink and drugs and I was simply working to feed my habit. I bunked the train to work and bought a jumbo box of cornflakes for 50p each day, so I could have a large bowl for breakfast and another at lunch.

I was walking to work along The Highway, heading to Shadwell. I saw a guy I recognised and asked, 'Did you used to be Pa Eames?' And he replied, 'I still am.' I said, 'You used to be a hero of mine,' and he laughed and said, 'Nice to meet you,' and bowled off.

Andy Manston: Around 2002, as the music changed, I started noticing that my DJ work was disappearing off the face of the planet. And that's when I started working for my mate as a labourer too. Me and Danny are both grafters so we did what we had to do. I'd gone from having a Top 20 hit and playing all over the world...to a building site. The boys I worked with couldn't believe I'd ended up there. And I had to start from scratch, I didn't even know how to hang a picture.

Danny Clockwork: It all came to a head for me at the V Festival in August 2003. I was in such a bad way I thought my brain was going to split. When I woke up the next morning I opened my eyes and just had the feeling that it was over...that the addiction had gone. I was very lucky I could just stop like that. Then all those feelings and emotions that I had suppressed over the years came out. I built my way up from a guy who knew nothing on a building site to running jobs ten time bigger than the job I started on, managing more than a hundred members of staff and working with dozens of contractors every day.

Andy Manston: We both started at the bottom and worked our way up. Danny became a project manager, and I became a site manager. Through Clockwork, and what they now call transferable skills, we already knew how to manage large events and organise people, so thankfully we were able to progress through the construction business.

As the years went by, Danny and I went on camping holidays together with our families, and most nights we reminisced about Ibiza and Clockwork's heyday. I'd always float the idea of doing a renunion party but it never got past the conversation stage.

AND THE CLASSICS JUST KEEP ON COMING.

When a rock music fan from Chicago was upsold $7,000 worth of studio equipment at his local guitar store in 1985 his friends thought it was hilarious. Twelve months later Ron Hardy, Larry Levan and Frankie Knuckles were playing his first track several times each night...and Marshall Jefferson was able to quit his night-shift job at the post office, and was catapulted into a DJ producer A-List circuit of house pioneers.

I was into Led Zeppelin, Black Sabbath, Yes, Deep Purple, Van Halen...rock music, man.

I saw The Beatles on *The Ed Sullivan Show* in 1964 when I was five years old and got into The Monkees, then Cream and Jimi Hendrix.

But dance music attracted a lot more females than rock and roll so I'd play disco and European stuff at small local bars.

I was studying to be an accountant at college, and looking at a starting salary of $12k. I took a summer job through the night at the post office on $21k and quickly quit college.

A friend of mine needed a ride to our local music store, Guitar Centre, so I drove him down there.

The guy at the store was trying to sell him a Yamaha QX1, which was a sequencer.

'You'll be able to play keyboard like Stevie Wonder,' he said. 'Even if you don't know how to play at all...'

So I said, 'Wow, that's just what I need.'

I'd already decided to buy it there and then, and asked how much?

'Thirty five hundred...'

'Oh, I haven't got that much...'

'Where do you work?'

'The post office.'

Which at the time was just about the most secure job you could find. You could work there for years and years with lifetime benefits. There wasn't an email in sight at that point.

So the shop gave me a £10,000 credit line right there and then.

I was ready to rock out of the store with my QX1 and go home and play with it.

But the guy was like, 'Where you going? You need a keyboard.'

'What?'

'Yeah, you need the keyboard too...and you also need a drum machine...'

'Yeah, I do need me a drum machine...'

'And you need a mixer, so you can hear everything...'

'But I'm a DJ, I got me a mixer.'

'Nah, you need a recording mixer. See, this here has eight channels, so you can hear eight instruments at the same time.'

'Yeah, that's what I need, I need a recording mixer...'

'And you need a multi-rack tape recorder, so you can record everything.'

So I got a TASCAM Portastudio...

And then this guy sold me a bunch of other stuff...another drum machine...and just before I walked out the door, he said, you need a DB-303 to make your baselines.

'Sure, I'm a DJ. I need baselines, I need a TB-303.'

I got all this stuff home and my guitar-playing friend was nice enough to tell all of our friends, and so they came over to laugh at me. They took the piss out of me for hours.

'You stupid mother fucker, you don't even know how to play...hahahahaha...you're going to make a hit record...hahahahaha.'

I made my first demo track two days later.

I was trying to make dance music that sounded like Elton John, who, for me, was the coolest man on the planet. He had so much soul in the '70s they had him on *Soul Train*. I wanted to play piano like Elton John, so that's where *Move Your Body* came from.

About a year after I walked out of that guitar shop, *Move Your Body* was out there and DJs were hiring keyboard players and telling them to play piano like Marshall Jefferson. I had never played an instrument before, just air guitar.

And because of the piano there was also a lot of people saying, 'Erm, this ain't house music'. I was like, 'well, it is now.'

Part of the reason I added *(The House Music Anthem)* to the title was two fingers up to everybody who said it wasn't house music. It was upsetting at the time. Ron Hardy, Larry Levan and Frankie Knuckles playing your record multiple times each night was my definition of house, right there.

I recorded *Move Your Body* in September of 1985, but it was nine months before it came out in the June of 1986. Between that time it had gotten all over the world on cassette. That was viral back in the day.

But I must be a very non-threatening type of guy, because all my friends thought they were smarter than me. That is definitely an American thing — confidence and arrogance.

Mike Dunn, Tyree Cooper and Lil Louis, all those guys, they saw me playing all the instruments on all my records. 'If Marshall did that, we can do it too.' So they did.

When I went over to England, and people saw me making music, a few of them picked it up, but most just went out and hired a keyboard player, and I was like, 'No, man, you can play everything yourself. Look how easy it is.'

I do joke about the confidence levels between American and European artists. I can produce a European vocalist for eleven hours and they're like, 'I've got to get it perfect, run it back, run it back,' when it's already sounding amazing to me. I go back to the States, the vocalist fucks up every note, comes out the booth and says, 'Ain't that the greatest shit you ever heard?'

*****

At the post office I was working the graveyard shift, midnight to 8.30 every morning. Prime partying hours. The day *Move Your Body* was released I left the post office, a job I loved. I wasn't even playing decent local bars and clubs in Chicago, but now I was heading straight to New York, where it was all really happening. It felt like I'd gone straight to playing stadiums, the change was that big.

I wasn't even used to a crowd because I'd mainly been DJing at home by myself with no audience — except the neighbours. I had a huge system and the entire block would hear me. And they weren't exactly receptive.

The New York club scene then was like no other, and there hasn't been anything like it since.

It was the most extravagantly financed club system in the world. You had Studio 54, Paradise Garage and Better Days, all these gigantic clubs, which the mafia were laundering their money through. Cash was no object. All the main DJs were getting three thousand dollars a night. They were the only DJ at their club and each club had that DJ's sound.

I played at the second Studio 54, not the original one. There was another Warehouse after the original Warehouse, and I played at that one. These places had separate sound systems for the DJs and the live acts. I'd get put up in a nice hotel and they gave me a limousine service for every gig. You don't see that anymore. We used to get limos to MacDonalds, man.

For every 400 gigs in New York, I'd get four gigs in Chicago. Because Chicago wasn't money laundering it couldn't afford me. One weekend in New York I played nine times at three grand per booking. One year I think I played 300 different times in New York.

The bottom fell out of all that in about 1988. The IRS came down on the mafia and cleaned them out. Most of the venues in New York closed. It was like The Sound Factory with Junior Vasquez was the only club left in town, and that's why it blew up. Midnight to noon.

When the club work dried up in New York, Marshall realised he wasn't earning the royalties he should be, considering *Move Your Body* had done so well. Several other tracks he'd been involved in had become hugely influential, if not pioneering.

I suddenly noticed I wasn't earning anything from the royalties of record sales. I had so much money in my pocket, I hadn't been paying as much attention as I should have.

I was now heavily involved with Trax Records. I'd produced *I Lost Control* for Sleazy D three or four years before in 1985. I was thinking Black Sabbath, that was my motivation. There was nothing out there like that...nothing.

I thought it was going to be big in Ron Hardy's club The Box, and a lot of people think it was the first acid house track. However, I believe the first acid house record was *Acid Tracks* by Phuture, which I also produced. The difference was *I've Lost Control* didn't start a movement, but *Acid Tracks* did.

SOME PRODUCERS MADE ONE TRACK THAT WAS SO HOT THEY DANCED TO IT AS WELL. THEN THEY COULDN'T LEAVE THE PARTY. LUCKILY, I CAN'T DANCE, SO KEPT MAKING MUSIC.

People were like, 'Aciiieed, aciiieed house.' They started wearing smiley T-Shirts.

Every producer wanted a TB-303 because it was the acid house machine. Phuture bought one when they heard *I've Lost Control*. However, they had the same problem as me; they didn't know how to work it. That's why weird stuff came out, instead of a nice organised baseline.

Phuture gave their tape of *Acid Tracks* to Ron Hardy, who gave it to me. I went to the studio with Pierre and we made the track. And I knew what it was about, because the precedent had been set with *I've Lost Control*. Now I knew exactly what to do with it.

I'd paid $150 for my TB-303 and was getting offered five times that amount, so I wound up selling mine to Bam Bam for a thousand dollars.

Open Your Eyes, under my own name, Marshall Jefferson Presents The Truth was huge in the summer of 1988 too.

Some people made one track that was so hot they had to dance to it themselves, then never left the party. Luckily I can't dance, so kept on making music.

In fact, when I was touring *Move Your Body* with vocalist Curtis McClain and Ruby Forbes, we were on the same bill sometimes as JM Silk (Steve Silk Hurley and Keith Nunnally) who had their big house track *Music Is The Key*. Keith had to teach us some basic dance moves because we were complete novices.

Royalties were and always have been a problem with those early records. Sleazy D died without getting a royalty cheque. Gary D from Adonis died without getting paid for *No Way Back*. DJ Spanky from Phuture died without getting a royalty cheque. It's the same for Daryl Pandy: he saw no money before he died.

I only just got money for *Move Your Body* in 2020, and I now finally own the rights to it because of the 35-year rule in America. It's a process, man. A lot of people put their hearts into their music and the record companies steal that heart away. They don't care, but I don't think it's all about money — it's about ownership. Record companies just want to own you. Over the years it was difficult to take, but you get used to it, and you move on to other things.

One other thing Marshall Jefferson had been working on was Ten City, but that side project was just the tip of the iceberg.

Ten City started out with me and Byron Stingily writing songs together. On one DJing trip to New York I took Byron with me. He'd just made a track called *I Can't Stay Away* under the name Ragtyme. That weekend he performed it at all the clubs I played at.

At the end of the weekend, Byron said, 'Hey man, let's stick around, let's stay another week and try to meet some record labels and play them our work.' I was rich, so I said, why not!

Somehow Byron managed to schedule meetings with every major record label in town. By the end of the week, everything I had got signed. Ten City to Atlantic for an album, the CeCe Rogers' single *Someday* also to Atlantic, a Kym Mazelle album deal with EMI. There were also labels that wanted Paris Brightledge, but he had signed to DJ International, and Curtis McClain, who sang *Move Your Body*, but he was already signed to Trax Records.

One way or another everything got signed. Nothing was even finished with Ten City. In fact, we didn't even have the name Ten City yet.

Byron is a likeable guy, so Atlantic told us to go away and come up with our first release. We actually wrote it days later on a double date back in Chicago. One girl was feeling me because I had *Move Your Body* out, but the other girl wasn't giving Byron anything, so he started singing a song at the table, to try and impress her. I said, 'Man, that's a jam.' So the next day we took that melody and came up with *Devotion.*

I thought of the name Ten City, short for Intensity, and then Byron was saying Ten is the perfect number, so Ten City is the perfect city and all that stuff. So that was the concept.

Ten City was just supposed to be me as the studio guy and Byron performing, but he had stage fright. He didn't like being out there on his own, so he brought in two of his friends, Byron Burke and Herb Lawson, and they became Ten City

I was a songwriter on *That's The Way Love Is*. I thought it was going to be a hit from the start. Just before the album came out the label said *That's The Way Love Is* would be the first single. I was originally down as a songwriter, but I didn't like the mixes done to it, so I asked the label to take my name off. I was going through an artistic thing at the time. I think I was on as a songwriter when it first came out, but it doesn't say that anymore, so that's a lot of money I lost out on. I do love the song, though, but in general I hate remixes of my work.

Right Back To You, the New York Mix, is the one I really like. With the long trumpet solo. That's one of my favourite instrumentals I've ever done. Herb played guitar and Glenn Morimoto was on trumpet.

We also had an old session guy on bass called Willie. Now, Willie was old school and he just didn't get house music. He was always telling me that I wasn't a proper musician. He would say, 'This shit is weak. You know why it's weak? Because you don't know what you're doing.'

We use to laugh so much in the studio.

Marshall Jefferson with Jonny C.

with Matt Emulsion.

and with DJ Sterling and Mickey Moore.

Willie would add something like, 'But you know what, this freakin' bullshit is so weak, it's going to sell...'

Willie played amazing bass on *Right Back To You*; he really ripped it up. And we called Willie our good luck charm, because if he said it was weak, we knew it was going to sell. It was funny, because when we did the second Ten City album, when Willie started saying it was now sounding really good, we said, 'Uh-oh...'

I'd got talking to Kym Mazelle at a club in Chicago. A girl came up to me, saying she could sing her ass off, and Kym said she could too. I invited them both to the studio the next day, but Kym was so much better.

The album deal that we got in New York was a big deal for her. A young Simon Cowell working at EMI looked after the project.

CeCe Roger's manager Billy Prest had been wining and dining me for a while in New York, giving me the use of his limo and booking me nice hotels. Then he started to talk to me about CeCe and asked if I could write a song for him. I went home and I was thinking a lot about South Africa and Apartheid, so I wrote some lyrics - 'Someday, we'll live as one family in perfect harmony'.

Billy loved it and booked flights to Chicago for CeCe, who was the ultimate performer. The greatest house singer of all time, in my opinion. Certainly the greatest I have ever heard and seen. He could be in a room performing to two people and he'd have them both screaming with their hands in the air. CeCe was also a virtuoso pianist and had been told not to play in front of me, the producer, because I was just a keyboard player. Billy Prest didn't want him to embarrass me. However, CeCe walked into the studio and, probably to impress the beautiful backing singers sat there, jumped on the grand piano and started to play Rachmaninoff. CeCe's so competitive, man...the ultimate show off. Then he sang *Someday* and the girls were literally crying it was so powerful. I was sat there thinking, this is going to be the greatest house vocal of all time. I thanked CeCe, but he said he was just warming up. I was ready to go home, the first take was that good.

CeCe was saying it was terrible, so I said to the engineer, 'Let him do as many takes as he wants, but don't touch that first tape, I'm going to MacDonalds.' When we got the Atlantic Records deal CeCe still wanted to do more takes. They flew him back to Chicago for another session, but I still used that first take. He was pissed off at the time but we're best friends now.

Marshall moved to the UK in 1999 because the vast majority of his DJ work was in the UK/Europe.

There was no work in Chicago and no major work in the United States since New York shut down, so I decided to move to London in 1999. First off, I rented in Chelsea, where I was paying thirty five hundred a month for an apartment. I worked out that I'd get much more for my money on the outskirts of town and moved to Billericay, where I had five bedrooms and two bathrooms for nine hundred a month. So it was economics.

I really liked Essex.

My friend's girlfriend was from Brentwood and she was such a snob. We went to a nearby town in Essex, and she said, Uurgh, can you smell that?' And we said, 'what?' And she said... 'It's Basildon.'

Poor old Basildon gets a hard rap.

Marshall is no stranger to *Centreforce*, having visited the studio several times, as a guest of DJ Sterling.

At *Centreforce*, I trust the DJs. It's as simple as that. I was a guest on DJ Sterling's show four times. I met Danny, Master Pasha, and I was so impressed. I would be so proud of a son if he did what Danny has done, running the station like he does. It's amazing.

I'm now back in the States, New Jersey. I wanted to be closer to my family and concentrate on production.

Byron and I also wrote, produced and released a new Ten City album called *Judgement*, signed by Ultra Records, 30 years after we last worked on any new Ten City material in 1989.

Byron has finally gotten over his stage fright and Ten City is now back to just me and him. We were really excited to sign to Ultra. I hadn't made any new music since the mid-'90s because I had been DJing every weekend all that time.

I knew *Move Your Body* would be a big hit and that my early house music would last; you know that arrogance you have as a kid. I can remember thinking that in 30 years time I would be the first inductee into a House Music Hall Of Fame. I actually thought *Move Your Body* would be a lot bigger and I'd be a lot richer. I really did. I thought I'd be a multi-millionaire by now. But it's been all right. I can't complain.

Hippie Torrales learned his DJ apprenticeship at block parties in New Jersey in the early'70s, quickly progressing to regular spots at the local rollerskating rink at the age of 15. Within five years he would be the opening resident at the legendary Club Zanzibar in Newark, rubbing shoulders with house music royalty...but it would be another decade before he produced one of THE classic piano house anthems.

My family moved from Puerto Rico to New York when I was a baby, relocating to New Jersey when I was six.

When I graduated from 8th Grade in Jersey City at the age of 14, ahead of going to High School, the local nightclubs allowed students into special parties to celebrate their graduations. We went to a club called El Centro and a guy there, DJ Angel, showed us around the DJ booth.

'These are two turntables, this a mixer and this how it works.'

It was 1972 and I was like, 'Wow, this is what I want to do.'

And from that point on it was all about collecting music and finding a way to start DJing.

Then we moved to Newark.

There were a bunch of mobile jocks who would literally DJ on the streets. I bothered one guy, Nelson Butchie Nieves, every week and he eventually gave in.

I threw on some records, and I'm absolutely sure there were some horrible mixes. I was playing things like *Love Is The Message* by MFSB and *Rock The Boat* by Hues Corporation.

Fortunately, Nelson worked out I had three older sisters, who could bring a lot of girls with them, so in turn a lot of guys would come. He was like, 'Okay, this guy already has a following.'

So now I was officially part of his mobile set-up, *Traveling Disco Sounds.*

I started to play for Nelson at Branch Brook Skating Rink with its DJ booth next to the office on the second floor looking down on the rink. I was getting recognised among the, mostly, Puerto Rican/Latino crowd. We started hosting parties with another local group, Mark Four Disco, the first time I played to black crowds. A mix of Latin-rock, stuff like *Woman* by Barrabas and early disco records.

In 1976, when I was 17, Butchie opened a club in Newark called Docks and I was resident alongside him. That helped me get a gig in The Limelight in New York, the original one on 7th Avenue & 9th Street.

I began playing Thursday nights at the iconic Lincoln Motel, which had 200 rooms and a ground floor nightclub called Abe's (as in Abraham Lincoln). Our resident DJ Gerald was a music man and reached out to Richard Long, who had created the soundpost at the Paradise Garage in New York...which Miles fell in love with. He said, 'I want to take this to New Jersey', so Richard did the system in the first floor club over again and now we had the best sound in Newark (and better than most in New York). In fact, us and the Garage now had the best sound on the whole of the east coast.

When the club upstairs re-opened it was renamed Zanzibar.

Miles asked me to open the first Friday and be the weekly resident. I was 20-years-old. Amazing.

The opening night, August 29 1979, was some spectacle. There were real tigers and lions in cages, pythons, body-painted dancers, magicians ...and a monkey called Zippy who could roller-skate to disco music.

A guy came up to me in the booth with a record he said had only been played once on a radio station in Texas. 'We really want to break this record in the New York area,' he told me. I listened through my headphones and liked it, so I threw it on...and that was the first time *Rapper's Delight* was played in a nightclub anywhere.

After the first three months we were able to bring in Larry Levan, as long as it was a Wednesday. Larry had a strict contract with Paradise Garage which meant he couldn't play anywhere else in the New York area, but he could play for us on a Wednesday because it was in Jersey.

Larry and I hit it off and he invited me to his apartment in New York, a really nice loft. He always gave great advice.

'Listen, you have to have attitude. If I like a new song I don't care if the audience likes it or not when it first comes on, because as long as I like it, and I get it, if I play it enough times, they're going to get it too.'

And that's what Larry used to do, play a new track early in the night, then play it again, and again, up to about eight times some nights. By that time the audience was screaming the song. 'Oh, that's Larry's new song.' Now they got it.

Larry showed me that you had to be like a teacher to the crowd, especially at that time with all the amazing new music and songs coming through. You had to feed the crowd.

I remember a limo arriving to take us a few blocks to the cinema. Larry was on that level. He could make a call and get most things done.

I wasn't even close to what Larry was earning, and he would say, 'Man, you need to get yourself more money. You got to do better than this.'

He told me 'They (The Paradise Garage) pay for my apartment. I get $1500 a month wages and all food and living expenses covered too.' That was a lot of money in the early-'80s.

Meanwhile, my arrangement with Miles at Zanzibar was $35 a week and a room in the Lincoln Motel.

While I was at Zanzibar, I won Billboard's Disco Forum 8 award for Best DJ in the state of New Jersey, the time they held that award, 1980. The winner for New York was Larry Levan. I told Miles I needed to make more money and got a raise to $250 a week but I had to move out of the hotel.

I started doing remix work for George Rodriguez, who owned a local record pool, sending out promos to his roster of jocks.

Our biggest mix at that time was Jimmy Ross – *Fall Into A Trance*, which became a big pop record on the radio. Then on my own, I did The Clark Sister's – *You Brought The Sunshine*, which was a huge gospel anthem in the New York area. It got me a #1 record on New York's local radio station *WBLS* and a Grammy nomination that year in the Best Gospel category.

I left Zanzibar because the management at that point wanted the whole atmosphere and the jocks to be more gay. I wasn't gay, so that was that. I didn't fit the pattern, but I was okay with it. I was being offered opportunities on the Shore, so I moved there to take up new club residencies.

That was a whole different scene by comparison. The beach and it only being a summer season made it feel like Ibiza.

I was always welcomed back at Zanzibar to play guest spots or one-off events. Tee Scott had taken over the weekends, a young David Morales was guesting and then Tony Humphries heard the sound system and saw the crowd acting just like they did at the Garage and was like, 'Oh my God, I've got to play here.'

When we first heard house music we called it club music. It started in 1983 with Boyd Jarvis and his first track *The Music Got Me*, which is recognised as one of the first early house records.

The next time I came back to Newark and Zanzibar from the Shore, the music had been named 'house'. I heard people like Tony Humphries playing 'house music', and I was like, 'Wow, this is pretty cool.'

The main difference between disco and 'house', for me, was the drum machine, everything more synced up. I started getting into it in 1984,'85, taking house down to the Shore, and training that audience up on it.

*****

I knew the owner of a record store in Newark called Music Village well. Joe Rogriguez also had a record label, and in 1988 he said to me, 'You've been doing this a long time and playing house for a while now, Hippie. Why don't you try to do your own song?'

So, I said, 'Okay...' And it sowed the seed in my head.

I borrowed a keyboard and a drum machine and I put down a simple baseline. And then I started to write the lyrics and I'd never done lyrics before, but I just wanted to keep a little rhyming scheme going.

I don't know where the theme for the song came from. I wasn't even going through a relationship like that. I hadn't just broken up with someone. I hadn't even been in a relationship recently. The first record I ever bought was *I Heard It Through The Grapevine* by Marvin Gaye, a record famously about relationships and cheating, so maybe that influenced me.

Soon I'd written and produced a basic version of *You're Gonna Miss Me.* I wrote the song in a day and a half. And I took it to Joe and he said, 'Yeah, let's do this,' so he put up the money for the studio time and I recorded it. I put my own vocal down on it because I wanted someone else to sing it, not me.

But Joe said, 'Nah, it works, leave it like that.'

'You sure, singing is not my thing?'

'Yeah, let's keep it...'

Hippie Torales

I mean, I used to lead the choir but I stopped singing at the age of 15. I was now 29-years-old.

So I put down the vocals again.

A female friend of mine recorded the phone call at the end in Spanish, and then I talk to her in English, which I thought was nice an unusual tagline at the end. My friend Paul Scott, a great musician, played all the keyboards again. What I couldn't play I would tell him. I want trumpets like this, so he would play it on the keyboard. We put all the music and the arrangement together and released the track under the name Turntable Orchestra on the Music Village Records label. We sold a couple of thousand copies locally, and we didn't think much more about it.

Then a friend of mine came back from England, and said, 'This song is huge in the clubs. It's being played all over, it's like an anthem over there.'

'Really?'

A day or so later I got a call from Dave Lee, aka Joey Negro, from Republic Records, saying, 'Listen, we really want your track.'

So we signed a deal with Republic. A week later Virgin Records called up and said, 'We really like *You're Gonna Miss Me*, we want to sign it.'

Reluctantly, I said, 'Sorry, you're too late.'

Republic Records brought me to England to do some gigs. At every club the lines were all the way down the street. We did a party with Pete Tong from FFRR.

I was very lucky that Joe was a decent guy. I discussed the publishing rights with him and he said, 'Listen, it's all you, I don't want any of that.' So he took his share of the sales at that point, and I've owned the track ever since. So it wasn't because I knew what I was doing, I was just very fortunate. I also think that working for Miles Berger from Lincoln Hotel/Club Zanzibar helped make me much smarter by that point.

When *You're Gonna Miss Me* blew, I travelled more internationally and left the New Jersey and New York club scene. Over the years the record has gone on to sell two million copies.

Hippie also left Turntable Orchestra behind too, joining forces with New York producer/A & R man Mark Mendoza to become MenTor Productions, remixing the likes of Jocelyn Brown, Evelyn 'Champagne' King and Lisa Stansfield.

Fast forward to 1997 and MenTor remixed a song Prince had written for a new Motown artist called Rosie Gaines, who was less than enamoured with the outcome.

We were told Rosie cried when she heard our mix of the track, *I Want You*. She said we had 'munchkin'd' her voice because we'd sped it up. She hated it.

Motown didn't use our mix on the release, but my friend Camacho had some gigs in London and asked if I had anything new for him to play, so I gave him the Rosie Gaines mix.

A few weeks later I got a call from Camacho saying he'd played it to Paul Trouble Anderson, who told him, 'I need this track.' I said, 'Sure, give it to Paul.'

And Paul Trouble made that mix an anthem on his *Kiss FM* radio show. Suddenly Motown UK in London were on the phone, saying they needed to release the mix. We did a deal and it put Rosie on the house map.

But then Rosie got dropped, and Scottish label Big Bang picked her up and were on the phone asking if we'd mix her new single, *Closer Than Close*. And the rest is history...our mix gave Rosie a huge hit, going on to sell eight million units.

When Turntable Orchestra took off, there was acid house, and it took off because it was different, and the same thing happened with Rosie Gaines because when that came out speed garage was big at that time, and *Closer Than Close* was a little different too, and I think that made both tracks do so well.

*****

I'm still making music. *Funk The Formular* with Koffee Paige did well on Tracksource recently. I've presented a radio show on cyberjamz.com every Tuesday for the last 15 years so people can check out there what I'm up to and into musically these days.

From Jersey I moved to Florida with my ex-wife. When we got divorced, I was heading back to Jersey but my family were living in South Carolina, and they asked me to come here for a couple of months before I went back to Jersey...and I just stayed. It's pretty decent here, nice weather, we don't have the winters we have up north. I've been here ten years.

I just cannot believe the lifespan of the Turntable Orchestra track. All the airplay on *Centreforce* is amazing. I'd been on some journey already before I even made that first track.

I always say to people, you just don't know what you are good at until you try. Never give yourself doubt about anything, because you might do something that changes your life. Always be ready when opportunity knocks.

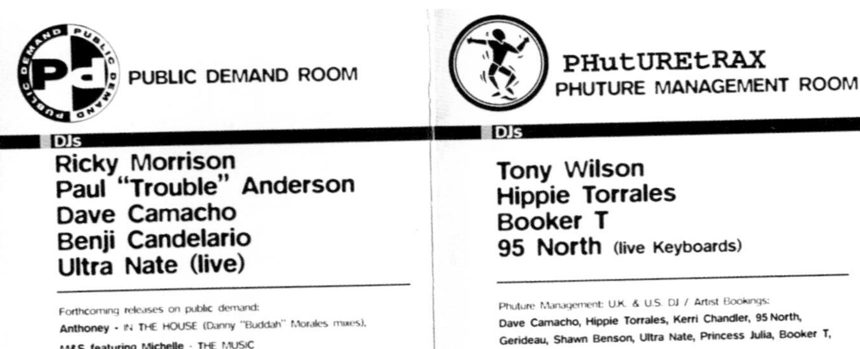

A Public Demand/Phuture Trax event flyer from WMC, Miami, March, 1996.

Right Before My Eyes by Patti Day is an unlikely club classic, given song-writers Michael Zager and Alex Forbes' brief to create a pop hit.

Bruce Forrest was resident DJ at New York's primarily black gay club Better Days club in 1988 when he produced a remix for the 12 inch single package, which crossed over so emphatically to the UK's dancefloors.

When I caught up with Michael and Alex in Florida and New York respectively on a Zoom call more than 30 years later, they were still wondering why Forrest didn't use all their vocal hooks in his dramatic and mostly a ccapella intro.

Michael: We thought the hook was catchy but when they did the remixes it seemed ridiculous that they didn't have the full hooks in there.

Alex plays the track on YouTube and sings the missing 'Right Before My Eyes' hooks.

Alex: It's so much more pop, the way we wrote it, but it's so much more club the way Bruce did it. I do understand why, though, because a big empty gaping space is no problem in a club song but with a pop song, you have to fall right in and find the melody straight away.

Michael: It was supposed to be a pop song, and be radio friendly. We knew there would be remixes for the clubs but our brief was to get Patti's records played on the radio.

Alex: The radio is where we made our bread and butter.

Three decades later, the track has stood the test of time and is a firm *Centreforce* anthem, but Michael and Alex are struggling to remember, exactly, how they met.

Alex: How we got together reminds me of the famous Sammy Cahn quote about which came first, 'the lyrics or the music?', and he said, 'the phone call.' And that's like us, right, Michael?

Michael: I'd had a bunch of dance hits and I got a call from the record label, Star Way. I think they were starting the label and they wanted me to meet with Patti.

Michael's 'bunch of hits' began with his eponymous Michael Zager Band project.

In 1977 the single *Life's A Party* featured a 14-year-old Whitney Houston on vocals alongside her mother Cissy. Then in 1978 Michael's worldwide chart-topper *Let's All Chant*, a No 8 UK hit, and a No 1 on the US Billboard disco chart, went on to sell more than ten million copies.

In 1980 Michael had two big medley hits with The Spinners. Firstly his own remake of *Working My Way Back To You* segued with *Forgive Me Girl*, a new track also written by Michael, which reached No 1 in the UK. The follow-up, a new version of the Sam Cooke hit *Cupid* mixed with I *Loved You For A Long Time*, another original song by Michael, peaked at No 4 in the UK Top 40.

Alex: Michael, with *Let's All Chant*, am I right in saying that you invented the sound that goes, 'Ooha, ooh'?

Michael: Yes, I did. And it's still getting ripped off now.

Alex: And you started Whitney Houston?

Michael: Yeah, we had a huge club hit for Cissy Houston with *Think It Over,* and Whitney had been singing background for her mum. I was making *Life's A Party* and I asked Cissy if Whitney could do her first solo for me on that track. Cissy later sang all the back-up on the Patti Day album.

Alex, meanwhile, came from a pure songwriting background and her big break came in 1985.

I began writing a lot of folk/rock stuff, but then I came under the influence of the Madonnas and the Chaka Khans of this world, so my first success was a dance hit, a track called Too Turned On for Alesha. Shep Pettibone's mix went to No 6 in the club charts in 1985, got a lot of radio play and made me some decent money, considering I hadn't made a cent yet. I got to quit my day job as a graphic artist, which was fantastic.

They called it a 'freestyle classic', which meant I wasn't pigeon-holed to one particular genre now.

I began working with Ric Wake, Taylor Dayne's producer.

Wake produced the Bros hits *When I Will Be Famous* and *I Owe You Nothing* around the same time and the 12 inch mix of *Love Will Save The Day* for Whitney Houston.

He was also the producer behind Degrees Of Motion anthems *Do You Want It Right Now* and *Shine On*.

Alex: I met Ric when he was 19 years old, and I was in my late 20s or something really old like that. But he was definitely coming up and very ambitious and he had discovered Leslie (Wunderman) — aka Taylor Dayne. He was stockpiling songs for her, and that's how he ended up with *Tell It To My Heart,* a No 3 Billboard chart hit. The track I wrote *Don't Rush Me* was the follow-up single and it went one better to No 2.

Michael: That's maybe why I wanted to write with you.

Alex: Michael is a songwriter, who also does all the production. And also had a band. I could write good melodies, lyrics, chords, but I wasn't a great singer, producer or even an arranger. So when Michael and I started working together on Patti Day material it was a good fit and, in terms of our influences, it was perfect timing. We wrote three tracks in total on that album.

With my own search for Patti Day or a contact for her amounting to nothing, I wondered if Alex or Michael had any ideas?

Alex: Patti Day seems to have disappeared, but I never actually met her when we wrote the song.

Michael: I don't know where Patti is now. I've tried to find her on *Facebook*. She was a nice girl, very sweet. Maybe she got married, and her name changed. Maybe that was her stage name anyway.

Alex: It was the first time we worked together. *Right Before My Eyes* was our first record baby.

Michael: I remember the pre-chorus, the section leading into the chorus. We didn't have that in our original version. I remember the writing session for this song clearly. I started playing some chords and then Alex started singing 'Just a touch away…all I need to do, all I need to say is baby…' so we added that in as the start of a bridge, before the pre-chorus.

Alex: The result is very dramatic for a club song. So it is quite sophisticated for 'a boom-boom'. It's a bit more chordally complex. It wasn't like I walked in with an idea. A lot of the time us songwriters bat around ideas. We might walk in with a title or something, but in this case we just mutually contributed ideas. I think Michael played something on the keyboard and I threw out a melody and sang a lyric and then we went back and forth. And in those days you'd have a cassette player and tape the whole session and just see if you come up with anything great. I do remember being excited about the song. It was super catchy from the get-go.

In 1998, Grant Nelson, under his N'n'G guise and featuring Kallaghan on vocals, scored a No 12 UK hit with a UK garage version of *Right Before My Eyes.*

Alex: To this day, we also get publishing from the N'n'G version. It's crazy. It must all come from the UK because I don't think *Right Before My Eyes* is a thing here still. We still get cheques, so it's great.

Michael: Somebody else plagiarised the hook. We won't tell you who it is. It was a really big record, and I heard it and called Alex. I wrote out our melody for the hook and I wrote out the other melody side by side in the same key. It was note for note.

Alex: It was exact. Just the melody, not the rest of the song.

Michael: I called the record company, a major label, and said: 'You plagiarised us.' It never went to court. They settled with us and we got a third of the copyright. It was a huge hit here on the radio and in the clubs. They had to pay back royalties. It was a lot of money.

Alex: It was a great day. And the derivative song did better than Patti's version and still does.

Michael moved from New York to Florida in 2002 to take up the position of Eminent Scholar position as the Head Of Commercial Music Programming at Florida Atlantic University.

I wasn't looking for the job but I got offered it and I figured I might never get a chance like that again. I really enjoy it at the University. I'm always really busy. I think the students enjoy my experiences and stories. I also write textbooks for schools. I'm finishing my sixth book.

Alex is still active in music and is a published author and songwriting coach.

I find the subject of songwriting fascinating — I'm passionate about it. I care deeply about pre-choruses and lyrics and melodies. So for me, teaching is an extension of doing it all the time, and both are really fun. I run workshops for ASCAP (American Society of Composers, Authors and Publishers), our version of PRS. It's a great life, I have no complaints... zero. My book *Write Songs Right Now* is on Amazon, and there's an Audible version too. It's hopefully an inspiration for people who want to write songs, but who are afraid to try. A lot of us want to express ourselves and be creative with it. It's about kicking it into gear, as opposed to sitting on your couch thinking about wanting to write songs.

Those lost on the dancefloor at the Hacienda in Manchester or raving in fields illegally in and around the M25 may have wondered about the mysterious female vocalist on The Beat Club's haunting anthem *Security*, which quickly became a mainstay of the acid house scene in 1988.

Few would have expected that exotic-sounding 'spoken word artist' to be a middle school teacher from Miami much more into classical music and a member of the church choir. Mireya Rodriguez wasn't even a Rodriguez yet. She had only been the girlfriend of successful South Florida freestyle producer and artist Ony Rodriguez for a few months.

Ony had met Cuban-born Mireya at a mutual friend's house party and wrote the lyrics soon after, inspired by how comfortable he felt in her company.

Ony: It was 1986, I was in a band called The Voice In Fashion, signed to Atlantic Records. Our first single was on the radio and doing really well. We were part of the new Miami freestyle scene.

At the party I just felt like Mireya was going to be my wife. I knew that on the spot. It wasn't a 'love at first sight' moment. It was more, 'I'm just really comfortable around this woman, she has to be my wife.' It was the familiarity. They say the sense of smell is the sense that triggers memories the most, hence the line, 'A certain scent, controls the air'.

I'd just watched a TV documentary about reincarnation and spirituality, so I put that and my experience of meeting Mireya into writing *Security*. It's only five lines.

Mireya: My friends were saying, 'It's Ony from The Voice In Fashion, but I hadn't heard of him or them. I liked jazz, classical, opera and big band music. This one girl was all over Ony, but he wanted to talk to me. Another guy told her he was Bruce Springsteen so she went off with him. Good job Ony didn't tell me that night he wanted to marry me, because it would have freaked me out. We really didn't date much in 1987, because Ony was touring with The Voice In Fashion. It was late '87, early '88 when we hooked up seriously.

After a stint in a progressive rock band in the early-'80s Ony embraced British new-wave bands like Human League and Heaven 17.

Ony: I was into guitars and synthesisers and prided myself in my musicianship. I always had my own studio set-up, even if just a little four-track cassette or an eight-track reel-to-reel.

Then I got into The Buggles and, for me, Trevor Horn was THE man. I was into everything he was doing. When I heard *Video Killed The Radio Star*, as a pop song, the sheer quality. It really got me into new-wave, all the ZTT records and Frankie Goes To Hollywood, of course.

In 1984 I released my first solo project, *The Dream World EP* as 'Ony' but as the freestyle scene evolved there was now something to attach my music to. I started The Voice In Fashion as a side project with some friends. As the name suggests, we were being quite sarcastic with it, but it took off and we were surprised when Atlantic signed us. Personally, coming from a progressive rock background, being in a pop band wasn't what I'd planned, so I kept going with my own solo project, which I had now named The Beat Club after a venue we used to go to in Miami, which played a lot of the new-wave British music coming through.

I was touring with The Voice In Fashion, and I really didn't want to leave my pals in the band, because they were my best friends. Our first single *Only In The Night* had been produced by Lewis Martineé, the man behind Exposé. Lewis was working with the Pet Shop Boys so we actually provided the All day, all day' backing vocals on the single *Domino Dancing.*

I thought, well, I can do my little pop thing, and also focus on The Beat

Club, which I had set up a studio for in the warehouse district. It wasn't a commercial facility, but it was a place I could experiment and share ideas. For The Beat Club I thought, let me try something with spoken word...and that's when I came up with *Security*. It had a four on the floor beat and it was more like a house number, so there was something interesting there.

Mireya: I had a friend from college called Susan, who was one of the singers with Company B, who had a big hit with *Fascinated*. At first she agreed to work on *Security*, but then she said she was too busy. So Ony asked me to come in the recording booth and speak the lyrics, not too high-pitched, to try whispering them, do something different.

Ony: Fortunately, Mireya was hoarse that day from shouting at kids at school all week. Trevor Horn had produced the band Propaganda in 1985. They had a big hit with *Duel*, which I loved, so I asked Mireya to sing that to see what her voice sounded like. But I think *Security* was always meant to be a spoken word track.

To be absolutely honest, it was better that Mireya did the vocal, because I wanted to keep the project in-house as much as possible. So it was so much better that my girlfriend signed the deal and kept it in the family. *Security* was the first big track in my new studio. I had bought some new gear. It was now 16-track analogue. It wasn't really high-end — I didn't have loads of money to spend on it, but it was a very efficient studio.

My friend Avy Gonzales, a club DJ, loved *Security*. He brought in Keith Johnson from hip-hop act DJ KJ And Da Fellas to help with some beats, which were incredible. I had always been a fan of Kraftwerk, and now *Security* had that machine sound.

We spent about a month more working on this track, at a very slow pace, trying lots of different things. Avy also brought in The Whiz Kids (Wayne Walters and Kevin Flounoy) to do 'razor blade' edits. We locked them in the studio and said we'll see you tomorrow. What they did was amazing too.

We went to clubs and DJs we knew with this new version and then fine-tuned the track after any feedback. All the clubs had reel-to-reels still, and the DJs were very cooperative, mixing different parts of the song into other tracks so we could see how it worked on the dancefloor. It was great to have access to that immediate reaction.

Security came out in the US in the summer of 1988 on Atlantic and sold about 60,000 copies, which was really good for a 12 inch.

Because *Security* had done that well, let's just say, I needed to go ahead and exercise my lease option with Mireya, who I'm pretty sure was the only middle school teacher from Day County to be a major label recording artist at that point.

Mireya: We weren't married yet, but Ony had proposed by now. We now had gigs also, but I have horrible stage fright. Ony and Avy were trying to coach me. The makeup I wore and the sunglasses were a mixture of being a huge fan of Siouxie And The Banshees and not wanting my principal to find out what I was doing.

Ony: There is a promo shot on our Bandcamp page of me and Mireya, and I have a beard and hair. I was still in The Voice In Fashion, so for the gigs it was just Mireya on stage with two dancers. We were making very good money doing the shows at local nightclubs like 1235 and Club Nu. In New York, we played Studio 54 and Roseland.

Mireya: And Cocacabana, where I was a big hit, because they thought I was a transvestite.

Ony: There was a period of a year or so when we were doing at least three or four club PAs a month. When I was not travelling with The Voice In Fashion, I would go along, otherwise Mireya would do the shows on her own with the dancers. My old rock band would get $150 a show, but with *Security*, we got $2500 for a basic PA. I did struggle with that, because part of me is very serious about my musicianship.

Mireya: It was crazy to hear my voice in the club and also coming out of big boom boxes or huge bass bins in the trunk or on the back seat of cars. My voice blasting out as they drove by,...'no existe, solo existe el amor.' The heavier the traffic was, the more stereo it would sound, as the cars vibrated. There was a radio station called Power 96, and they had it on rotation.

Ony: I licenced the record to Champion Records' sub-label Base Records in the UK in late 88, via a US distributor called Alliance. I was hesitant, but I thought what the heck and unfortunately I lost control of it and didn't even receive a copy. I was now purely a session player for The Voice In Fashion, but a remix of their second single, *Give Me Your Love*, which we called *Give Me Your Bass* and was more in keeping with The Beat Club was popular in New York clubs.

While Ony's marriage to Mireya was finally confirmed, his relationship with Atlantic was fractured at best due to a change in management.

Ony: In September 1989, this guy calls me up and says, 'Hi, I'm Frank

A SUBTLE WINK,
FAMILIAR SMILE
A CERTAIN SCENT,
CONTROLS THE AIR
ANOTHER DAY,
ANOTHER NIGHT
ANOTHER PLACE,
ANOTHER TIME
SECURITY...

Callari. I'm a DJ in New York, and I'm thinking of relocating to South Florida'...and then he said, 'You know your track *Security* is really blowing up in Manchester.

'Do you mean, Manchester, New Hampshire...or Manchester in England?

'Yes in England...do you know the Hacienda?

'No...'

'Yeah, the club by New Order...you know New Order, right?'

'Sure, they're one of my favourite bands.'

'Yeah, they own the Hacienda, and you know what, Bernard (Sumner) is a really good friend of mine, and he loves *Security*, and he wants to work with you.'

'What?'

Suddenly I was on the phone to Bernard Sumner, telling him my Atlantic Records sob story.

And Bernard said, 'Well, maybe there's something we can do, because our manager Rob Gretton is starting his new record label, Rob's Records.'

Now, bear in mind, it wasn't until I saw the film *24 Hour Party People* many years later that I realised what was going on with Factory Records at that time.

So I said to Bernard, 'I'm not really doing anything right now, I'd love to work with you.'

It was crazy, because the people I looked up to were Kraftwerk, Trevor Horn and New Order.

Bernard asked if I'd fly to the UK and I said, 'Do you think you can put us up at your place?'

And Bernard said, 'Sure.'

So I went to Manchester. Mireya stayed behind. We had been married just three months. Bernard is so focused, so in tune with music and a workaholic. Instead of releasing *Dreams Were Meant To Be Broken* as the second single, which had been my preference, Bernard wanted to re-release *Security* again and he wanted to New Order-it-up. I suggested he add some vocals. That was my contribution. And then Bernard came up with the hook. He actually recorded the new version at Johnny Marr's house, so I also got to meet Johnny, and I was such a fan of The Smiths, too. I had literally been fast-tracked into the Manchester scene.

I really loved what Bernard did with *Security*, but that was all him. I was just basically a tourist. I was in Manchester for two weeks. I kept extending my stay so I could see the thing through and finally when it was ready to be mixed I said, 'I'm going home now.'

Bernard then brokered us a deal with Rob, who was great.

Rob said, 'I'll take care of this,' and he paid for all the production to be finished. He flew out to Miami a couple of weeks later and I tried to impress him. I used to drive a Porsche back then and I had a big studio so that helped. I sat Rob down and showed him the tracks I'd been working on. I wanted him to understand I was not just a club act; I was a producer that wanted to make songs and music.

Rob liked what I played him, and said, 'We'll deal with Atlantic. We want to put out Bernard's version of *Security*, and I want to manage you and sign you to my label.'

And I said, 'Whoa...'

I never really had a manager. Up until that point I had been mismanaging my career myself. I knew a little bit about Factory Records. Rob was an independent. He told me I could do what I wanted and he would back me. I was so anti-major record labels by that point; I thought this is the first time an industry person really cares about me as an individual. Rob and Factory didn't believe in contracts, just a handshake, and that appealed to me.

And instead of an advance, Rob just worked out a monthly budget so we didn't have to worry about money.

So he released Bernard's version of *Security*. It was the first record on Rob's Records, November 1990, and that's how The Beat Club became a Manchester band.

I really have to thank Frank Callari for setting up the whole Bernard Sumner thing. He went on to have huge success as the manager of The Mavericks. Rob wanted us to move to Manchester, but by now Mireya was pregnant. It meant we missed the momentum of the Manchester scene, but now we know what was going on with Factory Records, we know there were problems.

I travelled back and forth to Manchester from Miami a bunch of times, and I was in the Townhouse Studio in London and mastered an album but it was never released because Rob was too tied up with what was going on with Factory...and then the thing fell apart.

Rob was very professional; he wasn't like he was portrayed in the movie. OK, he was a little bit like that, but he didn't try and beat me up over the table like he did Tony Wilson in the film.

Back in Miami we regrouped and refocused. I put together my own 'debut' album for The Beat Club, *Electrobeat Introduction,* and we did a label deal with Alliance, the biggest distributor in America at that time.

Mireya was so good with people, I said, 'You know what, you're now the Managing Director (and Sales Manager) of our own label Electrobeat Records. She was so good — Alliance offered her a job.'

Today we concentrate solely on our independent digital releases. For me, it's about producing music. I'm not really business savvy and now the internet allows me to release my music for free, when I've made it for free. I've got my web page, and I'm happy doing that and selling the music online myself through Bandcamp or iTunes, and also to develop our *YouTube* channel. Needless to say, *Security* is still our biggest seller. And *Security* is obviously the thing that attracts people to what we do now.

Mireya: Ony had a vision with *Security,* but he also allowed friends and hired musicians to have their inputs. I very rarely heard him say, 'I don't like that, you ruined my song.' The fact that he let go of his ego really endeared me to him. So *Security* had a lot of positive energy to it.

Ony: It's definitely the longest I've ever worked on a project. One whole month on one track. And that's why I think it stands the test of time, because we put so much work into it. At the time I didn't think *Security*, with its airy-ness and haunting sound, wasn't like anything I had ever heard before. I was going for a four-four beat, as opposed to a broken beat, and it came at the right time, when people were looking for that. Everyone was so receptive and then it just happened to resonate in the UK at that crucial time in 1989 too.

I read something that Stewart Copeland, the Police drummer, said... that every now and then things sync up, so you have to make sure you're ready for the world to sync up with you.

Mireya and Ony Rodriguez. Photo credit: Electrobeat Records

This underground house anthem began life in a shelter for unmarried mothers run by the family of producer Ben Cozmo D Cenac, at that point better known globally as the frontman of electro/hip-hop outfit Newcleus. It was a curious dynamic, which somehow created one of the purest soulful vocal house anthems of our generation.

As a teenager in the mid-'70s, Brooklyn-born Ben explored various routes into music.

I first started DJing in local parks under the name Cozmo Disco. When hip-hop became prevalent in 1977 I shortened it to Cozmo D. I was playing guitar and singing in a cover band, but I was a better DJ.

In 1979 I bought an Electro Harmonix mini-synthesiser — a little plastic thing with membrane keys and a bit of cardboard on the back, and a Boss DR-110 Dr. Rhythm Graphic Drum Machine and started making some very crude and noisy recordings.

I made a track that very night — a funky thing with a pop vocal. It was my first attempt at writing a vocal song, and I sang it as a duet with my girlfriend Yvette (Lady E). Those tapes are long gone; I was just a kid trying something for the first time.

I began working in a law firm in Manhattan as a messenger...then selling tickets on the subway. I certainly couldn't see music as a career yet. It wasn't until I was able to make what I was hearing that I thought I could make money doing it.

I was DJing any place they'd pay me to play. In the parks was for free, but we'd get paid to do block parties, house parties, wedding receptions and the odd small bar where we brought in our own mobile systems. We had Technics 1500 Mk2s and a Numark mixer, and speakers that we bought and made ourselves, with folded horns and scoops.

The music I was making in 1980 is hard to explain. There was a lot of weirdness and some 20-minute tracks, definitely shaped by the equipment I was buying and what I listened to, like Jean-Michel Jarre and Giorgio Moroder. Not much Kraftwerk until the *Computer World* album hit in 1981...then loads of Kraftwerk.

It was just me for the first couple of years. Then I made a deal with my cousin Monique, aka Nique D. If she helped invest in a TASCAM Portastudio, so I could make multi-tracks. Then I agreed to work on music with her boyfriend, Bob, aka Chilly B. We had already worked together in a couple of bands, Thunder Funk and Reggae Metal — me as a singer and him on bass, so it made sense.

When I got a Roland TR-808 drum machine everything changed because I was now able to produce the beats that were in my head. A total game-changer. The first record I made was called *Thank You Lord.*

I was working for the parks department in 1981,'82 when I made a track (with vocoded rapping) called *Computer Age* about machines taking over the future. 'I'm no longer in control, I can't program my machine, now it wants to take my soul, stop it or it will proceed!'.

Planet Rock was on the radio and I said, 'If that's a hit, then *Computer Age* is a hit. Why sit around and waste time? Let's get it out there.'

That's when I started to shop my music. It gave me the confidence that what was happening was now catching me up. There wasn't many rap records out at the time so the list of labels I could approach wasn't that big.

It was ironic that a track I was doing as a joke, really, would actually become our first single. Salvador Smooth, one of the DJs for our hip-hop crew Jam On Productions, was always on at me to do a rap song, but because I didn't think much of the rap records I was hearing on the radio, I decided to do a parody jam instead. One record label guy heard it and lost his shit. He said he'd make us half a million dollars in the first year.

Me, Lady E, Chilly B and Nique D were recording under the name Positive Messaging at the time, which was meant to be Christian in its outlook and helping to change the world, but we'd got this record that became *Jam On Revenge (The Wikki Wikki Song)* and it ain't got nothing of that, so out of respect to God we changed our name to Newcleus to denote our three families coming together.

Jam On Revenge was originally recorded in 1982 and finally came out in 1983 on Sunnyview Records after support from airplay on _WBLS_ in New York. The record reached No 23 on the Billboard R&B charts and charted all over the world, including No 44 in the UK charts. _Computer Age (Push The Button)_ was released in 1984, the same year as _Automan_, which was sampled by Snap! in 1992 for their hit _Rhythm Is A Dancer._

By 1985 we were still waiting on that half a million dollars, and we still are. The people behind the record label were crooks. They paid us a wage, but stole hundreds of thousands of dollars of our money.

I went back to putting on my own promotions and started making house music in 1986. And house fit me right away. I'd started out as a disco DJ so it was natural that I liked the early house that was coming out.

In 1986 I did a song called *Pay Me*, a house jam, channelling a lot of MSFB, with horns and all that, and I got a deal to get my own label at Warlock Records.

Pay Me was supposed to be the first release, but I was convinced by an engineer I'd worked with on Newcleus to change the drum beat and make it a freestyle record. And then the vocalist, who I got a job as A&R at the label, the first thing he did was to decide not to put out his own record, because it wasn't a house record anymore. But, otherwise, that would have been my first house record in 1986.

I finally released the house version in 2013 on the *Ben Cosmo D Cenac presents Cosmic House EP*, using the same 12-track recordings we did back then.

My style of house was influenced by Newcleus more than anything. It's the same instruments and ethereal feel. Sweeping building emotional pads and space, because I don't believe in clutter in music, period, and especially in dance music. I like a funky baseline to come through and have room to move your heartbeat so that every movement of the track can be appreciated. You can fit a lot of emotion into space. If there's a whole bunch of stuff going on it's almost confusing.

All of which sums up _I'm In Love_ perfectly, but the track was a couple of years in the making and there were a few changes in personnel before Sha-Lor actually materialised.

While we were still doing Newcleus, my mom was running a shelter for un-wed mothers at her house and my studio was in the basement there. One of the girls staying with us and her friend from high school came to me wanting some studio time. Neither of them could really sing but because it was something for the girls to do, and to please my mom, I agreed to work with them. But the friend got kicked out, another came in, she left, then the original girl staying with us got pregnant again, so she left.

So now I had completely new girls, and they brought in another two, including one who could halfway sing, but more importantly she could write. Her name was Sharmelle. Then another girl left and another one got pregnant and we were back down to two. Sharmelle said she had a cousin who can really sing. So this girl Lori came in...and, sure enough, Lori could sing her ass off.

So now I've got Sharmelle, Lori, and another girl and she gets pregnant. Now I'm left with a girl who can sing her ass off and a girl who can write and sing a bit. After three years we were finally making some headway. So we did a freestyle record called *Hot Love* which Sharmelle wrote. Atlantic were going to sign it but they changed their mind. I said to the girls, 'Right, we going down the house route.' I had the idea to put the Sha and Lor from the girls' names to create Sha-Lor.

I'm In Love was my idea and it was an easy song to write. With all my music I make the track first, starting with the baseline and then build the chords and melodies around it. Then I feel the emotion the music points me towards and let it paint the picture and write the story.

And Lori did sing her ass off and killed that vocal, with Sharmelle doing all the ad-libs.

The track didn't do much here in America, but it blew up in the UK, and in 1989 Deconstruction, the subsidiary of BMG, licensed it. I remember it well because it was on my label now, Gertie Records (my grandmother's name) and out of Jump Street Records in New York, and it was the first time since the Newcleus situation I was looking at some money. I've owned every master I've made since then.

Now Sha-Lor were in demand in the UK and Deconstruction Records were keen for the girls to visit to promote their underground vocal house anthem.

I didn't know anything about management. I'd been sort of managing these girls but I'm not the sort of person to pretend to do something I've never done before, so I suggested they get a professional artist manager.

I swear, within a day of that discussion, Sharmelle told me she'd met a guy on the train who was now Sha-Lor's manager. This guy got on the

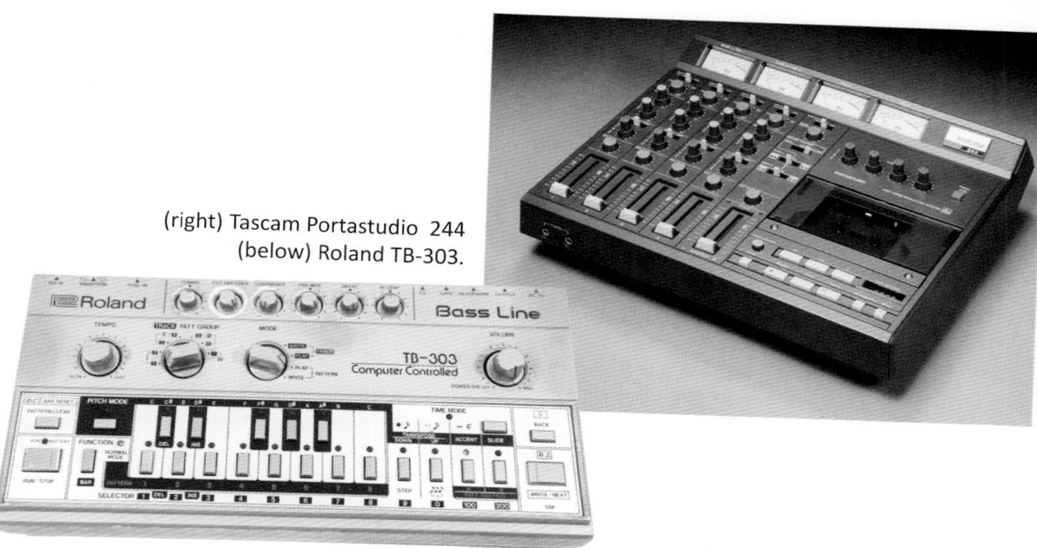

(right) Tascam Portastudio 244
(below) Roland TB-303.

phone to me, wanting to cut my throat. Why haven't these girls got a contract, why haven't they gotten paid? Blah, blah, blah, this and that and so forth.

I said, 'Listen, please, you go ahead and manage them, draw up the contracts.'

I didn't go to London because nobody asked me. It wasn't like I was making a tonne of money. I got $7,000 for the licence of Sha-Lor from Deconstruction. It seemed like a lot of money at the time, but not enough to book a trip to the UK. So the new manager took the girls to the UK for their gigs and then rang me from London and said, 'You know these girls can't sing...' I said, 'Well one of them can...'

The girls told me years later, because I still pay them their royalties and we're in touch, that their 'manager' abandoned them in London. Fortunately, they had family over there, but they had to find their own way back after a few months.

Apparently, Caron Wheeler from Soul II Soul told them while they were in London to look after their producer, but I wouldn't work with them again. I owned the record, I wrote, produced and played everything on *I'm In Love*. I even wrote Sharmelle's ad-libs.

Deconstruction had an option for an album, so if the girls had gotten themselves together, who knows?

They had another track out the following year called *My Love (Has Gone Away)* on Fourth Floor Records out of New York, but that was nothing to do with me. And I think Lori worked as Lori Lava for a while.

I even stopped signing other people to my own labels because the relationships always became strained. I just thought, well, I know I can trust me.

At the same time, Nique D and Chilli B went through a divorce and then me and Chilli B went through a professional divorce and I stopped working with him.

On the label, it says I'm In Love was produced by me and Chilli B, because I shared the credits with him, even though he wasn't around to do anything.

You learn to regret lots of things later, but it's all a learning thing.

So my next release, and a declaration of independence that 'now I'm working on me', was *Push/Pull - Bang The Drums*, the first time I showed my love of jazz with a house music feel and heavy tribalistic drums. It could have been mixed better because the drums weren't warm enough but apart from that, I'm very proud of that project.

After that I did *My Love Turns To Liquid*, which became the *Dream 2 Science* album on my Power Move Records label.

In the early-'90s I started moving back to hip-hop and producing various artists, but again I wasted a lot of time when I should have been doing my own stuff.

It wasn't until 2004 that I decided to bring Newcleus back on our own Jam On Productions label and since then it's been more lucrative than it ever was. We were trying to finish a new Newcleus album, which we came close to doing, until the pandemic hit and I learned bad habits of laying in bed all day rather than getting up and working. But while I didn't make much music during the lockdowns, I did do a lot of good business, and was thankfully able to get all the rights back to my Newcleus publishing thanks to the 35-year-rule in the States.

And *I'm In Love* is still out there too. I have to say I'm not shocked at its success. I didn't expect it, but I'm grateful.

Regardless of what I said on Computer Age all those years ago, technology is an amazing tool, as long as you put it to the right ends. It's like I said in the track, back then. Don't let the technology run you, you must run the technology.

I've always embraced new tech. When CDs came out a lot of people were resistant but I wasn't. Then I started giving away stuff on MP3. Now we do well out of streaming. I embrace whatever pays me.

You can't stop technology, it's the future and you can't hide from the future.

Kevin Saunderson's New York cousins had heard all about the electronic music and its developing scene in his native Detroit, but they had other ideas.

My mum was away so I had a 'graduation' party at our house in the suburbs. My pal Juan Atkins brought a whole new clique of kids from Detroit. I hadn't seen people like this before. All black kids and more progressive in their way of thinking. They dressed differently, they smoked differently and they just seemed to have a cooler approach to life. It was all about the music for them and almost in an egotistical kind of way.

It was a really cool party. Juan was on the tables the whole time playing amazing music, including his own new material, so I massively drew inspiration from him that night.

But then I went on to college and at the same time I was going to New York a lot to see my father and other relatives.

In 1982 one of my cousins Berry White said to me, 'We're going to take you out, we're going to get some New York in you.' So at the age of 17 he took me to my first nightclub, The Paradise Garage. It's hard to beat that, I guess, and I went about six times in total in that period.

That first night we had to be picked from the queue. As we walked through what seemed like a tunnel to get to the main room we could hear the pulse of the bass. Amazing lights. The sound system was the biggest sound I'd ever heard at that age. Larry Levan up above. Mainly men dancing below.

Larry took sections of records and repeated them over and over. He could use bits of one record, with a copy on each deck, for like 40 minutes. His mixing was non-stop and so smooth. You couldn't even tell he was cutting in and out of different copies of a track, or when another record was coming in. The transitions were seamless. I was amazed.

It was dance wherever you want and just be in your own world. I hadn't been around a predominantly gay crowd before. I was intrigued by the way these guys were dancing so flamboyantly with soul and were into the beats, in a different way.

We walked out into the bright sun around midday, an unforgettable memory. I saw Liz Torres sing live at the Garage on another visit, as house music took off. I never got to hear Larry play one of my records in later years, but I'm told by others that he did. And that is an amazing honour for me in itself.

There were many pieces of the puzzle that inspired Inner City, including Larry Levan and my trips to New York, but I also made many road trips to Chicago with friends around that time to see Ron Hardy play.

Growing up, I was massively inspired by a radio DJ in Detroit called The Electrifying Mojo, who had an hour called The Midnight Funk Association. Derrick May, a mutual friend of Juan and I growing up, turned me on to Mojo. I heard music I'd never heard before. Parliament funk, Prince, Kraftwerk, Tangerine Dream, New Order. I was used to listening to disco or Motown in the car with my mum.

Disco had always given me this four to the floor pulse growing up. Soul automatically. Then Mojo started playing Juan's music, his Cybotron stuff. It was so inspiring.

I wasn't even a DJ or thinking of making music at that time. That wasn't even on my plate, but I had this love for it. I'd thought I was going to be a pro-footballer, but it didn't work out and I gave that up.

Around '83,'84 I noticed a change on the radio. It sounded so different. 'Time to jack' and 'jack' this and 'jack' that.

I was hanging around with Juan, Derrick and the cool lot from Detroit. I'd watch them mixing at their houses, I wouldn't dare try myself, so I would just watch closely.

But sports had made me competitive. I wanted to excel at this too, so I made my own path after being inspired by others.

I saw an advert in a music publication saying, 'Do you want to learn how to mix? It was a DJ clinic in Ohio, about a four-hour drive away. I booked myself on and went down there, not telling the guys. And that's where I learned the basics. The course was very forward-thinking, they had Technics SL1200s and the latest mixer at the time. I took a hotel room because it was 10am-6pm over two days. I was taught how to count BPM, they talked about the one beat, the breaks and where to mix. I hadn't learned that from any of the others, I daren't ask.

I came back and bought me some cheap belt-driven turntables, and if you can mix on belt-driven, you can damn well mix on Technics 1200s.

From that point I practised and practised. I didn't even go to college anymore; I forgot all about school. All I wanted to do was be a DJ and make music. I'd visualise myself as a DJ on campus, playing at the frat parties.

Then I made a plan to join a fraternity, with the sole objective of being their DJ. But it's not as easy as that. There was an interview, then you had to be selected by the fellowship of brothers. Then you have to pass the test of whatever is set out for you over weeks, not days, to show your commitment. All the time practise, practise, practise on my decks. Then I was finally accepted. I pledged and became a brother. And only after that point did I say, 'Can I DJ at the next party?'

Now I had somewhere to play, somewhere to make mistakes and learn on the job, playing for up to a thousand people at frat parties, and then for the same fraternities at other universities.

Suddenly everyone was like, who the hell is this Kevin Saunderson?

Then the next phase.

I was playing Kraftwerk, and it was great, but it's not really dance music. It's great synth music and futuristic sounding, but it's not dance music. I was always thinking about how I could replicate what Larry had played at the Paradise Garage. Records like *Supernature* by Cerrone. Vocals, but a different kind of music, mostly always four on the floor.

At that point, I didn't think there was enough music to keep the scene going for much longer.

I started bringing a drum machine, a 909, when I was playing out.

I could make drum patterns, but I didn't know about hooking it up to a sequencer. I didn't understand what MIDI (Musical Instrument Digital Interface) was. But I quickly learned that's how you bring these instruments and sounds together to have the potential to create your own music and to replace a bass guitarist or a keyboard player.

So I started taking the drum machine with me to play when I was DJing at a party to give some variation. But even that variation got boring after a while because you come out of a track into drums, and there's only so much you can do with drums. You can't play one drum pattern after another after another.

I realised the next progression was to make music. So I started raw. How do I take a baseline and make that work with drums? I had parts and ideas and a mixing board that gave me eight tracks at a time but I didn't know how to bring it all together. So I called up Juan Atkins.

Before that I hadn't really connected with him on all this studio stuff, just admired from a distance, so it was a case of, 'Whassup?'

Juan was great. He showed me how to mix a record on the fly, to two track tape, marking sections and then editing per section. Sometimes you could make good mistakes. Then mix it down, record it, get it mastered and put it on vinyl.

By 1987 Juan Atkins has been prolific as Model 500 and Derrick May had already made the soon-to-be-seminal *Strings Of Life*, as Rhythim Is Rhythim. It was time for Kevin Saunderson to step up.

My early records were all collaborations. The first in 1987 was *Triangle Love*, under the name Kreem on Metroplex Records, a vocal house record I wrote with a guy called Arthur Forest and for which I used the name Kevin 'Master Reece' Saunderson, the Reece being short for my middle name Maurice.

Even *Big Fun* wasn't all me. It was a collaboration with James Pennington, who was two years younger than me at Belllville High School. Yes, it was my vision and my idea, but James played on it too. It started off as an instrumental. Just the baseline, the chords and the drums and we were really excited about it. But I just felt it needed a vocal. The girl I used on *Triangle Love* didn't feel right for it so we sat on the instrumental for a year.

Over those 12 months I had been connecting with different people in Chicago and a guy I met through Chicago Warner, Terry House-master Baldwin, had done a couple of tracks with a singer called Paris Grey. He came to visit me in Detroit and listened to *Big Fun* and said, 'Man, if you're looking for a vocal for that I'll hook you up with Paris.'

I said, 'Aight, let me see where her mind is at.' We had a conversation on the phone; I told Paris the kind of vision I had, the types of tracks I liked and that I wanted to create uplifting vocal records with those magical moments that touch people.

Paris was from the church, so I liked that. I gave Terry a cassette tape and he took it back to Chicago. Within a few weeks, Paris called me back, and with the instrumental playing in the background, sang the vocal she had written back down the phone to me, and there was *Big Fun*.

I was all in. I could tell right away. I wasn't thinking in terms of the magnitude of the hit it became, but I was thinking, this sounds great. As a producer, you always need that vision to be able to hear something rough and imagine what it could become, and what it will be like when it's polished, but you could never imagine how big it would become. I said, I want you to come to Detroit, which she did, and she knocked it out. And that was the beginning of Inner City.

Juan mixed that record and was pivotal because he was the most experienced guy I knew. It was so different for him, because Juan hadn't been doing vocals, but he understood music theory and arrangement, how to make it work and his *Magic Juan Mix* became the go-to mix.

A guy from Birmingham in the UK, from a label called Network Records, and a consultant for Virgin Records making a compilation album, arrived in Detroit. He was looking for one more track to complete his project, *Techno! The New Dance Sound of Detroit. Big Fun* isn't really techno, it's just a great track, but when I pulled it out for Neil he loved it right away.

***Big Fun* had just made the cut and was on its way to the UK.**

I pressed it up as a white label for KMS (Kevin Maurice Saunderson) Records and got it to as many of the right people as possible. I took a copy to Tony Humphries in New York. I gave one to Frankie. Any DJ who was on top of their game got one. The DMX guys and various distributors. Sometimes I'd drive to Chicago in my car, pitch up at a record shop, play them *Big Fun* and they'd say, 'Hey man, give me a couple of boxes.'

I couldn't keep up with the pace, the demand was so high. We sold 35,000 copies of *Big Fun* on KMS very quickly, excluding the copies that were booted.

Virgin, which had 10 Records at the time, had the rights to licence *Big Fun* for the compilation only, but now they wanted to do a single deal for the UK because the track was blowing up over there.

I actually caught my pressing plant booting red-handed, when I popped in there one day unannounced. At that point I realised this record was bigger than me, so I did a deal with Virgin. Even before *Big Fun* was released they were talking about a follow-up, and that's why

Good Life came so quick, because there was money on the table and I needed something. I toured the UK during the summer of '88, playing seven cities promoting the compilation, and so saw the amazing reaction to *Big Fun* first hand.

I was so inspired by the pirate radio stations in London. They weren't polished but they played music that was real, that was important, and it

Kevin Saunderson

felt like something special was happening. This was so different from what we had in the States. It helped the whole movement in the UK and maybe without that, it wouldn't have happened the same way.

I came back to Detroit from the UK after the summer just as *Big Fun* was about to be released there in the September/October. James Pennington had disappeared on me. He had a habit of doing that. I wanted to work with James, because that combination had created *Big Fun*, but I needed to get a follow-up done, so I did the music myself. I didn't actually hear from James until eight months later, which was a lot of time back then, with what was going on. He didn't even know what happened with *Big Fun* and Inner City.

I wanted the next track to sound in the same family as *Big Fun*, but not a complete copycat. *Big Fun* was so successful, why not make it related? So I came up with the main riff for *Good Life*, put the bass down, put the string part down, the percussion parts and built it all up. And then I spoke to Paris and said, 'We're going to keep it similar, keep it uplifting, keep it happy.'

This time I mailed the track to her priority post. She wrote it real quick and sang *Good Life* back down the phone to me a few weeks later, the same way.

I was trying to make music that was strong, that stood without a vocal, and that would only be improved with a vocal. Thankfully, Paris was inspired, and I don't think you can write a better follow-up. Again I heard it straight away. This time, I said, 'That's a hit,' because this sounded better than *Big Fun* to me.

I felt *Good Life* had better potential. It's actually a little more polished, a little more poppier, but not intentionally. I just felt it could go even further than *Big Fun* did, which at that point of the process was only just becoming a hit. This was October, and by the December we were back in the UK doing Top Of The Pops with *Good Life*.

Kevin's assumption was right, but only just. While Big Fun peaked at No 8 in the Top 40, *Good Life* was the highest climber in the week Inner City performed their second single on *TOTP*, climbing 16 places to No 6, and eventually peaking at No 4.

I actually recorded *Good Life* in Chicago in a studio Steve Hurley worked out of and hooked me up with. I was in touch with him by now. I flew Juan and Derrick to Chicago to do mixes and Steve did one too.

At that point, it felt like whatever vision Juan had years earlier...was coming around, and that there were going to be lots of opportunities and Detroit wasn't only going to get recognition for Motown now. It gave opportunities to other people, like Jeff Mills and Carl Craig. These are all guys who were inspired by us, because things were moving so quickly.

The success of Inner City in the UK and globally was quite different from how I thought it was going to happen. I thought I was going sit back in Detroit and develop my production skills. I didn't think I'd become a recording artist touring and appearing on TV pop shows. That wasn't on my plate, but I adapted. I did *Top Of The Pops* about four or five times. I was forced to in a way. I could have said no, but my management and the label said it was a better career move. First of all, I'm not a textbook standard musician who can play continuously. I learned to do some of that, but you're still never going to see me play a baseline on the guitar all the way through a song, because that's not what I do.

Back then you couldn't recreate your studio on stage, and control the different parts of the music, certainly not on those pop shows. Even when we went out on tour I had to hire traditional musicians to repeat parts of my songs. In my mind I'm a producer with good ears, and good vision of sound, who knows what works, but I'm not a musician.

So there was a lot of anxiety to 'perform live' because it was so new. As a DJ I'm playing two pieces of vinyl of other people's music, but on *Top Of The Pops* with Inner City I was miming playing vinyl so you feel silly. Appearing in videos also wasn't our thing. Both *Big Fun* and *Good Life* were shot in London because we spent so much time in the UK from the summer of 1988 onwards, which is also when I met my first wife, Ann, who is from Birmingham.

While touring the UK in 1989/90 any appearance on pop commercial TV shows were contrasted by the raves that Kevin and Inner City were exposed to, including an appearance at Raindance in 1991.

It was actually so inspiring to see a totally different type of vibe and crowd compared to America. We were used to playing to either a black or a gay crowd. White people didn't really play or dance to our music. First it was blacks, then the gay community started to support techno music. The gay community had always danced to disco through time. We didn't even have a vision that white people would ever dance to 'our music'. Then when we went to the UK, it was the opposite.

Music for us had always been about segregation and, of course, we grew up in segregation. We didn't have mixed fraternities at college. The white fraternities played rock and roll and pop and it was about drinking beer not dancing. We expected it to be the same in the UK, but

WATCHING THE BRITISH PEOPLE PARTYING THEIR MINDS OUT, ON THE SAME PULSE AND RHYTHM, BEING TOUCHED BY THE MUSIC, WAS BEAUTIFUL.

it wasn't like that at all. Loads of white people dancing at these raves, everyone on the same pulse and rhythm and being touched by the music in the same way. It was totally shocking to me, but beautiful too. Now, at the same time, I know a whole bunch of ecstasy was being taken, but people have been doing drugs since who knows how long. Watching the British people partying their minds out all night was just amazing.

Meanwhile, Inner City needed an album to cope with the demand, particularly in the UK, and they weren't short of record label offers.

Virgin didn't have an option for the album at that point, and we had loads of companies pitching to us, but I felt comfortable going with Virgin because they had their teeth wet in it. We'd had a couple of hits with them, it was early in my career and the money was good — especially for back then, so I thought it was the right move. It also covered the States too, so it seemed easier to deal with the same label.

Once the album deal was signed I bought a 24-track mixing board. After *Good Life*, my wife-to-be Ann came back to Detroit with me and I moved from the suburbs into Detroit to a warehouse space, the first time I'd lived in the city before. I set it up as a live-work-studio, with different entrances and that's where I produced Inner City's first album, *Paradise*.

And 1989 was another amazing year in the UK for Inner City. *Paradise* reached No 3 in the UK charts and gave Kevin and Paris another three Top 20 hits with *Ain't Nobody Better* (10) *Do You Love What You Feel* (16) and *Whatcha Gonna Do With My Lovin'* (12). The singles were national chart hits all over Europe, with four No 1s in the US Billboard dance chart too.

I just loved Stephanie Mills' original version of *Whatcha Gonna Do With My Lovin'* so I thought, let me do a cover, something different. I asked Frankie Knuckles and David Morales to do a remix and I thought they delivered an unbelievable mix, with that amazing breakdown halfway through which sampled Marshall Jefferson's *Move Your Body*.

The scene was moving so fast you didn't even have time to think about it. There was a terrible structure to the deals for artists back then, and if I could do it over again, I'd probably have released the Inner City stuff myself in America. One thing I will say for Virgin is that they went back and improved my royalties for now, based on how bad the deals were back then.

At the same time, in 1989, I had this thing going on with *Rock To The Beat*, a record I made with my fraternity friend's brother Santonio Echols. He was more like a protege under me, but he had a drum machine and a few other tools I didn't have at the time. We started making some stuff, but *Rock To The Beat* was really all me. I had my sister Latonya come in and repeat the vocal over and over, and the track sounded powerful.

Around the same time I did a track under my own name called *The Sound*, which this guy I'd never heard of called Todd Terry sampled. He took the main riff from *The Sound* for his track *Bango (To The Batmobile)* and that blew up for him. I decided if he was going to sample my track, I'd sample it back and put it out as a different version of *The Sound*. I thought, he can't do that, so I'll do this. I was doing a deal with FFRR in London with Pete Tong for *The Sound* and I threw *Rock To The Beat* in as part of the deal, and it became a bigger hit. Then the Belgians (*Maurice Engelen of Praga Khan)* covered it, and added a European flavour. I didn't even know what was going on half of the time because I had all this mainstream stuff happening with Inner City, and then all this underground stuff coming out that we'd also been working on.

It was a record I had forgotten about, then a French publishing company popped up and offered me $120,000. Apparently, a TV pop show in France was using it for their theme tune. It must have done some numbers out that way because I recouped that advance and still earned from it. All because a guy in Belgium couldn't buy a copy, but you never know how what you create will inspire somebody else.

Two more Inner City albums, *Fire* and *Praise*, and more anthems like *Hallelujah*, *Pennies From Heaven* and *Till We Meet Again*, followed in quick succession as the early-'90s unfolded.

I was always trying to experiment with downtempo tracks. Paris wrote *Till We Meet Again* also and it might be the favourite song I ever recorded. It can make you both happy and sad.

My (now ex-wife) Ann had written some stuff for the second album and got on well with Paris. I had created a string patch for a track and then together they wrote the song *Pennies From Heaven* and it just worked perfectly. Paris sang lead as usual and Ann sang some backing vocals, for which we also brought in a Detroit group called Members Of The House, who were awesome. I did the main versions with additional mixes from Tony Humphries. Again, everything worked so well. In 2001 Ann sang on the huge house anthem Black Water by Octave One, which is an amazing track. We still work together and are great friends.

Fast forward almost 30 years and the Inner City sound is still as fresh and timeless as ever. In 2019, Kevin started to tour the band again with his son Dantiez heavily involved and a new singer Steffanie Christi'an on board.

We actually released an album during the pandemic on Defected, which included *No More Looking Back*, a collaboration with Idris Elba who came out to Detroit to work with me.

Paris has opted to spend some time out currently, but will hopefully be making some guest appearances on future projects. I've tried to modernise some of the music, but all the key components of the original tracks are there, with all the hands in the air moments. It's great to have Dantiez involved. He's very talented and reminds me of a young me. Stephanie's from Detroit and an amazing performer. The show was received really well in the UK, including at Glastonbury and across Europe. It's amazing to be out there touring and DJing still after all these years.Hopefully, people don't think, ah, well, they were great back then...and they're more like, ah, nice they're still here, doing their thing.

Watching Ten City, Kym Mazelle and a certain Marshall Jefferson perform at The Dominion Theatre in London in 1988 inspired a Swedish film student to write one of THE most iconic vocal house tracks.

I wasn't sure if it was tacky, but I wanted to play on the theme of 'house' and 'living', but without using the word 'house'.

I had this feeling that house music was really music that you move into and it becomes like a home. Because if you're into house music, you go to clubs all the time and you just dance and you feel comfortable in that space.

As Lars Kronlund sat in the bath in his Camden flat, the morning after the night before, he drafted those legendary lyrics...

After that show at The Dominion I went straight back to my flat and sat up all night and at one point I came up with the piano riff for *Where Love Lives*. When I discovered that riff, you know it just clicked. I knew I had something. I liked it so much I just played it repeatedly on the keyboard. I wasn't really a piano player, but I dabbled.

I already had the structure of the song and the chords that became *Where Love Lives*, but it was on a Fela Kuti type groove, up there in that same kind of tempo.

But I had just been to a concert and heard live house music for three or four hours so I was impregnated with that groove, and I guess the idea of playing a riff on a piano just happened. I'd always loved clavinet riffs, the German keyboard used by Stevie Wonder in *Superstition*), with its heavy 'Afro-Cuban' sound and influences.

That's The Way Love Is really blew me away when it came out. That was like a 'Whoa!' moment. It felt like Marshall Jefferson was doing house music heavily influenced by Norman Whitfield and that '70s psychedelic orchestral music. Marshall was bringing in the wah-wah guitar which hadn't really found itself into house music at that time, because most of it was programmed.

In London, I had a sampler keyboard, a TASCAM Portastudio recorder and an Atari 1040 computer, so I could programme a bit. When you come up on a decent riff or baseline, in that moment, you know you have something.

What I had felt solid and something that should have lyrics so the next morning as I sat in my bathtub they came to me. When you write a song that works it feels amazing...and even better when your idea the night before still sounds good in the morning. And, of course, the whole environment and era I was in the middle of...and living in, it was just so exciting.

I was never going to sing the track myself. I had a stint as a busker in Paris, standing around playing electric guitar, singing The Cure and The Doors. And then I thought, well, if I can't sing like Marvin Gaye, then fuck it, what's the point? And if you're going to try to be like Lou Reed instead, then there's no point if you haven't got all that charisma. I admire people who are big artists who must know that they really don't have much of a voice. Most of all of the really big artists, mainly white people, they're not really good singers. Bob Dylan can't sing to save his life, but because of his lyrics and the way he delivers them, it worked.

Lars came to London from Stockholm in 1984 and lived there throughout the rest of the '80s.

Those were the good times. There was so much great music in the early '80s, especially in the way that black and white music was mixing a lot. You had bands like Talking Heads and The Clash who were really influenced by black music - funk and disco and Fela Kuti, so all of that was a big inspiration. I had played in various rock bands and had made a record with my own band before coming to London from Stockholm, which I guess was a funky Talking Headsy kind of thing. Prince was a huge influence at the time, and Rick James. I was a big fan of Chic too.

I was really into the boogie disco that was happening at the time, and it seemed to be easier to find that on the radio in London, and usually on pirate stations. I had always been writing songs. My father was a jazz musician. But I'd had no training musically.

In my early 20s I took a three-year diploma course at London International Film School in Covent Garden and hung out a lot at the ICA (Institute of Contemporary Arts) nearby.

I was doing a lot of film school art, listening to house music, and going to all the clubs. There was a fashion show at the ICA one night, in 1985. It was really raining that night. You know when it's really pissing down in London, like hailstones, coming at you sideways...that kind of night. I lived in Notting Hill Gate then and my friend had just cooked a really lovely meal and we'd just rolled a nice spliff and I was like, 'I think I'll pass on the fashion show, I'll just stay in.' But something made me go, so I braved the elements.

The fashion show featured people from Hyper Hyper fashion market on Kensington High Street and Judy Blame, the guy who did jewellery for Boy George and Neneh Cherry. It was a groovy-type fashion show with dancers and singers.

A female sat on a massive swing, wearing a frock that would blow in the wind, and sang *God Bless The Child*, the Billie Holiday classic. It's one of my all-time favourite songs. I was smitten by the singer's artistry, so I went and spoke to her after the show. She told me her name was Alison Limerick. Alison and I stayed in touch and we made some demos while I was still at film school, some boogie disco stuff.

House music was something I first came in contact with in 1987 by listening to radio stations and going to clubs like The Mud Club, The Fridge in Brixton and Camden Palace. And, of course, I knew about *Centreforce* when that came on.

After film school, Lars took a job working for a company called Commercial Music in Soho, doing just that, making music for commercials. It was a studio run by Paul Carter and Manda Glanfield who were signed to the Rhythm King label as The Beatmasters and went on to have UK Top Ten hits with *Rok Da House* with The Cookie Crew and *Who's In The House* featuring Merlin, which is maybe why Lars was so intent on not having the word 'house' in the title of *Where Love Lives*?

I gave Paul and Manda a tape of some musical ideas that I had, and they hired me. The great thing was that they had a 16-track tape machine

A RECORD LIKE *WHERE LOVE LIVES* BELONGS IN A CLUB, IN THE MIDDLE OF THE DANCEFLOOR, WITH THAT MAGIC AND THE EUPHORIA. THAT ONE PERSON YOU FANCY. WE CAN'T EXIST WITHOUT THAT.

and all kinds of fantastic equipment so I would stay after hours, often spending the whole night at the studio, working on my own stuff.

A few years had passed and I was also working with Claudia Fontaine, who had performed backing vocals on The Jam's *Beat Surrender*, on Soul II Soul's *Back To Life (However Do You Want Me)* and Elvis Costello's *Every-day I Write The Book*. Claudia was amazing and I really loved her voice.

I actually presented *Where Love Lives* to Claudia but she said she didn't want to do house music. She'd also had lovers rocks and R&B hits previously so I guess she just didn't think house was for her. So I called up Alison, who I knew *Where Love Lives* was perfect for.

Alison came to the Commercial Music studio in Wardour Street, which is where all the production houses were then...and how we got work from all the advertising agencies, which would be further up towards Oxford Street. I played the track to Alison once, with a really bad demo vocal that I'd done myself, and she said, 'All right, I get it...' then we cut the initial version.

I knew Titiyo, the sister of Neneh Cherry. She had just done a deal with Arista Records, so I met somebody from Arista at The Coach & Horses across the road, and gave them a cassette.

I had already sent demos to all the major record companies, and got lots of rejection letters, with stock answers, some not even signed. They said things like, 'This is interesting but you should work on the lyrics... keep us posted.' I wish I'd kept them.

Then I was asked to meet Chris Cook, Head of A&R at Arista, who loved the song. He was the first person to believe in it. Chris presented it to BMG, and I was able to sign a publishing deal on the strength of that song. I got an advance, which meant I could quit working at Commercial Music full time. I was able to say, 'No, somebody else will have to do that yogurt advert...'

But I was a bit miffed with them, because I had brought Alison to the label and I thought I would be working with her, but they signed Alison on her own artist deal. Luckily, I had a good lawyer and I signed a production deal for *Where Love Lives*, because it was 100% made by me.

Chris Cook connected with Frankie Knuckles and David Morales for the remixes, which was such a blessing and a really smart move.

The version I produced, the Sauna Mix, is on the album and is much more how I envisaged the record. It used some of the ad-libs from the demo because Chris loved them.

Alison is the kind of singer who doesn't want to repeat herself. She's like, I did that. And I was like, 'Yeah, but that was on 16-track one inch track. We're now on two inch, so can you please just fucking sing it again like that.' And she would say, 'No.' So we had to use some of the ad-libs from the demo.

We went back a few times to fine-tune the original mix, but it was never released initially without the remixes. Chris was really into remixes and this was the day and age when everything had to be remixed, but I'm really glad that he got Frankie and David involved and I think they both loved working on the song.

But Frankie wasn't happy with the first mixes. He said he could do better, but everybody was like, 'no, it's great.' But he actually booked a studio and paid for it himself to redo the Classic Mix.

A lot of the Classic Mix was really close to my original idea so it was very respectful.

I was in The Milk Bar, early 1990, with some friends when I first heard that Classic Mix in a club. It was Danny Rampling's night. It got to 2am and we decided we should move on somewhere else. I went to the bathroom and heard the song come on, and I was like, 'ooohhh'. And then I came out and it was complete madness. It really blew me away, even the staff were dancing on top of the bar. A girl came up to me and said, 'Why are you not dancing? You are the only person in the club not dancing, why are you looking so sad?' But I guess I was just taking it all in.

Records like *Where Love Lives* belong in clubs. There's always that one person that you fancy. It's the magic. That euphoria. We can't exist without that. That's what's it all about.

I had another situation at The Sound Factory Bar. When I arrived at around 5am Frankie Knuckles, always such a wonderful, warm-hearted person, gave me a hug in the DJ booth and said, 'Oh, this is perfect timing. You gotta see what happens when I play the song.' Frankie mixed it in, and everybody went nuts. At The Sound Factory Bar, the booth was one floor up, and you can really look down and see everyone going crazy down there. I started crying. But when you see the appreciation of people dancing to your record played by a DJ, as opposed to watching you perform it live, there's something about it which is just more pure.

At that point, *Where Love Lives* was at the top of the dance charts in both the UK and in America, so I used to go and hang out at BMG Publishing with head honcho, Mike Sefton, go out the back with the staff, smoke a spliff, have a beer. And most importantly, Mike would let me use the phone. I didn't even have a phone in my flat, let alone a mobile phone. One time I was there Mike took a call and he said Lati, which was my nickname, it's for you. It's Arthur Baker from New York and he wants to talk to you.

And I was like, 'Arthur Baker, wow...'

'Hi, it's Arthur, I really like your song, I'm coming to London and I think we should work on something together.'

'Okay..erm...great.'

Two days later there was a knock on my front door and Arthur Baker was stood there holding a pile of records.

'I think we should sample some of these, I have some ideas.'

There was no, 'Let's have a cup of tea, let's talk about it. It was like, switch on the studio, let's do this.'

And that's typical Arthur. So Arthur and I wrote Alison's second single *Come Back For Real Love.*

I think I went a little bit too far with that one, in that I wanted it to be retro, so it was 114 BPM, which was perfectly fine if you were making boogie disco but house music was definitely going in the other direction. *Where Love Lives* was a 121 BPM and throughout the '90s the tempo of house music only increased, all the handbag stuff was even faster. So we probably didn't help ourselves by making the track so slow.

It's not as strong a song anyway, but I think it would have been stronger if we had done it in a different way.

But it was fun to work with Arthur, we really hit it off, and he suggested I go to New York to work with him. I had just split up with a girlfriend so I said, 'Why not?'

At that point I'd been in London for nine years and I felt that the opportunities for me in New York were really exciting. So I moved there, worked a lot with Arthur and lost touch with Alison.

Alison had a third single, *Make It On My Own,* which did well and went Top 20 in the UK charts, which I was not part of.

The crazy thing for her was that she was dropped by Arista. She made a whole album with Frankie Knuckles, which wasn't released.

I was told that Arista in the US, who had that big deal with Whitney Houston, didn't want to have non-American black female acts. So they said, we'll go with Lisa Stansfield, but we'll pass on Alison Limerick. So *Where Love Lives* was never released Stateside. It still went to No 1 in the US dance chart as an import but that's probably one of the reasons they dropped Alison, because we were never going to have the support we needed.

When they re-released *Where Love Lives* in 96 it did even better than before and was a Top Ten hit in the UK. The label rang up Alison and said, 'Ah, erm, can you do some, er, gigs, for us? We need you to do some PAs to support the record and to go on *Top Of The Pops,* and Alison said, 'But you fired me.' Of course, she did it, and she's been able to do gigs with that song until this day.

And it's great, because since a few years back, I'm close to Alison again, because she is now a singer in my band Brooklyn Funk Essentials, which I originally set up with Arthur Baker.

We've made six albums, the last one in 2019 including a re-recording of *Where Love Lives*, which really went back to what the inspiration was for the song. It's still house, but it's house that is very much connected to funk and disco, which is obviously what house was in the first place. And everything is played live.

When we first started everybody either lived in Brooklyn or the East Village of New York. Today some of us live in Stockholm, and the other three live in the UK, including Alison in London and two others in Birmingham. We're signed to a label called Dorado Records, which has an office in Soho, and our A&R guy Ollie lives in Miami, so works for us. We play a lot of jazz festivals and were due to support Grace Jones at the Hideaway festival in Chelmsford in 2020 which was cancelled due to the pandemic and also didn't happen in 2021. I also write music for films.

*****

I actually terminated my publishing deal with BMG towards the end of the Noughties when BMG became Universal, and I managed to get my catalogue back. I was able to leave them and I'm now with a small admin company in the UK.

I must reiterate that my original lawyer Nick said to me from the start, the most important thing is that you have an 'out' clause, because when people are keen to sign you they will say nice things to you, but one day your A&R guy won't be there any more. So thankfully Nick managed to get some clauses in my original publishing contract that we could use later on. I would love to be able to speak to young people today, and point out the pitfalls and the dangers, because at the age of 20 you really don't think like that when someone wants to release your music. You're like, 'Oh, wow, they played it on the radio.'

I'm still with Nick 30 years later. If you find someone who is on your side then don't mess with that.

Back then I wasn't trying to make something with the longevity that *Where Love Lives* has enjoyed, but you obviously always want to make something that will matter for a long time.

The song has a good melody and lyric. When you see people singing along to it on the dancefloor, you can see that it means something to them, and that is important. When it's played on the radio alongside something contemporary or current, it never sounds old, so in that respect, its longevity is not surprising.

And the Classic mix is that Frankie sound which is just so timeless, with that Frankie heart in it. We wrote a song together in 1995 for Frankie's second album, *Welcome To The Real World*, with Adeva on vocals, called *Whadda U Want (From Me)*, which was a Top 40 UK hit.

In 2013,'14 Frankie was doing a director's cut album with Eric Kupper of all his famous mixes and we discussed doing one of *Whadda U Want (From Me)* but two months later he passed.

I once posted the link to *Where Love Lives* inclusion in an all-time house music anthems chart on social media and Frankie replied and said it was his favourite all-time mix and he felt so privileged to work on it, and I replied, 'Oh, Frankie.' I think in the mid-'90s Marshall put out a list of his favourite tracks and *Where Love Lives* was included, and that was so great, because it meant that the track mattered to the guy that inspired me at that time, all those years ago.

I stayed in New York for eight years and met my wife there, and then we moved to Paris and had two kids, but we're now back in Sweden because Sweden is a good place to bring them up.

Where Love Lives has been everything to me. It opened so many doors. I didn't want to go out that night to the fashion show at the ICA but I did and met Alison. It's often those split-second decisions, those moments that can change everything. It's a testament to, 'fuck sleeping, fuck watching Netflix, go to clubs, enjoy yourself and meet people.'

Alison Limerick and Lars Kronlund perform with the Brooklyn Funk Essentials.

As Steve Silk Hurley sat in a studio in Milwaukee in 1989 preparing to start his latest remix project, a Roberta Flack track, he was struck by both the enormity of the task in hand and the esteemed company he found himself in.

For a start Roberta Flack was one of my favourite female singers… and this track had been produced by Quincy Jones. Man! Quincy Jones productions inspired me to even get into music. Michael Jackson, George Benson, Heatwave and Rod Temperton, those guys. Such great music. And now I'm sitting here with these two digital tapes. Quincy Jones' digital tapes. Wow.

I'd had to drive 90 miles from Chicago to Milwaukee because my studio was just a 24-track and a fancy digital studio was needed for these 48-track tapes. It was ridiculous. In total there were 90-something tracks of music and percussion. I spent the first day just wondering where the hell to start.

And Quincy had all his top people working on this track. Jerry Hey, one world most-renowned horn players, and Greg Phillinganes, one of the best keyboard players out there. And wait a minute, let's see who wrote the track. Oh, it's Ashford and Simpson — they're not small potatoes either. One of my favourite song-writing duos who made some of the most timeless, up-tempos records. Gee, they wrote *The Boss* for Diana Ross.

So being surrounded by all this music royalty was daunting.

The track in question was *Uh-Uh Ooh-Ooh Look Out (Here It Comes)*, one of the stranger song titles Steve Silk Hurley was ever given to work with.

I was trying not to insult the record and the music legends performing on the track...and then I spent three days coming up with probably the worst remix I've ever done. An extended version of the original R&B track.

Before I left the studio for my long drive back to Chicago I made a nice bounce of the percussion from the track and took any bits of music I thought I might need. I had unfinished business.

When I got back to Chicago I didn't even go home. I drove straight to my own studio and said now I'm going to do a house mix.

I used the percussion I'd made and sped the record up to 120 BPM. I put the vocals on and then started playing different music parts. Suddenly I had created a whole new track that had nothing musically to do with the original track. So that was a monumental time for me, because a switch flipped in my head and I realised I was on to something. It actually became the way people remix now.

I had done stuff for Ten City before that. When I did their track *Right Back To You,* I mainly used Marshall Jefferson's parts, his baseline and a lot of the music, but I changed all the drums and then added samples, using my Akai S1000, to do a lot of sample triggers, and then I did actual tape edits, with reel to reel tape, including turning the tape backwards.

When I started on that Roberta Flack house mix I was able to let everything go, because I had already done the R&B mix. That's over there and this is over here. I felt free. I was like, yeah, people are going to be able to dance to this. This will take Roberta's song to another audience who appreciate house music.

When I sent it to Merlin Bobb and Dina Perera at Atlantic the reaction was, 'Yeah, the house mix is cool'. I don't think I even have a copy of the R&B mix now. I don't even know if they released it.

On the 12 inch release they put my track on the B-Side and Arthur Baker's mix on the A, and Arthur was another person that was legendary and who I was heavily influenced by growing up, with all the stuff he did like Afrika Bambaataa's *Planet Rock*, etc. I didn't mind being on the B-Side, I just was happy to be on the record. The test pressing came out and all the DJs started playing my version and it hit No 1 on the Billboard Dance chart. I didn't know what was happening on the UK side of the pond.

And sometimes in the UK, a track that doesn't hit the charts can still have a massive impact, and that's something I didn't really understand then. I've certainly had a lot of people over the years over there telling me how much that Roberta Flack mix meant to them.

Like I get a lot of people from the UK mention the Simply Red mix, *Something Got Me Started*. Nobody from the US ever talks about that. Or my mix of The Pasadenas' remake of *I'm Doing Fine Now* by The Spinners — every time I see people from South Africa, they mention it. Or in Ukraine they talk about my Debbie Gibson *We Could Be Together* mix.

But Roberta Flack was definitely a turning point, where I started to give as much as possible from myself, musically, to the record, as opposed to just tightening up the drums and making it hit a bit harder.

I believe that's the art of remixing: to realise the intent of the artist and take it in a direction they wouldn't think of, without taking it too far away from the original idea. I want them to still be proud of it, even if it was a ballad and it's now a dance record. Roberta Flack actually called me up to thank me, because the track went to No 1 on the dance chart and she hadn't experienced that before.

Later, it got to the point that I would have to remix even my own stuff in that way. Like Shay Jones — *Are You Going To Be There* in 1991, for which I was actually infleunced by Soul II Soul, because they were one of the hot sounds the year or so before.

I noticed early on that the more I put into my remixes the more I got a response. Remixing in the late-'70s/early-'80s was the domain of engineers like Francois K, Tee Scott, Shep Pettibone and Tom Moulton. When I started DJing in '80, '81 I was doubling back into '78, '79 and finding amazing extended remixes where the claps were louder, the kick-drums were heavier and there was just more energy in the track generally.

Steve Silk Hurley is a name probably better known to the masses in the UK for his trailblazing No 1 *Jack Your Body* in 1987, which is renowned for lyrics that are both far from inspiring and pioneering at the same time, the like of which the commercial charts had never heard before.

At school I loved basketball so I went through a phase of wanting to be a pro baller. I didn't know until I started DJing in High School that

that's what I really wanted to do. And back then it wasn't even a career so you can imagine what a struggle that was with my father. I wasn't the best student because I was so focused on learning how to DJ or how to play basketball.

I tried to be a civil engineering student because my father was involved in designing the expressways in Chicago, but then my music started to take off and I got interested in gadgets and devices. I was the guy at the picnic with the boom box, playing cassette tapes I'd made from the radio. I was very influenced by Parliament-Funkadelic, George Clinton, Chaka Khan. Anything Quincy Jones. The Jackson Five, and anything Michael Jackson. Soulful disco like Stephanie Mills and the Philadelphia sound.

Then as we got into the '80s I started liking the garage music that was coming out of New York and the New Jersey area. Stuff like D-Train, *You're The One For Me*.

I borrowed the money from my dad to make the JM Silk record, *Music Is the Key*, which I recorded with my vocalist Keith Nunnally, and it went to No 9 on the Billboard Dance Chart. It was one of the first vocal house records to chart.

That was our first big break, 1985, and we were signed to RCA. We were booked to perform live and I went through that whole process of becoming an artist...and quickly realised I much preferred being the mad scientist in the studio. And that I wanted to concentrate on production and making music for other artists...to get up every morning and go to the studio, rather than go to a rehearsal space and work on live shows. Over time I became a better and better producer.

A remix I did of the pop hit *Funky Town* by Pseudo Echo for RCA in 1986, where I added some piano and drums, really helped my profile.

Keith Nunnally and I split off because he wanted to be an artist and I wanted to be a producer.

But if Steve Silk Hurley was looking to stay in the background, the groundbreaking track he'd invented in his 'laboratory' was only going to bring him more attention.

I was always looking to do something different on a record, which is how *Jack Your Body* happened. I was trying to do a blues arrangement on a house record. One of my managers knew how to play the blues and so I asked him to show me how to change the chord progression, how to take my baselines up and down to make it sound like a blues record, which made the record sound the way it did. Almost by accident, with the right speed, it was suddenly different enough but also musical enough to work on UK radio.

I had been playing *Jack Your Body* out at DJ gigs as a demo from my four-track for two or three years. At the same time I was out doing live PAs with Keith as part of JM Silk, learning how to be a performer, getting good money, but I just didn't want to be part of a vocal group.

I still wanted to be a mad scientist, so *Jack Your Body* was my ultimate mad scientist record. I decided to experiment and come up with another version of the four-track version. Eddie Murphy was the hot comedian at the time and he was always imitating James Brown and Mr T and a guy from a classic comedy TV show called *The Honeymooners*. It was pretty vulgar, but a funny routine.

So the 'Huerrgh' was the nod to Eddie's James Brown impression and the line 'Jack It Up Out There' that was the Mr T reference. All the vocals on there were me, I was just experimenting. I was thinking how can I be more innovative, to do something that hadn't been heard before, as opposed to trying to conform. I was in a studio where I could record whatever I wanted, playing around with a hot beat. I was just seeing what happened. It was done for fun, it wasn't done to be a big record. I didn't set out to make a load of money. I couldn't wait to get it to my DJ friends, that was about it. It wasn't like I thought it was going to be a commercial hit. *Jack Your Body* was just another one of my four tracks that I made in my bedroom.

Steve was then living in a rundown neighbourhood in Chicago, having moved out of the family home in a much more desirable area of the city in a bid for independence...and so he could concentrate on his music away from any discouragement from his parents.

When *Jack My Body* came out my flatmate was another DJ, Farley Jackmaster Funk. Along with Jesse Saunders and vocalist Daryl Pandy (RIP), Farley ripped off another of my demos, *I Can't Turn Around*, a cover of the Isaac Hayes disco track. I wouldn't wish any ill on Daryl or those guys but they pretty much took my idea and ran off with it. And they got their version out before we could get ours out. Like *Jack Your Body*, I'd also been playing my version of *I Can't Turn Around* from my four track, mixing it live at parties, for the last few years and anyone who was going out in Chicago at that time will tell you that. They took the direction of what I did, added some lyrics and changed the title slightly to *Love Can't Turn Around*. Their version was a UK Top Ten hit in August 1986, the first vocal house record to do really well in the UK. It ended up being a blessing in disguise because that track opened up the doors for *Jack Your Body*, which became the first house record to top the UK charts.

I still speak to Farley. We're still okay, civil with each other. He's apologised. I still DJ at the big festivals Jesse puts on in Chicago. We're all cool, but it doesn't change what happened, and our relationship is not what it used to be or what it could have become. I took it as a learning curve.

When *Jack Your Body* hit No 1 in the UK, my manager got a call from *Top Of The Pops* but had already said no to them before he even told me. I guess because I was in the process of finishing the JM Silk album and he was getting paid off the back of that album being completed. He told me we had to prioritise because we had a deadline. And my head was just down doing remixes and making tracks. There was no internet to go and search for *Top Of The Pops.* I didn't know it was an influential BBC TV show: I thought it was like a dance chart or something so I was on the same page as him, but if I had known the significance, I'd have been like, 'Sorry everyone, I'm out of here. I'm going to London. I'll be back in three days.'

I think the *Top Of The Pops* producers got the impression that I didn't want to come. I also got married around the same time so on the show they actually said, 'Steve Silk Hurley got married instead.'

When *Jack Your Body* took off that was the first time I was really recognised at that level. It made me sit back and think, but only for a second. It was 1987 and I was only 24-years-old.

Then remixing Inner City's *Good Life* and *Right Back For You* for Ten City really got the ball rolling for me. Being asked to remix New Order's *Fine Time* was another big break for me. That was all in 1988.

When I first remixed Ten City they had just signed to Atlantic. They didn't have a lot of money and I didn't have a lot of experience, so it was a good fit. Then they didn't forget me when it came to the remixes for *That's The Way Love Is.* All these little breaks stacked on top of each other and it started to snowball from there.

Michael Jackson was another big break. To be able to remix *Remember The Time* and also to be able to work in the studio with Michael on his next album was just an honour. His producer Teddy Riley was another hero of mine. Those people were untouchable back then. Even though we didn't come up with anything suitable for Michael, just to get through to that part of the process was amazing.

In the modern era there is actually a lot more communication from the artists because it's easier for them to get in contact.

Of course, the technology and the way we work has changed so much also. Now I've got all this equipment at my disposal. When I was coming up I was using reel-to-reels. These guys today don't know how lucky they've got it. I was using turntables, these guys have got controllers. I'm a turntable lover, but now I use controllers too because I like to embrace the technology. I don't want to be that guy stuck in the '70s or '80s.

Every day I get a notification that there's new software or a device that's going to help me. I always try to remain humble and remember being in my bedroom at my parents' house on my four track. I had to borrow a drum machine first and eventually saved enough money to buy my first synthesiser.

As the 1990s got underway, Steve Silk Hurley was a name already ingrained on the house scene but there was no time to dwell on his success.

I would say from '88 to '93 my head was just down and I was doing records. As producer, musician or an artist, or all three. I wasn't looking back to see how that last track was doing. I would see that some stuff had gone to No 1 on the dance charts and was getting a lot of love, but I just tried to stay focussed because I realised I now had people's attention. I just wanted to keep that momentum going and keep delivering.

And deliver he did, with 1991 a particularly good year for Steve.

I wrote a song called *Too Blind To See It* and produced it for Kym Simms, at around 90 BPM, again influenced by Soul II Soul. When we didn't get any bites from major labels I said, 'Let's put the track out on our own, but now it's house time, forget about the other mix.' I started adding totally new music and pretended I never had anything to do with the original. The new mix started to hit the dance charts and then Atlantic swooped in and signed Kym as an artist, purely on the back of the house mixes.

I don't know where the lyrics came from. It was like a female anthem, but maybe I picked up on stuff going on to people I knew. I think if women love a track they mostly love it for the lyrics or the vocals. They want to walk away with something. Guys, we can fall in love with a track even if it's not saying anything at all.

When remixing *What Would We Do* by DSK came on the table, it was another project where I thought, wow, this is already a hot track. I would play that anyway. I just didn't feel *What Would We Do* was a record that needed to be saved, I just enhanced it and came up with something different. I decided to go in two different directions, one more melodic, *Hurley's Extended Mix*, and one more aggressive, *Hurley's House Mix*. I prefer the melodic one personally, but I would play the aggressive one when I'm DJing if I was in that mood.

Like my own track, *The Word Is Love*, for instance. I did about five different versions before I came up with the one that took off, *The Anthem Mix*. In order to get to that version, which was the more disco driven record, I did one called *The Original*, and there were even several versions before *The Original*, which had a more melodic baseline. Then I found one part that I liked, that I could loop and then I was like, 'Oh, I should make a dub mix,' and that ended up being *The Anthem Mix*. But it took all of that struggle to come up with the one that everyone knows best now.

The Steve Silk Hurley production line continues to roll-on, with the man apparently never happier than when he's making music or talking about making music. More recent projects include an intriguing rework of a D-Train anthem.

Working on our version of *You're The One For Me* was another honour. I loved that baritone voice of people like James D Train Williams, Teddy Pendergrass and Colonel Abrahams, but I decided to mix it up by having both a male and female vocal for the remake. Christopher Williams from *New Jack City*, who also had a hit from the film called *I'm Dreamin'*, and Caroline Griffey, who is part of Shalamar now, and whose father, Dick, owned Solar Records and started Soul Train.

In the studio, I try to be very critical of myself, and never think, 'Oh, I got nominated for a Grammy, now I can do the hell what I want.' I am a mentor to a lot of people but I still have mentors myself.

Sometimes you work until 4am and you say, 'Man, this sounds terrible, let me go to bed.' And then you listen to it when you get up and you're like, 'wow, this is great.'

That's just the nature of someone who is trying to create something that they want the rest of the world to fall in love with. That's artists; we're so insecure.

Over the years I've learned to let go...if I'm not happy with one mix or track I don't have to finish it. I can move on to the next version. But you've got me thinking, I might go and do another mix of that Roberta Flack track...

When a 17-year-old Sally Rodgers arrived in London from her native North-East in 1986, her first stop was the Wag.

It felt like I was straight off the bus at Victoria Station with all my worldly possessions and into Gilles Peterson's Monday night party Wah Wah Acid Jazz at the Wag. I joined a band and we became semi-residents for Gilles, playing for him once a month.

I was a Saturday girl for Pam Hogg at Hyper Hyper and in a gang of musicians who worked at Kensington Market over the road on Ken High Street. I met Paul Daley, a percussionist, through a band we both auditioned for, and formed A Man Called Adam with him and Steve Jones, who had moved to London from Coventry to study graphic design, and who played piano accordion.

We were all Bossa Nova jazz kids, living in Camden. When Gilles launched Acid Jazz Records with Eddie Piller in 1987, we had already started to record at a place called The Basement Youth Club in Covent Garden, where Jerry Dammers used to put on his legendary Triple A (Artists Against Apartheid) parties.

Our engineer, Mat Clarke had just bought an Akai sampler, so it was the first time we'd got our hands on one. Our debut release was on Acid Jazz, the A-side was a live samba track called *A.P.B* and the B-side, *Before You Know It,* was the result of that sampler.

At this point, we were real connoisseurs of TV and movie soundtracks, as was Adrian Wright of The Human League, who was a fan of the band. We became friends and had also recorded in a tiny little studio in his fancy house in Chelsea.

So the first release for Acid Jazz was a big percussive keyboard workout, which sampled American '60s TV cop shows.

A friend from my home town kept saying you really must come to an acid house party. A bit of that Ibiza thing had already filtered through to London. Shoom, etc, was already happening, but it just wasn't our scene. We were more about DJs like Paul Guntrip, another Wag resident, and Jay Strongman...hanging out at Dingwalls or going to rare groove warehouse parties in east London. Not being able to get taxis home because they wouldn't come to Shoreditch.

We'd already made *Techno Powers*, a B-side our second release on Acid Jazz, *Earthly Powers*, when my friend finally got us to a rave in Cambridge in the autumn of 1989 called Blast Off. And I don't think we could have had a better first experience of ecstasy. A 60k rig and a party in an amazing stud farm in beautiful countryside, Loleatta Holloway and 808 State both performing. We were 'Johnny Come Latelys' and certainly didn't experience the first wave of it, but we were instantly converted to this new kind of world.

Techno Powers was a Lonnie Liston Smith-style track we'd deconstructed with a sampler. DJs like Harvey and Choci and the Tonka Soundsystem guys got behind it...and *Centreforce*, always on in the car at the time, also picked it up.

We had a tape cassette recording of *Techno Powers* being played on *Centreforce* and the DJ said, 'Time to get right on one.' We just loved it and always wanted to use that line on a record. It never happened, but I've still got the tape.

For a little while, everyone was so loved up, and feeling good about everything, that any trouble stopped. Class, gender and racial division disappeared.

Steve and I were from working class backgrounds but we were art-school drop-outs. Creatives in a hip jazz scene. Now we were spending our weekends partying with plumbers and plasterers with that amazing rapier wit they possessed.

It was a little shining moment when we experienced proper cultural integration for everyone.

Then Gilles and Eddie Piller had a parting of the ways, and we did one record for Eddie's new label, Ritmo Records, which had a cover of a Sergio Mendez track, *Love Music*, which we called *Musica De Amor* on the A-side. Again the B-side was electronic, this time a house track called *Amoeba*, which included a tiny vocal sample that said, 'No happy faces', which was a nice twist on the acid house smiley face at the time. That record also did well on the scene and was another *Centreforce*-type record.

We still had one foot in the jazz scene, but by now we were working with Lisa Loud, who had her PR company Loud & Proud, and her good friend Lisa Horan, who became our manager. Two great women of dance music.

Then we made our next record, *Barefoot In The Head*, which was really our version of *Tears*, and the first house record we released that was THE track...not a B-Side. It still had those kind of jazzy inclinations, but the lyric was about ecstasy and it's much more about our use of samplers and sequencing, the 909, the 808, the 727...all of it. And the acid house scene got behind it.

We signed a deal with Big Life Records, a new label set up by Jazz Summers, who had worked with Wham!. With hindsight that was probably a mistake, and we should have gone with a smaller label.

Big Life had signed acts like The Orb and The Soup Dragons, so they were picking up interesting types of electronic and indie music, but they also had Lisa Stansfield and Yazz. And as a female singer, I guess that's the mainstream mould they had in mind for me, so it was always a battle with the middle-aged white men of pop. I didn't want to wear make-up or have a stylist.

I was still only 21, full of myself, very confident, very ambitious, but I underestimated that as a relatively attractive woman they wanted me to be a pop star, whereas I wanted to be Shaun Ryder. I was like, why can't I be like him?

A Man Called Adam's inclusion in Channel 4's *A Short Film About Chillin'*, which followed Flying promoter Charlie Chester and acts and DJs including The Farm and Andrew Weatherall to Ibiza, was not exactly encouraged by their record label. Unavoidable, though, was the impact already of *Barefoot In The Head*, with its now iconic 'I put a seashell to my ear...' vocal sample of American poet, actor and singer-songwriter Rod McKuen.

Big Life were like, 'What the fuck is this?' They had to be persuaded but eventually and begrudgingly gave us £500 to get to Ibiza. The Farm's manager Kevin Sampson and director Angus Cameron had put the whole thing together and that was where the real money came from.

Both *Techno Powers* and *Barefoot In The Head* sold well at the Flying Records shop and we'd done PAs for Charlie at his parties at Queen's in Slough, so we were in and around that scene, but the two Lisas also insisted we had to be involved in the trip and the film.

Steve took his Tandy keyboard his dad had bought him, that had given us the choral sound in *Barefoot In The Head*, wrapped in a blanket because he didn't have a case for it.

We were all in weird shitty little apartments in San Antonio, but we just had the best time ever. It was my first time to Ibiza, and you kind of forgot that people were following you around with cameras because it was pre-reality TV, as we know it today.

The classic interview is of Steve completely tripping on acid, and everybody loves him because of that interview. Apparently, there was loads of footage that Channel 4 wouldn't use...including some of Andrew talking about ecstasy, which would have been amazing to see.

At the time it seemed incredibly radical and I was told it was one of the biggest youth TV audiences ever. I have friends who were a bit younger and said they couldn't go out because they were 14 or 15 and so would sit at home and watch it again and again on VHS recordings.

We were coming out of Thatcher and all that stuff, and that is why I have a little bit of a problem with Sade. Everybody loved her, and I loved her voice and as a person she's lovely, but, for me, those records represented that yuppie, loads of money, '80s thing that kids on the dole were excluded from.

Acid house was us expressing ourselves, and so I think that little bit of film for a lot of people was saying, here are people like us having a brilliant time on a beach listening to amazing music. It was and still is so powerful.

People are always trying to organise panels and streams and interviews around *A Short Film About Chillin'* and whenever I'm out and about or DJing somebody always comes up and talks to me about it.

There was a 30th anniversary tour planned for 2020, which Andrew was meant to be involved in before he sadly passed, but then Covid knocked the whole thing into the long grass anyway. Maybe another time...or in 2030 when 40 years later the film will no doubt resonate even more.

By now Paul Daley had left to form Leftfield with Neil Barnes, who was a uni friend of Steve, and who Paul had already been working with at The Basement Youth Club studio.

Paul was on the first three records with us...he was involved in *Barefoot In The Head* but not as involved as the first two, so there was already a parting of the ways.

Steve and I were now electronic music producers rather than the jazz kids we once were, but with us still having lyrics and melody and Paul being a percussionist, I guess he was always going to go towards that harder sound.

And it's strange because at the time those Leftfield records seemed really hard, but now they sound quite gentle.

Following the release of a debut album on Big Life, *The Apple*, Sally and Steve left Big Life and formed their own label Other Records. In the mid-to-the late-'90s AMCA became darlings of the Ibiza chill-out genre with various contributions to the Cafe Del Mar compilation series and also recorded as alter-ego Beachflea. A second album, *Duende*, was released in 1998, including more 'Balearic' gems like *Estelle*, *Easter Song* and *All My Favourite People (Stay With Me).*

We were still in touch with musicians and percussionists from the Latin jazz scene, so on *Estelle* we worked with Eddie Parker and it became a big Ibiza chill-out record on the back of *Barefoot In The Head*'s success as a Balearic house anthem. So it felt like we were constantly evolving and becoming parts of different connected genres, but always close to our jazz roots.

In the late-Noughties, Steve and I both went back to education to do Masters degrees and PHDs. Mine was in Creative Writing and Modern Poetics, so about lyrics and poetry and how capture and recording technology has changed that, ranging from the Romantics to hip-hop to memes.

Steve now lives in France and his PhD was about 'New Creative Practice with Mobile Technology'.

I guess for a while we felt like we were repeating ourselves and we just wanted to have more skills and knowledge and understanding of where we fitted in the continuum.

When we both finished our studies I was itching to make a new record so in 2019 we released *Farmarama*, which I like to think is a decent solid electronic dance album.

Steve is an ally, we talk a lot, and that's maybe why we've always been able to work together. We have our own lives, but we still enjoy making music together, and I guess we'll carry on as long as we do.

Now as a woman still involved in the music industry I'm having to navigate the whole Woke thing and reflecting on what I experienced.

I speak to young people getting into the business and it's refreshing because they're like, 'Fuck that shit, we're not standing for that.'

*****

I don't believe in creative blocks...it's like boredom, nobody should ever really be bored, but when Covid struck there was an element, for once, of not being able to write new music because we'd just been completely side-swiped by the whole pandemic.

At least Covid made us step back from the relentless commerce.

We have dozens of old floppy discs with half-finished tracks or tracks where the mix was a bit shit...or a nice little song that nobody has ever heard, so we spent the lockdowns working on a couple of albums worth of rarities and oddities. We worked mainly remotely, and Steve came to the UK for two or three months at a time.

We still self-release and we own our entire catalogue now, so we are masters of our own destiny. *Barefoot* and the stuff on Big Life was previously owned by Universal but we got everything back in 2011.

There are about five or six titles in the catalogue that always get used...and now it's about making new ones that get used...so it's about catalogue-building.

Steve and I both want to be more experimental again and not be worried too much about vocals. We're really enjoying having a dozen tracks on the go and not having any limits or expectations on what we're making.

I've had a bit of therapy over the years and I've learned it's about externalising your feelings, and, for us that's what music is...an externalisation of your inner life, and you can't put a price tag on that.

All you can hope is that your music resonates with someone else's inner life, and occasionally it did. *Barefoot In The Head* is a great example of that.

Maybe we'll make some new music and it will resonate with a bunch of confused middle-aged people somewhere along the way.

Danny 'Dany' Losito admits the global success of his first studio production was overwhelming.

I started from a little place in the south of Italy, and my record went all over the world. It was too much for me at times. I had to be strong.

I had wanted to make music all my life, but for my first track to be a big hit like that was just unbelievable. I used to look up to the sky and say, 'Hey God, are you sure?'

That little place was Gioia del Colle, a town in the city of Bari in southern Italy, famous for its mozzarella. Danny Losito's friends knew his DJ and singing act would appeal to the owner of Italian nightclub Green Leaves, a five hour 500km drive away.

Green Leaves was a historic club in Porto Recanati on the Adriatic coast in the city of Ancona. It had been a very important disco since the late-'70s.

And that's where I met Davide Domenella, the other D.

*****

Radio inspired me to become a DJ. As a child, I would always listen late at night in my bed, and when the music came out of that box, it just felt like magic. I started to imagine. I used to play instrumental records and sing over the top, so I thought, maybe I really can sing.

I was DJing at my local nightclub from the age of 16 in 1983. A lot of friends growing up were musicians, so when I started at the club some would come and help make the first part of the night with live music. This was always a big influence for me.

I liked a lot of Teddy Pendergrass, Kool In The Gang, Steely Dan, Luther Vandross. Stevie Wonder, but I also liked Italo disco.

The first part of the night was always mid-tempo, then some disco. I used to play a lot of English music, Level 42, Pet Shop Boys and Curiosity Killed The Cat. When I saw Ben Volpeliere-Pierrot on the TV I used to say, 'I want to be like that guy.' With the hat and the way he danced, he was so cool.

I remember the first time I showed my mother some cash I'd earned at a nightclub and she said, 'What is this?' And I said, 'Mum, I don't want to go to school anymore, because I now play music in the club. I sing on the mic and people like it. This is me now.'

Lots of my friends had been to Green Leaves. They came back and said, 'You have to come to this club. They will love you.' And thankfully they did. After my audition one Sunday after a long drive the owner said, 'Okay, you can stay here, phone your mother and tell her you have a job.'

By 1988, I was playing some house music in my set, still singing over the top, but I still didn't know that much about house.

I met Davide at Green Leaves and we went into the studio to try and make a track, some samples, a drum beat, then me trying some vocals like, 'yeah, yeah…whoa…ah,..yeah yeah.'

I couldn't write songs in English at the time…but my brother, Leo Losito, we called him Ninni, was an English teacher in Wisconsin, U..S He offered to help me with the lyrics for *Found Love*.

Davide and I had never made a record before. The only experience we had was using a keyboard or sampler while we DJd at Green Sleeves.

When we got in the studio we tried to arrange everything in the right way. We used samples like we did salt or herbs when we cook. A little bit here, and a little bit there. Some nobody spotted or knew where they came from. We played the track and we knew it was powerful. Then we saw the people dancing in the club when we played it, but went back to the studio and made it better and better.

The night we finally finished *Found Love* we sat in the car on the way home from the studio, playing the record on the tape player. There was a fog, we couldn't see much, but we saw a bar and stopped at 4am to have a drink. I said to Davide, 'Is this really our record?', because I got the same feeling as when I listened to other popular records I played in the club. It was exciting because I knew the track was good enough.

*****

After months of shopping the record around it was eventually signed by a new label, Irma Casadiprimordine - 'First Class House' in English' - whose fitting name came from the popular brothel which had been located in the same building as the label offices in Bologna in the 1950s.

Many labels turned *Found Love* down. It seemed nobody wanted the record. But two guys from Irma, Alessandro Staderini and Caludio Moz-Art (both later from the group Jestofunk) were DJs and producers on the label and they knew the track would work on the dancefloor. It's Claudio Moz-Art's son in the video.

The record was originally released as a white test-pressing and then as the first release on Irma's new sub-label Onizom. All the DJs started playing it, particularly the Fullhouse Mix, which I think was really popular in the UK. My brother rang me from America and said, 'Hey, your song, people know it here. It's being played on the radio. I've been explaining the lyrics to my students.'

I told him, 'Don't be silly, you're crazy.'

But Tony Humphries had got hold of the record and was playing it on his radio show in New York. It was a big moment for Italian productions at the time. In 1990, everybody was doing music with samples and it was at the moment that Italians started to make house music. There were not many singers or full songs in house, so I guess the record was maybe unusual.

My brother said I should visit him, to see for myself, but I never did go to America. My life had changed: there was too much happening all the time. The record went to No 1 in the U.S. Hot Dance Music/Club Play chart. Then Epic Records signed *Found Love* for America, and I was like, 'Are you crazy? The label of Michael Jackson has signed my record, really?' It was just too much at times. Danny Tenaglia did a remix for that version also.

It was incredible. You know the story about the young guy who dances in the mirror, singing into his hairbrush. I was dreaming, I still am.

I had been in London in 1989, but I didn't come in 1990 to promote the record. Irma was a very small label. We were not really ready for the management of this track. It was like a bomb exploded in our hands. There were no instructions.

I didn't really like the video. I saw other songs out there with a big video, big production and I thought, wow, I have a better song and I don't have a big video like that. And then I told myself, at least I am in the game.

And Double Dee was certainly in the game. *Found Love* reached No 24 in the Italian charts and follow-up singles, *Don't You Feel, Hey You* and *People Get Up,* all reached the Top 20 in Italy, with *Found Love* also Top 40 hits in France, Holland and Belgium, earning Danny a platinum disc. The track also reached No 33 in the UK when it was re-released in 1995.

And then everyone was asking me, 'Why can't you make another record like *Found Love*?'

'C'mon guys, I can't do that again.'

Then I said, 'I'm going to sing Italiano.' So I did a track with an Italian hip-hop band called Sottotono, *Solo Lei Ha Quel Che Voglio*, which was a big hit in Italy. It means, 'Only her have what I need.'

I was also lucky enough to work with Ben from Curiosity Killed The Cat, the hero of mine, and now my friend. Unbelievable. Our project was called 2 Men 4 Soul.

And it seems there is still plenty of music to come from Danny Losito. In 2020 he was involved in a new house release on Solomon's label, Diynamic - *Rain* by Matteo Bruscagin, Angelmoon & Visnadi featuring Danny Losito. And new remixes of *Found Love* by David Penn and Dimitri From Paris were released on Defected Records.

During the pandemic, Danny also formed a new virtual band called Quarantina, featuring British soul singer Omar. He also hopes to return to Ibiza with his band Mash Machine, which held a residency at Blue Marlin on Cala Jondal beach for three consecutive summers in 2014, '15, '16.

We'd make a mash-up of the music live. The band would play Disco Inferno and I'd sing another track over it. Of course, I would sing versions of *Found Love* too.

It's strange, I said to a friend in 1990s when people only talked about *Found Love* that I didn't want to sing the record anymore and he said, 'Hey, you will sing this song for the rest of your life and it will follow you forever. You won't understand this now, but you will appreciate it one day,' and it's true, because I always remember his words.

I feel so lucky. I knew the song was big, but I couldn't imagine it would last for all these years. Me and Davide still own the music. You hear a lot of stories about artists having their music stolen, but we are very fortunate that is not our story. Davide and I still work together from time to time. He does his own thing, and I do mine.

Found Love was an important part of the Italian house scene. I am friends with many of the other guys, Marco Fratty from FBI Project and Daniele Davoli from Blackbox.

I still live in Porto Recanati and I DJ and perform in a beach club ten minutes from where I live. Life is good.

You know, I love music and every time it seems music shows me the way. Sometimes I stop to look back, and I think, how is it possible that I do this? But I think it's about passion. It must be. It's passion and fire that got me here.

Danny Losito

When Richard Goldman heard Marshall Jefferson's *Move Your Body* in 1986, he realised you could make a song with just three chords.

I was a drummer in bands from the age of 15, long before I made dance music. Then when I learned how to play the chords to *Move Your Body*, that was like an epiphany. I was like, wow, that sounds amazing, I can play that. I realised you don't have to be Beethoven to play a house record. But at that point it was still very much an American thing: it hadn't come across here to the UK mainstream yet.

And when I think about that Marshall Jefferson track, when the drum roll goes, and it says, 'Gotta have house music…all night long,' it still makes the hairs stand up…to this day. That record still makes me say, 'Oh my God.'

It takes me back to a time when everything was new and we were discovering all the time.

There are a lot of things I like about being middle-aged, but I miss being impressionable. There's not much that amazes me now, but back then we were blown away every day.

Before the rave scene happened we had rare groove. That for me was the beginning of acid house. Acid Jazz, which Eddie Piller had started, which was a blend of what was going on in America and what was going on here. In 1988, I can remember wearing a leather jacket, a polka dot shirt and a bandana, being in to The Pasadenas and Inner City, *Big Fun*, at the same time. I loved it all.

By '88 I'd got friendly with some DJs in my local pub in Enfield who were involved with the Caister Weekenders. One Friday night I stood there in awe, the Technics 1210 decks they were playing on were like gold bars to me. I needed a pair so much.

So on the Saturday morning, I jumped on the tube to Tottenham Court Road. I walked up and down and in and out of all the Hi-Fi stores, to see who would give me the best deal? I've still got the receipt. Two 1210s for £500. All the other shops were saying we can't do it for that but one would.

Looking back I can't believe what a one-track mindset I had. The sheer naivety of carrying two 1210s home on the London Underground with a piece of string tied around the two boxes. Any DJ will know how heavy just one is. But I proudly walked back down to Tottenham Court Road tube station, navigated the escalators, changed at Holborn and made it to Southgate where my car was parked. I'd been through Wood Green and Turnpike Lane. Somebody could have taxed me and I would have been none the wiser.

It was amazing to be young and have tonnes of energy. I was intent on getting those decks back home and set up because I was so sure I was going to be a DJ. Growing up, I always auditioned for bands, but nobody wanted a 16-year-old drummer.

I was lucky. My family were very musical. My sister a classically trained pianist, so there was a piano from day dot. But I gave up learning as a kid because I heard my sister play and thought I don't like that stuff. I wasn't into pianists like Elton John either. It was house music and Marshall Jefferson that made me want to play the piano.

I'd started to hire equipment at the weekends, and dabbled with drum machines, samplers and keyboards, because I thought I needed to take it all on. My ambition when I left school was to be a musician, or at least a music maker. Fortunately, the rave scene and house music allowed me to do that.

I got a few DJ gigs in pubs where I grew up, using the name Richie Malone, in Enfield in North East London and in nearby Cheshunt.

I was acutely aware that people like Marshall weren't musicians, but they had a love for music, some equipment and a few ideas. I didn't need to write a whole song of piano chords, I just needed a riff.

I had to find a studio so I looked in Melody Maker. Back then, that's what you did. I found Synchronised Studio in Tottenham on the High Road, near the football ground, in a garage behind a shop. Synchronised found me a female singer from Islington, a good session vocalist, and we made a track called *What You Want*. It came out pretty well so I sent it to some contacts I knew but heard nothing back.

*****

I went to The Astoria pretty much every week in 1989. I'd run straight to the dancefloor and be there all night. There was an article in *The Independent*, with photos from The Astoria, including one of me. I look like I'd taken about 20 pills, when I never took drugs at all. The look on my face is not exactly one of happiness, but I'm just so in the moment. The music was so amazing and that photo just summed it up for me.

I'd stand behind Pete Tong at The Astoria with a pen and a bit of paper and luckily he would show me every piece of vinyl after he played it. I used to walk out of there with a list and spend every penny I had getting all those amazing records from Music Power in Ilford and City Sounds in Holborn. And that's what the scene did to me.

There's the romantic view that because of the rave scene and ecstasy, football hooligans stopped fighting each other and started hugging each other, but that definitely happened. I remember going to an Energy rave near Colchester in September 1989 with 25,000 people and not a hint of trouble and thinking a year ago there would have been fights throughout the night.

I saw an interview with the head of the Essex police back then and he said that the people who ran the raves were as good as any military outfit. The way they organised people and were able to move them around...he was almost in awe of them.

And I think it was all those elements. The music makers, the DJs and the party organisers, who together, caused the explosion.

In my head I was hearing records from people like S-Xpress and Bomb The Bass and thinking, I can do that.

So besides the whole raving thing, there was this real desire to make music, and the best thing was that the music in that scene was so simple.

*****

At the end of 1989, I went back to the Synchronised studio. This time I met a guy called Martin Spreckley who, like me, was trying to make dance records with samples. So we joined forces, partly because money was tight and together our limited funds could get more studio time. Martin was from Basildon and said he knew a girl, Lizzy D, who could sing.

'Great, bring her in.'

I was actually late the day the Lizzy came in. Martin had already got her singing the line 'Move your body, higher, higher h-h-higher.' So I started to lay down some drum loops. I played the chords in, and at that point we had a bland track which I didn't think was very good. Also, I was feeling really awkward that the song had the same key words as Marshall Jefferson's track. But we had no other vocals to use. There weren't any a cappella albums, they hadn't really come out at that point.

We did a couple more days in the studio, but I still wasn't happy with the track. I knew the piano sound for the chords was not quite right. I knew I needed a big sound to make an impact.

Then it hit me. I had always loved the keyboard sound in Van Halen's huge hit *Jump*. I'll use that as inspiration. These days there are hundreds of thousands of dance music records to be influenced by, but then there wasn't that many. For me, only Marshall Jefferson and a few others stood out.

The guy in the studio who was engineering created a sample of the bright synth sound used in the Van Halen track. He put it in an Akai 900 sampler and set the MIDI up. I told him it must have lots of delay and reverb. So he put the effect on, pressed play and fuck me, that riff came out. It was a Eureka moment. From that moment the record started to work.

I took a rough demo into Street Level Records in Tottenham where I shopped and asked the guys what they thought.

And they said, 'Is this you?

'Yes.'

'Fucking hell, this is great…'

I really wasn't expecting that reaction at all.

The Street Level guys said they were setting up a record label called Optimism and they'd loved to sign the track, which was now named *Move Your Body (Elevation)* by Xpansions. A couple of months later, February 1990, they had it out on white label.

But over the next month, nothing really happened.

The guys at Street Level told me to be patient and over the next few months, I started to hear more DJs play and chart it.

While the momentum was building I was still out and about handing out flyers for my own little parties and trying to blag myself DJ gigs. I got to know the Raindance guys, Paul Nelson and Ray Spence, and I'd pester them all the time.

NOT MUCH AMAZES THESE DAYS, BUT BACK THEN WE WERE BLOWN AWAY EVERY DAY.

Richie Malone (back left) and Xpansions.

'Please let me play, please...'

Back then Fabio and Grooverider always played at the Raindance parties, a DJ duo I really idolised.

I was on the pirate, *Lazer 94*, at the time and a guy from there took me to a DJ agency in west London where we went to blag promo records. I knew the agency represented Fabio and Grooverider so I was more than happy to pay them a visit.

Then on the August Bank Holiday Sunday in 1990, Paul Nelson invited me to the next big Raindance event, a big rave in Cambridge, with a Fabio & Grooverider, Mathew B, Slipmatt and Ray Keith headlining. Paul said, 'If one of the DJs doesn't turn up, you can play.'

Wow, this could be my big chance.

At about 3am in the morning, with the rave in full swing, I got the good news. The next DJ hadn't turned up. All my last few DJ gigs and parties I had put on had flopped for various reasons. I was getting a few bookings at places like Rifles in Enfield, which was probably my best gig, but that was it. Now I was about to play in front of 5,000 people in a huge circus top, with only minutes to prepare.

I would never shirk an opportunity like that. I always felt ready because it was what I wanted to do.

But I still wasn't sure about playing *Move Your Body*, simply because it wasn't a big record at that point...but I knew I had to play it.

Halfway through my hour set it was time. The moment had arrived. When the riff kicked in, well, it nearly took the roof off the tent. I can remember putting my arms in the air, which DJs still didn't really do back then. I blushed with embarrassment because nobody knew it was my record, then turned round, head down in my record box and quietly said to myself, 'Fucking hell.'

And *Move Your Body* got that kind of 'hands in the air' reaction all the time. A perfect example, and captured amazingly in black and white footage on *YouTube*, is the track dropping at Quadrant Park. An amazing hands in the air moments from the entire dancefloor and the club itself. *NB - Search 'Quadrant Park 1990's Xpansions - Move Your Body (Elevation)' to find it.*

Over the next two months, the track built momentum. Then I got a call from Optimism. They had received three offers. Sony, CoolTempo and Arista all wanted to sign the record.

And I thought, that's it, I've got where I want to be. A major record deal.

*****

When *Move Your Body* was released by Arista in the autumn of 1990 it failed to make the Top 40 leaving the label pissed off they didn't get the hit they expected.

It was still hard to get house music on to the radio then because, commercially it was still a new thing. So Arista said, go and make another track, we still believe in you.

So I made the next single and in the January of 1991 Arista said they were going to re-release *Move Your Body*...and I said, 'Why?'

'Because we're getting tonnes of orders.'

Arista had deleted the record ahead of the re-release but the more people heard the record in the clubs or on pirate radio the more requests the record shops were getting from it. The shops were ringing up the distributor and asking for it.

So I rang up Dave at City Sounds and asked him what he thought.

'It's definitely going to go this time, mate.'

So Arista put the record out.

This time the midweek chart had the record at No 41 so we were told we needed to make a video a.s.a.p.

It was the start of a crazy few days. *Move Your Body* entered the chart at No 29 on the Sunday, we shot the video at Bagleys on the Monday and that night as we were packing up we got the call to say we'd be on *Top Of The Pops* on the Thursday, so we'd be filming that on the Wednesday.

Everything was happening so fast I was just going with the flow.

I was excited about *Top Of The Pops*, but by the same token my cool factor was asking me, do I really want to do this? At 22 I wasn't sure if I wanted anything to do with a pop show. But I also didn't want to piss the record label off or the other members of the band who *were saying,* 'This is going to be amazing.'

And it was a great day. We hung out with Kenny Thomas and Shovel from M-People and had a great laugh.

Then Arista said we had to appear on Children's ITV at the weekend, *Motormouth* on the Saturday morning, and I said, 'Fuck that, I really don't want to do it.'

I was assured that we wouldn't be interviewed, we would only have to perform. And it was actually good fun. I didn't have to speak and I was at the back on my keyboard, so I was fine with that.

Next, daytime Children's ITV wanted to interview us live. By that point, I knew I had to keep playing the game. Keep everybody happy and my music career will continue. So I went up to Birmingham, did the interview, which was horrible. It was 3.30 on a Monday afternoon, and it was like 'Hi, we're joined by Richie Malone from Xpansions.' It was very nerve-wracking because it was live TV and I was worried about swearing and I just wasn't comfortable because I was worried about my credibility. It was always in the back of my mind that I didn't want to be pop, I wanted to be underground. In that moment, I probably would have given it all up to be either Fabio or Grooverider. They were the kings for me.

Fortunately, that was as bad as it got, really, other than the under 18 gigs. I didn't really enjoy those either, but I was also aware that things could be a lot worse. *Move Your Body* had reached No 7 in the UK charts by now so I had a coveted Top Ten hit to my name.

Some of the gigs were freebies because they were for radio stations, others were decent money. It's strange, I like nice things and money as much as the next person, but back then I wasn't driven by money. The main thing was that I wanted to be cool.

*****

Within weeks I received the call that made me think, now I've really made it. The DJ Agency who represented Fabio and Grooverider wanted to represent me. It meant so much to me at that point. A year or so earlier I'd been on the dancefloor of Rage at Heaven looking at Fabio and Grooverider in the DJ booth thinking, I want to be doing what they're doing, and I ended 1991 sat on a plane with them flying out to Rotterdam to play at a huge New Year's Eve party in a venue the size of Wembley Arena.

In fact, I was getting such good DJ bookings I just wanted to be a DJ. I didn't want to be in Xpansions anymore. You could still be a DJ and hide in between gigs then...and that really appealed to me.

At that stage, I would have quite happily stopped the train and said, 'Take me back to the underground. I don't want to be involved in the mainstream, trying to make commercial records.'

In my mind *Move Your Body* was a fluke because it wasn't intended to be a hit.

By now I was tied into a commercial management contract, floating around trying to find singers. I was into so many different styles of dance music too. Jungle and hardcore had started. A lot more US house had come out...and I liked it all. I'd be asked why I'd 'used that breakbeat' and I say, 'because I like breakbeat.'

I'd stopped Xpansions in its tracks and parted company with Martin and Lizzie D, but some promoters wouldn't book me as a DJ because I was deemed too commercial.

A side project - *Out Of My Head* as Marradona - I'd started in late 1992 with a good mate Scott Rouse, was finished in mid-93. Scott came up with a really good breakbeat and we built it from there. We both loved beats so after developing the drum track everything else was just messing around with ideas. Like Xpansions, I didn't think it would be much more than a club tune, but Graham Gold played it at Peach at Legends one night, and it went off, so he signed it for his new label, which was PWL-backed. The track reached No 38 in early 1994, which was a massive achievement for a record that started in my bedroom.

*****

Being involved in two crossover hits, at either end of the Top 40 was a great learning curve, but I felt like so much of it was out of my control. My biggest mistake was not sticking to one genre. I was too young, not musically knowledgeable enough, far too controlling and I wanted it all my own way.

I should have let other people guide me, but I was very precious about music. I have had so many conversations with people who have made the same mistakes as me so I know I'm not alone.

The problem with the mainstream is that you can't turn it on and off when you want.

I tried to make it as a songwriter but struggled to get a break, and had a lot of bad luck with certain artists along the way.

I'm the classic story of someone waking up one morning, no money, broke. What happened?

I started to ask why I haven't had any royalties. I realised there was money out there that I didn't know about. I suddenly asked questions and with the help of a good lawyer, I got the money. Around £100,000. And in 1998 when you're broke, that's a lot.

I realised there must be other people in my position, so I started speaking to other artists I knew. And that began a 20-year journey of learning exactly how the music business works and operates. Knowing intimately how and where every penny moves.

Richard is now one of four directors at Performance Rights Limited (PRL) alongside his long-time friend Andy Bailey from Street Level Records and Andy McQueen and Dave Loader from Notting Hill Music, who publish people like Will Smith. Together they look after 'neighbouring rights income' and have above 400 different singles, producers, DJs on their roster.

I'm very lucky now that 30 years after *Move Your Body* came out I can work in this side of the business.

We have clients like Marc Almond/Soft Cell, Jonas Blue, Wretch 32, Eric Prydz, Kevin Saunderson (Inner City) and Kevin Hedge (Blaze) — a real cross-genre of big clients built up by approaching people and saying, 'You're not administering your catalogue properly, we're the experts, let us do it.' And they say, 'okay, great.'

My selling point is that I can say, 'I've been an artist, it happened to me, I've been you.' And they trust me.

I helped N'Joi. They were signed to the same label as me, and so they had the same problems as me. And they have become close friends. And they're still getting paid now.

There are lots of people who don't realise that there are multiple incomes from music, not just from record sales.

I get amazing satisfaction from getting people royalties they couldn't get before or didn't know existed

DJ Luck and MC Neat is a case in point. We've got them into a position now where they are making fantastically good money from their music. Even I am shocked how well their records stream.

*****

I'm as surprised as anybody about both the rebirth of my record and *Centreforce*.

I can only put it down to people growing up, their kids growing up, and they've got the time and the money. They're desperate to relive that era, because it was so amazing. Life became tedious, hard and boring, going through the motions of normal life, and all of a sudden they had a bit of freedom again.

I was a massive fan of *Centreforce* back in the day. I got totally swept up by the pirates, whether it was *Centreforce*, Fantasy or Sunrise.

For *Centreforce* to come back after so long and to see the demand and for them to be so successful, it's a great thing. It's a bit of a phenomenon, but maybe we shouldn't be so surprised, because the scene was so huge.

*****

I made a new Xpansions record with my production partner Phil Drummond when *Move Your Body* was used on a Suzuki advert in 2019, and I was happy to be back making music for fun, without the pressure of having to get on a playlist.

And I'm making music for film and TV because there's none of that political bollocks about, 'you're too old, you don't look right, you're not hot.' They only want the right piece of music.

Thirty years later I still regret the shit deals I signed because I get bad splits. I don't own the record, Sony owns it for life. The publishing is with somebody else for life. Yeah, I get royalties and I get income, but I know that I'm getting severely ripped off.

At 52 I still hate the music industry. It never has your best interests at heart, but from having no money in 1998 I'm grateful that I am now secure and that out of adversity I have been able to build a career in the business.

My whole purpose was to be successful as a DJ or as a musician, or both, and for a while I did it all.

Geoff Hibbert was surprised to see a new place on his tour. But it would be the 22-year-old's last gig. As Cyclone, or Rhythm On The Loose, he vowed never to 'perform' live again.

I looked like a complete tit miming to 500+ people in a sweaty club in Leicester, plink-plonking away like Les Dawson. As I walked off stage after my set, the rubber 'play' button on my crappy sequencer was jammed and played the last track again. I quickly ran back on and turned it off as the DJ mixing his next track in glared at me. So that was my live career over. Way too much stress.

It was time for Geoff to regroup. He had earned some early recognition as Cyclone for releases on Birmingham-based Network Records, but it would be under a new alias that he cemented his own place in house anthem folklore. And it was his love of rare groove and samples used in hip-hop that inspired him.

From the age of 15, around 1983, I was into hip-hop and electro.

I started messing around with a crappy old turntable and I made my own very basic mixer, because I was really into scratching. Eventually, I bought a pair of Technics 1210s and had a stint DJing in Leicester at a club called Helsinki.

I left school at 17 and got a job as a trainee land surveyor. In 1987 I was able to get a loan and buy an Akai X-7 sampler. Every bit of kit that came out then cost around a grand so I'm sure it cost about that. When you're only earning about £5,000 a year, spending a grand on a sampler was a big deal in those days. I was always getting loans and buying various bits of kit.

I started messing about with samples, because hip-hop and house had crossed over into hip-house, and I thought, I really like this.

I loved rare groove growing up, and because a lot of people were listening to rare groove just before acid house appeared, samples from those great tracks suddenly were all over house tracks. I went to the Wag in London to a rare groove night and I thought it was the coolest thing ever. The hip-hop I loved always had lots of samples. Nobody really cared back then: there were no comebacks, everybody was sampling everybody else's records, and I just thought that was great. One of my favourite hip-hop groups were EPMD and they sampled *(It's Not The Express) It's The JB's Monaurail* by Fred & The New J.B.'s for their track *Let The Funk Flow.* It was absolutely superbly done, so that was a big influence.

Because I always had a full-time job the music side of things was always a hobby, but as a clubber, I lived and breathed dance music. Not always at the coolest clubs in the Midlands, but I visited the Hacienda regularly and one of my favourite clubs was Venus in Nottingham. I had the long hair and the uniform of leather trousers, white shirt, maybe a waistcoat. I loved Venus and the progressive house played there, and it prompted me to go in a different direction musically.

I made a bleep-house record under the name Cyclone called *A Place Called Bliss,* named after the Leicester club we used to hang out called The Bliss. I knew the DJ well there, and he played it once a night and even announced it for me.

I sent a cassette tape to a few labels I liked. Kool Kat Records in Nottingham, who I really respected, but they didn't even respond. Then I got a call to my work number from Network Records in Birmingham saying they really liked the track and wanted to sign it. I thought it was a wind-up.

So I went to meet the Network Records boys, including Neil Rushton, who had been a consultant for Virgin Records and had compiled the influential compilation album *Techno - The New Dance Sound Of Detroit.* And I was delighted, because *A Place Called Bliss* was an underground hit. The BBC2 TV show *Dance Energy* had it at No 1 in their buzz chart at the time, and I was No 1 in the buzz chart and I absolutely loved anything like that, being so immersed in the scene.

I started out wanting to cultivate a Sheffield-esque bleepy house sound, but house itself was changing all the time over that period. The second Cyclone track *Love & Happiness* was actually inspired by the hands-in-the-air piano vocal sound that was so popular. But fans of the original Cyclone were getting confused, so I came up with the silly name Rhythm On The Loose and I started to work on the track a new track. I was influenced by two big tracks that summer, Moby's *Go*, because of the strings, and Cola Boy's *7 Ways To Love*, which I didn't particularly like, but I did love the honky tonk keyboard sound to it.

I had a particular keyboard, an Ensoniq SQ80, which again I paid a grand for, and made a sound that I loved and no other keyboard made. Adamski used it on all his tracks, and I was a huge fan of his stuff. His *Liveandirect* album was awesome, so I had to get one of those keyboards. Adamski used the standard keyboard sound, which is really nice but if you tilt the module slightly it turns it into the honky tonk sound that I used on *Break Of Dawn*.

I wanted to create something with those influences and find some cool samples. I'd paid a lot of money for a vocalist for a Cyclone track that I wasn't really happy with, so for *Break Of Dawn,* I decided to go down the sample route.

I'd recently bought an album of a cappellas and I heard the First Choice *'I'm surprised to see your suitcase at the door, remember the good times, don't you want some more?'* sample and thought, that sounds great, I'll give that a go. Nothing more complicated than that. The Lynn Collins *Think About It* sample? Well, that drumbeat, it's just so good. To get the desired effect I had to take two parts of the record because it occurs at different times.

The original 1991 version of *Break of Dawn* was recorded in my bedroom at my parent's house.

Everybody thinks the title of the track refers to the sun rising after a rave or a party, but it's actually about a girl called Dawn I met on holiday in Tenerife in 1991. It should have definitely been 'Suitcase At The Door' because that's what most people think it's called anyway.

I'm sure Dawn, a holiday rep working on the island, hasn't got a clue. It was a nice little holiday romance, and when I came back and finished the record I thought I had a nice break and so I named the track after her. We did write to each other for a bit, in the days of letters, but that fizzled out. She came from south London, I think.

In 1991 Network initially just released a thousand copies on an

Geoff Hibbert, then and now.

offshoot label of their's called The One After D, a drug reference, which didn't take a lot of working out. They had no idea how it would do, but it got good feedback and the interest grew.

And eventually four years later, with some remixes, it got into the Top 40, No 36 for a week, then straight out. A career highlight. Those versions were recorded in my mate's home studio, Mark Archer from Altern 8.

My other claim to fame is that I think I contributed to the demise of Rednex, the Danish group that made that awful track *Cotton Eye Joe*. After the 1995 chart success of *Break Of Dawn,* I was asked to remix The Rednex new track, a version of the *Can Can.* I said, absolutely no way. Neil Rushton argued it would be five grand for a day's work and I said, 'When do I start?'

I'm not proud of my version, it was absolute gash. Yes, I took the money and ran, but at least Rednex split up very soon after that release. I like to think of it as my service to humanity, but it probably helped the demise of my music career as well.

*****

I dip in and out of music. Around 2015 I got massively back into it. I did a load of remixes for Pianoman and one or two up and coming artists and some re-edits like the Geoff H Disco mix of what I finally called *Suitcase At The Door*. I did a few new Cyclone mixes too.

I stupidly sold a lot of my equipment around 2002, when my wife and I moved into our first house, and which I hadn't used for ages: the Ensoniq SQ80 keyboard, my 909 drum machine, a TB 303 Baseline, that I got good money for, and all sorts of vintage synths, that I also got rid of. Now I'm like, 'Why the hell did I sell them? We didn't need the room that much.' Fortunately in 2021, after two decades of regret, a new version of the SQ80 was released so I was able to buy one and be reunited with that Break Of Dawn sound.

*****

I worked my way through the construction industry and I'm now a design and technical director for a national house builder. It's quite a high-pressured job that doesn't leave a lot of time to work on music, but I will have a tinker from time to time.

People do often find out at work. I'll be in a board meeting and suddenly someone's got *YouTube* on and they're playing *Break Of Dawn*. I get so embarrassed, I just want to hide under the table. The younger ones are like, 'what you?' And then I show them pictures of me in the early-'90s with hair down my back. It freaks them out.

I'm still constantly amazed that there is still so much love for the record, after all this time. If I look at the comments on *YouTube*, I'm always so grateful for all the kind words. It's wonderful that it always brings back so many memories for so many people. Thanks to everybody at *Centreforce* for their support.

Dorothy and Phil Fearon have been around the world twice with each other's hit records. Their music careers are definitely the gifts that keep on giving.

When there were still only four TV channels in the UK, Dorothy had already fulfilled most aspiring singers' dream of appearing on Top Of The Pops...as backing singer for husband-to-be Phil's early-'80s pop-disco outfit Galaxy, which had Top Ten hits with *Dancing Tight, What Do I Do* and *Everybody's Laughing*.

Phil, born in Jamaica, moved to north-west London with his family at the age of five in the early-'60s, and his music success was a No 11 UK hit in 1979 as a member of soul group Kandidate with *I Don't Wanna Lose You*.

Dorothy grew up just down the road in Neasden and remembers...

When we left school my mate and I used to go and watch a boy band and the guitarist knew Phil. He told us Phil was leaving his band Kandidate and was looking for some backing singers for his new project.

Suddenly we were auditioning and freaking out because we loved the

Kandidate stuff. We were nervous as hell, but thankfully got the gig. At the time we were both working in travel, but as Galaxy took off Phil asked if we wanted to be in the band properly. We said, 'Yeah,' and we both left our jobs. Before we knew it we were performing on *Top Of The Pops* and flying around the world.

Ten years later the couple were married and had started a family. Phil launched his own label, Production House. It would soon be Dorothy's turn to be lead vocals.

Phil: When I started doing well with Galaxy I bought the house next door to the family home where I grew up in the Queen's Park area of north west London, and later set up Production House there. The logo said 'Rooms Have Rhythm' because every room had music and noise coming out of it. I had friends and relatives coming in and out all the time.

We were also lucky to have some great up-and-coming artists come in off the streets and cutting their teeth. Kids I'd grown up with. My brother, Dorothy's brother, various friends. We gave them the keys and let them crack on, so Production House was an easy label to get in with and on. Go in there and do what you like. You can record 24-7 and we'll put it out. If it goes nowhere then there's nothing to pay. If it does something, then you pay your studio time. Nobody needed to watch the clock, so it was a lovely atmosphere. A crazy, vibrant house of music.

We launched in 1987 and got into our stride around the time *Centreforce* came on. Both Ratpack and Slipmatt would come in now and then.

I wanted Production House to make all kinds of dance music, but we found ourselves gravitating to rave music. That was a big learning curve and transition for me. I was just funding the label and keeping it going. I hadn't been going to the raves so I didn't fully understand what was happening on that scene.

Dorothy: I was always around Production House because we lived as a family next door. Jungle and hardcore acts like The Brothers Grim and producers like Acen were hanging out there.

One half of The Brothers Grim was Floyd Dyce, who became a backing singer for Galaxy and was also part of a soul group called North West Ten signed to Ensign Records.

Phil: The Brothers Grim wanted a feature vocalist for a track they were working on. And D was just there, packing boxes of records or doing whatever, so she stepped in. We didn't know what to call her so I thought, well, her nickname is now D. She's mad about babies. Let's call her Baby D. We threw it together, really.

D: It's true, I was literally pregnant at this point and in the middle of having babies. On the early Production House records it felt like I was either pregnant or breast-feeding.

Then Floyd Dyce came up with a new idea, a rave track called *Let Me Be Your Fantasy*, which seemed perfect for Baby D.

D: It was completely different to anything else I'd ever done. The beats were so ridiculously fast. I just did what I had to do and ad-libbed where I could. It was a mad track to record.

Phil: Floyd Dyce came up with the *Fantasy* track, and it sounded great, but at that point, it was just another Production House release. But as Fantasy started to pick up, and I became D's driver for her PAs at the raves, I saw the appeal and potential of it. And the genius and joy of that track was that it crossed over. D could perform at a house club or a jungle club and it went down equally as well. You couldn't plan that. Floyd Dyce did himself proud with that track. He was a reggae/soul boy, really. He was fresh out of school when he joined us. I have to say the rave scene was the happiest one I'd ever come across, because everywhere you went it was just pure love and pure joy. It was beautiful.

We put *Fantasy* out on our own label and we had our own distribution. In the early days Cleveland Anderson, a *Centreforce* DJ in the recent times, was a very powerful influence on Production House Records. He insisted that we do our own street sales. We had been messed around by other distributors previously so Cleveland said, 'Let's do it on our own,' and it was a phenomenal success. Cleveland was very knowledgeable and a great A&R man, in terms of saying a track needed a little more of this or a little less of that.

The sales team were amazing. My cousin Raymond Wright and a girl from Yorkshire, a loudmouth ginger girl called Jane, who was on another level. And my school friend Laurie. And a very clever guy in accounts, who ran the whole label on an eight thousand pound overdraft.

D: When 'Fantasy' came out I was doing a few random club PAs. The rave scene was so exciting I never knew where I was going to be next week. Little by little the track was getting bigger. I could be in a small club or in front of 10,000 people. Fields, warehouses, wherever. But more and more random people would come up to me before the show and ask for 'Fantasy'. Slowly but surely it was getting more loved. And then we

(main photo) A Baby D press photo from 1992 (above) Dorothy 'D' Fearon performing live in recent times (right) her husband Phil Fearon of Galaxy fame.

couldn't keep up with the demand for gigs.

Phil: We put *Fantasy* out first on Production House in 1992 and it stayed in the UK Top 200 for two years. We were doing so well out of it, that when we were approached in 1994 by London Records label Systematic to try and make it bigger, part of the deal for us was, if you can make it a bigger hit than we have, then great, but if you can't, the rights come back to us. Systematic were so confident they agreed to that and they were right because it went straight in at No 3 and then went to No 1 the next week. Our company still owns half of the publishing so it was a great deal for us.

D: They were very exciting days. We got this second wind with *Fantasy*, it was mad. In fact, our kids are quite jealous of us. They haven't done half the things we have.

And the *Let Me Be Your Fantasy* success story has never waned since. The record was in the Top 20 best selling UK singles of 1994, also peaking at No 5 in the Eurochart Hot 100 in December of the same year. It's been featured on hundreds of compilations since, and Baby D also won Best Dance Act at the first MOBOs in 1996.

D: I was pregnant when I went up to get the award — I was literally about to pop. And the live bookings just keep coming. 2020, before Covid hit, was set to be Baby D's busiest year ever for gigs. When we're out there we always stay back and chat to the fans and we never get tired of hearing their stories, what the track means to them. They tell us they got married to it, had babies because of it, and it's both amazing and sad how many people tell us they want *Fantasy* played at their funeral.

Phil: People bring their kids to the shows, it's beautiful to now see the different generations enjoying the music together.

D: If someone had told me in the mid-'90s that I'd be still PAing *Fantasy* in 25 years, I'd have said, 'Yeah, right...' It's just unreal. And I am forever grateful. I get 'endorphined' every single weekend performing that record. I just love the interaction with the crowd.

And it's not just the fans. Meeting up with the other acts on the same bill as us is such a privilege too. One Saturday in 2019 we had three gigs that night. I was going from up north back down to south London to do Soul Town, and when I got there I looked at the posters outside the venue. I saw my name and then screamed. Evelyn Champagne King was performing too. I was so excited to meet her. I was like a little kid, complete fan worship. Backstage Evelyn said, 'Wow, it's Baby D,' and I started freaking out. I was like, I can't believe you know who I am. And then I started singing *Love Come Down* and she joined in. It was magic.

Phil: We know we're blessed in this business. At one gig in Spain this guy lifted his top and *Let Me Be Your Fantasy* was tattooed across his stomach. At the gigs some people say it looks like I'm having more fun than D is. Normally we kick the music in and then drop the volume for the first line and everyone always sings along. It gives me goosebumps every time.

Phil has also enjoyed a renaissance with Galaxy, often booked alongside Shalamar, including a London Palladium show, unfortunately cancelled due to Covid.

Phil: I've known Jeffrey Daniel for years, back to the old days with *Soul Train*. When we hooked up again it was like old school friends meeting. We sat there for ages catching up. I'm a huge Shalamar fan so it's great to work with them. I was bragging to everybody that I was finally going to play The Palladium. Hopefully another time.

But it's great, when D is doing her gigs I'm the driver and carry the bags, but then I'll fly somewhere to a Galaxy gig, and there's someone to do everything for me.

One weekend in August 2021, a couple of weeks after Freedom Day, I drove D to a gig in Swindon, and then on to another in Southport. Then the next day I drove down for a gig of my own in Essex, handing over tour managing duties to my daughter, who took D to Lincoln, Rotherham and Manchester. That was a typical weekend again.

D: There's some really good new music on the hard drive which should have come out by now, but we just get so caught up with touring the old tracks.

Phil: D and I feel totally blessed for what happened musically to us. It was a fantastic time when *Let Me Be Your Fantasy* came out and we'd go back there in an instant. It was a rollercoaster ride of fun and creativity and enjoyment. We thank the fans and the *Centreforce* listeners, because they are so passionate. They are what's kept us fed all this time and we are very grateful.

A 19-year-old Victor Simonelli rang Arthur Baker's studio in New York every week for nine months before he was finally offered an internship…and then spent a year running errands before he was actually allowed to work on any music.

My first day was spent helping move Arthur's out of his apartment in New York, up-state to a new place in Woodstock.

It slowly got better, and I got into the studio…not producing, but working as an errand guy, answering the phone, picking stuff up. I was like, whatever you need doing, just dump it on me.

Victor possessed a steely determination, probably developed when the Simonelli family relocated to Utah because of his father's Government contract.

Dad had been such a huge influence on me musically, a real collector of vinyl records. My earliest memories are going through his collection, picking out things I wanted to hear, usually because of fancy cover artwork a child's eyes would naturally be drawn to.

My dad would ask how each record made me feel, what lyrics I could remember, which instrumentation stood out and thoughts that came to mind, and that really got me listening to music on a deeper level, always dissecting it.

Then I saw a cover that was so plain it stood out from all the rest, a simple burgundy-coloured sleeve with a sky blue centre label. It was a 1976 release, *Dance & Shake Your Tambourine* by the Universal Robot Band, which was one of the few 12 inches in his collection and the first one I remember touching. I found it intriguing, one single track on one side of a record.

I started to shop for 12 inches and started listening to mix shows on the great radio stations we had in New York like *WBLS* and *WLSO*, tuning into certain DJs like Tommy Musto & Tommy Sozzi.

My dad would rent out a dancehall and throw parties for the local kids. It was the first time I was exposed to the dancefloor.

Then in 1980, after spending the first 12 years of my life in New York, Dad was transferred out west to Utah and the disco and the electronic music I was into just wasn't there, so my interest levels only increased. I asked my friends to send me tape cassette recordings of the radio shows I was missing.

It felt like I was at boarding school: a whole new environment and a way of thinking, but it made me hungrier and set me up for travelling in later life.

Thankfully I was able to come back to New York in my late teens and enrol at The Centre For Media Arts.

By now I was a huge Arthur Baker fan. Between 1981-85 he was banging them out, one after another. *Happy Days* by North End, *I.O.U* by Freeze and *Planet Rock* are obvious examples.

I read in Billboard Magazine that Arthur liked to give young talent a chance so I went to his Shakedown studios and asked if there were any internships available. I was told no, but to keep in touch. So I did. Every week.

And if there's any advice I can give to anyone trying to get in the music business, or any business, in fact, it's consistency. Not giving up, not taking rejection personally and remembering that people are busy.

My thing was always...you're not going to find anyone who will work as hard as me. In my experience, talking doesn't get you very far, but giving and working hard does.

I gave it more than my all. I basically moved into the studio. I never left. Arthur would go home at night and come back in the morning, and

I'd still be there. He never asked if I was tired, or I wanted to go home, he'd just give me some more tapes. Christmas and Easter would come and go. It was work, work, work and I guess that's how it was coming to him, and so that's how he put it on me. And I wouldn't have it any other way, I just loved what I did.

I was not even 20 years old yet; I just remember thinking, this is my chance.

I made sure I told Arthur and the studio manager that I felt comfortable editing. That I understood it was a mathematical process, taking the best parts from the various stripped-down versions of each track Arthur had recorded across multiple tapes.

The previous editors were Latin Rascals, Tim Scott, Junior Vasquez, Benji Candalario, Danny Krivit...

One day Arthur came in and said none of his editors were available, did I want to work on a Will Downing track called SOS, which had just been signed to Island Records? And Arthur was very happy with the outcome.

I learned to do tricks, what we called shot-gun edits, dissecting each beat, inserting different sounds or the opposite, silence, into the measurement of a beat. At the end of the process, I'd be buried under scrap tape.

And Arthur just kept giving me more tapes.

Eventually Talking Heads, Quincy Jones, Chaka Khan, Diana Ross, Rolling Stones, Hall & Oates and New Order. I also edited Arthur's version of the Roberta Flack track *Uh-Uh Ooh-Ooh Look Out (Here It Comes).*

I was lucky to get an editing credit on the majority of the stuff I worked on. It's amazing to have my name on such iconic records.

My friend from the same neighbourhood in Brooklyn, Lenny Dee, had been working at Nile Rodger's studio, Skyline. Arthur put us together and gave us a name, Brooklyn Funk Essentials, that he'd already produced under, but let us experiment with it.

Then I worked with Arthur and Lars Kronlund, the man behind *Where Love Lives*, and we produced a track called *Why Can't We See* as Blind Truth.

Next, I produced a track on my own for Nu Groove as Groove Committee, with similar drums sounds, called *I Want You To Know*.

And this was a turning point for me because I'd been editing since 1987...almost five years, but after *I Want You To Know* I started to get calls about my own music, which hadn't happened before. I was booked to play in Japan, my first gig overseas.

Around that time, Todd Terry gave me some great advice. 'Just do it again, do the same thing.'

And so I did. I went back in the studio and did *Dirty Games*, again as Groove Committee, the same sort of concept, which Nu Groove signed... and then I did the same thing with *Feels So Right*.

With all those tracks I was inspired by what I was hearing out at places like Zanzibar with Tony Humphries, Shelter with Timmy Regisford and The Loft with David Mancuso.

And *I Want You To Know, Dirty Games* and *Feels So Right* were all done on the same mixing board (which I still have) and this was pre-computer, with a sequencer. And all three tunes loop like they'd play forever. And, if you hear any reverbs or delay throws, that's all live and unplanned.

What Todd said made so much sense. He did *Party People* and then *I'll House You* for the Jungle Brothers and then replicated things again and again in that era. Having a friend and a colleague point me in the right direction, when I was in the middle of it all, left, right and centre, night and day, was invaluable.

Victor Simonelli

And *Feels So Right* really did feel so right. Victor was into his stride now and had inadvertently developed his own trademark 'Simonelli sound'. So right that everybody wanted to release it, whether they had permission or not.

The first release of *Feels So Right* in 1992 was unauthorised, on a label in New York called Illegal...can you believe that? I gave the guy some white labels because he was interested in releasing some stuff. I was speechless when I found out he'd just gone ahead and done it without any further conversation. Finding him was impossible back then, his office had shut down. It's sad there are people out there who did that, but you had to try and remain positive.

It led to another authorised release on an Italian label called Under Control.

It wasn't until a few years later that I was able to get a handle on what was going on, because I was making so much music and travelling all the time. Back then your track could get a life of its own and go in its own direction. I compared it to a child, which over time grows and ultimately you're not always in control of what it decides to do or become.

In 1996 a UK label, Soundproof, put in a good offer and that was the first legitimate release of *Feels So Right* that I was in control of, and thankfully these guys cared.

From that point on I've owned all the publishing, and I absolutely still do now. For anyone who got ripped off back then at least there's the 35-year rule. Original writers and creators should always own their music.

I recently put out a 30th anniversary release of *Why Can't We See* on Tracksource - it must be one of the most sampled tunes ever. I've got around 125 versions of it, and they keep coming. Armand Van Helden and Chris Lake contacted Arthur and me to do their own version recently, and now that's come out, called *The Answer.*

Thankfully I have a massive catalogue of my own material and control several labels, spanning over 30 years, but keeping on top of it all is a full-time job. And then there's uploading...I could do with some help for that.

*****

Over the last few years I've become friends with DJ Texsta. When he took me to the *Centreforce* studios a few years ago, I was introduced to Andy Swallow, and I recognised him from somewhere. Then I put two and two together. Back in 1996 I was with the management company Release The Pressure, for the UK, who brought a group of us over for some gigs, me, CeCe Rodger and Lenny Fontana, and put us up in an apartment block in Maida Vale in west London. Lenny was going into the Public Demand office one day and took me with him and that's when I first met Andy. Me and Lenny ended up doing a remix for Andy together, the L & V Classic Anthem Mix together of a nice tune called *We Got Love by* One Family..

It was great to see Andy again and how he'd brought *Centreforce* back. The whole pirate radio thing in the UK is fascinating, because in America it was very rare as there's a completely different mindset back home. I find *Centreforce* amazing, a station with such enthusiasm.

Loose Ends' frontman Carl McIntosh believes support from pirate radio was crucial at the start of the band's career.

As we chat, *Centreforce*'s Sunday-morning-early-afternoon DJs Phillo and Steve Kite fittingly play his hits *Hanging On A String* and *Gonna Make You Mine*. Roger The Doctor, a huge fan, dedicated one hour of a recent show to the *Zagora* album, while Loose Ends performed at a *Centreforce* Sessions party in Romford during the *Time FM* era.

When we began making music, particularly as black artists trying to break through, we were always conscious of having to water down our sound. Pirate radio allowed us to be as pure as possible.

You could never compete with national airplay, but pirates always had a strong soul music ethic, and if you were getting a lot of pirate support, there was a chance national stations would pick up on that.

As kids, James Brown was in our family's record boxes, and we thought radio just played a different type of music. We didn't know James Brown wasn't getting played because an old guy in an office at a radio station didn't know what the hell he was talking about.

Maze came over and sold out Hammersmith Odeon two days in a row, with no national airplay...and added another date when they were here. And that was the power of pirates like *Horizon* and *JFM*.

I remember pirate radio evolving from CB radio, which back then was like having a free phone. People had handles, talked to each other and hooked up through CB radio, then that gave birth to the shout-out. Pirate radio was everywhere and when our music started getting released I heard pirate stations play it everywhere: in my local West Indian shop, if I was sat in the launderette when somebody drove past in their car, on the train on someone's Walkman. It was crazy. I'm from Hackney so, of course, I can remember when *Centreforce* came on later.

Carl played bass in reggae bands at Upton House School in Homerton. One classmate at school inspired his early songwriting.

I was in the sixth form with Jean Adebambo, who was already known to us as having an amazing voice through performances at school. I wanted Jean to sing in my band, so I started crushing on her, but she

Carl McIntosh

told me I was too short, and that if we were out dancing and she had heels on it just wouldn't work. It broke my heart. I went home and wrote *No Stranger To Darkness, Dial 999* and *Choose Me*, which became initial Loose Ends singles and album tracks. Jean recorded her huge lovers rock track *Paradise* while we were still in the sixth form at school, and went on to be a big star in that scene.

A few years later I took my mum to the market to do her Saturday ting, and Jean and her tall, good-looking boyfriend pulled up next to me. It was two days after I'd first been on *Top Of The Pops*, and Jean was like, 'Hey, we've been looking for you, maybe we should work together...' I had to smile.

Working in Philadelphia with producer Nick Martinelli (and a Roland TR-808 drum machine) helped hone what would become Loose Ends trademark post-disco Brit-funk sound. Top 20 albums *So Where Are You*, *Zagora* and *Look How Long* delivered hit after hit throughout the '80s and into the early-'90s.

The trio were formed in 1980 by music and drama graduate Steve Nichol, a trumpet and keyboard player who toured with The Jam. Carl joined on guitars originally but soon became immersed in songwriting and vocals with lead singer Jane Eugene.

In 1985 Loose Ends became the first British band to top the American R&B single charts.

When *Hanging On A String* came back it didn't sound right. It was produced like a neo soul track — nice and warm and cute, but it wasn't feeling like a single. The record company said they really liked it, though, so asked Nicky (Martinelli) to look at it again. When it came back — wow, he'd brightened it up, worked on the intro, it had a really nice bottom end, and now it just sounded like a hit.

Steve and I had come up with the original arrangement and music for the track, as we did most of the time.

The lyrics were myself and Jane, but by this point we had become more than friends, probably because we spent so much time together over a period of a couple of years, including a lot of time in Philadelphia working on the first two albums with Nicky.

I remember sitting down to write Hanging On A String with Jane, and she sang the line, 'I've waited oh so long, for you to come to me...'

And I'm sitting there thinking, oh, that sounds nice...

Then she sang, 'What did I do wrong, it's all a mystery to me?'

It sounded like a great lyric to me, so I just sang back replying to what she was singing about...

'Baby, I feel it too, what am I supposed to do? Maybe I've just changed, or could I be wrong for you?'

And we were off, *Hanging On A String* was born.

By the time we'd also shared vocals on hits like *Magic Touch* and *Slow Down,* I began to realise there was definitely something going on here. And when you look back at most of our songs it is glaringly obvious that there is a theme running through them.

The promotion for *Hanging on A String* in America was relentless, but at least the accommodation had improved. When we made the first album the record label put us up in the projects, but when we came back to do So *Where Are You we* were in a lovely condo in Rittenhouse Square. We got a hamper sent to our homes that Christmas, and it was those little things that your mum noticed that made you realise things we were doing well.

The promo tours were all aimed at getting us to No 1 in the R&B Billboard charts. Tiring 18 hour days, driving to local radio stations and record shops in New York or wherever for three months straight, talking about yourself so much, all day, every day, you forgot you were a musician. We'd come back from one area and they'd say, '*Hanging on A String* is No 52 now, we're going to LA tomorrow,' and we'd be like, wow, what do we have to do to get it to No 1...but we did eventually.

I think a lot of the Americans we met respected our British soul sound, because they could hear that it was different.

In 1989 Nichol and Eugene left Loose Ends and Carl continued with new members Linda Carriere and Sunay Suleyman, and soon after released the band's fifth album, *Look How Long*, and the single *Don't Be A Fool*, also both Top 20 hits. Two years later a Frankie Knuckles remix of *Hanging On A String* also charted, at 25.

It's a shame. When I auditioned in a block of flats all those years ago, I was more impressed with Steve than the idea of Loose Ends. He had flex, was very charismatic and worked as a model. He was also the first person I'd met who had been to university. He knew how to engage and talk business and what he wanted the band to look and sound like. As far as I was concerned, Loose Ends was Steve's band. He'd put the whole thing together. We'd just returned from supporting Freddie Jackson in America, which Jane put together through her contacts over there. Steve and I had a disagreement about a few things, and one day I was told he was leaving his own band.

Jane went off and her did own thing too. She moved to America and signed a solo deal with MCA. She later did a Loose Ends Reunion tour out there...with herself. After that, I went out and did a few shows with her and I think Steve did too.

Our publicist Erskine Thompson came up with the concept of our 1992 remix album, Tighten Up Volume 1, based on the Trojan Records reggae compilations of the same name. When *Hanging On A String* first came out in 1985, Nick Martinelli introduced us to Frankie Knuckles, who said he was a big fan of the track. So it was an honour and a privilege when he agreed to remix it seven years later, because he was the man of the moment by then. And Frankie's mix is brilliant. He kept a lot of the lo-fi elements of the original song, with real horns, and didn't just put a four to the floor wrapper on it, keeping it around 109/110 BPM. Other remixes for that project came from David Morales, Gang Starr and PM Dawn.

A new Loose Ends album will be out in 2022, plus acoustic versions and re-edits of some of the old stuff. We're also working on a 40 year anniversary remix album, including some new house mixes.

I'll also be back out on tour in 2022.

I haven't been able to get the three of us back together for any live shows yet but, for me, that door is always open.

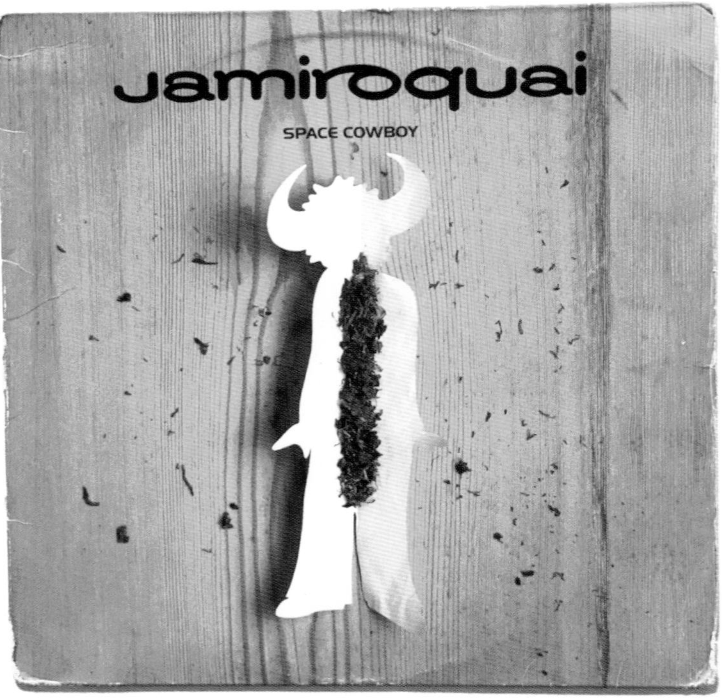

David Morales only really wants to talk about the game-changers...and his remix of *Space Cowboy* certainly falls into that category.

To think that my remix was Jamiroquai and Jay Kay's biggest track. The record label told me he hated it. And I understand, from an artist's point of view, because I trashed everything. Jamiroquai is a band, a proper band, and Jay Kay's a proper songwriter. I have the ultimate respect for him, his shit is organic, he's like Stevie Wonder, but he was probably thinking, how dare somebody come in and fuck my shit up like this?

Morales is not averse to ruffling a few feathers...or daunted by filling big boots. Stepping in as cover for Larry Levan one weekend at the Paradise Garage in 1983 helped set the benchmark for his prolific DJ and production career.

I was a street kid from Brooklyn and they asked me to play at the fucking Mecca. I knew its importance because I'd been there and heard the amazing sound system. I'd stand and look up in awe at the DJ box, and say, 'Oh my God, oh my God.'

When I first played the Garage people were like, who the fuck is this? And of course, they were going to compare me to Larry. He was one of the Peech Boys, he was Man Friday. One of the very first DJ-producers in the game, who started the evolution of playing demos in a club, six or seven months before a track came out. Larry Levan was the king and queen of the Garage. Case closed.

*****

I'm a DJ first...I've been doing that for more than 40 years. I was always interested in music when I was an adolescent, but the first time I started to mess around with decks was between the ages of 13 and 14. It was the evolution of listening to music and finding out about the 'non-stop-disco-mix'...then thinking: how do I mix between two decks so the music never stops?

Coming from Brooklyn, there was more cutting up going on, but nevertheless always a seamless flow of mixing two records together. As a teenager, I wanted to DJ at any party I could. Around 1980/81, aged 18, 19, I'd go to the Garage to dance...one of those kids there from beginning to end.

I got into editing on reel-to-reel tapes, what I called my 'mash-up master mixes', which I'd pass around and were well received because of the shortage of promo records. I got into editing professionally for various remixers, creating 12 inch radio and dub mixes from the multiple tapes they'd give me. But I was a DJ. I ain't ever taken music lessons. Writing and producing records is a whole different game. I lived in the studio five days a week.

I started my own parties and residency at The Ozone Layer in Brooklyn on Fridays and Saturdays. Straight to the club most nights with edits and mixes I'd been working on, shelves stacked high of reel-to-reels behind the decks. There was just one style of music back then...it wasn't house music, it wasn't this or that, it was just music, proper music.

*****

When I was 21 in early 1983, I was lucky enough to join Judy Weinstein's record pool. I hadn't even played in Manhattan yet. My neighbour Kenny Carpenter, who had been a resident at Studio 54, and was now at Bonds International, a huge venue, got me in. To join I needed a letter from my resident club, with a corporate seal. All the best guys were on the pool — Jellybean Benitez, Francois Kevorkian, Tee Scott, Shep Pettibone, Bruce Forrest — the list was endless. The creme de la creme. Such an honour.

Then the biggest moment of my life at that point. I remember when the phone call came through to my house like yesterday. I thought it was a joke.

'Hi, I'm Michael Brody, I own a club called The Paradise Garage and I'd like you to play for me.'

'Yeah, right, are you fucking kidding me?'

There were so many other great DJs who deserved to play before me, including Kenny, but I think they wanted someone who wasn't involved in the politics.

Larry Levan could be temperamental and he treated the club like it was his own...and, in retrospect, it was his club. He played what he fucking liked, which is really how a DJ should be. You'd stand there thinking, what the fuck is this? But when Larry played that one track, that he had exclusively, that you couldn't wait to hear, it was like some-one had lit a fucking bomb and a firecracker at the same time. The place went ballistic. To me, he could seem inconsistent, but Larry had balls, and now I've gotten older I realise he was one of the best at telling a story.

Since then I've cemented my position in the game and become one of Larry's peers, but at the time everyone was in awe of Larry. I didn't appreciate the huge pressure that came with the position he was in.

I played October 14 and 15, 1983 at the Garage. Midnight to 11am on the Friday, with Jocelyn Brown performing live, and another 11 hours on the Saturday. Almost 24 hours over that weekend.

They put my name on a banner at the entrance of the venue, with 'The Ozone Layer' printed underneath, which was a nice touch, because it meant my home club got props for me being there too.

The following February in 1984, I was booked for two more weekends in a row, playing around ten times in total. And that established my standing in New York. People were like, how did you get to play at the Paradise Garage? Whose dick did you suck?

In 1986 David remixed the Blaze track *Whatcha Gonna Do*.

I had David Cole of C+C Music Factory/Clivillés & Cole come in and do some additional keys. At this stage, for me, a remix meant adding a couple of parts, maybe changing the baseline, adding a solo, some extra percussion and a snare, but I really tried to keep as much of the original as possible.

Around the same time, I remixed the Imagination track, *Instinctual* for RCA in America. Leee John and the group and the producer, Arthur Baker, all thought the record was off-key. Josh Millan from Blaze played keyboards on it for me, but once they saw the reaction in the clubs, they had to put it out. Leee John became a good friend, and we've worked on each other's stuff a lot over the years.

I had a big underground record in 1987 with David Cole, Robert Clivillés and Chep Nunez, fittingly called 2 Puerto Ricans, A Black Man And A Dominican.

Next up was Whitney Houston, and this was when Whitney was Whitney. Jellybean produced her track *Love Will Save The Day,* and then her label, Arista Records asked us both to remix the track. This was my first remix with a household name, but the label thought it was too dance, and too black, even. In 1987 you have to remember that mainstream record labels didn't know jack-shit about house music, because house music was a culture that your average regional promotional man for a major had no idea about, because he didn't go to those clubs.

Somehow DMC got the rights and put it on a compilation, and it did appear on the *Whitney Houston - Unreleased* album in 2000. There was a dub that we did which was really sleazy but it went missing. I'll have to ask Jellybean about that...

From that point on the remix offers just started to pour in.

In 1987 David and Judy Weinstein, now a consultant for Polygram Records, A&M Records and MCA Records, joined forces to set up Def Mix Productions, an all-singing, all-dancing exclusive DJ agency and management company. It was soon a case of 'when David met Frankie...'

Frankie Knuckles was moving from Chicago back to New York, where he'd grown up, to play at a club called The World. They paid for his move and his apartment. Me and Frankie hit it off immediately — it was like we already knew each other.

Knuckles had 'discovered' Satoshi Tomiie in Japan, and persuaded him to move to New York. He became a welcome addition to the stable, which was increasingly becoming known for its 'Def Mix sound'... Frankie and David's Def Mix of Inner City's *Whatcha Gonna Do With My Lovin* a perfect stripped-down example of that.

We began to work together under the Def Mix banner but neither of us wanted to look like a team because we each had our different styles.

Frankie had a very sophisticated sound, whereas mine was a bit edgier. We didn't want people to think us working together was the standard, and looking back I don't know if that was the best thing or not. We were both growing so fast at that time that it just happened the way it happened. We travelled the world together, we never had a fight, a disagreement, or two bad words.

As I started to make some money, I got a 16-track at home which I remember writing *I'll Be My Friend* on with Satoshi and Robert Owens.

As remixers, we mainly worked in Quad Studios in Time's Square. They had a lot of floors and I used to have the B-Room on lockdown, renting it for years.

Another big remix of mine around that time was *Dirty Cash* - The Adventure's Of Stevie V. I was already playing the original at my residency at the Red Zone in New York. I had a meeting with the A&R director at Polygram, and he said, 'The record's not really doing it for us.' It hit No 2 in the UK pop charts by the time I was done with it. People ended up playing my 'Sold Out' mix, and then Mercury Records in America picked up the track and it got to No 25 on the Billboard 100. I also remixed another track, *Jealousy*, from Stevie V's album.

In situations like that, I started to get ticked off, because if it wasn't for me there wouldn't have been a second Stevie V album deal. The record label was about to drop that project altogether. Then it would have been nice for them to share the love, and get me involved in that second album, but there you go. That was normally the case with a lot of people that I mixed and made rich. The one person who was really good about it was CeCe Peniston.

In 1990, me and Frankie were asked to remix Alison Limerick's *Where Love Lives*. It was an amazing record: you heard it immediately. Because we were in the business of remixing, by then we had both worked on so many records that were just okay. But with *Where Love Lives*, the result, the first 'Classic Mix' we did, is one of my favourite remixes I've been involved in. Easily top 5, maybe top 3. We didn't stray too far from the original, because it had that amazing piano line. I would usually let Frankie do his thing first, then I would come behind him with the drums. I mainly handled the bottom part of the track and he handled the top. And we'd usually be at opposite ends of the huge console at Quad. We would somehow compliment and vibe off each other.

I even went back in and did a bleepier version of *Where Love Lives*, with 909 drums and snare rolls, which is wicked. I play it out sometimes to spice things up. Alison Limerick is just amazing, brilliant. I would love to work with her again one day.

The following year, 1991, was an interesting one.

On one hand, I did the Club Mix of *Always There* by Incognito featuring Jocelyn Brown, eight years after she performed with me at the Garage. It was special to work on a track by Jocelyn, and Bluey Incognito is such an amazing musician.

But in 1991 I also produced the radio edit of *Mr Loverman* for Shabba Ranks: the biggest, most successful remix, and the most-selling record I ever made. And nobody can believe it was me.

It would be CeCe Peniston's *Finally* that became David's signature tune and sound of 1991. The 12" Choice Mix and subsequently the 7" Choice Mix quickly replacing the original mixes, and have been industry and airplay standard ever since.

In 1992 Frankie and David teamed up again for a Classic Mix of Luther Vandross and Janet Jackson's *The Best Things In Life Are Free.* Then in 1993, an emerging superstar was called in to re-record her vocals in David's studio.

I did the *Finally* remix with Satoshi, sampling the drums from *Let No Man Put Asunder*, and playing a similar baseline to CeCe Rogers' *Some-*

day. We didn't think too much about it, at that time it was really just making records from a DJ's mentality. After *Finally*, thankfully, it was a rare situation when the record label included me on some future productions of hers. Appreciated.

I didn't get to work with Luther or Janet, but I did meet Luther, a great guy and that smile, wow...always positivity on his face. I would have loved to work with him, I wish I had the chance, he was taken way too soon.

Then I was offered the *Dream Lover* project for Mariah Carey. I told Columbia Records I couldn't remix the original. Too bubblegum, too poppy, but can she re-do the vocals with me? I was just putting it out there, speaking off the cuff, I didn't think the label would agree to it. Nobody had come in and re-sang any vocals for me before. My job was to bring the record to the dancefloor but I couldn't do anything with that record. I couldn't do anything with it as it was.

When they said, 'Okay,' I was like, 'Really? Alright, let's go...'

Mariah came into Quad studios and sang the record over. Amazing. I came up with a completely new track, nothing like the original, a ten minute Def Mix. Everybody was blown away. Nobody had heard Mariah Carey like that before. She came in the studio, this skinny young pop girl, now we heard the diva.

I'd never worked with a singer of that calibre before. I'd worked with Robert Owens and Byron Stingily, but not someone who was becoming one of the biggest pop stars in the world. This was not someone coming to make a record in my bedroom or sing in my bathroom. It was another level. It was one of my favourite remixes, but hard to come by in America. Again, the label thought it was too housey. The UK put it out commercially but America wouldn't release it because they didn't want Mariah to be known as a dance artist, which was a huge shame because with the vocals re-sung and so different I'd negotiated royalties on that remix.

David's first solo album project was written and recorded in 1994 in Jamaica by an ensemble he formed called The Bad Yard Club, with producers Sly Dunbar (of Sly and Robbie) and Handel Tucker, keyboard players Eric Kupper and Peter Daou, vocalists CeCe Rogers, Donna Giles and a young Anastacia...and dancehall rappers Delta, Papa San, Stanryck and Natural E. Then in 1995 much closer to home, David hooked up with Andy Swallow's Public Demand label to remix Robbie Craig's *Special*.

Most of The Bad Yard Club album was recorded and written in Kingston, Jamaica, and I spent an amazing two weeks there working with Sly on it. Again, it was the remix of the single *The Project* that became popular. Another big one that year was *Caught In The Middle* for Juliet

THE ARTIST IS

THINKING,

HOW DARE

HE FUCK

MY SHIT UP

LIKE THAT?

(left) David Morales
(below) That Mariah Carey remix...
(bottom) The Paradise Garage; photo by Steve Howlett.

Roberts, a great British singer. I produced a Def Mix radio edit and 12 inch mix which helped get that track to No 14 in the UK charts in the summer of '94.

Yes, Robbie Craig. I have very fond memories of working with the Public Demand guys, and in particular the producer Ricky Morrison. I did a similar drum pattern on that to *I'll Be Your Friend.*

For many, the soundtrack for the summer of 1995 was that remix of Jamiroquai's *Space Cowboy.*

It was major surgery. If you look at the original, it sounds nothing like the remix because it doesn't flow the way I got it flowing. Back then it wasn't the norm to flip an artist's record, 360, without telling them. Sure, the artist would throw a fit. 'Where's my fucking record, what have you done to my fucking record?'

Space Cowboy was a lot of work because the original isn't really a proper song. It was more like a jam session: Jay Kay kicking out some lyrics and the band vibing on their instruments.

So I had to take a lot of parts and make them feel like a song. The extended vocal stabs at the beginning of the Classic Club Mix were taken from Jay Kay's ad-libs that appear towards the end of the original radio mix. I edited all that in the sampler to create that intro.

I completely reconstructed both *Dream Lover* and *Space Cowboy*, but the Mariah track was easier because she came in to re-sing. With Jay Kay I had put his vocals in another time. I did *Cosmic Girl* too, but it was nothing compared to Space Cowboy...which is certainly one of the remixes I'm proudest of.

But I really understand as an artist if he hated it. You have to remember he's a creator, he's a painter...and somebody took his canvas and fucking threw paint all over it. Jamiroquai are a band and Jay Kay is THE man. Suddenly the record was all machine made, but nobody could do anything because that shit was banging. Jay Kay has respect for me for sure, because I made that boy a lot of money. And when he goes to perform that record, everybody knows it, hands down.

I try to talk to David about his Club Mix of Jaydee's *Plastic Dreams*, in 1997, and how he reworked the haunting original anthem from 1992, but I'm politely moved on.

It was alright, but it wasn't one of my game-changers, not an 'Oh my God, oh my God' moment. What else you got?

***Ain't No Mountain High* - Jocelyn Brown? David's face lights up again.**

Jocelyn came into re-sing the vocals for this, and to have Jocelyn in the studio with me at that point, well, she may as well have been Aretha Franklin, it meant that much to me. Because I didn't grow up with Aretha, I grew up with Jocelyn Brown. The first record I played of Jocelyn's as a teenage DJ was *I'm Caught Up With A One Night Love Affair.*

It was such a pleasure to finally work in the studio with Jocelyn on *Ain't No Mountain High*, with all its history dating back to Marvin Gaye in the '60s and it also being Diana Ross' first solo record. I also managed to get Vince Montana Jnr from MSFB and Salsoul Orchestra to come in and play strings. Wonderful.

And I was lucky to work with Aretha, the biggest name to my credit, the ultimate. You're talking about the greatest African-American female singer in our lifetime.

David fittingly ended the '90s with his own production, *Needin' You* — David Morales presents The Face, a huge hit for him.

Needin' You was the easiest record I ever made and it's made me the most money too. How about that? Sampling *Let Me Down Easy* by Rare Pleasure, it took me about three hours.

We shot the video all over Ibiza, including Pacha, Space and Pikes. I knew Tony Pike very well and I love that hotel. I was about to board a plane home at the airport one visit and I realised I'd left $14,000 in cash on the bed at my room in Pikes. I rang the hotel and sure enough the cleaner had found it and they had already put the money away safely for me. That sums up the family spirit that Pikes embodies.

The full vocal version of *Needin' You* came out a year later in 1999 because Danny D came to me with an idea involving Juliet Roberts, and it was great, because it extended the life of the record.

I've got a remix of that version that I've never put out that is absolutely crazy, so maybe I could do a 20-something anniversary re-release.

The pandemic saw David, like many DJs, saw David get into streaming, the merry-go-round of regular bookings and constant touring suddenly a thing of the past, but it could have been a lot worse for the Italian-based Morales.

In mid-February 2020 I was about to leave my house for the airport. Bags packed, car ordered, on my way to Ibiza for a few days, then

New York, and on to the Winter Music Conference in Miami. But they were already cancelling flights, so I changed my mind at the last second, and I thank God I did. I probably would have been stuck outside of Italy for months, because everything fell apart within a few days, and the airports in Italy closed down.

I saw the way streaming was going, that in the moment it would be the only avenue to have contact with my audience. First it was *Facebook* and *YouTube*, then it was *MixCloud*, and then Twitch, which I started to do exclusively. Every week my 'Sunday Mass', all kinds of music from ballads from the '60s to reggae to R&B to house, gospel house to classic to new stuff. Then I started a 'Diridim' show, the name of my label.

Upfront music, more about the 'boom, boom, boom'. Guest-wise, I tapped into new guys already on Twitch...a 14-year-old kid from New Jersey called Just The DJ, who is just amazing. And a fantastic guy from Wales called Sam Tweaks, who only plays 45s. So many gigs got cancelled: thank God for my Twitch channel. I built a new streaming room, like a mini Boiler Room set-up for ten people. Mirror balls, fog machine, moving heads...it's proper.

A new David Morales album, his fourth solo project, is signed to Nervous Records featuring collaborations with the likes of Mike Dunn and vocalist Michelle Herrera.

I think it's one of my best albums — if not THE best. I've also released more of an instrumental, jazz fusion, percussion kind of album called Parkside Avenue.

I still get loads of remix offers, but I'm very picky. I turn down more than I take, because there's so much rubbish out there. I might remix one if I like it, or approach an artist or label myself, but I'd rather spend time making my own music. They say I've done more than 500 remixes. There are some you forget and that fly under the radar. I'm not so sharp that I can remember all of them. It's just nice to know I had such an influence on the British market and people.

I'm discussing the romantic notion of sitting in your car, parked up by the M25, waiting for instructions and directions to that night's rave with Hardsoul's Rogier Van Bueren.

I was crying out for a radio station like *Centreforce* in 1989 telling me where all the raves were. Man, I was crying out for some raves even! That's just insane, I love that shit.

Growing up in the Netherlands in the late-'80s wasn't the best place for a would-be house music producer and future connoisseur and mentor of the genre.

Now, more than 30 years later, Rogier — aka DJ Roog — is a leading tutor at *The School Of House* in Amsterdam, an official educational programme.

In between, Rogier and his brother Greg created soulful vocal house anthem *Back Together*.

When I was a teenager most people into dance music in Holland liked harder house, trance or techno. There just wasn't a soul or disco tradition. I was always trying to incorporate more soulful sounds into my DJ sets.

I'm the older brother by four years. Our dad and his brother were musicians, classical pianists, always making music and big jazz heads, so I was brought up on Miles Davis, and Greg and I both played piano to a high standard when we were younger.

I had a mobile drive-in set-up and I would play disco, funk, rap...a bit of everything.

We started buying synthesisers. We had heard house music but we didn't know how to play it or make it.

In the late-'80s I was going into my local record store hearing records like Inner City's *Big Fun*, and I was like, 'I love this. Electronic, yet soulful at the same time.'

The first time I heard a DJ play house the whole night was at a club called The Roxy, which was the birthplace of house music in Amsterdam, really. I always describe it like that scene out of *The Blues Brothers*. The venue is like an old church. I saw the lights and I was like damn, you can play house music all night? These guys play four to the floor all night?

When I tell my students this, they look at me thinking, what is this guy talking about? They have no idea how revolutionary this was at the time.

I tell them I had no clue how to get that house sound, because we had no internet, so I couldn't Google it, and all these young people look at me and say, 'No internet?!' I could have gone to the library but there wasn't a book yet about how to make house music.

It took me and my brother years to find out that the drum sound we were trying to make on a Kawai drum computer ame from a Roland 909, and that it was actually impossible to get that sound from any other machine.

These days you can download all the settings of a Roland 909 and 808 instantly.

I still hadn't been able to afford a 909, so we were sampling drums and we were working with lots of musicians. I had always played in bands. So I was half in the live world, and the other half a DJ. Even the bands were always soulful, nowhere near as good, but trying to do stuff like Incognito.

It took Greg and I six years to make our first record, and me personally about ten years to establish myself with the sound that I wanted to play as a DJ.

Our first Hardsoul remix was a Lakeisha Berri track called *Like This And That* and it ended up on a speed garage compilation in the UK. When the label in Amsterdam, Outland Records, told us we said, 'What are you talking about?'

Then I realised it was all linked to my DJ sets. To satisfy the Dutch crowd's thirst for a faster and harder sound, I had been speeding up dub mixes of US soulful house records in my sets to around 126/127 BPM because those crowds were into at least 130 and above.

Then I began trying to make music in that kind of range, like a hybrid with more energy than the American stuff from New York.

So based on the success of the Lakeisha Berri mix, I thought let's find out more about speed garage, and so I flew to London and found myself in Blackmarket Records in Soho. They had all these speed garage white label vinyls and I was like, damn I love this. It was still four to the floor and it all worked perfectly for my set because it was energetic and still had the soulful vocals. So I said to them, 'Give me all you've got.'

I started doing monthly trips to London and I became, probably, the first speed garage DJ in Holland.

Then I got invited to play at The Roxy. It was literally a dream come true.

On a Sunday night, they had a combined speed garage/house night. An article in a Dutch magazine that came out about speed garage being the new hip thing, mentioned me. Everybody was like, let's book this guy. But I had been DJing ten years so I was already very experienced and knew what I was doing.

So, that was my big break, by accident.

And, of course, I still want to make and play soulful house, so a couple of years later when speed garage went into 2-step, I said, 'Oh no, this is not my thing, I need my four to the floor.'

So we went back to playing and trying to make more classic house sounds because we loved Masters At Work.

We were lucky to have some support from Brian Tappert and Marc Pomeroy from Soulfuric Records in the US. We sent them some demos in the late-'90s and they loved the tracks and started to release them.

I put all the money I made from DJing and selling records back into making more records. We were able to hire the best musicians from Amsterdam, all these top cats from concert orchestra bands, because back in the early-2000s, when you could still sell vinyl, there were big enough budgets to be able to use these guys. Nowadays I can't afford to have all these musicians so it's just me in my studio.

Back in the day we programmed a beat, and then asked the guys to jam and see what sounded best. We would guide them towards what we wanted. We had a really small studio so we could only have a keyboard player and a bass player at most in the early days. Just to get the human interaction going was amazing, and then we'd keep the best parts. And it was hiring all these great musicians that meant we were able to create the backing music for *Back Together*.

But while we have wonderful musicians in Holland...we don't have a lot of great singers.

Fortunately, I had already met Ron Carroll when he DJd at The Roxy in 1999. I was blown away by what he did behind the decks. He picked up the mic a few times and sang, just amazing because I hadn't seen that before. Wow, a guy who can play and can sing. I knew I needed to do something with Ron. He didn't really have much music out so I was like, 'Dude, we need to make a record.'

We stayed in contact and then I sent Ron the music to *Back Together*. He loved it so we would chat on the phone and he would sing some ideas down the line. Nowadays we can do it on a video call, but then you could still jam vocally over the phone and steer people in the direction you wanted.

A few times our publisher has sent us vocals and songs to potentially place over music we've already made, but it's never ever worked too well, because I always have a certain vision of how it should be. And it was the same thing with Ron Carroll. When he sent us *Back Together* it wasn't a surprise, because I knew the idea that we had been working on.

We loved it, but at the time we all said that the track was not great for the dancefloor, because it was too slow. It was 122 BPM, it had a verse, a chorus, a verse, a chorus and a bridge. We thought it was just too musical for the dancefloor.

Normally we would write a song and then break it down and remix it to make it more dancefloor-friendly. But this time I emailed it as it was to Brain Tappert. Now we had internet. It was the end of February 2003.

Soulfuric had already given us our own sub-label, Hardsoul Pressings, which was amazing, so I said to Brian, 'We've got this track, but we're not sure.'

Within a few minutes of receiving the record, Brian called me and said, 'I love this. Don't change anything. We're going to put it out like this.'

At the end of March, we were at the Winter Music Conference in Miami. Back then there weren't so many parties at WMC. The Soulfuric one was always a hot ticket, though. Every big American DJ was there.

The track was still a demo so Brian played it from a CDR.

At the start when the strings came in the whole club just erupted, but nobody had ever heard it before.

Then I saw Tony Humphries and Louie Vega running to the booth, both asking, 'What the fuck is this?

Brian pointed at me and Greg, and then Tony and Louie rushed over to us and I'm like, 'Yeah, it's our track but it's really not finished yet.'

It was insane...our heroes were Masters At Work. I will never forget that moment. Crazy.

And it was one of those rare times when a DJ plays a track that nobody knows but the crowd goes nuts. I saw it also when I was in the room with ATFC (Aydin Hasirci) when Masters At Work played *Bad Habit.* I was standing next to Aydin and he started crying. It was such a lovely sight, and I could totally relate to it. When your heroes play your track that's the most gratification you can get.

After that *Back Together* was an instant club hit.

*****

We haven't worked as Hardsoul since 2015. I'm now working on my own as Roog, but always in the soulful style. We stopped Hardsoul because after 20 years it was at the height of the big EDM boom here in Holland so it just sucked up everything else. We did an album at the time, and it did nothing, so we were like, whatever.

We were putting so much time and effort into making songs and people weren't just interested, so my brother started doing other stuff and I have always been a DJ so I can always work. We may revisit Hardsoul at some point.

And the EDM was just horrendous. I mean, I can appreciate a lot of things, but it was just horrible. To listen to it is just painful for the ears.

DJs like Tiesto make a lot of money playing trance and EDM and good luck to them. I wish soulful house got that big and we were invited to Vegas for $100,000 a gig, but we're not.

I'm working a lot with Low Steppa now. We fit together because his sound is taken back from the '90s, a speed garagey style that's so cool, that's come back around, that we make now with a little bit more house. I also put my music out on his label because it seems like a natural fit. We have the big bass sound in there, and it just works.

Greg and I also signed a deal with a Ultra Motor in Holland, who own back catalogue, with a view to releasing new mixes.

I have a side project called House Quake, which is pretty big here in Holland. We do all the big festivals. It's a big room sound but it's never ever going to be EDM. I like DJing and reaching people with my music and soulful house is such a niche thing here, it's not something you can do full-time and make decent money. So with all these other projects, I can finance the making of the music I love.

And there's also Roog's work with The School Of House to keep him busy.

The guy that founded ID&T (the huge festivals Mysterylands, Sensation, etc) sold it to SFX for 100m Euros, or something like that.. Then he said, 'I need to give something back to the community,' so he put some money into the educational system and founded *The School Of House.*

He called the top guys from trance, techno and house (that's me...) and we try and give our knowledge to the younger generation.

*****

I can never quite believe how well *Back Together* has done because for me it's still a demo. And even how big it became, it was never going to be a Top 40 hit, it was always an underground track. We have since tried and tried to make a more stripped-down version, but I couldn't change it because the vocal is glued to that arrangement. I tried for a year to remix it, but I came up with nothing. But it's so cool that so many people have done mixes of it. I mean, Frankie Knuckles did a mix. Damn it, that's insane.

DJ Roog

'A sad banger,' is how Greg Dowling perfectly describes one of house music's most enduring anthems.

Those melancholy lyrics for *The Cure & The Cause* were written by singer-songwriter Tracey K when she started working with Greg and his partner Shane Johnson on their debut album project in 2006.

When a distributor in Canada offered to send the track to a producer friend in New York, the trio soon forgot about it when they heard nothing back. But Dennis Ferrer had contracted Lyme Disease, unable to work for the best part of the year. When he did return to the studio, the Fish Go Deep track he'd received was the first thing he worked on. When Ferrer sent back the track underpinned with that irresistible rolling baseline the trio couldn't believe their ears.

When the mix came back to us we were like, 'What the fuck?' We hadn't heard anything like that. Dennis' mix was not representative of what we were making or playing. Our DJ style is pretty deep; we wouldn't have been playing any big bangers like that.

The Cure And The Cause is a great song, but, actually, like a lot of house anthems, it's a sad song. I guess there's no better place to be when your heart is broken than the dancefloor.

We played it at Fast Eddies in Cork, the first time it would have been heard in a club, and the reaction was phenomenal. Then the pirates in London started hammering it, and that's when it really took off.

We put it out on Go Deep Records, our label, and we were pressing vinyl at our distributor Chad's plant in Canada for his label Ultrasound. When the track caught the attention of Simon Dunmore at Defected Records we were asked to go in for a meeting.

I remember Simon saying to us, 'You do know this is a classic?' And we just looked at him, kinda going, 'What?' And he said, 'You know, this is forever...this will be played forever.'

We knew it was doing well, but we weren't thinking that big, but Simon said, 'no, no...this will go on and on and it will be one of the house classics,' and he was right, so it turns out.

When Simon signed it for Defected, he had to stop us pressing any more vinyl and also get to the bottom of all the bootlegs that were appearing in the record shops. I've always thought if someone is bootlegging your record, that's a good sign.

The success of the track was a shock, and it changed everything for us.

Greg admits that people are surprised when they find out Fish Go Deep are from Ireland. Even the name Fish Go Deep is a curious one but it made perfect sense to Greg and his partner Shane Johnson, both veteran Irish club promoter/DJs.

We had a record store for a while in a food market in the centre of Cork. It was next to the fish section so we decided to call it Fish Records. We were getting into production and the idea was that we'd put out all types of music. Fish Go Tech, Fish Go House, Fish Go Jazz, etc.

We met Tracey K, a very accomplished singer-songwriter from Kerry, through friends at an after-party. Shane and I were writing an album idea, and we started sending stuff to Tracey. Bit by bit it started coming together. We all clicked. Tracey was living in Dublin at the time and started coming back with her own songs. *The Cure & The Cause* was one of those.

Greg and Shane had no particular designs on being producers when they started promoting small events in Cork in the mid-to-late-'80s.

The very reason I got into the whole club business was to be a DJ, because back then you were just that....a DJ. Someone who presented other people's music. Now the DJ is meant to fuck about with the music too.

We didn't grow up thinking we wanted to be DJs because DJs were over there in the corner somewhere...probably where we should have been, rather than standing up in the middle of the club with our hands in the air.

In the early days, around 1986, '87 I started putting on parties locally, playing a bit of everything. Indie, some hip-hop, the odd early house record. There was no particular music policy at the time, it was all over the shop.

Back then we were just happy to get two records together sounding okay, and hopefully get some people to come to the club.

The manager of a bigger venue in town, Sir Henry's, asked me to do a Thursday night. Shane joined me and we called it *Sweat*. It was that old concept of doing a weekly night to the same crowd each week. We eventually moved it to a Saturday, but it took ages for the Saturday to take off, because everybody liked the Thursday.

We never really had guests, but one week we had Mike Pickering come over from Manchester. The whole Hacienda thing and the house music club culture was kicking off and Mike had all these records we had never heard of.

*****

Pre-'88, in my 20s, I had loads of different jobs. Working in bars, living in different countries. I was a bit lost, I'd say, but always in the back of my mind was music.

I played the guitar when I was younger and I worked as a tape operator in a studio for a bit. I was always on the edge of music, but I didn't really know enough to make anything.

We only got into producing in the mid-'90s when we thought it was the natural progression from being a DJ. *Sweat* ran at Sir Henry's for 13 years, so we had a lot of time on our hands during the day and week. From 1988, that's all we did: putting on parties, DJing and later production.

We'd have guests at *Sweat* once every six to eight weeks. People like Kerri Chandler, Laurent Garnier, Cajmere. But the guest was just something to enhance the night, to give it a shot in the arm. It wasn't the mainstay of the night. Between the two rooms, Sir Henry's was about a thousand capacity. Down the back Stevie G was playing hip-hop, which he did really well. His room had a whole crowd that never came to the house room and vice versa. It helped make the night very strong, with two different successful identities.

Record stores were so important back then. You either had to go back to the club where you heard the record the next week, and try and find out what it was called, or try and sing it to the guy in your local record store. It was vital in those days to try and find the right music, but now it's just all there in front of you.

I'd regularly head over to Manchester to visit Spin Inn Records. Russ there would be getting tunes together for the guys at the Hacienda, and he'd sort out the same bag of records for me, so I was getting such fresh incredible music. Every week another box of records, all future anthems.

When we opened our own shop later we were selling American twelves and whistles and stuff for the ravers, in this really small shop in the fish market for about two or three years. Then we moved to an actual shop, and we were there until about 2000. There were so many records that we weren't into, which we probably could have sold 400 copies of. We only really sold the stuff we liked. It was your classic Nick Hornby record shop. I've got an amazing house music record collection, though. Lots of the really obscure records, that we only got two or three of, and obviously kept one each for ourselves instead of selling.

Without that devastating Dennis Ferrer mix, maybe *The Cure & The Cause* would have been one of those obscure records.

We were so lucky that Dennis worked on that remix.

You could feel it at our gigs after that. You could see people standing there thinking, when are they going to play the Dennis Ferrer mix? Then we'd play the mix, and they'd all fuck off.

Dennis' mix and the stripped-down versions all work well. There's a mellow mix from the album that we play and people love it. There's also a Charles Webster mix, which is strange and electronic but still sounds amazing. And there's an acoustic version, with just some strings, which I play at the end of the night sometimes.

The song certainly seems to have a magical quality: one of those tracks, no matter what you do to it, which way you mix it, it remains the same in some ways. It's very unusual like that. Tracey always says, if you write a really good song or make a really good track then it belongs to the people. It's their song and each person has a different reason why it's their song.

I can see from royalty statements that it's still played on radio stations all over the world so it's nice to see a track still out there working for you. And in Ireland we have something called artist exemption, where you're allowed to earn up to so many thousands Euros on artistic work without paying any tax on any music you make, so it actually encourages people to try and make a living artistically.

So what's next for Fish Go Deep?

Tracey has pulled back from the music thing more recently. But as Fish Go Deep, Shane and I continue to work together. We still have good relations with Simon and Defected and still send them stuff, but we also go down the Bandcamp route as well to press vinyl to take out the risk. There's no reason why you can't do everything on your own now, unless you have a huge anthem on your hands like *The Cure And The Cause* and need the weight of a bigger label.

Up until the lockdowns, Shane and I were still DJing in Cork, doing monthly residences, but we pulled away from promoting ourselves because we felt like we'd done that. To book a decent guest these days you have to go really big. Huge fee, huge door price and huge production. I'm hoping Covid causes a re-set where it goes back to being about a dark room, a good PA, great music and just getting on with it.

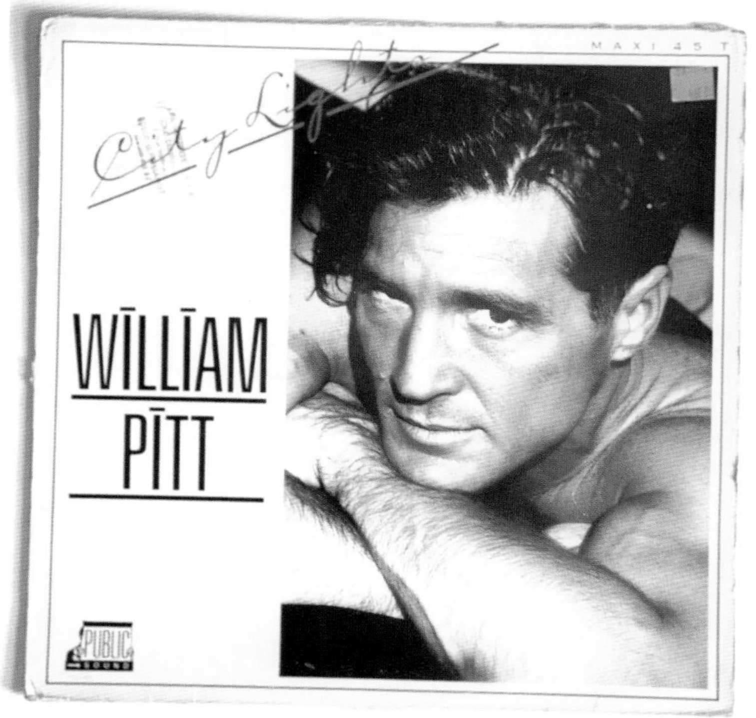

William Pitt and *City Lights* was somebody else's dream, not mine,' insists the other William...the real William...William Frederick Pate.

I managed to contact the enigmatic American singer-songwriter-rhythm guitarist in Geneva, via the unlikely source of a community project he had supported in Yorkshire.

'The three years I spent playing the role of William Pitt were less than fulfilling and certainly not enriching.'

Which is a huge shame, as those are just two ways to describe such an enduring so-called 'Balearic' anthem.

It was even more disappointing to discover that after, 'bopping around Europe on Boeings ceaselessly the only place I would have loved to go was the UK. No one invited me, no invitation from Ibiza either.'

William explained he has been reluctant to talk about 'long-forgotten events', but like all the amazing records and mixes featured here, I was intrigued to discover the story behind the music.

So I was delighted that William agreed to share his thoughts.

MT: How was your childhood in Seattle and what were your early musical influences?

WP: Until I had my first car, an old MGA, Seattle could have been on another planet. Some 15 miles away, it was unnecessary to me. Nature was my favourite world. Sitting alone high up on a branch of 'my' maple tree, overlooking Puget Sound, I was free and at peace with the world.

My awakening to humanly-elaborated sound began at home. My mother had been a Hollywood starlet, an opera singer and a very talented pianist before falling prey to the gallantry and good looks of my father, a staff reporter at the *Los Angeles Times*.

Music, especially classical music, was a major part of the sound environment of our home, except when there was a heavyweight boxing match on TV. The variety shows on TV also exposed me to the crooner force of the day.

Then came Elvis Presley.

Then came my Sears & Roebuck Harmony six-string. And one day, I traded my magic glowing-in-the-dark ring for an even more magical homemade crystal radio.

Then on they came, so many wonderful musicians, singers and songs that it's impossible to enumerate them here.

Then came The Beatles!

MT: What took you to Paris?

WP: A true flower child and largely unconscious of my interactions with worldly life, I very rarely took decisions but rather let myself be swept along by the whims and waves of destiny.

Kendall Kardt, a great songwriter and friend of mine, called L.A. the 'City of Lost Angels' and justly so. They came from everywhere, all those beautiful young people, hoping their wings would carry them into the skies of fame and fortune. I was one of them, although my mode of life and priority was always about having fun.

After six years of fluttering above Sunset Boulevard in a fantasy land traffic flow with the others, living countless, crazy and dangerous adventures until my wings were singed, it was time to fly away, with the few feathers remaining. It's amazing what a human body can survive!

As improbable as it was, I got myself engaged by a travel agency in Beverly Hills as the vegetarian cook onboard a mythical racing sloop named Barbara, anchored in Curaçao, and soon after left Hollywood behind me like the faithless mistress she was.

This was the beginning of many Caribbean adventures, and following the shipwreck of the West Indies sloop I was on in Puerto Rico, I found myself miraculously singing at the Yacht Club of St. Barth's. There was an older French lady with sparkling eyes who came to listen often. At the end of the evening, she always offered me a bottle of champagne. She said that I had to go to Paris where I would be immediately successful as a singer and offered me a one way ticket.

She was there, waiting for me at Charles DeGaulle International Airport on the 13th of October, 1979.

MT: How did you get involved with the band French Kiss?

WP: After two weeks of dedicated full-time 'joie de vivre' celebrating (champagne with breakfast, lunch and dinner, and, and, and...) in Paris then Cannes, then back to Paris, Madame 'Sparkling Eyes' cracked, and while I was still sleeping in my room, paid the hotel bill, took a taxi to the airport and got on a plane back to St Barth's.

Call it luck, destiny or whatever you like, one evening I came upon what seemed a sympathetic bar and met Jacques Humbert, who adopted me, took me to his flat, put a guitar in my hands, listened to me sing a few of my songs and declared that we were going to make a band.

It took a few years before French Kiss was really a group and could do gigs, make some money. In the meantime, I busked in the Metro without great success and gave English lessons sometimes. I worked in a couple of restaurants as a waiter (even onboard the Orient Express for a while!) but my heart wasn't in it, and as long as Jacques and I had something to eat and some wine, well, the important thing was the music. In a seaside resort on the west coast of France, Saint Palais sur Mer, we shared a little beach house, had our own cook and played every night in a bar-restaurant which soon after our arrival was joyfully jam-packed. This was a good time in life for all of us - on the beach every day then on stage again - just for the fun. Simply glorious.

Back in the eternal traffic jam of Paris, the group faded away like our suntans.

A friend of mine said, "Why don't you become a model? It should be an easy job and well-paid." I laughed heartily at the idea but the following day presented myself to the biggest model agency in Paris. Nearly immediately, everything changed!

I had by then completely forgotten the 'demo', as the producer called it, of *City Lights* my lead guitar player had convinced me to sing and talk on some months previous. I was encouraged to sign a contract, the contents of which I couldn't read, due to my very rudimentary French. There was a promise (between friends, of course) that it wouldn't be binding if I was ever unhappy with the evolution of future events.

MT: How was your experience as a model?

WP: 'At forty, it is a bit late to begin a career in modelling,' said the co-director of Paris Planning, the biggest model agency in the city.

For my first casting, I was intimidated by the number of younger men waiting to meet the photographer. He asked me to put on a coat waiting on a chair. I did so, then with a smile, he said, 'Hello, Dartagnan!'

Next stop, the Castillo country of Spain, in the middle of the desert. For the sake of billboards all over Germany declaring the wonders of Dinkelacker Beer, we (being myself, an English Shakespearean actor and a top English model) were the Three Musketeers.

Soon after, I posed for famous fashion photographer Klaus Wickrath for the Spring Men's Catalogue of Gianni Versace.

After that, work came easily and often - as long as I stayed in Paris. Later, when I went to New York by demand of Manner Models, I discovered the rude reality of not being a professional model. Until then I had been hired for my physical characteristics and I simply followed the instructions of the photographer. In New York, however, I discovered the command of 'do your thing.'

No one had ever shown me how to 'do my thing', which was to take a series of poses in a rhythmic manner, changing facial expressions, and knowing where and how to put my hands, etc.

Being an unprepared photo model in New York brought me just enough money to stay alive and relatively well while I was there. In any case, during several years of my life, I was 'used' for a few major publicity campaigns, tons of catalogues and at least thirty TV commercials, all over Europe.

My agency in Paris called to tell me that I had to go to Milano the following weekend for the big Versace Men's Fashion Show.

'No way, I've never done a fashion show and remember what the artistic directrice of Balmain called me — a midget — no way!'

'You have to, it was Gianni himself that called.'

Walking down the runway, unbalanced in shoes way too big for me so stuffed with wadded paper, I knew this was not going to be one of the greatest moments of my life. Before I was able to turn around at the end of the runway, I heard Mr Versace and his assistant laughing loudly.

'He doesn't know how to walk!'

Followed by a dry 'Ciao' from Mr Versace himself.

The message was more than clear. Humiliated, I left. I walked (yeah, I knew how to walk!) to the Magenta Bar, where all the models usually went. It was empty of course. I drank a few pints of Guinness, went back to my hotel room and stayed there until Monday morning.

MT: What are your fondest memories of the 1980s?

WP: I love the sun, the sea, the wind.

'Fond' is a difficult word for me in the context of this interview. Fondness is a sentiment I would feel looking into the eyes of a child, petting my dog or my cat or something like that.

I love the sun, the sea, the wind and automatically the word 'holiday' or 'vacation' flies into the sky of my thoughts like a careening seagull.

I loved my vacations in Kiaton, Greece and in the Greek islands, especially Amorgos. I loved my illegal extended stay in Bali and Jakarta. I loved my vacation in a little stone house with no electricity and a water well in Ibiza (before *City Lights*). I loved my first vacation in Corsica.

Wondrous is the memory of discovering gold at the Departures bar of Linate International Airport in Milano. There she was, in a designer trench coat, with a panini in one hand and a draft beer in the other. It was 8 o'clock in the morning and snowing outside, and I was in love. She was Béatrice, my future life partner, wife, goddess, lover, guru and best friend.

If Versace hadn't laughed me off the stage the preceding Saturday I would have stayed in Milano to do some castings, maybe land a big deal. Bless you, destiny.

MT: What do you remember of the actual recording of *City Lights*?

WP: Allow me to preface this with an anecdote...

'We've found a good name for you.'

'But I have a good name...my name,' I said somewhat perplexed.

'Like it or not, P-A-T-E will be pronounced in only two ways in the French-speaking world: pâte or pâté, and in both cases, we're talking about something to eat, not something to listen to.'

The costume and makeup department had decided I was no longer ME but had suddenly become an actor in a play. And thus began a fictional life that lasted for three years.

As for the recording of *City Lights*...I remember very little. The studio was small by comparison to what I was used to. They were using my favourite microphone, the famous Neumann U-47, so for that, I was happy. The work of getting the spoken part just right was a bit long but interesting, technically speaking.

MT: Whose idea was it to talk as well as sing on the record?

WP: The song had been conceived and constructed as such and I think that's what sold the 'demo' to the eventual record label. It took me many years to formulate a positive interpretation of the lyrics, but once I put them in the scenario of someone foundering in a sea of borderline autism, I was happy to have been the instrument for a sort of encouragement to 'get out'.

MT: How surprised were you when it became a hit across Europe?

WP: Completely surprised. Nobody around me, myself included thought the recording would go anywhere at all, much less across Europe.

MT: Were you aware that City *Lights* was/is a 'Balearic anthem' in and around the eclectic club scene in Ibiza from the mid-to-late-'80s onwards...or of its popularity in the UK?

WP: No, I was not aware of *City Lights* having any particular popularity in Ibiza, or in the UK. Considerably later, DJ Alfredo from Ibiza contacted me via *LinkedIn* and we communicated for a while. I did notice, with great astonishment, that on one English Top 100 chart, *City Lights* was at 50.

When *City Lights* hit No 1 in Spain I was invited to Madrid for some promotion work. The three days spent there with the promotion people of Zafiro Records was just delightful. They took care of me, and of Beatrice, with real kindness and respect, and that was unique in my experience of *City Lights* promotion.

After three years I said, 'Stop! I want off,' but it cost me the vacation of an incompetent lawyer and all the money I would have made in mechanical rights - forever.

MT: Despite an 'unfulfilling experience' in the role of William Pitt you seem to have found spiritual enlightenment in the face of that adversity. What, with hindsight, if at all, can you take as a positive from the whole William Pitt experience?

WP: I have been very blessed in this life to 'taste the tastes...' as Donovan said in one of his wonderful and luminous songs.

To experience earthly pleasures unto satiety, and then, satisfied by the acquisition of one's desires, retire peacefully from futile pursuits, one can finally concentrate on the work of self-realisation.

I am currently enjoying what is referred to in Hindu tradition as Vanaprastha - the period of one's life when one retires, usually to the forest, in order to realise the otherwise hidden dimensions of one's self.

I have discovered I have much work to do purifying negative tendencies, thought patterns and knots and chains, be it from past lives or this one, that prevents one from being truly and entirely free.

With each day, I abandon more and more the notion that I (the ego, William) am the one doing things, thus allowing God (Source, Essence, Brahman, Allah, Ishvara etc.) to work through this body and mind with greater efficiency and harmony.

And Beatrice and I are sharing this experience, the long-awaited time of my life to look upon life as happening within.

MT: What endears you most to Switzerland and Geneva?

WP: Soon after the dissolution of the William Pitt enterprise, of which I was a sales representative, Beatrice and I fled, with two bags each, to New York. We spent a frozen winter there followed by a carefree springtime in San Francisco, then our hearts called us back to Europe. Pages of scribbled and sketched life flew off into the wind until one day we fled France once again - this time from the lovely city of Fontainebleau which was becoming less lovely - and arrived in Beatrice's hometown, Geneva.

Beleaguered as we were, Geneva took us in, took care of us and then appreciated us for what we both were and had to offer. Thus began a new and very different life.

Switzerland is a physically beautiful land, its people cultivated, healthy and courteous in general, its government wise most of the time. A place of peace talks and direct democracy, it's a good place to live, an island in a stormy sea.

MT: How did you get involved in Estelle Brown's Incredible Edible community project in Yorkshire, UK?

WP: The news first arrived as an article in French ELLE magazine. Something wonderful was happening, not only in Yorkshire but in cities of France as well. Veggies growing in the most unexpected places — all over town! People taking a big step out of the industrial food chain. Hallelujah.

I had just finished writing a song called Plant A Seed and nothing seemed more appropriate than sending a rough unplugged version to Estelle, as a thumbs-up. She liked it and made a lovely video clip to go along with it and here we are.

MT: You seem to have been prolific with the songs you have posted on your mx3.ch page over the last two decades?

WP: In fact, the songs on my mx3.ch/justcallmewilliam page represent a selection of many, many comprising the work of my life. I began the creation of the oldest among them, *Open Your Eyes*, fifty years ago, seated on a rock with my acoustic guitar at Point Lobos, California.

I'm happy and satisfied to post my songs on this marvellous Swiss streaming platform, without seeking any financial reward. They are far from being professional productions, but it's my dream come true to be able to offer these little musical cartoons to whoever may wish to enjoy them, no strings attached, a simple offering of love.

William Frederick Pate

BACK FROM THE PAST...

There were rumblings on the airwaves across east London. A frequency very close to home had been sourced and behind the scenes discussions had taken place. Could it be true?

Jonny C: I can remember exactly where I was. Summer 2007. Sitting in my garden in Grays, a beautiful sunny day. My best friend Russell Newton called me and told me *Centreforce* was back on. Jimmy Low, who he knew, had started it up again on 88.4FM. I went indoors, tuned in my radio and there it was, blaring out old school, sounding like the old *Centreforce*. It was a 'wow' moment. Something I didn't think I'd ever hear again.

I had to get involved, so I called Russell back. A few minutes later he came back to me. 'Saturday. 10am for two hours.'

'Amazing.'

Russell picked me up on the morning. We were on the A13 and I had that, 'Yes, we're driving into London to the studio' feeling. Blue sky. The city coming into view. *Centreforce* blaring...

Then we pulled off at Barking and drove through an industrial estate to a large scaffolding yard, at the back of Barking and Dagenham market...and there it was, the studio. In a shipping container. Inside, just a table and a set of original Mark 1 Pioneer CDJ decks, the little silver ones with black jog wheels on them.

Ramsey: Jimmy told me he was thinking of bringing *Centreforce* back. That he'd run it past Andy. I had brought MC Creed into the mix because the 88.4 frequency was his. Our mate Micky put the original rig up. Jonny C got involved, it was a collective thing.

Jonny C: I played an old school set from '88 for that first show and it went down well. I met with Jimmy after and it was nice, because we got on well and we were both on the same page. I had something to offer because of my pirate radio background. I started doing a weekly show and brought in my own Mark II CDJs. Then I got more involved, updated some of the equipment and got it sounding a bit better. We had a huge 400 watt rig with a double stack, coming off Shooter's Hill in south London. By now I was getting more and more involved, also sorting out shows for Jimmy.

Steve ESP: There was a lot of excitement that *Centreforce* had come back on 88.4. When I heard Jonny C was involved, I asked if there was any chance of getting on. When he said yes I was like, 'Really?' It was hard to leave *Force*, because I loved it, and they were like family on there, but when I told the guys where I was going they understood because they knew *Centreforce* was 'bucket list' for me. My show was Sunday mid-mornings, playing old school, but not much hardcore, because even I don't want to listen to hardcore at that time on a Sunday.

Mete: In 2007, Wayne and I were asked to come on the new version of *Centreforce* in the container in Barking. We had listened to *Centreforce* first time around, even though we were mainly *Sunrise*. We were on Jimmy's mailing lists in the '90s and knew Andy Swallow through football connections so it was nice to be asked, especially being South London boys. The shows were going well, but one week Wayne got on the mic, and he can get a bit gobby. He put on *Hooligan 69* by The Ragga Twins and said, 'Because we're in bandit country, this one is for all the Millwall out there.' As the record started playing, the phone went crazy. The *Centreforce* massive were not happy.

'What did you do that for, Wayne?'

Then the management called. 'Put Wayne on the fucking phone.'

It was a case of, 'You better leave the studio...now.' Or words to that effect. And that was that, we had to leave *Centreforce*.'

Bubbler: My contact at *Flava FM*, Chris Low, called and said his cousin Jimmy had put *Centreforce* back on. Because I was up on the roofs all the time with *Chillin'* they wanted someone trusted to get involved. I was happy to help and also did a couple of shows on 88.4. Shooter's Hill is one of the highest points in London. However, the signal was so strong it meant *Centreforce*, with its history was always getting taken off, often daily.

Jonny C: The DTI, or Ofcom, as it now was, the newly formed Office Of Communications, kept cutting our power at Shooters Hill, so we wired into a pylon at the tower block, which they hate, and because they won't climb those, they came for us at the studio. We moved on to the latest technology. Instead of leaving a laptop in a sandwich bag on the roof of a tower block, I had small single-board computers, like a Raspberry Pi device, built into the transmitters.

Ramsey: I did a lot of shows from that shipping container from 7am, playing 89ers and a bit of garage. One day Jimmy turned up and thought the studio was on fire, but, fed up with going to the cafe every day, I'd brought in a little burner and was cooking burgers. We had some great times on 88.4, but we were getting hit quite a bit, so it began to fizzle out.

Steve ESP: We got raided loads on 88.4, which was unfortunate, but not surprising, because everyone seemed to know where that studio was.

Jonny C: When it got on top at the Barking site, around the Spring of 2008, we moved to a converted chicken shed on a farm in Harlow, where we could have it as loud as we wanted. We announced we were coming off FM, that we were becoming an internet radio station, and we distanced ourselves from the pirate side of things, and made sure there were no shout-outs referring to people being in their cars or any reference that would show the pirate side was still running,

Peter P: I'd been going to West Ham for years, so I knew Andy to say hello to. I got a call from a fella from the old Bank Of England ground in Loughton, which was now called The Academy, asking if I'd come down and have a look at the grounds. When I got there, it was Andy.

I heard *Centreforce* had started back up again as a pirate on 88.4 and managed to blag myself a show. When we moved to the farm and on to the internet we now had to say, 'Centreforceradio.com'

Jonny C: At the start of 2009, Jimmy decided to close down *Centreforce*. It was time to re-group. A few months later, a bailiff turned up at his house, collecting for an unpaid parking ticket. Jimmy got talking to the guy, who was also a DJ on *Time FM 107.5*, a legal community radio station in Romford, broadcasting across east London and Essex. Further talks led to a proposal for '*Centreforce* Sessions' to host weekends and weekday evenings at *Time FM*.

Bubbler: Jimmy Low was thinking of trying to go legal when the *Time FM* opportunity came up. I was concerned that a legal station needed to be more polished and we'd have to speak in posh voices. I could see when we visited the *Time FM* studio that the guys in the office had genuine fear in their faces, as if we were going to rob them. I don't think they'd met the likes of us before. But the response when we started was amazing, and I thought, do you know what, we can actually act like a pirate as part of a legal station. I went on to do 10pm-midnight on both Friday and Saturday, and brought in Rooney too.

Rooney: Coming off *Chillin'* on to *Centreforce* Sessions at *Time* was just so nice. We were still playing a lot of vinyl then, but always so worried on a pirate that we'd get raided and have our records confiscated. It happened at *Flava* one night 20 minutes after I left. The station got spun and they took all the DJ's tunes. But on *Time* it was such a great feeling being in the lift going up to the studio knowing it was all legit. Happy days.

Peter P: Suddenly we were legal and the authorities didn't like it. Andy was involved at the start, but it wasn't really for him so he took a back seat and Jimmy ran it. On *Time* we started on Friday nights, straight after veteran Essex radio presenter John Leech's Dance Decades show. We were on from Saturday and Sunday from midday and every midweek night from 8pm, branded throughout as *Centreforce* Sessions.

Kenny Ken: I knew Jimmy from back in the day and we became good friends. I'd played a few sets for *Centreforce* in the container in Barking and got to know Jonny C. I also played quite regularly for Jimmy on Time.

Slipmatt: I did once a month for Jonny C and Jimmy on *Time FM*. In the '90s I'd done a few mixes for *Radio 1* and some drum and bass shows for *Kiss*, so it was nice to be asked and to do some more radio.

Peter P: The whole of Romford was buzzing with it so we did a gig with Loose Ends at Branighans in Romford, and another one with Omar. My Soul Syndicate show was midday-3pm every Sunday, which was one of the most popular shows, and I had a Wednesday night 8pm-10pm house show too. I did that for about four years and I think that's where I really developed as a presenter. For most of us, we were in a professional studio for the first time. I'd done a lot of radio by then so I already had the bare bones of it, but I polished my act at *Time.*

Darrell Privett: It was great to be asked to do a show on *Time FM.* The set-up was good, but very different from a pirate, because of the news, weather and travel.

And now the tables had turned. *Centreforce* was getting a taste of its own medicine.

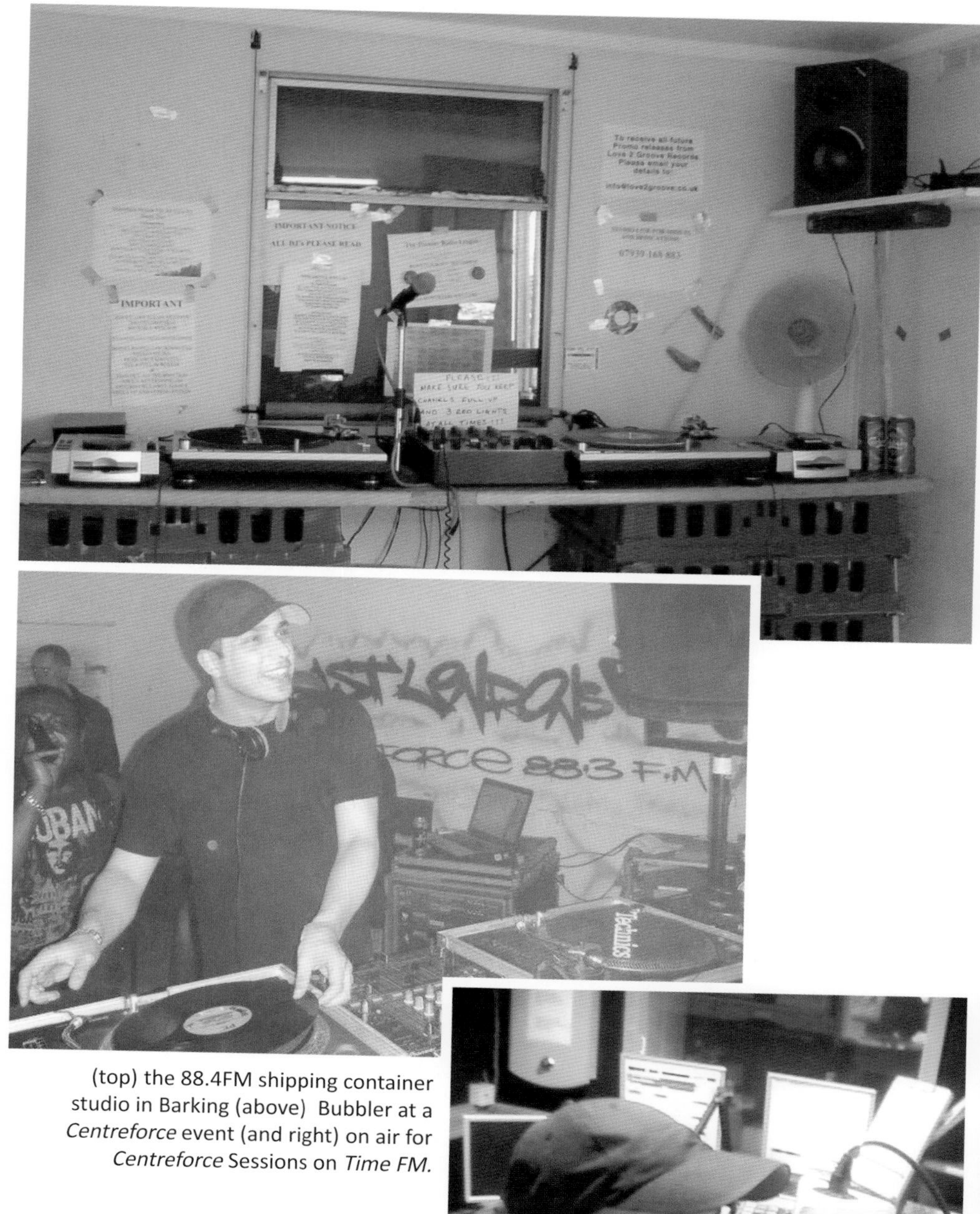

(top) the 88.4FM shipping container studio in Barking (above) Bubbler at a *Centreforce* event (and right) on air for *Centreforce* Sessions on *Time FM*.

Bubbler: We were getting so much trouble from other pirates. As a legal station, which had to stick within its stipulated boundaries in the Essex and the east London area. *Time FM* had around 100 watts of power, whereas pirates on the other side of town had 200, sometimes 250 watts. That meant they were inadvertently bleeding into our signal and loads of listeners were complaining about the sound quality. We tried to call those pirates, and put feelers out, asking them to move somewhere else on the frequency, but they were like, bollocks to you lot, and who could blame them...certainly not us.

Ironically, we decided to go back to our pirate ways to deal with the problem. But we couldn't just start ripping aerials down. We had to go through the proper channels, and run it past Ofcom. They were fine as long as one of their officers came with us and we booked a regulated security firm — that's when we contacted Britannia Security. The boss, himself, Danny Lines, came down with a dog.

We'd take one station off, and then another one would pop up right by the same frequency. There was a trick years ago to find exactly where a pirate was located. Take the aerial off your car and if the radio is still clear you know you're very near to the transmitter. Look for the nearest tower block and you could usually spot the 30 foot aerial, if you knew what you were looking for. But now we could use the technology that was available. It was very strange having Ofcom on our side for once as well.

Rooney: We tried to do our bit, sorting out pirate stations frogging over. Some madness going on, given our backgrounds. Bubbler driving around with a tracker and Danny arriving at a block with his dogs. Then Peter P would go up on the roof, mix up cement and fill in the offending rig. Guerrilla tactics, but it did clear up the problem. I think at that point, thanks to us, *Time* was more pirate than *Centreforce* is now.

Danny Lines: We were called The Concrete Crew. It was unreal. I got a letter of commendation from Ofcom. In the end we were so successful at taking pirates off, and providing the security when it was happening, because we were licensed operatives through the SIA, Ofcom employed us, and that massively helped us for the future.

Bubbler: I got chatting with Danny and we realised we knew the same people from Manor Park. He was in with the *Centreforce* boys back in the day so we stayed in touch, and he started to come up to the studio when I was on air. I let him do a few shout-outs and then he got on the mic more. Just before *Centreforce* parted company with *Time,* I could see it coming, so I left to go on *Kool FM*. That's when Danny and Rooney got together and developed their double act.

Rooney: Me and Danny Lines got on well and one day at his house I saw a photo on the side of a lovely kind man I recognised from when I went to a remote control car club as a kid in Plaistow. Turns out he was Danny's dad, who used to fix my cars, and then we remembered each other when we were aged 12/13. It was crazy. Danny started hosting on my show, and we've been together since then.

That period on *Time FM* showed how big *Centreforce* still was. The one thing that held it back was *Time* just being a local station and their reach just not being far enough. After *Time* finished I worked five years as a paramedic. I did a few guest shows on *Kool FM* with Bubbler, but I could never commit to a weekly show because of my shift patterns.

Master Pasha: When *Centreforce* was at *Time FM* Jimmy, who is my godfather, took me up there regularly so I knew all the DJs.

At one of Jimmy's house parties, Peter P asked me if I wanted to have a go on the CDJs. Pete taught me a few little things and I played for the next eight hours. Garage music had been in my life since I could remember so I knew the tunes. Artful Dodger and Majestic, people like that were there. I loved it.

I'd been around the studio when my dad was working with Craig David and Robbie Craig, and my mum was a singer, songwriter involved also. Up until that point I had never thought of music as a career for me. Then I became obsessed with the idea of being a DJ. But I didn't want to do the graft. I just wanted to be given everything. I didn't want to practise — I'd rather be on Playstation or knock around with my mates. I was given opportunities through our family connections. I warmed up at Garage Nation at The Scala when I was 15, and had a residency at Club 195 in Epping when I was 16 but I'd turn up and play a mix CD, usually pre-recorded for me by Artful Dodger. That's how arrogant and ignorant I was. I didn't give a fuck.

Peter P: I think *Centreforce* Sessions came to an end on *Time FM* because of jealously. The regular *Time* DJs had to up their game, and couldn't pre-record so much because we never did. When we left there were placards and protests in Romford town centre and *Time* got a lot of hate mail. A *Facebook* page called Save The Soul Syndicate popped up, with a thousand people on it, and there were other petitions.

Andy Swallow: Jimmy had two good attempts at bringing *Centreforce* back. Both times I went down with Keithy Mac and we did a show, but on each occasion it didn't feel right.

Jimmy wanted me to be one of the first DJs on *Time FM*. I went down to the studios in Romford with Keith and we some took some vinyl. We were taken into the studio and told all the rules. You can't touch this, and you've got to do this, and you've got to play the news feed on the hour and the travel every 20 minutes. We did the show and as we left I said, 'Nah, Keith, this is not for me…'

And Keith said, 'Fuck that…that's not *Centreforce* Radio.'

We didn't go back. It just wasn't our thing. I had learned in the music business by then that if you're not into it, don't do it. I realised I would only be involved with *Centreforce* again if it leaned towards the old school side of things.

Danny Swallow learning the ropes at a family party in the late-Noughties.

TIME OUT

Within weeks of buying The Opera House, the global economic crash of the late-Noughties ripped the rug from under Sam Supplier's feet.

Takings were up and down and people were picking and choosing what nights they went out. Then as things began to pick up, the Tottenham riots, which caused the whole of London to riot, started on our doorstep. We had to close for the next two months. It ruined the business and we were back to square one.

Then it hit me. What had happened to the kid who jumped on the mic at United Dance at 15? Making money had taken over. I needed to reinvent myself. I didn't want to be one of those older MCs, running round stage shouting, 'Oggy, oggy, oggy, oi, oi, oi'.

Around 2012,'13 there was a newer version of deep house coming out of a scene which by then was a mix of grime and electro, and it sounded quite garagey to me. By now I could mix okay, so I became Sam Supplier, the DJ. But the house music scene wasn't going to let in this old garage MC from years ago that easily. I had to work for it.

I was looking at the people above me, and they were playing all over the UK, and I was just playing around London. Then I realised they were all making music. I was still living on top of the club in a four-bedroomed flat. I bought whatever equipment I needed to make music, cleaned out one of the rooms, and just sat there, learning and learning and learning. I invited any of my mates round who made music and said, 'Use it as your studio, for whatever you want, just so I can pick up what you're doing,' They were like, great, sweet. My pal Tony was really helpful. I made some stuff and people were supporting it. One bootleg of an Adele record got plays on *Capital* and then *Radio 1*. I started to get booked all over the country, and it snowballed from there.

In 2011 Laurence Bagnall launched a new night with friends Yankee and Mark Radford and also became part of a new festival.

We did really well with Audio Rehab at the House & Terrace in Greenwich (now Studio 338), a night Mark still runs now.

With another partner I set up Sundown festival, with our first show in 2012. Ten years later we attract 25,000 people over one weekend at the start of September, including 15,000 campers. We're now partners with U-Live, who bought into Sundown four years ago.

I go to a lot of festivals, and people are blown away by them, but it's never far away from what Jay did with his World Dance events almost 30 years ago. It's great that young kids are still experiencing it today,

I'm also part of a management company called Maximum Boost with DJ Swan-E. I look after Low Steppa and DJ Zinc, who is an absolute legend. The festival once a year and the management company is perfect for me.

As her husband finished his DJ set at Pacha in Victoria in 2011, Sarah LP had a lightbulb moment.

Brandon Block was on next and I watched Brett struggle to get his last CD out of the deck because he'd a few too many drinks and I thought, if he can DJ in that state, I should have a go myself. So I told our friends that I was going to be a DJ. Nobody took me seriously. They were all like, yeah, alright Sarah. And that was the best thing for me, because if you tell me I can't do something, I'll do it twice.

I was a teenager working behind the bar at Futures in Deptford when I met Brett, who was the club's resident DJ. We've been together ever since and have four kids. Brett always DJd alongside running his scaffolding business and I became a sign-writer and launched my own printing company. I'd always loved house music, from going out, to places like Club UK in Wandsworth. I love the big clubs, I'm the type of person that wanders off on my own. Stars in Greenwich was another regular haunt.

And then I stopped going out, and calmed down a bit, but turning 30 kicked it all off for me again...and I was back out. One of the main clubs was the Bon Bonne. It's weird, I'd never heard of Martin at that time, but I was never really interested in who was playing.

I'd always messed around on the decks we had at home. Now, after my big announcement I practised with vinyl, CDs, we had it all. I was around all these male DJs but none of them would help, and I didn't know any female DJs I could ask. So I watched mixing tutorials on *YouTube*. Thankfully, a friend of ours, Dave Simpson, who promotes Shudderfunk parties, offered to help and taught me to mix. Then Dave booked me to play at his New Year's Eve party. I was in the toilet at Arcadia, a small venue in Bexley Heath, before I went on, thinking, why am I doing this to myself? I nearly didn't come out of that toilet, but I fronted it out and it went okay.

I didn't really push it, but our friend Paul Crane who runs Kinky Malinki booked me and that opened a lot of doors for me and I went on to do five summers in Ibiza and Marbella between 2012 and 2017. I actually played the last ever set at Pacha in Victoria around that time, which was ironic as it was where I had decided I was going to give it a go. My son was horrified and said if any of his mates saw me playing out he would deny I was his mother. My daughter came with me to Marbella one time, and couldn't believe my last gig of the night was at 3am and we had to stay up that late. My younger two have grown up with it so don't know any different.

Our surname is La'Porte, so I decided to call myself Sarah LP, to distance myself from my husband, who had always used our name. I play a lot deeper than him, so it worked out okay. After a while he decided to stop DJing because all his contacts were booking me instead and all his mates were taking the piss out of him and saying I was a better DJ.

I think it's much easier for guys to start DJing, but once you've learned how to mix and get your first bookings I think it's easier to progress as a female DJ because we're still a bit of a novelty. I'm sure I was getting booked as the token girl DJ, but I didn't mind —I just took those opportunities when they came.

I can't stand seeing female DJs abroad, playing topless, with a CD. I mean, I'm all for promoting female DJs. She can get her top off if she wants, but she should make sure she can mix, because there's plenty that can.

Ramsey: I'd done a few guest shows on *Time FM,* but me and Fen were getting really busy at that point. The usual bits in Tenerife, Ibiza and Majorca, but also in Amsterdam for the Dance Valley Festival and anywhere from Germany, Turkey and Switzerland to Miami and Japan.

Then we were offered a show on *Choice FM*, which had become the first legal black music radio station in the UK years earlier. It was an offer we couldn't refuse, a great slot on Choice, 9pm-11pm on Thursday nights. It was a brilliant four years there, before the boys in suits came in and the Global Group bought them out and the station was rebranded as Capital Xtra in 2013. We moved with them for six months and it was good for a while. Lovely studios overlooking Leicester Square. Beautiful leather settees, Chris Tarrant in the lift. Nice. But they gave us 3am-6am on a Sunday morning, when we were meant to be out earning money. They wouldn't let us record, so we left. They couldn't believe it.

A few years later Mi-Soul got in touch. Fen went up there to meet them and he came back with another 3am show. I said, 'Are you mad? We've not long left an air-conditioned FM station and they want us to go to south London on a DAB?' Back then nobody had DAB, people weren't listening to it yet. But Fen took the show, so he slipped in on his own.

I was getting busier with my own annual promotion in northern

(left) Steve Kite (above) Mete and daughter, Yasemin Alpsakarya with the Guinness World Records mixing certificate (below) Alex P at Party In The Park, 2020. © Sharpscape Photography.

Cyprus called The Mid Summer Ball, which I started in 2005, taking all the big garage boys over there, which is still going strong.

2012 was a huge year for Mete's Dance Aid charity, breaking a DJ Guinness World Record at the Ministry Of Sound and visiting Prime Minister David Cameron at 10 Downing Street.

And all because Chris Doulou is so hairy! Many of the kids and adults we taught to mix were part of the world record attempt Sunday all-dayer at the Ministry. Our second Dance Aid party there, it featured an amazing line-up including *Centreforce* DJs Alex P, Dolly Rockers, Beckett & Casey and Trevor Fung, plus Grooverider, Jumping Jack Frost, Brandon Block, Angie Brown, Dominic Spreadlove and, of course, Chris Doulou, who I also threw out of a plane for charity one time.

Our aim was to create a new record for the 'most DJs to consecutively mix one record each' ...basically, without a clang. We had women, men, the young, the old, disabled children and some DJ friends stepping up to join in, including Chris Doulou, and attempt this record in front of a crowd of 800 people. We made sure everybody knew what they were doing and for the novices, 'Right, get your beats together. One, two, three, four, count yourself in. You ready? You're in, put the channel up.' And we smashed it, a total of 149 people successfully completing their mixes, almost doubling the old record of 81.

The David Cameron visit was organised by the MPs on the One Life UK board, so we went with my friend, the actor Tamer Hassan, X factor star Alexandra Burke and the Daminola Taylor Trust.

We had a seven minute meeting with Cameron, and then he put his arm round us for some official photos, to make it look like the Conservatives had actually helped us with our projects, which they very much hadn't. It was a bit like me finding out some local kids have done some good things in Bermondsey and then me saying, invite them round to Mete's house, I'll give them some sweets and have my photo taken with them for the local rag.

I managed to smuggle my phone into Downing Street, which you're not supposed to have on your person, so I could take a couple of photos, because otherwise who is going to believe that we got invited there.

Another thing I dreamt up was The DJ Factory. We taught Danny Dyer to DJ and took him on a club tour. We had a huge event in Sunderland and flew Danny up there with Tamer, his co-star in *The Football Factory* and *The Business*, and Bianca Gascoigne.

I'm an ideas man, I have lots of them. Don't get me wrong, some of them are shit, but most of the time we make some money and move on.

Danny Clockwork: As I approached 'the big four O' in March 2012, I started to post some old Clockwork photos on *Facebook* and Twitter. The reaction was amazing, and we'd never had the luxury of seeing that before because when we were flying in the '90s those social media platforms weren't around.

Andy called me up and asked me one more time, and I said, 'I've got the feeling back, let's do it.' It made sense to do something around my 40th so we announced a party at McQueen's in Tabernacle Street, a venue we picked because it was a 600 capacity so there wasn't so much pressure. We did a classic line-up of Brandon, Alex, Andy, Tony Nicholls, Keith Mac and me, and it sold out in a day. We still weren't thinking long-term.

Andy Manston: Our next party wasn't until a year later, at The Fire & Lightbox. The two thousand tickets sold out in a couple of days and then we thought, we might be on to something here. We had hit the market bang at the right time, when the old Clockwork lot had settled down, had kids and wanted to go out again. It was great to be back working with Brandon and Alex again. They put in the groundwork and the hard work to earn the status that they fully deserve today. They got us the foot in the door in Ibiza and DJd at my wedding. They are our mates, massive DJs, bloody good blokes and we've done a fuck load together over the years.

Danny Clockwork: When we did Fire & Lightbox I walked outside after my set. It was minus two and I thought it would be really quiet but it was rammed. I got talking to this young guy and I said, 'Mate, are you okay, you look a bit pickled?' and he said, 'You wanna see my mum and dad.' And that's when it hit me. The demographic was perfect. They'd become parents, they'd become grandparents, they'd got married, they'd got divorced, they'd got fat, they'd got bald...now they wanted to go out and party again.

Of course we couldn't have imagined coming back bigger than we were before, but somehow we did and Clockwork now seemed so much stronger, even though so much had changed.

When I got out of the club scene my little brother Ben started doing illegal parties in Shoreditch. It had gone back to basics, no flyers, no decor, no lights, no guest DJs. When Clockwork came back and he saw the production and the line-ups he said, 'Now I get it,' And if I couldn't have done it like we always did, I wouldn't have brought it back.

Alex P: A decade or so earlier, Millennium Eve had changed things and removed the foundations of the scene. Me and Blocko were getting pigeon-holed as 'legends of Ibiza' and booked to play the Lava & Ignites and the Time & Envys. They paid top dollar, but the punters weren't really into it, and there was an expectancy to play certain classics. It wasn't anyone's fault, these places just knew they could fill their club by booking us.

It was difficult to find a way forward, then I got hit by the tax man, investigating me for the previous five years. Rogue flyers didn't help. I had to prove I couldn't physically be in Cornwall when I was actually playing in London that night. It was a really tough time, and I only just avoided bankruptcy. I sold my house in Hampstead, and then moved to Dubai for a couple of years, to play for promoters I knew out there.

When we came back to the UK, taking my football badges to get a better overview of our son Zac's youth football led to me being offered a job working in The Foundation within the youth academy set-up at Tottenham. We helped players who had been released get back in the system at lower league clubs. It put me in a really good place, mentally. I also did a bit of building work, learning the tools, eventually running sites for friends like Danny Gould, if he needed some eyes and ears he could trust. At the same time, around 2009/10, I started playing at some smaller clubs in the suburbs, small pockets around the M25, some funkier, more underground parties. When Danny and Andy asked me to play at their Clockwork Orange comeback party at McQueen's in 2011, a few other interesting things had popped up and I felt like I was treading the boards again.

Martin Cee: A friend who was involved in Strongman asked me to host one of their events. I just fell in love with the commentating and being around these monsters of men. Then they asked me to commentate on England's Strongest Man, which was promoted by the company I work for now, Ultimate Strongman, which puts on all the *Channel 5* stuff.

I launched a *YouTube* channel called *The Voice Of Strongman*, because I wanted to make a statement in a world where I was unknown, and I got a million views quite quickly, which is actually nothing these days.

Mazda picked me up; I think they thought I was someone else, but they gave me a brand new car, with my name on the side and that helped get me known in the industry. I began to host events with people like Arnold Schwarzenegger and started making a living from it, alongside a bit of DJing. I also launched an online nutrition and coaching business with Terry Hollands, one of the World's leading strongmen.

In 2012 my mate Dean Alexander brought back *Juice FM*, which we'd done well with for a couple of years in the mid-'90s. Dean asked if I would mentor Sarah. When we met and I realised she was ginger...well, us gingers, we're usually quick to acknowledge each other's gingerness. We got on really well and quickly became friends.

Sarah LP: I got a show on *Juice*, and even though Martin eventually backed away from the station, we started working on a few different

(top) Ginger Alliance duo Martin Cee and Sarah LP at Party In The Park, 2020 (above) Tony Nicholls at Clockstock 2021. (left) Keith Mac, Party In The Park, 2020 © Sharpscape Photography.

business opportunities with my printing company and Martin's involvement as a presenter on Strongman. Then I moved to *Fresh Radio.*

Martin Cee: I was at *Select* with my mate Scotty Anderson, who over the years I've done Bonne Bonnie parties with. Then I got an offer from *Funky Essex*, which was rebranding as *Funky FX*. There was talk of me doing a breakfast show with a girl called Steph, and money being chucked at it. I knew me and Steph wouldn't gel, but even while the talks were going on Sarah was saying, 'You said we could do a double act together.' It was crazy, she had the right hump, it was like I was cheating on her. And she's a happily married woman.

Sarah LP: I always wanted to be in a duo. I love playing music but I wanted to explore more of the old school personality of radio. If Martin had been talking about doing it with Scottie, then fine, but if he was going to do it with someone else, then he could bloody well do it with me.

Martin Cee: I did a few solo shows on Funky SX but they run a programming software called Myriad. You don't know what record is coming next. It's terrible. Sarah actually sat in with me one day.

Sarah LP: We weren't a double act yet. It was always Scotty, Scotty, Scotty. Then there was Steph, I'm not letting that go...

Peter P: After *Time FM* finished, I had a residency at The Penthouse in Leicester Square and was flying back to Bali and South East Asia, DJing a lot abroad for a month at a time.

I was playing in Jakarta a lot, and met my ex-wife there. Indonesia was probably the last place on earth where the tobacco companies could sponsor events so Marlboro threw millions at it. Bob Sinclar and Tiesto were getting paid hundreds of thousands of pounds, and even I was getting first class air travel and five star accommodation and the great experience of playing with some of the best DJs in the world. Amazing beach parties and the clubs are second to none out there.

I came back to my hotel, the Carlton Ritz, after a day out and there was a press conference taking place for the Java Jazz Festival. I walked straight into it and stood awkwardly by the side of the piano. A guy started playing and I realised it was Herbie Hancock. Then George Benson walked on playing the guitar and started singing.

Tony Nicholls: By the end of the Noughties I knew the Romford club scene like the back of my hand. I'd been a resident at Pacific Edge in the market for five years and involved in promotions and management too.

I had also played the West End bar circuit a lot, like Pangea and China Whites. I played R&B and hip-hop, which I wasn't really into, but I had to make a living. I also took a full-time job running The House & Terrace In Greenwich, which was really successful at the time, and more great experience.

When the opportunity came up in 2010 to have my own club in Romford, I couldn't turn it down. On the site of the old Global Net Cafe, originally part of the Hollywood group, and later Bar Mango and Custom House, we opened Kosho. I teamed up with one of my brothers, Barry Nicholls, and our mate Ross Drogman.

It was a big leap for all of us. Collectively we had never owned a business before, let alone a bar or nightclub. When we got the keys I realised we needed to learn so much on the job, and quickly. With so many overheads and VAT returns to do, you have no choice.

In 2012 we bought The Opium Lounge in nearby North Street, and reopened it as The Buddha Lounge. We ran the two venues at the same time, both with late licences, and for two or three years it was a fantastic business.

After two years of running Buddha Lounge, we refurbed and reopened as Circuit in 2014. We had billboards on the A12 and on the *EastEnders* set. We put on some big house nights, acts like Secondcity and Sonny Fodera, and the first year was beyond all of our expectations. We were taking good money, but then our expenses went up and when turnover dropped profit margins started getting squeezed.

There was a power cut one Saturday night in North Street and we had to shut Circuit for the night. And it was literally as if somebody turned off the switch at the club. We had a few bad weeks after that, the numbers dropped and continued to. We hit a run of bad events, our takings halved, we struggled to break even and whatever we tried couldn't get it back to where it was. The power cut was a coincidence but at the same time symbolic. We came away from Circuit in 2016 and gave the keys to someone else.

Darrell Privett: I'd been appointed Head Of Music at Bethnal Green Academy, but after a while 'working for the man' was not for me so I reduced my hours at the school. Alongside my teaching role, I was always DJing and putting on my own parties, including Ce La Vie at The RS Lounge in Woodford with Brett Jacobs, who went on to do really well as a house producer and at Minx in Loughton, which became Luxe.

I also did a night called Couture at 195 in Epping and the Warehouse. We'd have a garage DJ play a set with an MC like Buzzard or Creed, and the next set would be full-on house. We were really mixing things up at that point. I did another night in Shoreditch called Dirtbox, which was deep and tech house.

In 2011 I was offered an events manager role at Luxe in Loughton where I'd been putting on a Saturday night called *Naive*. I accepted and tried to juggle two days at the club and three days at school, before I finally left teaching.

I also decided to use my real name. A lot of DJs I knew were moving that way.

In 2013 a friend asked me multiple times if I'd go to a casting of *The Only Way In Essex* with him. Reality TV had never interested me, but one day I gave in and we passed the screen test. After a while they stopped using my mate, but kept me on. I did a couple of seasons, probably cast more because I was a DJ/promoter than anything, but it really wasn't me. I just didn't like it so I stopped turning up. I hated getting asked in the street for photos, it just wasn't my cup of tea.

After I left Luxe in 2016, I was approached by Josh Hodges and Freddie Palmer, who had an idea for a new night with a Latin, Spanish vibe called La Fiesta. I've always had a lot of time for Josh and his ideas so I invested in the project and became resident DJ. The first few La Fiesta parties were at The Magic Roundabout in Old Street, which is not there anymore. In fact, the Old Street roundabout isn't there anymore. Up until the pandemic we were settled at 93 Feet East, which became home for us. Such a good vibe, and we always sold out in a few days.

Mete: Wayne and I were still DJing and had always played at our own charity events. In 2012 I was on *Kool London,* aka *Kool FM,* and then I was on *Select* for four years.

We were also approached by a mate with a boat to help promoting club-type events. I said to Wayne, if we're going to do this, we need to do it properly, so we trained to be Waterman of the River which, in technical terms, means we would be licensed to carry passengers on vessels on the River Thames. We had to take on a five-year Waterman apprenticeship to be officially received by officials wearing feathered gowns in a 15th century chamber in central London, because it's a proper Lodge type turn-out. We started running parties on The Hurlingham, one of the biggest party boats on the Thames, which we now own. It's like a club on water with two floors — and we now own and lease various other boats.

In 2013 we decided to wind down *Onelife UK* and our charitable exploits after raising a million pounds by that point. We had taken the initiative as far as we could, and were more than satisfied with the impact we'd made.

More recently I was walking my dog late one night and I noticed a

(top) Darrell Privett at his La Fiesta residency and (above) and (right) Carly Denham.

group of late teens on their bikes.

I heard 'Oi, mister,' and thought, oh here we go.

As I turned round, one of the youths continued, 'Mister, did you used to have a centre in Plough Way?'

'Yes, I did...'

'Do you remember us?'

And as he walked into the light, I said, 'Yes, Bobby, I do remember you, you had a younger brother, how is Billy?' And then Billy walked round the corner, and he was huge.

It's lovely to be remembered by young people and get that love back. The love of the people was always so rewarding, because if you've ever given your time to those who don't have much, even if you might think you don't have much yourself, when they give you that smile, or when they say thank you, it's beautiful. When you receive that, the material world doesn't seem so important.

Seeker: When Andy contacted me in 2013 to book me for a party he was putting on near Liverpool Street I hadn't DJd for the past 20 years. I had become so disillusioned with the whole scene and had lost confidence over that period. I agreed to play, but my performance set me back another five years. It was like I tried too hard and didn't relax into it. I was rubbish, I know I was. I think I even got taken off before the end of my set. The technology had changed. Everybody was on CDJs, which I'd never played on. Jonny C had been asking me to come back on the radio since the *Time FM* days and, bless him, he kept trying.

Tony Perry: In 2013 I entered a DJ competition hosted by Mister Jam and won, and was booked to played with him and Skream. The same weekend I had a gig at a Major Lazer after-party alongside Diplo. It was a big jump up for a bedroom DJ only playing out once a month.

A year later I was sent out to play at a ski festival in France and one night played a mixture of hip-hop, house and rock at the last bar to shut to an industry crowd. When I got home, an agent at the party booked me to DJ at an England rugby match at Twickenham.

I knew that stadium sports DJs were already a big thing in the States, so this was interesting. Then a booking came in to play during an NLF game at Wembley in front of 90,000 people as part of Live To The Bowl.

Danielle Montana: After about three years of not DJing I said, 'That's it, I can't stay away anymore.' I was lucky to have enough connections to get back into the business.

In 2014 with SW1 Radio, we held a ground-breaking reggae event at our local gallery, Tate Britain, headlined by lovers rock pioneer Lloyd Coxsone. It was hilarious when he rocked up with his Sir Coxsone Outernational Soundsystem. The Tate staff went into panic mode, worrying that the huge 40k rig would cause paint to fall off their precious artwork. I'll never forget their faces as the huge floor-to-ceiling speakers were being set up. But we were able to keep levels under control for what was an amazing local community event, and the first of its kind ever at the Tate, broadcast live on the radio.

Tony Nicholls was on verge of signing to Defected...and about to take on another well-known venue.

My Deeptrak production partner, Grant Richards, and I had remixed Todd Terry's *Jumpin'*, Victor Romero's *Love Will Find A Way* and NY Finest's *Do You Feel Me*. We were working on a re-edit of the UK garage classic *Girls Like This* by B15 Project, and waiting for them to do their own remix. We asked if we could put a short promo video up on *Facebook* to get some interest ahead of any release. It was just something Grant put together with funny footage of two boys dancing. Within two days we'd had three million views. It was crazy. MN2S wanted to send us to festivals around the world and also put B15 Project out on the old school garage circuit...as long as we signed for Defected. B15 Project eventually signed the remix package to Armada Music, owned by Armin Van Bueren, which were mainly putting out trance. We thought it was a huge mistake...and it meant, after years of working in the studio, we missed out on Defected.

Meanwhile, with my other partners, we bought The Warehouse in Edmonton. It was too much. We were expanding our portfolio but our management team wasn't evolving at the same pace. We kept The Warehouse name for a while, then renamed it The Box, but there were so many issues I moved away from that venue.

Around 2017 the lease was expiring at Kosho and the landlord said we could renew for another 25 years. I said to my partners, 'Look, we've had a really good run here, we don't owe anybody any money, the rent is paid, the taxman is paid, we can walk away from this with our heads held high. But my partners wanted to continue, so I stepped down and they signed for another 15 years. Business was very tough for them, and they were very fortunate to leave that venue debt free in March 2020... just weeks before the first lockdown.

Carly Denham: In 2014 I started a residency at The Brickyard in Romford, which lasted until 2017, when the venue stopped having DJs and concentrated on being a restaurant. By now I had retrained again and become a teacher, working for alternative education providers in the Havering area, currently working at an independent school in Romford, specialising in English Language, English Literature and History.

I think years of raving helped make me the DJ I am today. Hopefully, I've still got a good few years ahead of me. Because I love both my teaching and DJing I'm virtually teetotal now. I want to be able to enjoy and take both as seriously as possible. I'd burn out if I got nutted every week.

Lisa Nash: After *Clubavision* I moved into fashion TV and fitness. I worked in New York regularly and presented the Global Fashion Awards there. When I became a single mum I cut down on travelling, and having done martial arts to black belt level at a young age, the transition into fitness and personal training felt natural.

I also continued voiceover work on things like Pimp Up My Ride, The Osbourne Show, for CBeebies and a Kate Moss documentary. I was able to drop off and pick up my daughter from school and still have a decent career. I made two fitness videos with Frankie Essex, which led to running events which promote the importance of fitness and nutrition for mental health and well-being, which my old mate Brandon Block has taken part in.

Connie Runtings at *Centreforce*: Slip Back To '89.

Lisa Nash in a 2016 fitness video.

Roger The Doctor: It's mad to think, but I was at Faces for a total of 17 years. I left in 2015 when my old pal Lee Andrews offered me a job at his firm, DOC Cleaners, an apt name if ever there was one. It was the chance to have a regular job, a more family-orientated life for my new wife and young daughter, and it's the best thing I've ever done.

I'm now a regional manager, with 150 staff (who regularly get shout-outs on my show, by the way) and I'm able to do my thing at *Centreforce* and DJ out if I want. And if I want to go to a BBQ on a Saturday I don't have to worry about running back to the club to put the air conditioning on, or to let the bar staff in.

Dean Lambert: My wedding planning company in Thailand was going from strength to strength. After nine amazing years together, my wife Amy went into a deep depression shortly after her dad passed away. It peaked on Christmas Day of that year. Later that night she tragically took her own life. I found Amy on the morning of Boxing Day. I wouldn't wish anyone to go through that.

Eventually I came back to the UK to sort out some personal matters. My daughter lives in Thailand with her family, which is best for her currently. My life had been turned upside down and returning in those circumstances was horrific.

Andy Swallow: In 2015 I was invited to a party in the Stadio Olimpico in Rome through some contacts in the Lazio Ultras, who I am affiliated to. The party was being put on by Andrea Pelino, a good friend of mine, who is the co-founder of DC10 in Ibiza and its flagship night Circoloco, and the event was a co-promotion with the DNF Booking Crew, who represent a lot of their DJs.

I'd set up a meeting for DNF with some sponsorship contacts in London in the run-up to the party in Rome. Carl Cox was headlining so the boys asked me to come over, and I took Danny and Donna. We turned up at the stadium and a buggy pulled up.

'Andy, jump on, Carl wants to see you.'

We were driven round the stadium concourse, underneath the car park and there was Carl, about to go on. It was so great to see him.

'Me and your dad have got outstanding business,' joked Carl.

'Yeah, Dan, I still owe him fifty quid.'

Then I added, 'Carl, it's amazing, how have you done so well?'

'Well, I left you...'

Priceless.

He then told Danny to jump in his buggy and took him on stage with him, in front of thousands of people, which was a lovely touch.

...AND INTO THE FUTURE

Master Pasha: I'd given up on DJing and was trying to become a professional footballer. I was at Arsenal as a kid. Then I played for West Ham for a bit, and for Grays Athletic in the FA Cup. I left school and I got a football scholarship at South Essex College, earning quite good money and signed to Grays, as part of the course.

But I'm all or nothing, and if I'm going to be a footballer I want to be a top pro, so playing at that level just didn't interest me. My lifestyle was also holding me back and I knew I wouldn't make it. I enjoyed the football, but anger issues were getting me sent off each week. I had a few injuries, and woke up one day and said to myself, I can't do this any more. I had already told the club I was leaving, but I hadn't told my dad yet. It was even harder because he was now the owner of Grays. It was the first year of the college scheme, and I was leaving so it was a difficult phone call.

For the next five years I didn't have a clue what I was going to do. I worked in recruitment, at Dad's five-a-side centre...a gym. Anything.

My dad had taken over The Dovecote pub in Chingford and in the summer of 2017 we decided to do a *Facebook Live* stream for a young girl called Isla, who had cancer. I did a trial run with my dad a few days before, playing three on, three off, and I chatted on the mic a bit, and that was my first time talking on a stream or 'show'.

I set up the party for Isla with Jonny C, and got Majestic involved, and within a day we had a million views. A few days later, my uncle, Larry Manning died, and as he was a big part of the *Centreforce* family I asked Dad if I could do my own tribute show, which I really enjoyed.

We continued the *Facebook* streams, and because I was doing regular shows, I said to Dad, 'I need a DJ name.'

'All right, you're Master Pasha.'

And that was it. I didn't even question it, because I didn't know or imagine what would happen. And I could never have dreamed of being a radio presenter, because I didn't even know how to be a DJ yet.

Jonny C: As the streams evolved into '*Centreforce* Sessions', the first DJs on board were Peter P, Bonnie and Chris Phillips. With Andy often in Tenerife I tried to get a few of the older lot involved because I felt we needed a few originals to give the streams some authenticity, and it just grew. In the September, Connie Runtings and Hermit played, plus Swift and Zinc and Mickey Star Lewis. When Andy said, 'Let's try for a DAB licence,' I nearly fell off the fire escape.'

Master Pasha: I asked my mate, Danny May, a good friend of mine, who was working for us at the time, to make initial contact with the Essex DAB authorities, and when I realised Dad wasn't winding me up, and they were actually interested in talking to us, the possibility of *Centreforce* becoming a legal station suddenly became a reality.

Ramsey: Jonny C called me up and I took Matt Jam Lamont and Creed with me to do a show at the pub. We got 60K+ views. I also did a Force Of One / *Defection FM* tribute show with those guys, which was really popular too.

Dean Lambert: I wasn't in the best place when Andy invited me to the pub for a *Facebook* Live stream, and it was possibly the worst DJing I've ever done. I couldn't put two records together, probably too many beers, but luckily they were the right records. For four hours. I started doing one show a week, but I covered lots of others.

Max Fernandez: I met Peter P through the soul scene, at a Hayling Island Weekender. He was running his nights at The George (now The Rising Sun) in Hornchurch. So I'd go down there to see him and he asked me to do the warm-ups or cover for him if he was away. Soon I was playing on soul internet station *Zero Radio* in Southend, the first radio station I'd been involved in. I saw that Peter P was doing a *Facebook Live* from The Dovecote so headed down there. He introduced me to Jonny C, who was managing the sound. Then I got a message during one of my *Zero* shows from Jonny saying, 'Locked on.' That was so nice of him.

Rooney: When me and Danny Lines were asked to do a *Facebook Live* show for *Centreforce* I was doing the pirate *Vision FM* for Danny Bass, on the old 88.4 frequency that *Centreforce* had for a while. We had 50k views and 5k comments in the first two hours.

Master Pasha: Very quickly we had an initial agreement in place (above) Dean Lambert and Max Fernandez at Party In The Park, 2020. © Sharpscape Photography.

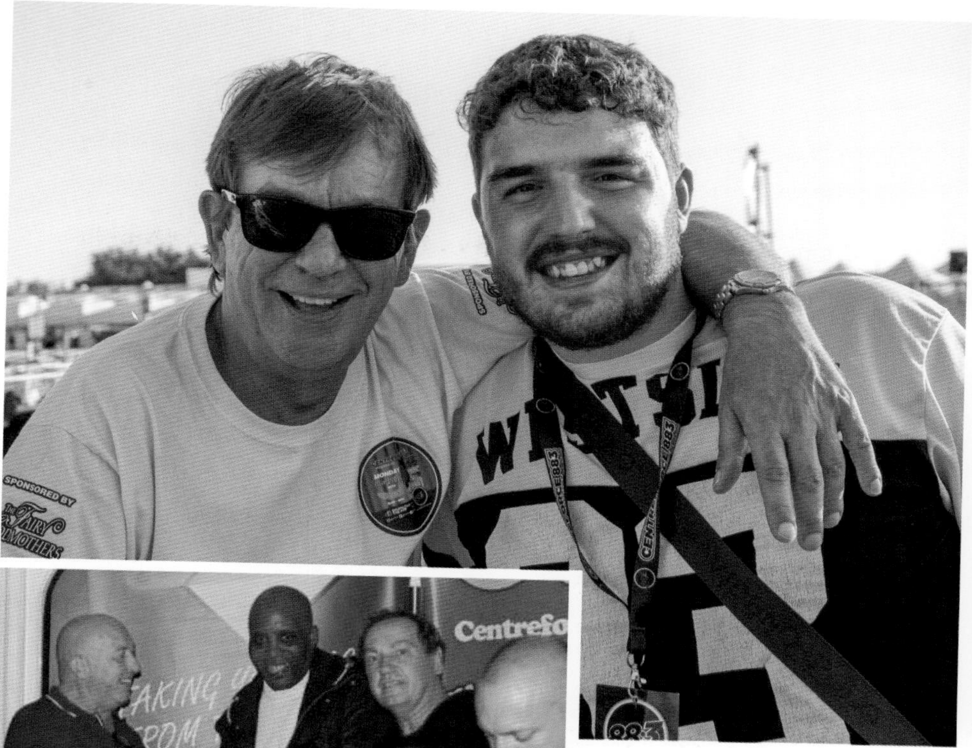

(above, from left to right) Gary Dickle, Fabian Runtings, Andy Swallow and Keith Mac at The Dovecote pub, 2017.

(right, from left to right) Matt Jam Lamont, Ramsey and MC Creed in recent times.

with Essex DAB. Things were moving fast, but we had no studio, no equipment and no DJs.

Jonny C: We were sitting going through the licence application, looking at the figures, and it was all a little bit jokey and still very much pirate. We were only going for the Essex area originally and then at the last minute, we said, 'Fuck it, let's go for London too.' And it was literally the next couple of days that the email came back. Piers is our guy at London 2 DAB Multiplex. At least 30 other stations applied during that period but it was almost like they were waiting for us. We became the only independent station on the London roster. My first question at the initial DAB meeting was, 'Do I have to play the news feed you provide?' They shook their heads and I said, 'Sweet.'

Master Pasha: The DAB licence approval was amazing news, we were in shock for a while. Yes, I now had a radio licence, but we were launching in six weeks. We had to sit down and conclude the London DAB contract negotiations , ahead of a review period, while the licence was finalised, and from that point a lot of it is a blur. We also had to raise initial funds for equipment, so a big thanks to a very close friend, who knows who he is, for his initial support.

On the back of *Centreforce*'s first official party for almost three decades at Bloc in Hackney Wick, a 700-capacity sell-out, a few months earlier, the station's latest event at Steelyard in the City in February 2018 was another huge success, with more than 1200 through the door. The same month the station was on the move again.

Jonny C: We had to set up a studio somewhere else because the DAB people could visit at any point, and we couldn't have them turning up at the pub. Andy spoke to his contacts at The Academy in Loughton and a deal was done to relocate there.

Steve ESP: I saw that *Centreforce* had been doing *Facebook Live* so I tapped Jonny C up again and he gave me 5pm-7pm on a Sunday, six months before they started on DAB.

Max Fernandez: I saw another post from Peter P about *Centreforce* moving to a studio in Loughton. Peter pulled some strings and messaged back, 'Come tomorrow and bring some tunes with you.' I was nervous heading to Loughton, thinking I might be on *Centreforce* and I was lucky enough to do a little back to back with Peter on his breakfast show. The response was good from Jonny, Andy and Danny and they offered me a 10am-1pm show every Friday which I did for 12 months, and continued in the Friday morning slot as the DAB licence approached.

Carly Denham: Andy saw some videos of me DJing with bongo player Matt Early and he invited us to do some *Facebook* shows together, which led to my own live streams and sets at *Centreforce* parties at The George in Hornchurch and at The Steelyard a year later.

Danny Lines: I used to dabble on the mic back in the day at after-parties, or sitting in record shops. *Centreforce* gave me the opportunity years later, and I haven't looked back. I was very happy to become *Centreforce*'s host at Academy and Dovecote parties and I've MCd at every event since.

Mete: After the 'bandit-country' incident on 88.4, I was shocked when my DJ partner Wayne rang and said that there was a chance we could go back on the new version of *Centreforce*. But everything had been smoothed over, and we started in Loughton, first on a Thursday afternoon, then on a Wednesday afternoon. Then Wayne decided to leave. Maybe it was the east-south thing. I had a word with Andy and he told me I was welcome to stay on.

Danielle Montana: I bumped into Andy Swallow in 2018. I hadn't seen him for 15 years or so. It was great catching up, and I was saying how amazing it would be if he ever brought *Centreforce* back. A couple of weeks later I got calls from Andy and Jonny C asking me if I wanted to get involved at The Academy. I said, 'Absolutely.' Andy already knew the DAB licence was in the pipeline when we'd met, but he hadn't let on.

Jonny C: A couple of months before our DAB launch, we went back online at Centreforceradio.com. We were quickly up to 10,000 hits daily to the website. I had to start building a roster of DJs, a mixture of past and present *Centreforce* favourites.

Bubbler: I was on *Kool FM*, because it gave me an opportunity to play my hardcore, jungle and drum and bass. A few of us went to The Academy and that's the first we heard about the DAB, which we really didn't know anything about. It seemed a small medium then, but suddenly everyone had DAB in their cars. Normally on a new station, a pirate, it takes a while to build it up, hoping you might get a few

(top) The infamous 'broom cupboard' at The Academy (middle) DJ Hugs and (left) Seeker, both from original *Centreforce* DJ crew, The Corporation, presenting an early DAB show.

messages, but *Centreforce* just blew up straight away. *Time FM* was really busy, but this was something else. I was really surprised.

Hornchurch-born entrepreneur Peter Faires was introduced to Andy and Danny Swallow by a mutual friend.

We had a conversation about the station trying to go legit. I wasn't ever massively into clubbing and never went too far afield. Hollywood and Ritzys, that was me. And I'm Tottenham, so maybe not the best person to be talking to the Swallows about *Centreforce*. I went to the five-a-side centre for a chat and saw the set-up in the corner of one of the rooms. They referred to it as a broom cupboard themselves, and I did wonder if Philip Schofield or Andi Peters were going to pop up at some point. We talked about the possibility of relocating the studio and discussed some figures. I looked at *Centreforce*'s history and thought, you just can't buy that.

Ed Simpson — aka Ed The Landlord, to listeners — had 'a heart ruling the head moment' when he heard *Centreforce* was back on air.

Me and my pals leapt around Echoes, wearing dungarees and Wallabees, thinking we were the nuts. When we came out of The Dungeons, we'd expect at least one of our cars to have been nicked.

Everyone we knew listened to *Centreforce*. We went to Sunrise and Biology in my Volkswagen Camper and were always upstairs at The Astoria. We were out all the time. Strangers in Woodford in the week, Camden Palace on a Friday. Then Limelight, Astoria and The Milk Bar on Saturdays and afters at Crowland Road in Tottenham, which was proper wonky. Without actually knowing that *Centreforce* put it on, we went to Woodstock. Also all-dayers at Shen-Ola in Hackney Wick, which was probably the first *Centreforce* 'do' I knowingly went to.

I worked in recruitment, then opened my own company in 1994. When I bought the Pixel Building in 2016, it evolved into a business centre, and home to more than 40 companies. I decided to set up a spin class studio for the employees in and around the industrial estate. I bought 30 bikes, and spent a fortune fully soundproofing an area at the front of the building but it didn't take off.

I was out in Majorca that summer, 2018, and a friend told me *Centreforce* was back, so I started listening to the station online while out running and it brought back so many memories of such good times, so I got involved in the shout-outs. I can actually remember thinking subconsciously at the time that I was going to be involved somehow, but I wasn't sure how yet.

Jonny C: And then came the day, which is still written in my diary on my computer as 'THE DAY RADIO CHANGED'. Saturday July 14th, 2018. *Centreforce* was broadcasting as a legal station, in its own right. It was definitely a wow moment.

Master Pasha: I was due to present the first show on DAB at midday, and the night before I was so nervous. I didn't sleep at all, and was sick when I woke up. As I drove to the studio at The Academy it was surreal, because Jonny was playing a test broadcast of one of my shows, so that was making me more nervous My way of coping with nerves at that point was to pretend to be someone else. Up until that point, I think I was mostly trying to be Bubbler. I couldn't remember a lot of my shows because they were all an act, and on that first day of the DAB, something changed, because I now realised I had two voices, my normal one and my radio one. I said it would never happen to me, so I was kicking myself.

Seeker: Jonny tried me again and wanted to get me involved around the launch of the licence. I told him I didn't have any music saved digitally, and he said I could play vinyl. I'd kept all my records but I didn't want to go to Loughton, weeks into the DAB and play a shit set on vinyl. I had bought some CDJs three months earlier, though, so I had been practising. Then Jonny said, 'If you don't come in and have a go, I'll get Andy to call you,' so I agreed if I could bring Hugs with me. Jonny sent me a USB stick with some tunes on it, which was so nice of him.

Ed Simpson: Back in the UK I got hold of Andy Swallow's number. I didn't know him personally, but we had some mutual friends. Andy fixed up a meeting with his son Danny to visit *Centreforce*'s set-up at The Academy. Danny referred to it as a broom cupboard, but I have actually seen bigger broom cupboards. It had just enough room for a set of decks and to be able to walk around them. There were a few banners up from their *Facebook Live* events. I also met Jonny and Dean Lambert, both lovely fellas. Maybe out of sheer naivety I put a proposal to Andy and Danny. I probably should have run a mile, given I had just thrown a load of money on the spin classes venture. There was just something inside me that said to them, 'Do you want a studio?' And it was definitely a heart ruling the head moment.

We arranged to meet at Pixel and I remember when Danny and Johnny C turned up. I don't think they could believe their luck, at the possibility of moving somewhere already purpose-built for *Centreforce*.

Jonny C: The move to the Pixel Building was another one of those moments. It was amazing to move there. Peter and Ed gave us tremendous backing. The concept of a legal station like ours had been around for a while, but nobody had the experience, knowledge and money to do it. The investors left me and Danny alone, and their backing allowed us to build a team and have access through the Tune In platform and to launch the *Centreforce* app, which would be vital for expanding the station's reach across the UK and globally.

The first broadcast at Pixel was on October 5th, 2018. Me and Rooney worked through the night, while a mix played, to get it up and running, and we were on air at 6am.

Ed Simpson: I feel an affinity with Danny because I set up my first company at 23. He's an incredible creative, a great people's person and he's been the driving force behind the growth of the station. Andy's musical knowledge, because of his involvement in the business for many years, is second to none, and you can see an awful lot of Andy in Danny.

Peter Faires had just committed quite a chunk of money, so I said I'd invest too. I didn't know anything about radio so I had to try and become fluent in the business side of it very quickly.

Grooverider on *Centreforce* with Chris Paul in 2021 as part of an Orange takeover.

A DAB HAND

Master Pasha: Starting the station up again was the biggest risk I could have taken. Forget financially, just in terms of continuing my dad's legacy. Not replicating it, but reinventing *Centreforce* — that was a huge gamble. There hasn't been a station launched again with a legacy like ours. *Kiss* have their own legacy, but it's a completely different station now, and the station they have become means that legacy is in the distant past. We are always enhancing our legacy by remaining authentic.

I wasn't even born when the original *Centreforce* came on air, but from what I knew and had been told, I was adamant that we could never hide the fact that we were a pirate radio station or where we had come from. I quickly realised I liked being the underdog when people say, 'You're mad, it won't work.' But I had to take the risk, knowing that if it didn't work out I'd have to hold my hand up and say I fucked up.

The last four or five years have been a massive rollercoaster for me. Dad was still around full-time when we first moved to Pixel before he moved to Tenerife to open a club and a bar, but from day dot he has said to me, 'Son, this is your thing.'

Jonny C: Out of all of us, Danny had the most pressure on him, having to live up to his dad and being the youngest holder of a DAB licence. Danny has spent most of life around us living and breathing *Centreforce*. I've felt so proud, watching him grow up and evolve. Any success we have had is because of Danny's vision.

Max Fernandez: One Friday, Danny was covering the drive-time show and asked me to do his shout-outs. We went back-to-back for a bit and just clicked, even though we hadn't ever DJd together or even hung out together outside of the studio. Behind the decks, it was like we'd known each other for years.

The phone lines were going off, and Dean Lambert came into the studio and said on air, 'Forget Masters At Work, these are the 'Boys At Work'. And the name just stuck. So we have Dean to thank for that. We love him, even though he's as mad as a March hare.

On the day of the Slip Back To '89 party at Hanger in March 2019,

Danny covered Peter P's Friday breakfast show we could run into my mid-morning show and do a six-hour warm-up show for the party. That became the first official Boys At Work show. It's been one of the best received shows on the station, and builds from soul and jazz-funk, some of the stuff that I was brought up on at soul weekenders growing up, through to soulful house and house. We're so lucky that with *Centreforce* we have the freedom to play what we want, unlike *Kiss* where they play the same records every three hours. Once you've learned the pattern you know at twenty past four exactly what they're going to play.

Alex P: Andy and I had always been in touch since I first met him at Land Of Oz at Heaven all those years ago. Then Brandon and I did the Clockwork Orange mix CD for him and Labello and also a few mixes, including Mandy Smith's *I Just Can't Wait* for Public Demand.

Andy was so enthusiastic about *Centreforce* coming back, especially when they got the DAB. I was delighted to get involved. I listened to the station and thought I could help attract a different audience, so I introduced a Battle Of The Bangers feature to my show, inviting guest DJs like Danny Rampling, Terry Farley and Jeremy Healy to come on to play music and talk about their careers, and that led to Jeremy taking his own show.

Hopefully, I was able to come in and steady the ship a bit, and shake up the schedule board. I spoke to all the DJs and reminded them that we're always there for them, and that they should support each other too. There were a few things that became apparent when I was driving about, that we needed to tweak technically from within the studio, so I hope I've helped take some pressure off Jonny C as well.

Master Pasha: The talent on the station is far more than I could have ever imagined when we first got the DAB licence. We're always looking at our line-up to see if we can freshen it up, but also want to remain loyal to the presenters who have helped us from day one and have always been the lifeblood of the station.

Personally, being around all these guys who joined since the DAB, like Jeremy Healy, Alex P, Andy Manston and Dolly Rockers. I'm taking little bits from all of them for my personal development as a DJ and a presenter.

Jonny C: The transition to DAB was such a learning curve. The transmitter and getting raided aside, back in the day, all we had to worry about from a technical point of view was the needle breaking. That and watching the door. Now I've got five computers running at any one time, so I'm dealing with engineers, liaising with the DAB team in Yorkshire and monitoring servers. For the first year or so Danny and I learned on the fly, dealing with the scheduling and all the Ofcom rules and regulations. At the studio morning, noon and night.

Keith Mac: Apart from that show with Andy on *Time FM*, I hadn't done any radio since *Centreforce* first time around. I still didn't feel confident enough on the mic, but Andy wouldn't leave me alone, always trying to get me involved. So I did one show at The Academy, just before they moved to Pixel and it went okay. Then I agreed to do Thursday nights, to get Andy off my back, really, and because I thought not many people would be listening. I became more confident and during the lockdown helped out on a daytime show. I was offered Friday afternoons, and I've done those every week since.

Rooney: Me and Danny Lines were delighted to be given Wednesday drivetime and Friday evenings when the DAB was confirmed. We were asked to move later on Fridays so a House Legends show with Colin Hudd, Trevor Fung and Ray Keith could come in, and I was like, 'No problem, I remember listening to Colin and Trevor at Spectrum, it's an honour to have those guys on board.' Unfortunately, it didn't work out for them, so we were happy to move back. We came up with the name The Super Smiley Show, which was a little nod to my old mate Simon James, who makes amazing 18-inch 'Super Smileys' and also dressed Oval Space for the 30 Years Of The Force party.

Danny Lines: I've been completely clean for years. I was untrustworthy, and not a nice person, when I was young, but I've been training martial arts for 25 years and it keeps me on a straight path, which allowed me to build up Britannia K9 Security after winning a contract for the 2012 London Olympics.

It was a massive buzz when *Centreforce* went legal. It's unbelievable to see the progression. It's powerful. It works because we've got the right people. It's a tight ship and we're family. I don't do it for any other reason than I enjoy it. I advertise on *Centreforce* too, of course. It's great being part of it. I also do regular meditation sessions online for the *Centreforce* family. Andy is the don of this. He's the man. My son's a massive West Ham fan, and a raver now. He carried the ICF flag with Andy when The Boleyn Ground closed down.

Dean Lambert: When the DAB was confirmed I was given Tuesday drive-time and Sunday afternoon. Master Pasha introduced me to Ed Simpson, who was talking to Danny about sponsoring my show initially, and then they did the deal to take the station to Pixel. Then for various reasons I came off air for six months, but I was pining for it the whole time. I was asked to come back and offered a Monday afternoon and from that point on I literally lived Monday to Monday.

(top) Danny Lines and Rooney in the Centreforce studio at Pixel; (above) DJ Freckles and (right) Danny Lines, both on mic duty at Party In The Park, 2020. © Sharpscape Photography.

Ed Simpson found himself on the radio briefly...

I am extremely mic-shy and I get very tongue-tied. I did a couple of shows with Dean called Soul On Sunday with Lambert & The Landlord. It was only a couple of weeks, and just a bit of fun. I'm more than happy to leave the presenting to the professionals.

Ramsey: When *Centreforce* moved to the Pixel I was doing quite a few shows, as well as sitting in the office ringing round contacts, trying to get certain DJs involved. Then I left to join a friend's new station set-up, which I was going to be cut in on, but that fell through, so I wasted a year or so. Both Andy and Danny Swallow welcomed me back, which was good of them.

The station's popularity had gone ballistic again...and every DJ wanted a show on there, so it was hard for me to get a regular slot that suits my music, because there are so many genres I play now. House, soulful house, broken beat, a little bit of tech, deep house and garage. Not forgetting new disco, which I play and also make. Me and Fen still play out together. I'm *Centreforce* and he's Mi-Soul, so when you book us you get double bubble.

Mervyn Victor: I heard *Centreforce* was back on so I called Andy up and asked if I could get involved, and he invited me down. I had a weekly show on a Wednesday afternoon up until 2020 and then took some time off but hope to be back on the station in the future at some point.

Roger The Doctor: A couple of years ago I was celebrating the 50th birthday of Samantha McCarthy, one of The Lovies, the group of girls from The Brewery Tap in Walthamstow where I had my first DJ residency in the '80s.

A guy called John Fleet was telling me that *Centreforce* was back on. Later that night he came and told me Andy Swallow wanted to see me. I thought, 'Am I in trouble?' It was like being told to see the headmaster.

A few days later I got a text from an unknown number. It was Andy asking me to come down and do a guest spot at the Pixel. I said I needed a few weeks to prepare because I only had vinyl still. The last time I'd done any radio was in Tenerife at Radio Biaha in 1993/94 when I had two shows a week. Andy kept messaging and sending me pictures of the studio. When I saw it for myself I agreed to do a Boxing Day trial show. Once I saw the feedback and how relentless the shout-outs were I was so impressed.

Jonny C offered me every week and I was chuffed... also later to be given a bi-weekly soul show on a Sunday morning because I love playing my 'snap, crackle and pop' vinyl, tracks that can't be Shazam'd. They message in and I say, 'Go on 883 TV and I'll hold it up for a few seconds.'

I'd say 90 per cent of the music I play on *Centreforce* is vinyl. Digital music may have b-lines and beats but for me it doesn't have the soul that you get with vinyl. My daughter Tiger Lily comes in and helps on my shows sometimes as Doctor Junior, reading out some messages.

I'll be on my decks at home and she'll ask me what I'm doing and I'll say, 'Well, I want to try something different this week. I've found these a cappellas and I'm trying them over these different records to see what works best.' And then she'll give me her opinion. For instance, Tiger Lily absolutely loves The Rah Band - *Clouds Across The Moon.*

The young DJs on *Centreforce* are amazing, the Max Isaacs and the Elysias. They work in the office day to day and are around so many DJs and different styles. It's such a great environment for their development.

Danielle Montana: When they got the DAB I moved with them to Pixel. I love the story, the comeback and every minute of it. It's great that I'm still working with Roger The Doctor, who is as lovely, as friendly and as funny now as he ever was.

I try to forget the cameras, because I can't help but dance, but then I always used to go out into the dancefloor and dance to my own DJ sets.

Darrell Privett: I used to box in the gym at The Loughton Academy, where *Centreforce* popped up again. I began speaking to Andy and Danny about a show while they were going for the DAB licence. They gave me a Monday evening so I took it on, and continued after the move to the Pixel. It's become one of the longest-running shows in the same slot. I was also one of the first DJs to go on there and play more new stuff, which on an old school station was a challenge anyway. When I first started I actually followed a football talk show. There'd be two guys sat there chatting and I'd come on and play upfront soulful house. It was certainly different. For the station to stay relevant there needs to be a decent amount of new material played.

At Party In The Park Part Zoo I was playing in The Hush Village tent at the top of Colesdale Farm. There was still quite a few *Centreforce* listeners at the front of my stage, yelling their 'shout-out' names at me and enjoying the new stuff I was playing, so it's great when the crossover works both ways. And I'm a big *Centreforce* fan. I listen to every show. I love Peter P's shows, and also Texsta on a Wednesday, he's been around for years... enough respect.

Martin Cee: *Centreforce* suddenly came back again in 2018 and it got my attention. Because I've always been a staunch West Ham fan, a lot of people said I should have been on *Centreforce*, and I'd always say, 'Yeah, well, they weren't on long enough, and I was happy on Sunrise.' But you know when that little thing has niggled away at you all your life. So I waited for the DAB launch and managed to sell myself in a long message to Jonny. It was great to sort something out. After a couple of weeks, I asked if I could bring Sarah in.

Sarah LP: Straight away on the show we had a laugh, because we always have a laugh as mates anyway. It's about being really comfortable with each other and picking up on body language for it to flow.

Martin Cee: About two weeks in we started calling ourselves The Ginger Alliance, but just referring to ourselves as that in and around the studio, and then Danny Swallow came in one day and said, 'You guys need a name for the show, it's got to be The Ginger Alliance.' The banter built and then it just clicked and we were off.

Sarah LP: It's how I always wanted my 'duo' show to be, off the wall, different subjects. I'm sure there are people who hate us and say 'God, not that bird with the annoying voice...'

Martin Cee: Lots of people think we're married. Sarah's other half said to me, 'All the grief she gives you means less for me.'

Sarah LP: I love it when we bicker on air. And they are genuine arguments that sometimes do continue in the car on the way home.

Martin Cee: I'm really pernickety. I don't talk over the vocals, there are certain fundamentals in radio that I won't allow to be broken. I play the idents in the right place, and they're not jingles, they're idents. I like to think our show is a throwback to when radio wasn't sterile.

Sarah LP: It's very *Carry On*. I can be quite near the mark. And I've been told by some listeners they tune in for my mistakes.

Martin Cee: Yeah, she still calls Plaistow...Play-stow, for God's sake. But people want something they can relate to. All right, I'm not university-educated, but there are too many formulaic, generic presenters on the radio.

Sarah LP: I'm university-educated but I still sound like a scumbag.

Mete: When I took over the Wednesday breakfast show I branded each hour. *Dusty Vaults*, focusing on a different genre each week; *Songs*

Of Raves - Iconic Clubs, the tracks of an iconic venue or rave; *Pub Quiz*, because that's one pub Covid can't shut; and *Make You Famous*, so listeners can send in their own tracks or dancing videos. Because I'm a salesman, I know how product placement works and I know how to package something. When I was given the Saturday breakfast show I introduced *Digital Bingo*. There are nine tracks on each card so when I play a tune, you mark it off.

From south London, I do a hundred miles and seven hours of radio each week, and I love every minute of it. Two shows, happy as Larry.

Carly Denham: I'd carried on my shows during the transition from The Academy to Pixel, and in the first half of 2019 I had the Friday afternoon show on *Centreforce*, which I was thrilled to have. But because of teaching commitments during the week and DJ bookings at the weekend, I had to go bi-weekly.

When I started on *Force FM,* I played old school garage and early Noughties funky house for those listeners, but more and more on *Centreforce* I've been into the tech side of things, but not if it doesn't go anywhere. I like my music to have big progressions and also vocals. And I'm a firm believer in playing new underground music. I'm not massively into tricks or being a wizard with effects — I believe that clean mixing and going on a journey is most important.

My son Taylor, who is 24 now, is my biggest fan and comes with me to gigs, which is amazing. He's a really good DJ, and won a *Centreforce* mix competition, but I did teach him from a really early age so we've grown up with it together. We did a back-to-back to mother and son set on the *Facebook Live* stream for *Centreforce*, which was a very special. We think in exactly the same way. Taylor will suggest I play a record and I've already got it cued up.

I've got my residency back at The Brickyard, because it reopened after the lockdown with DJs, a 500 capacity and a late licence alongside its lovely restaurant. I'm also programming the other DJs now too.

When I was asked to play at Clockstock it was the stuff that dreams are made of. Taylor was my + 1 and I bought a VIP ticket for his girlfriend, Stephanie, so could all go together. An amazing day. I remember going to Clockwork Orange at Hollywood in Romford on a Bank Holiday when I was 16 and it being the talk of the town. It may sound cheesy and corny but I literally feel blessed every day and extremely humbled that things are finally happening for me.

Paul Gullefer: After stints on pirates *Upfront FM*, *Shine FM* and *Select FM* as Dolly Rockers, Mark and I were asked to go on *Funky SX* in

Southend, the first legal station either of us had been on.

We were recommended to *Centreforce* by Ramsey, so sat down with Andy and Danny at Pixel and loved their plans...and joined the station four months after the DAB licence was secured. *Centreforce* feels completely different from any radio we've done before, with the name, the history, the fanbase and amazing DJs all in place. The pieces of the jigsaw came together. We walk into the studio just before our show and Andy Manston has more than 10,000 people watching on 883TV...on a Friday afternoon. Crazy numbers.

Wayne Soul Avengerz: Ginger was saying to me, 'You need to get back into it, and I was like, 'Nah, nah, nah...' And then he and Paul invited me on their Dolly Rockers show as a guest. I did an hour with them and instantly got my mojo back. I flew back home round the M25 on cloud nine.

I did another guest spot and Andy asked me to come on the station full-time. I used to listen to a lot of radio before I came on *Centreforce,* but it was just so contrived and planned. DJs talking over a 50 minute mix they've done on Ableton.

If Dolly Rockers had a show on Mi-Soul and invited me up, would I have fallen back in love with it? I doubt it very much. I just embraced the rawness of *Centreforce* and being able to play what you want.

Centreforce is just so fresh in an era where so much is premeditated. I've done shows on *Galaxy,* where I've had to submit a playlist two weeks before The first person who meets you at the studio is the producer, and you're like, 'Is it your show or mine?'

But you have to be careful on Centreforce. At the start I did play something with swearing on it — a version of Rene & Angela's *I Love You More*, with a Biggie Smalls rap — and, fair enough, I was banned for 28 days.

Centreforce has taught me that presenters being spontaneous has been largely lost in the digital age. I think about my radio shows all the time but I don't sit at home and plan them, that's the difference. I might work out my first two records on the drive there, but everything after that is on the fly, as I'm playing to a crowd. The 'tune', 'tune', 'tune' messages coming in are the virtual hands in the air, like the instant feedback you get in a club. Another message can make me choose a different record.

Mark Jones: I have big memories of listening to Blocko & Peasy's show on *Kiss FM* in the 1990s, so to be on *Centreforce* now with Alex is amazing. He's like an uncle to us. The likes of Danny Swallow and Max Fernandez are the future, and they make sure other younger DJs are coming through. We were in tower blocks running away from the police, so facilities the kids have now, still with a pirate edge, is fantastic.

Steve ESP: There are no bad show times on *Centreforce*. It's Monday morning Down Under on my show. Gary from New Zealand always locks in when he gets to his office.

For a few months in 2020, I co-presented on Saturday afternoons with my old mate Matt Emulsion, which was great fun. Hopefully, we can do a few more shows together in the future.

I'm really proud to have held down my Sunday night show for several years now.

Texsta: I hadn't been on the radio for many years, but went on *Vision* FM in 2017. I bumped into Ramsey, who was now part of *Centreforce*, and put in a great word for me. After being involved in so many pirates over the years it was surreal to be involved in a legal station, and fantastic to be part of *Centreforce* and their amazing team.

I was approaching 50 and I'd been through and seen a lot. The music industry is a delicate business. One minute they're holding you up on a pedestal and the next minute they're digging your grave and giving you a shovel so you can help, before you have to jump in.

I've been a personal security driver for movie stars and head chauffeur at The Hippodrome and in and out of the rag trade back in the day, but cabbing gives me the flexibility to work around my *Centreforce* commitments. Personally, I feel like I'm in the best place for my music now.

Within three weeks of my first show, through my contacts, and a lady called Miss T, I had booked Victor Simonelli, one of my real house heroes, as a guest on the show. Amazing. A month later Danny asked to pick up Louie Vega and bring him to the station. Wow. Then I met Arthur Baker at the studio and for the 30 Years Of The Force party, I was asked to pick up and be personal security for the night to Robert Owens. I was like, 'Guys, what are you doing to me? This man sung Tears.' But that's the power of *Centreforce.*

Danny is doing such a great job. It's very rare for me to look up to someone who is less than half my age, but he has achieved so much and is a lovely fella. He's lucky, of course, to have the old man behind him, with all his experience. Andy smashed it with Labello Blanco and Public Demand, so big up. His son is doing such a great job and is a credit to him.

My own dad would always say of my 32,000 vinyl collection, 'Why don't you sell all those records, you could buy a house?' I'd say, 'Dad, you have to understand, my record collection is my legacy.'

When the day comes, they will go to my daughter. She's got into mixing so thankfully, she knows that vinyl is not a frisbee.

Seeker: A Thursday in September 2018 had been my first show on *Centreforce* for 28 years. Two weeks later *Centreforce* moved to the Pixel Building. My shows were going okay, but I played a mixture of soulful house, afro-beat, tech and commercial and I think people were a bit shocked at how much new stuff I was playing.

Danny Lines, who I've always had a great connection with, came up to the studio to see me with Rooney, who I didn't recognise at first. He was 16 when he used to sit with me when the studio was in his sister's flat.

And that was the beginning of everything for me and Rooney. Love the Roonster. We exchanged numbers that day and just clicked. The geezer has helped me so much since, spending hours recording rare versions of tracks that I have on vinyl for me. He'd spend a whole day cleaning up one record or getting a crackle or swear word out of it.

Rooney: A couple of years ago I had a real go at digitally recording a lot of the old school vinyl so I know all that stuff inside out. If there are any tracks with something dubious on it, I put it in audio repair software — a wicked tool. If a tune has the line 'Back in the day we used to drop acid,' I replace it with something like, '...used to drop *Centreforce*.'

It's easy to get caught out, but as a DJ, especially on *Centreforce*, you've got to know your records, and sometimes you've got to think on your feet and mix another one in quickly.

Seeker: I started playing with Rooney on four decks on some shows. We don't practise, we don't look at each other, we just jam. I've never had a connection like that with anyone before. Out of all the DJs I've played with, Rooney's the best mixer.

I was now working as an air-conditioning and refrigerator engineer, up and down the country, and I tried out in a few different slots. Then in March 2019, I was asked to play at the Slip Back To '89 *Centreforce* party in Shoreditch. I went back to back with Hugs. Randall played and Corp Dave made a comeback too.

Dave went into producing in the early-'90s, soulful house and afro-beats, under his real name Dave Anthony, and has done really well with his own labels, Vice Versa and Kemet Soul, working with the likes of DJ Spen. Although we drifted apart in the aftermath of *Centreforce*, Dave loaded a music programme on my computer in the early-Noughties and has been on my case about production.

DJ One: I was involved when *Centreforce* came back as a pirate in 2007 but not with the *Time FM* sessions. I didn't jump back into it when it popped up again on *Facebook* or straight away with the DAB. I felt like

I had a DJ's form of writer's block. I get nervous in front of the decks now. I think it's because back in 1989 I was so much in the party all the time — that I just didn't care.

It's funny, I can remember Keith Mac when he started out DJing, just 16, asking me to hang back with him after my set at a party at The Gallery near the Blackwall Tunnel, when he was about to come on, because he was nervous. I still wind him up about that today, but now I'm the nervous one. Keith needn't have worried back then, he was always so talented, and now he's one of the main originals on the modern-day *Centreforce*. Well-deserved. Now I do fortnightly with my pal, Bob, aka Jack Bass, which suits me as he plays most of the music. Andy rings up and says, 'Ian, remember 30 years when you were DJ One, just be that person...' but it's not always easy to recreate that.

I love the Ginger Alliance, that's a proper radio, they both really gel.

Dave Tenacious: When trance started going down the EDM route, we moved back to making house and changed our name so I became Dave Tenacious on *Select.* Martin Cee had moved over to *Centreforce*, but I wasn't sure because I saw it as an old school station, which wasn't what we were playing or making. Then Dolly Rockers left *Select* for *Centreforce* so I started thinking we could make it work. When I saw the studio, I thought, wow, this is another level.

The DAB licence was a major factor and I spoke to Danny Swallow, and he insisted the station would have a short lifespan without new music. For us, it's just amazing to be on a station with so much talent. We're very grateful that other DJs on *Centreforce* like and play our music too.

It was a great honour to be asked to do a prime-time Saturday show. I'm very much on the radio/DJ side of Tenacious. I produce the show. My brother is the geek of the studio, he loves that side of it. He'll go back to back with me in the second half of the show, but he doesn't get on the mic. Lewis comes up with the baselines and the keys.

And since we've been on *Centreforce* it's like our production has gone up a notch. We signed to Ultra Music for our Blondie cover, *Call On Me*, and other bits and pieces to Champion's Cheeky Track, Something Progressive, One File Digital, Jeepers and PP Music.

Aston: I'd done a few guest spots for my pal DJ Fen on *MiSoul,* and wanted to get my soulful house sound on to a decent radio station. I'd heard *Centreforce* had come back on again so I arranged a meeting with Danny Swallow. We had a good chat, but the message was, 'We've got a million DJs wanting to come on.'

The car salesman in me was always going to back in with a new angle,

883
DIGITAL RADIO

SLIPMATT
30 YEARS OF RAVE

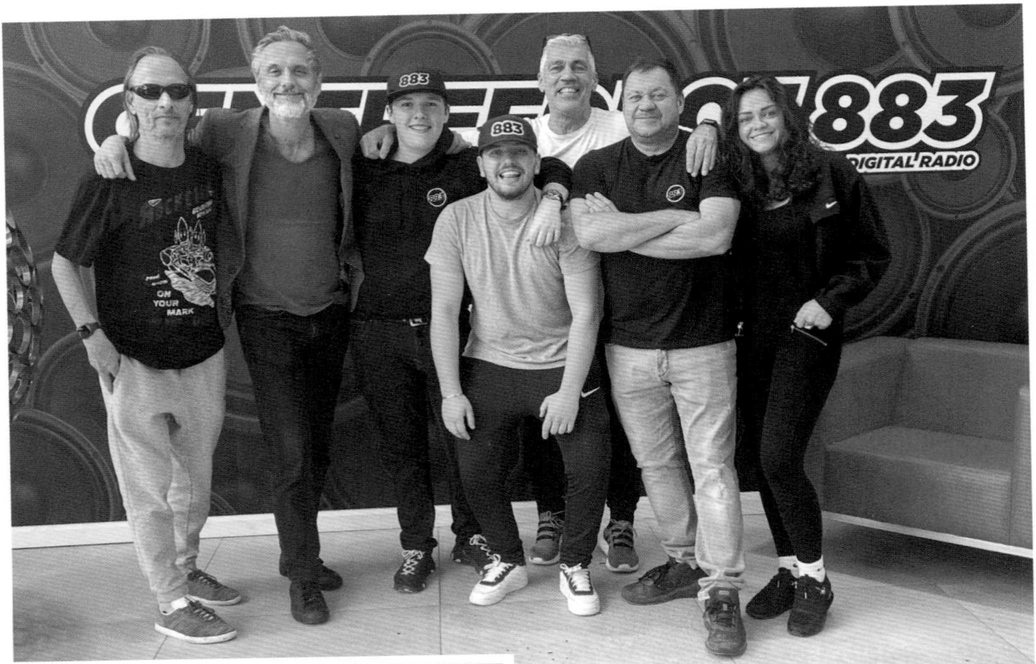

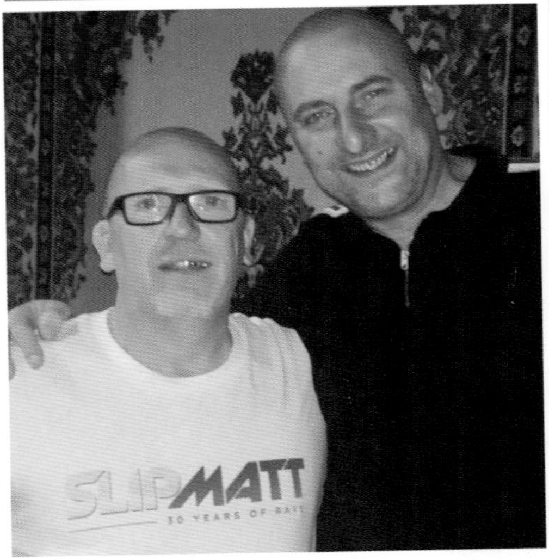

(above) Centreforce management team, left to right) Jonny C, Darren Clack, Max Isaac, Master Pasha, Alex P, Peter P and Elysia.
(left) Paul Larner and Slipmatt in Perth.

30 YEARS OF THE FORCE
1989-2019
SATURDAY 11 MAY / 4PM - 4AM / OVAL SPACE / LONDON E2 9DT
TAKING YOU BACK FROM THE PAST AND INTO THE FUTURE
MAIN ROOM
ROBERT OWENS
RATPACK ALEX P
LISA LOUD / KEITH MAC / DOLLY ROCKERS
ROGER THE DOCTOR / MR & MASTER PASHA
JOE VARNI / JOE BONNER / MARK SMEDLEY
BUBBLER & JOEY G / CHELSEA SINGH & RANDY C
THE TERRACE
JET BOOT JACK / DANIELLE MONTANA
JAMIE F / MAX FERNANDEZ
PETER P & ANDY SMITH
883
skiddle CLICK HERE TO BUY TICKETS

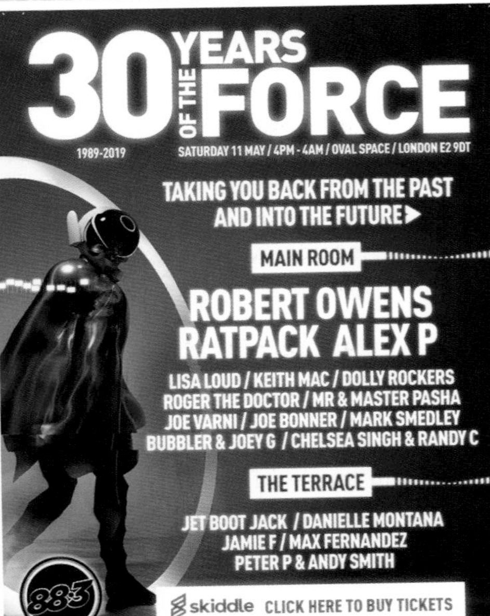

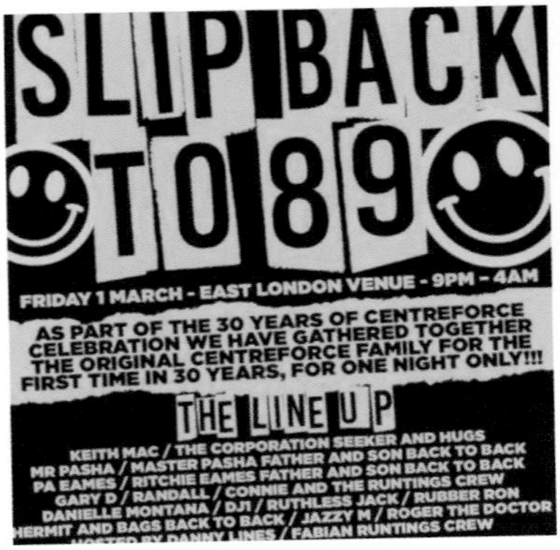

SLIP BACK TO 89
FRIDAY 1 MARCH - EAST LONDON VENUE - 9PM - 4AM
AS PART OF THE 30 YEARS OF CENTREFORCE CELEBRATION WE HAVE GATHERED TOGETHER THE ORIGINAL CENTREFORCE FAMILY FOR THE FIRST TIME IN 30 YEARS, FOR ONE NIGHT ONLY!!!
THE LINE UP
KEITH MAC / THE CORPORATION SEEKER AND HUGS
MR PASHA / MASTER PASHA FATHER AND SON BACK TO BACK
PA EAMES / RITCHIE EAMES FATHER AND SON BACK TO BACK
GARY D / RANDALL / CONNIE AND THE RUNTINGS CREW
DANIELLE MONTANA / DJ1 / RUTHLESS JACK / RUBBER RON
HERMIT AND BAGS BACK TO BACK / JAZZY M / ROGER THE DOCTOR
FABIAN RUNTINGS CREW

so I pitched a Hotbed show, because of my association with Kai Can't who runs Abode and its off-shoot Hotbed, and was given Monday nights. I have a little joke on my show that it's for the connoisseurs, there's no karaoke house. I have brilliant Hotbed residents like Billy Cocks, Larry London and Danny Langham coming in to guest on rotation, plus my boy Max, who I taught to mix in lockdown. Quality soulful house is my sound, I've always played it, I never step out of line. If you book me, that's what you get.

It's great that Victor Simonelli has an association with the station, all those years after we shared his tracks in Tenerife. After Knuckles and Morales, for me, in the '90s Victor was THE man.

Alex Little: I've known Jonny C for more than 20 years and had been talking to him about joining *Centreforce* since 2018, but my overseas work just wouldn't allow me to get involved. A year later, my full-time client, Paul Allen, sadly passed away so I took a security job in the UK and asked Jonny if the offer still stood? It's strange because I'd always hated my voice. I wouldn't even leave a voice note on *WhatsApp*, but I couldn't turn down the opportunity to join *Centreforce*.

I needed to get a demo to Jonny, so I made my daughter and her boyfriend sit in front of me, while I recorded it, which was a bit weird. I was given some midweek early hours shows, which became popular in Australia, especially via an old friend Marky Mark, who was a percussionist at the Juicy Tunes nights I was involved with. He told his pal in Perth, Paul Larner, that I was playing disco edits around their breakfast time.

As well as myself, there's Mick Turrell, Josh Watts and Anthony P, who also have a lot of listeners down under, because of the time difference.

Paul got involved in helping to promote *Centreforce* among its members. Australian producer Dr Packer sends advance releases, so I play loads of his stuff. Now Paul Larner has been presenting shows himself and is looking to bring some of us over from Centreforce to play at his promotions with Dr Packer whenever that's possible, which is just fantastic. It'll be amazing to meet the *Centreforce* listeners in Perth.

Paul Larner: Marky Mark told me there was this guy playing disco house edits, including Dr Packer records, on *Centreforce* at silly o'clock in the UK, but it's our breakfast time.

When I lived in Reading in the late-'80s, we used to drive into London and try and find *Centreforce* on the radio in our cars to find out what parties to go to or meet ticket agents.

And as for disco edits? Well, I've been to the local media in Perth several times, TV channels and newspapers. I tell that they have an international DJ/ producer in Perth who is flown out of Australia for three months of the year to play at some of the biggest clubs in the world, and still plays in our local pub to nobody. Would they like to interview Dr Packer, but they're not interested.

Because the radio here is like going back to 1970s Britain, there are no dance music stations in Perth. They play Aussie rock band Midnight Oil literally every hour. They also love ACDC, Jimmy Barnes and Cold Chisel and that's it...and Jimmy Barnes is the lead singer of Cold Chisel, so it's the same thing anyway.

That's why Alex Little has blown up here, because people are like, thank God for that. As a promoter, it was an easy sell for me.

A *Facebook* advert went out for Alex's show and got a lot of traction, so I started a group called the Southern Hemisphere *Centreforce* Family. I made some promo flyers and then began converting the schedule into relevant timezones on a spread sheet so it was more user-friendly for listeners down here. We've got some listeners in New Zealand too. The best known one, of course, is Gary.

When the listeners in the UK go to bed, we swamp the station and takeover. We have 200 people in our group, but I'm told there have been 1200 downloads of the Centreforce app in the Perth area. We are connected to certain listeners, and we all shout-out each other. Micky Moore, Eternal Nightshift Ravers, Silver Surfer — we all know when each other is online.

Paul is behind the SOS (Secret's Our Success) warehouse parties for the ex-pat community in Perth and has flown over some familiar guests.

In 2015 I started putting on SOS, which are illegal warehouse raves, and warehouses in Australia really are in the middle of nowhere.

In 2017 I flew Eamon Downes of Liquid/Sweet Harmony fame over to Australia...three months later I brought Slipmatt over, but because these parties weren't above board I couldn't announce the guest. I had to explain to one of my rave heroes, that I wasn't going to advertise him. Matt was like, 'Wait a minute, you're going to fly me to the other side of the world and not put me on a flyer? Mate, I'm in, I love that.'

In Perth itself there's more ex-pats than Australians interested in our scene, so there's a massive market there for the taking.

We had 400 people at the party — it was an amazing success and Matt invited us over to Ibiza in 2018 for his Slip Back In Time week, so 25 of us flew over. We've had Matt back again, this time legit, and for 700 people. And SOS is non-for-profit. Any money we make goes straight back into booking the next guy.

In March 2021 we put on a *Centreforce*-themed party here called On The Streets Of East Perth, outside a pub, with our DJs, a PA from Victoria

Newton, of *U Sure Do* - Strike/ fame, and had Mick Turrell from *Centreforce* playing a live stream for an hour from his shed in Milton Keynes.

It was an honour to be asked to present some shows myself, initially covering from various people. I got a call from Alex, Andy and Darren Clack, who I've worked closely with since I set the *Facebook* group up. They asked me to do a show the following day. I'm a promoter with no radio experience, but I made it work with a mix of old school rave music, 1990-93, disco edits and new breakbeat. I also had Greg, Dr Packer in for a very exclusive guest mix.

Ultimately I want to bring some *Centreforce* boys out to Australia... but we don't want the bigger daytime names, we want the middle of the night people, who we listen to live here...the out of hours DJs.

Jon Ulysses: Alex P invited me to come on *Centreforce* for his battle of the DJs. Apart from a guest mix and a bit of chat on Pete Tong's Essential mix, I'd never really done any radio, despite being on the mic all my life, it seemed. I approached Alex and he worked out a bi-weekly show for me. I like to think I provide something a little bit different within the *Centreforce* remit. And I can promote the new artists and my own material on my Uli-Bug label, so I'm really happy.

Jonny C: I'm on the DJs all the time so I know I can be a pain, but I hope I'm able to tune into each one of them and get their vibe. There's 80-odd DJs on the station so that's a lot of people to be in contact with. We've got so many *Centreforce WhatsApp* groups. We message to see who can cover shows for others and everybody mucks in. As soon as *Centreforce* became legal a lot more DJs wanted to know, but most of us were illegal all of our lives, so it's been a challenge. Some DJs have been and gone because they wanted us to blow smoke up their arses. There isn't time for that. Our DJs wouldn't be on the station if they weren't good enough. We are constantly looking to tweak things, so it's not a closed shop.

Like everyone involved, I've brought in my fair share of the DJs. Matt Emulsion stands out for me. He's been a fundamental part of dance music in the Essex area and part of the pirate story for years. He really picks what he plays and has the knowledge and experience we need. The stuff he was doing on *Force FM* for Bill was in a different league. Sonny Kane is a young DJ who came on with some other guys but immediately stood out. He has such an energy, is up for the crack and the banter and has taken everything on board. Danny Lines and Rooney, The Super Smiley Show, and Bubbler, they're on a different level too, that lot.

I also enjoy my own show so much. It's 4am-6am every Friday and I bill it as 'The Official Acid House Show For The UK'. I call my listeners

'Acid Owls' which is good fun and fitting for that time of the morning.

Peter Faire's business portfolio includes office fit-out specialists Choice Interiors, a chain of bars including The Vault in Shenfield and The Rising Sun, in Hornchurch, and the roll out of a group of boxing gyms under The Vault brand in the Essex area too.

Finding the Pixel, courtesy of Ed, and him being an old *Centreforce* fan and right in amongst it back in the day, made him a perfect fit as another investor, so we joined forces to work on the project together.

I started in the building game on the tools, and went on to develop my own team. We got a few lucky breaks along the way, including the contract to fit out the We Works group of buildings throughout Central London. My drive first is to succeed, and I know the rewards will follow. Someone once told me, 'Some people are poor, all they've got is money,' and I've always tried to remember that. I like the fact that both the bars and the radio station support multiple people at a time.

Ed and I are learning all the time about the radio business. We have to meet in the middle with the guys sometimes. Ed is naturally more hands on being based at the Pixel, but between us we try and offer whatever support or skillset we can to help.

Ed Simpson: There are enough of my businesses which aren't any fun at all, but it's hilarious down there in the *Centreforce* office. The stories, the banter and some real characters involved and passing through.

Everybody at the Pixel loves *Centreforce* being here. Anybody who gets shown around the building is taken into *Centreforce.*

The station has created its own family and its own set of values, and now, amazingly, is so much bigger than the first time around. I love the way *Centreforce* transcends generations too. I imagine an apprentice who puts on *Centreforce* at work listening to his boss, open-mouthed, as he recounts stories about the crazy nights and clubs that he went to and where all the music came from.

And it's great that the shout-outs, which were originally a vehicle for pirate stations to assess the reach of their signal, have evolved into an amazing support network and continue to keep *Centreforce* and its listeners so connected.

SMASHING THE GRAMMY OUT OF IT

Despite, and either side of, the Covid pandemic, these *Centreforce* DJs have been on the top of their game.

Mark Jones: When Paul and I went on our own with Dolly Rockers, both as DJs and in the studio, it took a while for us to build our kit and find our sound. We produced more than 100 tracks and remixes as Dolly Rockers and had five No 1s on the download charts. But looking back, those Dolly Rocker releases were 7/10s at best. We were doing remixes for the sake of it so there wasn't a lot of quality control. When we joined forces with Wayne Soul Avengerz in 2019 we needed to kick on.

Paul Gullefer: Wayne lives and breathes music but was disillusioned. The disco elements that helped him make his name with Soul Avengerz were coming back in, though. When he guested on our *Centreforce* show and heard what we were making, he said he'd love to go in the studio. It was perfect timing. Mark and I decided to create a new alias, Odyssey Inc, for the work with Wayne as it's not as heavy as the usual Dolly stuff.

Wayne Soul Avengerz: After being on *Centreforce* and getting back into playing music I naturally thought about producing again. I was still apprehensive, but it was such a giggle in the studio with Mark and Paul, and so refreshing to work like that. I think it shows in our music, and with us all able to keep our separate identities, not feeling tied to one studio project is really important. After putting out our first few releases on various labels, we decided to set up our own one, Trois Garcon, which simply symbolises, 'Three mates, three blokes, making music and having fun doing it.'

Paul Gullefer: Our *WhatsApp* group is constantly pinging with ideas so I don't think we'll run out any day soon. Most of the blueprint production is done at home, then we use bigger studios in Old Street and Elephant & Castle with regular engineers we gel with, to get things like baselines replayed. I think as experienced DJs we know what works, and what doesn't and all that projects back into our sound.

Mark Jones: We are much more selective about releases on Trois Garcon. Nothing gets released unless it's an 8/10 and I think that showed because all but one of first ten releases were Top 5 in the download charts. I was always told a decent single bought you a nice car and a successful album your house. It's a completely different business now, but we're doing okay.

We're very fortunate that Andy Swallow gave us carte blanche to remix anything from his Labello Blanco back catalogue, the first fittingly a Dolly Rockers Festival Mix of *Wishing On A Star* by 883 featuring Lisa May.

Highlights from those Wayne Soul Avengerz and Odyssey Inc collaborations include covers of Stephanie Mills' *Never Knew Love Like This Before*, re-sung by Vanessa Jackson, Respect by Adeva and *Heard It All Before* by Sunshine Anderson, both re-sung by Krysten Cummings, and Harold Melvin's *The Love I Lost*.

While *Centreforce* colleague Keith Mac has had two tracks signed to Trois Garcon, *Voices In My Heads* and *Got No Love To Give*.

Wayne Soul Avengerz: We set the label up because we were throwing 50% of each track away by giving our records to other labels. Now we're seeing records we turned down coming out on labels that we thought were bigger than us.

Brian Tappert at *Tracksource* advised us to do covers, rather than sample tracks, because then it's all above board and you just allocate the publishing to the right people. With that in mind, we try to pick records, like the original *Love I Lost* or *Never Knew Love*, that are vocal anthems, but there's no way a DJ could drop them in the middle of their set, because there's not quite enough BPM to keep the dancefloor.

With his and Odyssey Inc's cover of the Shawn Christopher classic *Another Sleepless Night* just weeks away from being released, Wayne Soul Avengerz was invited to a Zoom call with the producer behind the track, Mike Hitman Wilson, Shawn and their lawyer.

Wayne Soul Avengerz: They opened the conversation and said, 'You plan to release your version four weeks before we release the 30th anniversary release package, which includes remixes by Kevin Saunderson and Steve Silk Hurley?'

So I said, 'Okay, we won't release our version, then...'

And I think it kind of threw them, because they were probably expecting some big legal debate.

I continued, 'Listen, guys, I'm a fan. I bought the record first time around. We covered it because we love it. Do you think I'm going to sit here and embarrass myself, arguing about me copying your music?'

I could see them thinking, well, this is refreshing, and then Mike said, 'We really love your mix. If we send you Shaun's vocals, we'd actually like it to be part of the 30th package too.'

Wow...now I was taken aback. But then I thought, while we're on a roll, I'll chance my arm. So I said, *Don't Lose That Magic* must be 30 years old soon too. Any chance we can remix that also?'

'Yeah, sure.'

What a result! Minutes earlier I was looking at pulling our cover of *Another Sleepless Night.* Now we were involved in official remixes of both of Shawn's amazing vocal anthems. They also agreed we could recoup any costs and have Trois Garcon branding on any releases.

The meeting couldn't have gone better.

I added, 'Listen, guys, we make house music, don't we... house music at its happiest?'

'Yeah, yeah...'

'So, how can I make music like that, and then act like a wrong-un when it comes to the business side of things?'

For me, it's all about doing business the right way and being able to walk around and hold your head up high...haha...which is also a track I remixed when I was in Soul Avengerz.

Mike and Shawn's lawyer signed off, 'Wayne, one door opens, a million doors open.'

Forty eight hours later, I received an email saying our mix of *Another Sleepless Night* had been nominated for a Grammy, in the best Remix Category...our actual mix. I was stunned and sat on the news for a week before I told the Dollys, who were shocked and delighted too. I needed to get it checked out in case it was a wind-up, worried that five years later I'd still be known as the guy who told everyone he'd been nominated for a Grammy.

Sam Supplier's production career was also about to sky rocket, although it wasn't the smoothest of take-offs.

I managed to sell The Opera Club on and did okay, but pumped a significant amount of money into a festival that didn't happen, for a number of reasons. I ran to the toilet puking when it was confirmed I'd lost the lot. Fortunately, I'd been building a career as Sam Supplier, the DJ. I was still small-time, and had taken a huge wage dip, but I was living my dream again.

I was DJing at the Ministry before a Brazilian guy called Volkoder. If you had told me a couple of years before that I'd be playing main rooms like that, and at Fabric, I would have been, 'Whoa, yes please, let's do it.'

After the gig, Volkoder DMd me and asked about a tune I played, and added, 'I think it could be a hit, but there's load are of things I'd do differently to it.'

I was like, 'Mate, if you want to change anything, let's collab and make that hit.' So we did...and the result was the tech-house track *Volcano* (by Volkoder and Sam Supplier). Fisher, the Grammy-nominated Aussie based in Hollywood, who I DJd for in L.A a year earlier, signed the track for his Catch & Release Records label.

I knew *Volcano* was going to be big for a year or so. We were just waiting for the sample clearance, and then I was going to tour America and Brazil. But just as the track began to blow up in the States, I went from doing 207 shows in the twelve months before the pandemic, to two shows in the next 12 months. It was horrible. The most successful thing that could have happened to me, and I wasn't able to do anything with it. That success was actually more of a kick in the nuts in a strange way. I felt like I'd lost my mojo. I even got sick of making music.

The *Centreforce* Party In The Park in September 2020 at least gave me that feeling of being at a festival or an event, and that was amazing in the middle of the year we'd had.

I had to remind myself in the context of what was going on globally, that I was now being successful as an artist, and that became the most satisfying thing. I was now settled on making my own take on tech and minimal house and working with labels like Sony/Columbia in New York, CR2 worldwide and Global Underground.

I re-made an old hardcore track that I liked right at the start of getting into rave music — *Sound Is For The Underground* by Krome & Time. I basically turned an old hardcore track into a house track. I was trying to get clearance from Danny Donnelly, from Suburban Base, who lives in LA now and came to one of my shows in Hollywood. Danny was like, 'Mate, I love the record, fuck that, I want to sign it...'

The idea to just sign various single deals is deliberate so I'm not tied to any one label. I feel like I have an album-worth of material, but it hasn't been the right time to do it yet. Also, what I've learned from the music industry is that what seems like a good deal isn't always the best deal or the best label to go with. Some record deals for shit money are better than the ones with bigger advances because that label might do better for the record than the label with more finance. I've thankfully learned that money shouldn't always be at forefront of your mind.

If anyone had been smashing the 'granny' out of it...then it's the reborn and revitalised Clockwork Orange. The Ibiza weeks got bigger, including huge parties at Benimussa Park and culminating with a 25th birthday party at Amnesia for 6,000 people with a line-up of Paul Oakenfold, Jeremy Healy, Graeme Park, Seb Fontaine, Tall Paul, Smokin' Jo, Alfredo, Brandon Block, Alex P, Jason Bye, plus Andy and Danny. Selling out Fabric, Printworks and the Ministry also set new standards back in London.

Danny Clockwork: We had the best bar spend at Amnesia...ever. And they could have taken more, if they had listened to me. We've always had big bar spends, since day one. When we first did Clockstock the geezer suggested ten bars. I said, 'Make it 20.' He told me after the event, he was glad he did. Now we have 30 bars. When we approached Printworks about doing a party, the young booker said, 'Who are you?' When I told them we had £50 per head bar spends, his ears soon pricked up.

Particularly special were the two Clockwork trips to Australia. Amazing parties in the bush in Perth for a two-and-half thousand, mainly ex-pat crowd. It was amazing flying out there with Tall Paul, Seb Fontaine and Jeremy Healy, and spending quality time with those guys all these years later, especially someone like Jeremy, who was a hero of mine back then. I'll never forget the way he commanded the crowd at Es Paradis in 1998. Three thousand six hundred people in a 1900-capacity club, the entire crowd in the palm of his hand.

Andy Manston: We began to see a younger crowd coming through, loving the family Clockwork atmosphere.

Importantly, the music policy was evolving again too. We started to get interest from some of the cooler DJs in the modern-day house scene. I wanted the Clockwork Orange brand to evolve away from just old-school, and I began to change my own philosophy too, with a deeper, tech house sound. That didn't go down well initially with the older Clocky lot, so it was tough, but they came round. It does help with larger multi-arena events where you have the best of both worlds.

I'd already tried to get Eats Everything, but his agent knocked me back, saying it wasn't right for his brand. Then Eats reached out through Luke Neville and we met in Ibiza. He told us he'd watched footage of our parties and said they were 'sick'. He's used to everyone filming him all

(left hand page) The Clockwork Orange massive at Clockstock, Chelmsford, 2021 (right) Clockwork Orange duo Andy Manston and Danny Gould at Clockstock 2021.

(above) Dolly Rockers and Wayne Soul Avengerz at Party In The Park, 2020 with (left) Danny Lines and (right) Chalkie White.

night on their phones, so he loved the fact that doesn't happen at Clockwork. Eats rang his agent in front of me and said something along the lines of, 'What the fuck did you do that for?'...and thankfully he played for us at the rescheduled Clockstock festival in September 2021 on a line-up also including house legends Armand Van Helden, David Morales, Kevin Saunderson and Marshall Jefferson.

Danny Clockwork: Personally, everything that Clockwork is today originates from what I learned in my early days of sobriety and at AA meetings. Not on a holy tip, or anything above that, but the core message is...who are we to judge?

The Clocky Way. Treat a Clockworker the way you would like to be treated. If you find a phone or a wallet or someone's keys, hand it in. If you bump into someone and spill their drink, say sorry and buy them another one.

When we relaunched in 2012, I was a completely different geezer because I was nine years sober. In 2021 at Clockstock I was 18 years clean of drugs and alcohol. When we're doing Clockwork in Ibiza now, I wake up at 5.30am, have a coffee, turn my laptop and phone on and get on the socials as the sun comes up. Boom, that's it, I'm in...caffeine, a cigarette, blue sky...I'm buzzing. At Clockstock I'm there from seven in the morning, helping set up. Then the meet and greet as people start arriving...but because I'm getting on, I have a personal masseuse to loosen my back up every hour, then back into the throng.

Alistair Whitehead turned to me when he was coming off the main stage at Benimussa Park and said what a lot of people say...'I can't believe what a nice man you've turned into.'

Andy Manston: It's remarkable how Danny has turned himself around. I don't know how he does it. He is so strong because by being so involved in the scene still, he is always around people who are partying. But his drug is now Clockwork and making people happy. Danny is the best promoter, the way he orchestrates things. He's become the frontman, but I'm more than happy with that. It's a partnership and we make all the decisions together.

Sam, Andy and Danny were all welcome additions to the *Centreforce* team during lockdown.

Sam Supplier: Pre-Covid, Master Pasha asked me to guest on his *Centreforce* show, which I loved doing. When the lockdowns hit, Danny asked to do my own show and I could just tell that the station had got so much bigger. The listeners were bombarding the studio with shout-outs. I was like, blinking hell, it's livened up on here, I have to get involved more regularly. Due to my ban, *Centreforce* having such a pirate feel is a huge pull for me.

The concept for my Analog Records show means artists from my label cover me the weeks I'm unavailable. It's sick to go on there and play all the new music I've just made.

For me, *Centreforce* is absolutely just for the love of doing radio. I still feel I have the same energy for it as I did when I was 15.

Andy Manston: When we went into lockdown in March 2020, Andy and Danny Swallow approached us. They told us about the platform they created by relaunching *Centreforce* and asked us if we'd like do a weekend takeover to help raise money for the NHS.

Andy also explained that us bringing back Clockwork Orange so successfully had inspired him to relaunch *Centreforce*.

We started on the Saturday morning and I'd never seen anything like it before. Danny went on at 7am and there were 100,000 listeners. The server blew, and we went off air for a few minutes while they sorted out a new one.

I hadn't done any radio since a dodgy pirate when I was 17, but when I asked to do a regular show, I was like, why not. It was hard at the start, mixing and talking and doing all the shout-outs, but you get used to it. I just love the show. I think it's one of the best career moves I could have made.

My Friday drivetime show started out as 'Andy Manston's Start Of The Weekend'. My first hour always has a theme, a particular label or producer, and in the second I wanted to champion new squelchy house music, like I'd been trying to introduce at Clockwork. Then one of the listeners messaged and said, 'Mate, this music is proper filth,' which I read out. And then someone called me 'Dr Filth.' I said, 'We need a name for this show,' and someone suggested 'Filthy Fridays,' and I was like, 'Bang, done.' It's great that it evolved so organically from the listeners because without them the show is nothing. I have to be careful what I read out, though. The regulars try and catch me out with some of the stuff they message in, but it's all good banter. It does feel like I've brainwashed people, playing tech house at 5pm on a Friday, but now if I play something funkier they complain and ask for filth. I'm even booked to play out as 'Dr Filth' sometimes.

Danny Clockwork: I did my first show on *Centreforce* (for the takeover) at Keith Mac's studio. Straight after Andy rang Keith, who spoke to him, and then put the phone down and said, 'He wants you to do a weekly show on *Centreforce*.' I said, 'What do you mean, you're joking?'

I was so excited I was like a little kid.

Jeremy, Jon Ulysses and Tony Nicholls were also offered shows on the back of that Clockwork weekend. Jon has been a regular for us for many years and is an Ibiza legend in his own right….and we love Nicholls. Tony's a classy DJ and a classy guy.

I'd never done radio before, but I love it. I call mine the marmite show, for obvious reasons. I get to play the music that I love on a Saturday morning. The Balearic, alternative, eclectic mix that I fell in love with back in the day, and that's how my brain works, a little bit all over the show. I just try to be a bit different. I play around with the listeners' names, have a bit of fun with it.

I do it live from my loft, often in my pants, having a cigarette out of the window, hopefully as the sun shines through. I think my show works better like that, than in the studio standing up, which I think is much more geared up for a house show.

I still try and hunt for old *Centreforce* tapes and mixes, to try and hear that obscure old school record or rare Balearic B-side I'd forgotten about or never heard before, so I can play it on my show now.

Centreforce ignited my passion for house music, and started me on the road to Clockwork, then we came back and inspired *Centreforce* to relaunch. To be invited on and then offered shows is an honour and a privilege. It's gone full circle and that circle keeps spinning.

Jeremy Healy at Clockstock, 2021.

YOUNG GUNS

Max Isaac was destined for a mundane stint of work experience in an office when his mum's colleague asked his mate Danny Swallow if *Centreforce* could arrange anything. Within weeks, 15 year old aspiring Epping-based bedroom DJ Max was reporting to the studio at the Pixel Building, and opportunity quickly knocked.

I'd only been there an hour and a half when Danny turned to me and said, 'You're a DJ, right?'

I mean, I hadn't even set foot in a nightclub and wouldn't be allowed in one legally for a couple of years at least.

'Yeah, that's right,' I replied, as confidently as possible.

'Okay, cool, we'll go back to back on my show next week.'

It was a bold and generous statement from Master Pasha, only 22 himself...seemingly offering Max the chance of his short lifetime so far.

I can't lie, I was shit-scared at the thought of mixing live on the radio so I practised every night at home on my controller to make sure I was as tight as possible. They were using the original CDJ 2000s in the studio at that point, which I'd never used. Danny even said I could use my controller, but I thought, no, if I'm going to do this, I have to use the proper equipment.

Surrounded by rave culture growing up, Max started watching DJ videos on *YouTube* at the age of six.

I thought it looked cool so I downloaded an app on my iPad and learned to mix off that. It probably sounded pony, but I loved it.

My dad Alan, aka Big Al, listened to *Centreforce* back in the day and was into hard house and trance in his raving days in the '90s. When he was satisfied that I was really interested, he bought me a controller with a built-in sound-system, a Philips M1XDJ. It meant I could plug in my iPad, with all my music on, but I still didn't know about mixing with vinyl or CDs at that point. When I was ten I got a pair of Pioneer CDJ 400s and a mixer for Christmas but I didn't get on with them. It was like I'd stepped up too early. So when I was 12, I sold them and got the original all-in-one USB Pioneer controller, which had 'Record Box', and that's when I took it much more seriously and started to do parties at school and mate's birthdays. I'd do my homework when I got home and practise my mixing for the rest of the night.

My dad had been listening to the station for four or five months so he told me all about *Centreforce* and its history. All the other kids at school started their work experience on the Monday, but I started on the Tuesday because back then at *Centreforce* they had 'the three-day week-end' so nobody came into the office on a Monday. I did Tuesday to Friday for two weeks and my mates were already jealous about that.

In the office, then, it was just Danny, Jonny C and Hazel, God rest her soul. I couldn't have dreamt that I'd be on the radio so soon. The show went well and feedback was really good.

In the middle of my two weeks at the station, *Centreforce* also held their DAB first birthday at Hangar in London Fields so I also went to my first ever rave. Mental. Danny told me to keep in touch so I came back in a few times in the school holidays. I met Max Fernandez and the connection I had with those two guys was so important. Luckily, Danny told my school I could come in when I wanted, and my teachers actively encouraged it because it was such a unique kind of work experience. Then I started editing the *Centreforce* vlogs.

Danny also came down to the school and did a presentation to my class. I kept in touch with the guys and went to Slip Back To '89 Part Zoo at Oval Space, in November 2019, and helped out. The kids who were previously winding me up being on the radio were now asking me for guest list.

Then I left school early in March 2020 because of the pandemic. We got predicted grades and a lot of us had to re-sit exams because we just weren't happy with our results. When Covid kicked in, I was just at home doing nothing. Then Danny called and asked if I could help with the second Clockwork Orange takeover at the studio. I started coming in every week after that, doing business studies at college alongside it.

From that point on everything happened so fast. I started to do some cover shows, as Max The Apprentice, and then in the summer of 2020 I was given my own show, early on a Monday morning, called Wake Up With Maxwell, which was such an honour.

The run up to the socially-distanced Party In The Park at Colesdale Farm in the September was another great opportunity, being involved in an outdoor event for the first time. When things opened up again in 2021, I finally got to play in a club at the *Centreforce* residencies at The Green Rooms and The Playhouse. I only turned 18 in the November.

Max currently presents the early breakfast show on a Friday morning, which leads nicely into the Boys At Work show, hosted by his mentors, and now production partners, Master Pasha and Max Fernandez, who will probably always call him 'The Apprentice'.

Danny and Max are like older brothers to me; they've always been there for me...and the banter is amazing.

DJing will always be my first love, but I really love producing too. As The Boys At Work & Max Isaac, the first track we did for the *Centreforce* Records label was a rework of Brandy & Monica's *The Boy Is Mine*. We've got lots of other tracks in the pipeline and I'm working on a couple of my own tracks.

I can't thank Andy Swallow and the whole team at *Centreforce* enough for the support they've given me. But without Danny asking me to go back-to-back with him for that show, I'd probably still be a bedroom DJ. It took me out of my comfort zone and kicked-started everything for me.

As she stood awkwardly in the main room at Studio 338 in Greenwich and the entire room focused on the DJ, a 17-year-old Elysia Lee instantly knew her vocation in life.

I get excited just talking about it. It was my first proper rave, Abode. I remember the record the DJ, GW Harrison, dropped as I stood there. *They Don't Know* by Disciples. All I could think was, I need to do this. I grew up in the Havering-Atte-Bower and Collier Row area and had been to a few bars, but not a proper club night. I didn't even know what to wear to 338. I had on weird trousers and awful wedge trainers. I looked like an idiot, but I absolutely loved the night. I was just obsessed with GW and the other DJs, Jimmy Switch, Ellie Cocks and special guests Secondcity.

I went home and Googled 'DJ lessons'. I hooked up with the LSA (London Sound Academy) in Camden and had lessons with its owner Buster, who is great. Things happened quite quickly for me, with a couple of big gigs at Egg and Ministry Of Sound. But I was also in my first serious relationship and my boyfriend didn't seem keen on me being a DJ, so it was hard to progress. When we broke up a year or so later I thought, right, I'm going for my dream now, I'm going to face it. As soon as I put my all into it and concentrated on myself, my DJ career took off with gigs at places like BoxPark and back at Ministry. By early 2020 I'd started getting my name out there nicely. I'd also studied music production through the LSA, working on Logic, but had now moved on to Ableton, via Point Blank Music School.

Then Covid hit and it all came crashing down. It was obviously hard to take, but everyone was going a through a really tough time. I just tried to stay positive and think about what I could do to keep my name out

Let’s go, let’s go!
(main picture) DJ Elysia
(above) Max Isaac
(right) Ryan Willmott.

there and continue to grow as a DJ. I approached *Select Radio,* which was app-based at the time, and was given a Thursday night show. It was a great opportunity to try and develop both my DJ and radio skills, at a time when the country had virtually shut down.

The lockdowns were such a difficult time, but it gave me the opportunity to sit down and think about what I really wanted to do with my life. I left school at 16 and got an apprenticeship at a bank in Brentwood, and worked in the city for a while, before moving into recruitment. I was working from home, but also spent time setting up a mentoring business, aimed at helping young DJs and producers get into the business.

I knew of the *Centreforce* name, and that it had come on DAB. I got hold of Alex P's email address and sent him one of my *Select* shows. He offered me a late-night trial show, which went well, and I was given a bi-weekly with Carly Denham on a Tuesday. It was just amazing to become part of *Centreforce*. Then I was offered a role running the socials.

As 'Freedom Day' approached and DJ bookings returned it meant Elysia was able to take a shot at being a full-time DJ.

It was a tough decision, but I could tell it would become harder to juggle everything At the same time I signed a couple of records to Vivifier Records, including *Affection* and *In my Life*, which charted well on *Beatport*. The label has really backed me, getting me bookings at Bora Bora beach club in both Ibiza and Malta in the summer of 2021, where I did three headline shows. It was mad, because Bora Bora was the place I'd partied in Ibiza when I was 18 and now I've played there. I took my mum with me, so it was great for her to experience it too.

A few weeks after things started to open up again, I looked at my diary and realised I was booked up for the whole of August, which was a great feeling. *Centreforce* have been amazingly supportive too, and got me involved in as many of their events as possible. And now I've teamed with the station to co-promote a new event in Shoreditch, based on my own debut promotion at Cargo, which had to be cancelled when lockdown began. My event was called Audaz, which means Fearless in Spanish, but we've now launched a co-pro Audaz 883 to help showcase the talents of the younger DJs at the station.

Elysia admits being a female DJ definitely has its pros and cons.

Initially, I thought it was an advantage because I was probably getting bookings because I was a girl. But I've had two promoters ring me up now and say they have to take me off the line-up because their girlfriend was annoyed. I'm like, they actually just said that to me? It's ridiculous,

I hardly even speak to the promoters when I'm playing at their events, because they're so busy. The whole industry can be quite cliquey and sometimes you have to be one of the boys to get in with the boys, so that's when it can become harder, but I like to think I'm one of the lads anyway. And everyone is great to me at *Centreforce*, always great banter. Thankfully, there's so much more diversity and inclusivity in all walks of life now so hopefully that will continue in the DJ world too.

After getting knocked back from Ushuaia, with his parents already inside, the pressure was on a 16 year old Ryan Willmott to rescue his night out.

My mate and I didn't really stand a chance. We'd bought dodgy ID from eBay for a tenner, but they were fake actor's union membership cards. The Ushuaia security threatened to call the police so we legged it. We managed to swap our £100 pair of tickets with a street vendor for passes to Hi Ibiza across the road, but we weren't holding out much hope. There were at least a thousand people in the queue, and as we got closer to the front they seemed to be IDing everybody. Somehow the door staff were overwhelmed and we managed to walk through un-checked. We couldn't believe it, we were in. We daren't risk buying an alcoholic drink in case we got IDd and thrown out, so we bought a 13 Euro bottle of water, headed to the front of the main stage and stayed there for the next six hours listening to headliners Martin Garrix and Jonas Blue, and got home at 5am.

A couple of days later I went to the *Radio 1* live broadcast from Cafe Mambo. There was no age-limit to this event down at the front in San Antonio. Fatboy Slim, Claptone, Duke Dumont, Annie Mac and Danny Howard were all playing so it was a phenomenal line-up.

I was officially hooked. My parents had always listened to house music when I was growing up, and I knew older friends that were DJs. I bought a Numark controller for £100. It was all I could afford with any birthday and pocket money I had left. I spent every night in my room practising.

On a lads' holiday to Ibiza the next summer, Adam Beyer playing techno at Resistance at Privilege was a huge influence for me and the tech-house sound I now prefer. It really opened up a whole new world, because the music was so much more underground than I'd ever experienced before. Eats Everything and Patrick Topping played back-to-back for six hours. It blew my mind. I'd never heard a journey like that before, or even see two people play for so long together. To be sat in the cab on the way home to the hotel with the sun coming up was just the best feeling.

The dream was to maybe play music to a few people one day. The deeper I delved online the more I moved away from the generic dance music I'd been brought up on. I watched anything on *YouTube* that showed the technical side of DJing from different camera angles, and picked things up by trial and error.

I started recording my mixes and comparing them to pro DJs, but I was still a million miles away from what they were doing. At least I had a reference point. Slowly my technique did get better and I started to believe I might be moving towards what was expected in a club situation.

My first gig was through a mate of my dad's, Jodi, at his Catch The Feeling old school party in a marquee for a thousand people in Billericay. I played the warm-up spot to my mates, the staff and a few early-doors raves, but, importantly, it was the first time I'd heard the music I played on such a large scale. I also played at the packed after-party in a local bar and the feeling the next day was amazing, because when you start out you never think you're actually going to play to people.

I enrolled on a DJ course at the London Sound Academy (LSA), where I also learned how to play vinyl. It gave me so much confidence, and led to bookings through the LSA at the Ministry Of Sound, including the last set in the middle bar room, coming on after Maxine from Toolroom, which was a real milestone for me.

Soon I was getting at least one gig a month, although I have to say I was still usually playing for free. Then Covid hit and completely wiped out my schedule that summer, which included the We Are Festival. Ibiza was on the cards too and those months would have really kicked me on. But I had finished Business Studies at uni, so instead of writing essays I spent all my time learning how to use Ableton and produce.

Centreforce launched their breakthrough DJ competition in conjunction with Time Off Festival with a first prize of £1,000, two flights to Ibiza and a set of headphones, which I entered. By now I was a massive fan of the station, and played alongside a lot of the DJs, but as a young kid getting on a huge old school station like that seemed unrealistic.

Then in the middle of the lockdowns I was booked to play at Housework in Kavos. With the pandemic still at a critical point, my parents would only allow me to go if I isolated when I got back home. It seemed a sacrifice well worth making. I played on two boat parties in one afternoon, jumping between the two out at sea and playing after Rob Tissera and Slipmatt, which was daunting to say the least, now I was such a fan of his *Centreforce* show, and the techy 'Rave-House' sound he'd been pushing.

Back at home, my ten-day isolation began...in the cabin at the bottom of the garden. I was given a bucket, my dinner left outside, zero physical contact allowed with my family. A few days earlier I'd been DJing on a sun-drenched boat off the coast of Corfu. Now I sat in McDonalds in Benfleet to pass the time. On the third or fourth day I was allowed in the house to use the toilet.

Meanwhile, out of a hundred entrants I had progressed through the first two rounds of the *Centreforce* DJ competition, via remote half hour mixes. The semi-final was in a function suite in the grounds of the old Epping Forest Country Club, a live half-hour mix in front of an X Factor style panel including Alex P and Martin Cee from the station and reps from Time Off. It was nerve-wracking and unnerving at the same time with the judges in the booth at times watching and taking notes, and it's not like you can go on any kind of journey in 30 minutes. I made it to the final in Crawley, under the same format, judged on things like track selection, mixing ability and overall flow, and won.

Alex launched a Young Guns slot on *Centreforce*, midnight-4am, supervised by Max Ferdnandez, so all six finalists could take part, and Max asked me to do a guest mix on the Boys At Work show Friday breakfast show, which was a real honour. Then I was offered a bi-weekly Thursday 6pm-8pm slot alongside Jon Ulysses.

Rob Tissera became a studio mentor to me, advising me on my first release, *Give It To Me Baby* on Stash Records, so meeting him in Kavos made my quarantine in the garden even more worthwhile.

It was a whirlwind few months. To have a regular show on *Centreforce* is just amazing. The listeners are so fanatical. There are people in Australia messaging in to say they've set their alarms at 3am to listen to my show. Blimey. Being part of the *Centreforce* family and being able to get advice from all the *Centreforce* DJs and having that access is invaluable.

By joining *Centreforce*, Sonny Kane, 22, was able to reconnect his dad, Joe, with some old friends.

Dad grew up on the same estate in Islington as Wayne Soul Avengerz and Mark Jones from the Dolly Rockers. He messaged the guys on social media and said his son was on *Centreforce* and they were like, no way. They all knocked around together as kids, went to clubs like Ra-Ra's in Angel and hung out when Mark and Wayne starting DJing in the '80s. It's great they're all back in the touch through *Centreforce.*

My family has always been a big influence. The classics at family parties growing up would be *Show Me Love* and *Finally.* Nan would put a bit of Motown on, and then Dad would play *Tears* or The Nightwriters.

I was born and bred in Bethnal Green, then we moved out to

Chingford when I was 12. With a December birthday I was one of the younger ones in my year so started going out with my older brother first. One of his mates was an R&B DJ who taught me the basics when my mum suggested I get a controller for my 16th.

I emailed a couple of mixes to some local clubs and Club 195 in Epping came back and offered me warm-up slots, which was amazing.

In 2018 I went to the *Centreforce* party at The Steelyard and then two years later, just before lockdown, The Pineapple Disco at Village Underground.

When I was 19 I was booked to play at 632 Sessions, which is named after one of the guys' street numbers at his house in Chigwell. Another one of them was going out with a girl who was related to Danny Swallow so they managed to get a 632 Sessions show on *Centreforce*, Monday night/Tuesday morning, midnight-2am.

I'm a plumber and the other two were roofers so it wasn't ideal as we all have to be up for work at 5am, but I knew it was an opportunity to get noticed. When the other guys started missing the show more and more I did one on my own.

Jonny C, who we call Big Brother, because he is always listening, worked out what was going on, and I was offered my own show two hours earlier from 10pm.

Danny Swallow and the rest of the management started listening. I was thrown in at the deep end during lockdown and asked to cover a Bank Holiday Sunday show when everyone was at home and in their gardens. Again, I just took the opportunity.

There are so many people that would bite your hand off to get on *Centreforce*, and there's only so many shows and hours that can be filled, so anything they gave me I was all over it.

Danny Swallow has been amazing, giving us young ones opportunities, but then he knows what it's like to be a young DJ himself. He was quick to invite me as a guest to the Boys At Work show, which I did during Max Isaac's first week of work experience. He was bringing us in cups of tea so it's fantastic that he's got his own shows now.

Towards the end of the lockdowns in 2021, I was asked to move to 10pm-midnight on Saturdays, which was another amazing opportunity, and great exposure for me, especially during the pandemic, with everyone at home. I just asked if I could go back to midweek when restrictions were lifted and my DJ bookings started to come back. And Alex P was good to his word, moving me back to a midweek shot. I love being part of Wonky Wednesdays coming on after legends like Ratpack and Slipmatt.

And Sonny certainly needed his Saturday nights and weekends clear. As we spoke he had nine gigs over the forthcoming Bank Holiday August Weekend.

After 18 months of Covid restrictions it was so good to be booked again at festivals like House & Classics and in the *Centreforce* area at the We Are Festival. Also my regular work for people like Boat Club Events, who took me out to Ibiza, for what was also my first visit there, in 2019 for gigs at O-Beach, Wicky Woo and STK.

It's also great to be part of Elysia and *Centreforce*'s Audaz 883 parties with other young *Centreforce* DJs, especially as we don't always get to meet at the station. It's also a chance for the younger listeners to have their own party. The older lot might only go out once a month these days because they get written off for two weeks when they do, haha.

My plan is to finish my plumbing apprenticeship so I have a trade to fall back on, and then have a crack at being a full-time DJ. I don't suppose I'll still be DJing when I'm 50 or 60.

Well, you never know, Sonny. Just take a look around the *Centreforce* studio...

Sonny Kane playing for Boat Club Events.

LOCKED IN, LOCKED ON

YOUR ISOLATION STATION

Jonny C: As the first lockdown began to unfold in April 2020, only a certain amount of DJs were able and allowed to be live from the studio at Pixel, so around 40 others needed to present their shows from home. All that had to be set up remotely. Usually, I'd go round to their houses, but, instead, everything had to be done on the phone.

Each DJ required a hard-wired internet connection, a certain amount of bandwidth and two computers, one for playing the music through and another to access the messaging system. And a decent sound card, at £120 a pop, to be able to get the audio from their turntable or controller into their computer, a lot of which I had to clean up in the process. It was a full IT mission, from the ground up.It took ten minutes to get some up and running, and others four days. Some of the older lot, they stand behind the decks and they're DJ Gods, but give them a cable and they haven't got a clue. Thankfully I had the amazing support of my partner Jo throughout.

As I was in the vulnerable category, I wasn't allowed any interaction at the studio itself for a year. I was only allowed there on specified visits, for essential maintenance work, if the office was empty and there were back-to-back shows being done from home.

The socially-distanced Party In The Park event we were able to pull off in September 2020 was great. It was different, but it was so important to get an event away after the six months people had been through.

Peter P: Just before lockdown I went to A&E with chest pains and was diagnosed with pneumonia. I was sent home and despite being asthmatic, should have been okay with a week or so rest, but I must have caught Covid at the hospital. During one of my shows from home my oxygen levels were so low I called an ambulance, which at that point I was told would be five hours. Thankfully it turned up in three and a half because the hospital told me later that another 40 minutes and I wouldn't have made it.

But now the real battle began. I was in King George's hospital for three weeks, on oxygen for 19 days. There were ten beds in my ward, and 12 people who passed through died. The minute one had left us, another guy appeared. News reached me that Larry Foster, the hugely-respected Room At The Top resident DJ, had died from Covid during that period.

I was getting so many messages from listeners and friends, which was amazing, so I posted on *Facebook* from hospital to tell people this disease was real. After a while I could tell which patients weren't going to make it. They'd be a nuisance, not taking it seriously, not keeping their oxygen on at all times or not eating the hospital food. The next day they'd be dead. One night I felt like I was on my last legs, so I messaged my son, Harry. With visiting not allowed I was surprised when he appeared at the end of my bed. He'd come up to the hospital, and very luckily knew the security guys on the door from promoting parties in Romford. They got him protective clothing and smuggled him in. Harry sat with me and I cried for an hour. His visit probably saved my life. So far I'd refused to go to the intensive care unit because I hadn't seen anybody come back from there yet. After my son left, I fought with everything I had, and never gave into the ICU. When I was discharged I had a really tough four or five weeks at home, but gradually got through it.

On my first show back I started with *Staying Alive* and *Back To Life*. The welcome I received back from the listeners was unbelievable. I broke down and cried again after.

Master Pasha: When I tested positive with Covid, on reflection, it was a massive wake-up call for me. I was run-down and my immune system was low so I was vulnerable. I realised I had to change the way I lived. I needed to step up to the plate, and if I was going to make the station work, I needed to do things differently. And from that day I like to think I found a new love for it, and started to fully appreciate the opportunity I'd been given. I think there was a bit of arrogance there, but now there is much more appreciation and hopefully I'm much more humble.

After the first six months of the pandemic, being able to put on The Party In The Park was the icing on the cake for me.

Andy Manston: I remember being on our lads skiing trip and me and Tall Paul were like, whoa, what's this...what's going on? We had a Clockwork party on March 7th at Magazine, and the Monday after Boris said, you should stop going to nightclubs, and then clubs started closing down, and my world fell apart. We were still living in hope that it would go away before Clockwork in September. It was a tough couple of years, losing two festivals and two Ibizas.

Both me and Danny went back to our old jobs, for a year. In between, the only thing that kept me sane was the radio show because the feedback from the listeners was just phenomenal. The takeovers were great, people were having their own parties in their gardens. *Centreforce* got more listeners and Clockwork got a new audience. It was a win-win.

Peter Faires: The pandemic was obviously disastrous for the events side of our business but, in a big way, it helped the station because the listening figures went through the roof. I loved *Centreforce* during those horrible lockdowns. You whacked the radio on and it was always chirpy.

Jamie F: The pandemic was so hard for everyone, but the listeners always remained so positive After a long career in the print, I was furloughed from my graphic design job then made redundant. All my regular DJ work went too, like all of the other guys. There were dark times. Losing everything at once was soul-destroying, but my radio show helped keep me going. Gradually, things began to improve. I took a delivery job with Morrisons, then began re-skilling for a full-time role and, thankfully, as things began to unlock, the DJ bookings started to come back.

Our annual Summer Soulstice event was cancelled and didn't happen in 2021, but headliners Soul II Soul will thankfully appear in 2022.

Dean Lambert: In July 2020, I produced and released a tribute track to my wife called *Amy's Love*, with Andrew Galea, under the name D'Landy, which sampled her favourite Evelyn Champagne King record *I'm In Love*. With no clubs or events to play it at, thankfully I was able to play it on my show, and it got a great response from the listeners. It's obviously very personal to me. so will hopefully be re-released at some point.

Dave Tenacious: A lot of the guys streamed in from home, but I liked to go to the studio, because I felt like I was going out and doing something. It was also nice that Danny Gould rang us up and asked us to be part of the Clockwork Orange takeover. We did the midnight-1am set, and at one point we had 8,500 people watching on 883TV, which is amazing for that time of the morning.

Tony Nicholls: I'd had some late-night shows on a Saturday as part of *Centreforce* Sessions on *Time FM*, to promote my venue The Buddah Lounge. When I took part in the first Clockwork Orange takeover during lockdown, Master Pasha approached me about a weekly show and it was a privilege to be asked. What *Centreforce* is able to do, with no playlist and DJs playing what they want, is fantastic.

Lockdown was really tough, with the live side of our industry completely shut. I personally had 25 weddings, plus other 40ths, 50ths, etc, in the diary for 2020, and all those either had to be postponed or cancelled.

(top) Ratpack and (above) Peter P with son Harry. at Party In The Park, 2020 © Sharpscape Photography. (right) the cover artwork for Dean Lambert's *Amy's Love* release.

Joining *Centreforce* was so good for my mental health during lockdown. Just sitting down each week to work out my show was so exciting.

Martin Cee: Our show, particularly during lockdown, was like therapy for us, and hopefully the station is like that for the listeners. If you went legal before, you needed traffic reports and news. With all the apps available on our phone, we all know where the traffic jams are. And there's rarely any good news anyway.

Sarah LP: We deliberately didn't mention the word 'Coronavirus' once. Listeners were able to tune in and escape for two hours.

Wayne Soul Avengerz: Daydreaming during lockdowns gave me a chance to reflect and realise, do you know what, I'm lucky to like the music that I like. I could have grown up with Bon Jovi posters on my bedroom wall. Defected put up a post on social media that asked, 'What does house music mean to you?' And I would answer that, family and health aside, in one word..it means 'everything'. Because everything I have done and do revolves around house music. The way I dress, the clubs I go to...the books I read and the films I watch. Everything is driven around the scene I belong to.

Regular listeners of Jeremy Healy's show on *Centreforce* will have heard his tribute shows to the likes of David Bowie, Prince and Fleetwood Mac.

I was lucky enough to meet David in 2001 at an after-party for a Galliano show in New York. He was stood at the bar, but I think he was clean at that point and looked at our little lot, as if to say, 'Oh no, these guys are trouble.' So we chatted for a while, but he was definitely on edge and legged it soon after.

My first involvement on the station was as a guest on one of Alex P's 'Battle Of The Bangers' shows. I felt really relaxed and happy in the *Centreforce* studio with Alex. When he suggested I do a regular show I wasn't interested, probably because I'd had a bad experience with *Radio 1* in the '90s. They told me what to play and their conservative version of the scene was so regimented that I left after a couple of weeks.

When Covid happened I got back in touch with Alex to do a test show. I was asked to commit for three months, which at the start of the pandemic, when everyone thought it might be over in a few weeks, was still a big ask for me. I'm pushing 60 now, so I like to have as much time off DJing as possible. But I did commit, expecting to be back on the road by the end of it. I started off on Tuesdays with my friend Matt helping with the shout-outs, but moved to Thursdays, with Lisa Nash co-hosting, because I'm still recovering from the weekend on a Monday, when you'll only get a few steps out of me, a couple of sentences...and about four Deliveroos.

But I stayed at *Centreforce* because coming up with something new each week enlivens me, and keeps me focused. I also love it because at a club I'm usually put into a slot in the middle of the night when I'm expected to play certain tunes, but on the radio I can go way outside of that, like with the tribute shows. The feedback that I get through the messaging means a lot, and it feeds you. The Australian fanbase means a lot to me, because I love going there, and I love them reaching out on *Centreforce*.

I always felt that the connection with the crowd is the most important thing. I've realised over the years that the so-called cooler clubs aren't always that cool really, because they're usually full of people who take themselves far too seriously. These days I play in clubs for enjoyment, and I love playing for people who I have worked with over the years. Like Danny Gould and Andy Manston. Clockwork Orange was always my favourite club to play at in Ibiza, and the one I chose to play at when I could have played at all the others. It was just the best, most raucous rock and roll atmosphere. Danny hanging off the ceiling, throwing drinks at everyone, just brilliant. The sightline at Es Paradis was perfect because everybody could see the DJ and the dancefloor and we could see everybody too. It was funny going back there after 20 years with Clockwork... everything a little bit smaller, like going back to your old school.

Lisa Nash: I'd interviewed Jeremy Healy many times over the years for *Clubavision* and we'd always stayed in touch. When he and Alex P contacted me about his *Centreforce* show I was really happy to get involved. We started during lockdown, so it was great to come to the studio and have that outlet when everyone had been partying in their kitchens for 18 months. It's been great to get behind the microphone for the radio shows, and also at some of the *Centreforce* events. I'm also talking to the guys about developing 883 TV, which is exciting coming from my *Clubavision* roots. It feels like I'm part of a whole new family at *Centreforce* and I love the continued resurgence of the scene after all these years.

It's crazy that I'm on the station with people like Chris Paul. I went to his Orange parties at Camden Palace in the early-'90s when I was 15, 16. Straight to my job at the cafe in Valentines Park in Ilford where I'd fall asleep doing the ice creams.

After a stint on *Galaxy Radio* in the late-'90s Allister Whitehead was pleasantly surprised to become part of the *Centreforce* family.

I was living in London around that time and had an early evening Friday show on *Galaxy*, which was part of *Heart FM*, so I recorded my show there. I didn't really get on with it, the whole thing just felt too corporate, so I was happy when it finished.

We were in lockdown at the start of 2021 when Jeremy asked me to cover for him. That show went well and I was offered my own one. I'm based in Gloucestershire now, but it was just lovely to have a reason to travel and to get out of the house.

I love the fact that live radio stretches and tests a DJ so much. If you play two or three club sets in one night you can essentially play the same records each time so you can get lazy, but each radio show has to be different. I like to plan my radio shows, so that the mixes have longevity for those checking them out on *Mixcloud*. I see mixes as mini pieces of art, like painting a new picture each time.

They say you can't teach a new dog old tricks, but, actually, with radio you can, because you can be so creative, there's so much scope. I could just sense the ambition of *Centreforce* and quickly see what an amazing reach it had.

Whenever I tell people of a certain age what I'm doing now, they say, 'What... THE *Centreforce*?'

Steve Kite: In the run-up to joining *Centreforce,* I'd had stints on *Link FM*, a community station on Harold Hill, and the online version of *Stomp FM*, 2013 -2016. As we were moving into lockdown in 2020, I was offered a show on Morgan Khan's *Streetsounds* station. Max Fernandez heard me play a '90s house set at Caister and had been in touch and then Danny Swallow asked me about a Sunday afternoon show, so it was great to be able to choose *Centreforce* instead.

Slipmatt: Jonny C called in lockdown and asked if I'd get more involved, and I thought, I'm not going anywhere for a while, let's do it.

I'm playing a lot of new music, especially the tech-house side of things. And I'm all about #ravehouse, which is a new genre I'm pushing and producing too. My *Centreforce* show is making me download 25-30 new tracks a week and I'd say the show is 75% new music now, which is perfect, because I don't just want to be known for playing old school. It's great that *Centreforce* brought me back round to the housier side of things again and pushed me on again as a DJ.

Kenny Ken: Andy was always in touch trying to get me involved. We've always had a mutual respect over the years but I was hesitant. Andy wouldn't let it go, so I could tell *Centreforce* was going places.

Finally I agreed to present a show for the station's 32nd birthday and was adamant I would play house. It was my first time at the Pixel and I couldn't believe the set-up, it's proper in there. It was hard to keep up with the amount of shout-outs, and my inbox about it was crazy with people saying they loved the show. Even the guy who fixed my car was like, 'Ken, that set you played on *Centreforce*, everyone's talking about it.'

I've always collected house music and never lost my love for it over the decades, even though I wasn't playing it out. There's a few of us, Grooverider, Frostie and Bryan G, who still collect house music, because it's nice to have it sitting there in our collections. I've really been feeling techy, deep house more recently and I guess with my background in jungle and drum and bass, I would always lean to that side of things and bring it hard and tough. When I play drum and bass I need to get a reaction, and when I play house on *Centreforce* I don't just want to be another DJ playing old school. I know it works because when I played at a *Centreforce* party a few years ago in Hackney, I blended some newer techier tunes with the old school and it popped off in there nicely.

Production-wise, I'm working on mainly drum and bass, but if I get any brain-block I listen to some house to try and get some inspiration, and see if I can come back in another direction. I'm really happy to be part of *Centreforce*'s history and its future.

Tony Perry: I'd been doing some *Instagram* Lives for my mates to get through the lockdowns. I had a lot of time on my hands so I got a green screen, worked on graphics and spent some money on some voiceovers.

I'd just returned a Playstation I'd never taken out of its box, got a copy of Ableton instead, and started to rekindle production again, edits of the tracks I was playing, including a mash-up of Rozalla's *Everybody's Free* and Liquid's *Sweet Harmony.*

Danny Swallow contacted me about a show on Saturday mornings. I knew the station's rich history so I was excited to join *Centreforce*, later moving to Monday drivetime. I try to get a good balance between the old stuff, new mixes of classics and also new bits from people like Prosper and Vice, who I think are amazing. I definitely think there's a whole new rave thing about to explode, because it has commercial appeal, much more so than tech house.

I was delighted when my *Free For Sweet Harmony* track got such a good reaction on my show, but I didn't think anything of it. Then out of nowhere Mark Brown from CR2 Records DMd me on *Instagram* and I was like, oh no, does he own some of it? But he actually wanted to sign it. Turns out Mark had listened to *Centreforce* all through lockdown.

I wasn't sure how we'd be able to clear all the samples, but Mark suggested we completely re-make all the parts, so the track was a cover.

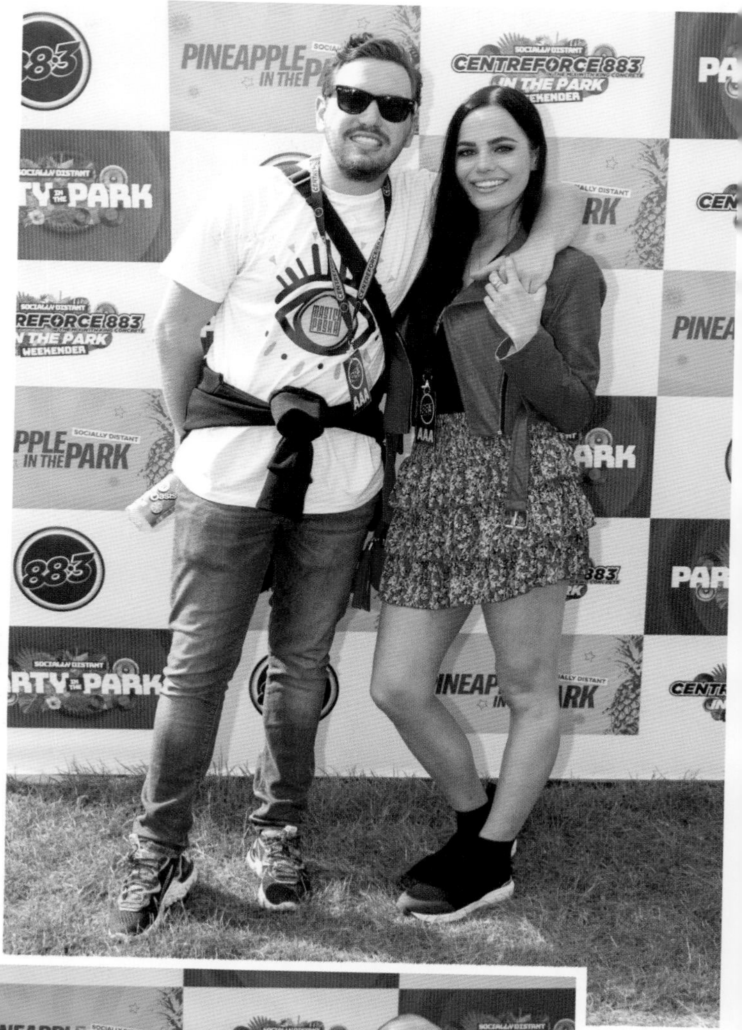

(right) Danny Swallow and fiancé Amber and (below) Keith Mac and wife Nicky (left) with friends, at Party In The Park, 2020.

© Sharpscape Photography.

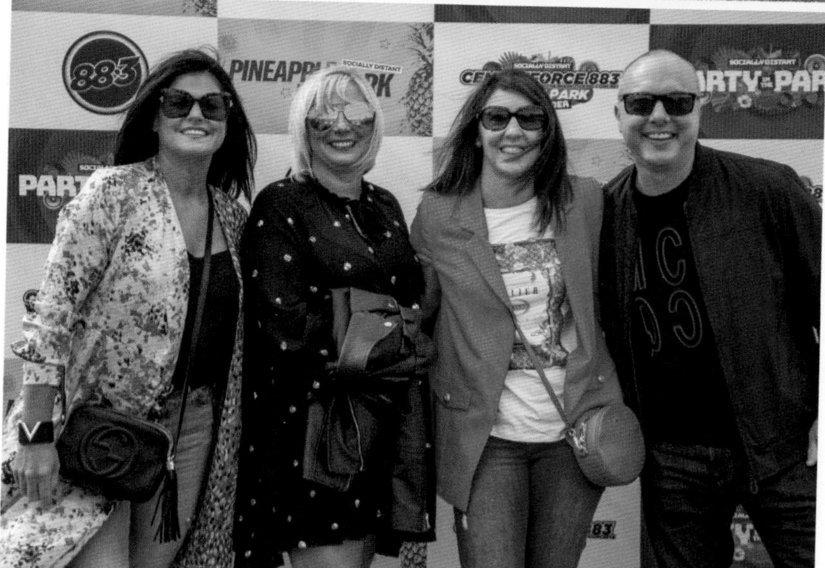

We did approach Rozalla to get involved, but she wasn't interested. We got it on *Kiss Dance*, *Love Island* and I'm mates with Ricky, Melvin and Charlie so they played it on *Radio 1,* when it got 4,500 Shazams in one night. It's crazy considering my cousin Eren made the Candi Staton/Frankie Knuckles mash-up back in the day.

At the same time, I was asked to be the official DJ at Wembley for the Euro 2020 (in 2021), virtually pitch-side near the corner flag, playing at all the major games including England's historic run to the final. It was a crazy few weeks. I was able to get my parents tickets to the final. After years of taking me to Sunday League football with my two left feet, there were plenty of jokes about finally going to see their son play at Wembley.

I like to think that I showed during the Euros that if you play the right records at the right time, you can make a real impact. There's huge potential, brand-wise, as well. I am booked by UEFA to play at the Women's Euros in 2022 and I'm hoping to do more work with England, hopefully at the Qatar World Cup and maybe closer to home with my team, Arsenal.

***Centreforce* business and commercial Darren Clack remembers the station accompanying him to his first rave, a Raindance event, aged 16.**

Waiting at the meeting point with my older brother and his mates, I was blown away by the amount of people gathered and still arriving. When the word came through, we sped off in Ford Fiestas, Vauxhall Novas and Austin Metros. Then the sudden realisation that every other car had *Centreforce* blaring from its open windows. It felt like our secret, an amazing shared experience with complete strangers we had everything in common with. When we arrived the thing that struck me most was the sound of the bass in my chest. After that night, at any rave, it was always that sense of anticipation, arriving at an event, the bass vibrating during the walk through an industrial estate or a field that got me. Raves at Grange Farm in Chigwell in 1992 were particularly special.

When jungle came through around 1993 I was 19, so that was perfect timing for me. I loved AWOL and it's been great reminiscing with Kenny Ken at the studio about those days.

I worked as a civil servant throughout the '90s, working for government ministers like Anne Widdecombe and Michael Portillo, then witnessed first hand New Labour's General Election victory in 1997.

I relocated to Australia in 2000 after a spell travelling down under and lived in Sydney until 2013. I put on parties and supplied DJs for fashion shows. I set up my own recruitment company and also worked in PR at Home nightclub, where Jason Bye, an old friend of my brother, was resident when he wasn't in Ibiza.

Growing up in Glasgow in the late-'80s didn't prevent *Centreforce's* in-house graphic designer Neil Shand from hearing the station.

Our pals worked as builders in London and stayed in Plaistow. They listened to *Centreforce* and went to The Dungeons. Every month they'd come back up the road with cassette recordings. It was clearly all kicking off down there, but not so much happening in Glasgow or where we lived just outside in Erskine. The first track I heard on a *Centreforce* tape was *Everything Starts With An E*, with that Hendrix-style intro. We'd been into Public Enemy, rap music, a bit of James Brown, so I was like, what the fuck is this? I haven't heard anything like that before.

Previously, my age-group had grown up with the New Romantics, so it was pretty grim in parts. And when the ecstasy came in, it was difficult being a group of lads in Glasgow who only drank water. Playing our *Centreforce* tapes became part of our night out, whether it was driving up into Glasgow or up to Sterling. We loved hearing the shout-outs on *Centreforce*. We didn't mind it being so London-centric. Announcements like, 'You need to look out for a guy in a black XR2i to collect your tickets,' sounded so cool.

Back at someone's place after a night at places like Sub Club, it would be, whose got a copy of the latest *Centreforce* tape doing the rounds? The fact the reception on the recordings wasn't the best, and it might have been copied several times, just added to the mystique of it all.

Our one attempt to go to a proper old school warehouse party was a trip to Newcastle, but the police raided it, and we turned around and drove home. There were some big legal events put on in Glasgow, but they just didn't have the same appeal as what we were hearing was going on down south.

When Darren at *Centreforce*, an old contact of mine, called up and said he'd hooked up with some West Ham boys who had relaunched their radio station, I was like, 'You're joking me? *Centreforce* is still as cool as fuck, and I always thought it had the best name. You'd be hard pushed to get a cooler name for anything. Even *Centreforce* Window Cleaners sounds cool as fuck.

Hamish MacLean is the voice behind many *Centreforce* adverts: his company Urban Radio produces those important few minutes at the top of the hour.

I had a hip-hop show on a pirate station in Luton called *Jive FM* in 1988 when I was 17, alongside DJs like Eddie Richards and Jon Jules.

The first I heard about *Centreforce* was in a James Hamilton article in *Record*

Mirror about pirate stations stealing each other's transmitters. Up until *Centreforce*, pirate radio had been very bland, presented in a formulaic style, inherited from local independent radio and, I have to say, *Kiss* was as well. *Centreforce* presenters sounded like a bloke down the pub, doing a DJ set in a club, on the radio. I loved the long adverts, with the phone numbers to secret events. It was like the underground had arrived. In a way, *Centreforce* democratised dance music, because loads of people found it for the first time.

I remember working in a pub just off the M1 in 1989, when a load of Millwall fans came in after a match, and they were joking about 'lots of orange seats flying around,' with reference to a trouble at recent Luton/Millwall game. I played *Oochy Koochy* by Baby Ford and they all started dancing and going mental, and that wouldn't have happened the year before.

I started doing adverts for reggae pirate stations and later did a lot of work for Select UK. A DJ I'd done some jingles for recommended me to Jonny C and I've been at *Centreforce* since 2017.

Ricky Cooper was a founder of the UK's first internet radio station Gaia Live with Mr C, which was first based in Brick Lane and later moved to The End nightclub.

I was involved with the free parties scene in 1993/94, with people like Spiral Tribe and DIY Soundsystem and then we put on our own Home-grown parties at Middlesex University with Mr C and the guys from *Freek FM*, EZ and Karl Tuff Enuff Brown.

For our monthly broadcasts with *Gaia Live*, I'd do American deep house, Mr C did the techno and then we'd have a drum and bass guest too, like Bukem or Goldie.

I was resident at a beach club just outside Lisbon in Portugal, then moved to Sydney in 2001. I owned a little bar, restaurant and club on Bondi Beach called Mocean, where Clacker (Darren) had a seat at the bar.

I'm now based on the Central Coast at Umina Beach, an hour outside of Sydney. I've run my Return To Rio three-day boutique electronic music festival on the banks of the Hawkesbury River for the last ten years. It's a Burning Man kind of vibe for 5,000 people and our first event out of lockdown sold out in 20 minutes. Mr C is our resident, and when I first booked him he wasn't aware until we met that I was the guy he set Gaia Live up with all those years before. Carl Cox, who lives in Melbourne, has played for us three times, the all-day Mobile Disco he does with Eric Powell. There's so much great Australian talent we book like Made In Paris and Dirty South, alongside the likes of Dixon, Ame, Acid Pauli and Greg Wilson. I'd say at least 60% of our crowd are ex-pats and most are old enough to remember *Centreforce* growing up back home.

When I was offered a *Centreforce* show, an early Saturday morning

UK slot, which means an afternoon show in Oz, it was a great fit for us. I play lots of new stuff, with a nice chilled vibe, from a nice little beach spot, when possible

Darren Clack: When I came back to the UK in 2013 and began working in football sponsorship I bumped into Andy and Danny Swallow through a corporate job at West Ham. We got chatting again at The Dovecote in Chingford when they were doing the *Facebook* Live sessions and after the DAB had been running for a while I offered to help with the marketing of *Centreforce*, which quickly became a full-time role.

I organised a *Centreforce* takeover of the Heineken Bar at the London Stadium on Rainbow Laces days with Artful Dodger and Danielle Montana performing. It was so busy we had to draft in Mickey Moore as back-up security. I had similar fanzone days lined up for Crystal Palace and at Millwall, with Mete, which I had to get special permission from Andy for.

I came in at a point when Hazel, who had been doing a lot of office management and admin, had tragically passed away, and various other people had left. When Peter P and Danny both got Covid it was a difficult time for all concerned. Alex P came on board as station manager and between all of us, we've managed to keep moving the station forward.

Everybody talks here about not wanting to become *Kiss*, i.e, a pre-programmed commercial station. The pirate sound we are known for is organic, but we set parameters because we are a commercial business and we have to abide by Ofcom rules. Covid was the best and worst thing for the station. The events side of our business was obviously decimated but the listening figures went off the scale and we've now had more than six and a half million unique listeners. As we came out of the lockdowns it was amazing to be able to put on unique events like the Party In The Park and Step Back 2 Back.

Our listeners are unrivalled. Their loyalty is the kind every major brand strives for. It's become almost a throwaway comment, 'the *Centreforce* family', but it really is just that. The shout-outs, which come in from all over the world, continue to play such a huge role in the success of the station, and still allow us and the listeners to appreciate just how far *Centreforce* reaches.

Andy Swallow: The *Centreforce* story keeps building and developing. We can only see the station becoming a much bigger network over the coming years. We have already expanded our reach on DAB to the north-west of England and North Wales. Further territories in the UK, other exciting expansion plans and new Global partnerships are all in the pipeline. We're really excited about launching *Centreforce* in Scotland, where we hope listeners will 'keep it loched'.

(above) The Eternal Nightshift Ravers (below) Jon O'Brien and friends, at Party In The Park, 2020.

AH YEAH...

Jonny C: *Centreforce* was the first acid house station to run 24 hours a day, seven days a week. No other station can say that, so the roots of the station are always there. A lot of people tried to copy it, and then when we came back on 88.4 in 2008, we were broadcasting pioneers again, changing the way the studio talked to the rooftops. I was looking at TV and live streaming even then, but the technology wasn't ready. We watched carefully as *Facebook* evolved, then used it to relaunch the modern-day version of *Centreforce.*

Our philosophy is always, 'If you're going to do it, then do it properly.' We don't try and go head to head with anyone, or battle anyone, we just do our own thing. When we were in that container in Dagenham, still a pirate, I couldn't have imagined we'd have a legal DAB station with millions of listeners just over a decade later.

Master Pasha: The last few years have been a crazy. Every day I wake up and think, thank God this has happened. It's the best, worst, most amazing thing I've ever done. If it had lasted one year or two years, I would have still been proud, but to have taken *Centreforce* to where we have is beyond my wildest dreams. I have got carried away at times with the station's success, but thankfully I've got my family to give me a slap down when they need to put me back in my place.

I want to continue to nurture young DJs and young people, because I went through a long time in my life contemplating what I wanted to do. It's also okay to not know what you want to do, but the pressure can be unhealthy. Then it's easy to get pigeon-holed into something that you don't want to do.

People may listen to me on the *Centreforce* and think that everything's fine with me, he's on the radio, life is good, but everybody has things going on in the background. I had opportunity thrust upon me, but that doesn't mean I haven't had to work for it. I've had a lot of good luck, I'll admit that, but I've had a lot of shit luck too. But when you get a break, you've got to put the work in to make things happen.

I would say to anyone who wants to be a DJ, have a look in the mirror and ask yourself if you have got the time to practise — all those hours when it sounds awful before it suddenly clicks. I'm still learning every day.

Wayne Soul Avengerz: For me, the essence of being a music lover is that it puts a smile on your face, and the next stage is that you want someone in the same room to nod to and say, 'Fucking tune this, innit?' That's what I get from *Centreforce*. There are people at the other end listening, and appreciating what you're doing. People are switching on because they want to listen to good music, whereas that hasn't been the case with a lot of nightclubs over the last ten years. You've got that Essex clique that just want to be somewhere because it's the place to be, irrelevant of what music is being played. When we grew up if you went through some shitty warehouse door and there were 800 people in there, we knew we were all there for the same reason.

We grew up listening to bootlegs that weren't polished, going to clubs that weren't polished. All the biggest tracks started out as raw bootlegs, some of them out of key, but they sounded great. Back in the day a track you had on white label would get signed to a big record company, get re-sung and re-played, all in the right key, sounding all prim and proper but it would lose its appeal.

So I see *Centreforce* as the white label bootleg of the radio industry. Somewhere DJs should be presenting, not presenters DJing. The other stations are the polished versions who have something missing.

Centreforce is in its own space at the moment and puts a lot of stations and the people who run them to shame for not thinking outside the box and following their own hearts. They must be secretly thinking, fuck man, I wish we were doing that. It's so nice to play a small part in something that is still growing. I love being around all the positivity.

Matt Emulsion: I feel so lucky to have stayed active and relevant in the DJ world, it's been a crazy ride and I've met some amazing people. I've played in both New York and Chicago, which ain't bad for a kid from Harold Park. One of the maddest things I've ever seen is Marshall Jefferson, an absolute icon, on the decks at an after-party at my mate's place in Basildon. It wasn't the nicest flat in the world, but Marshall stayed and played all night. Such a lovely fella. I was lucky enough to meet him a few times when he lived in Essex. I always bored him about the Chicago Bears, because I'm a massive fan.

All we dreamed of as kids was getting a DJ booking here or there. We could never have imagined getting continuous gigs all our lives, playing in front of so many people, and still being on the radio and on such a great legal station too. It's bloody amazing.

Texsta: All of the DJs on *Centreforce* have their own signature style — hats off to every single one of them. So many of us have 30 years experience in the business, then you look at someone like Max Fernandez and his musical knowledge is phenomenal. We need the younger ones coming through, 100 per cent.

Peter P: I've known Danny Swallow from a young boy and the way he's matured to where he is now, it's fantastic. It's great to see the younger guys come on, with the knowledge that they already possess, and grow into the presenters and men they're becoming.

Ramsey: You could see how big the new *Centreforce* would become when it came back for the *Facebook* sessions you could tell the listeners were there. If the same people running the station stay involved, it will never lose authenticity, because these are pirate people.

Ed Simpson: Hopefully *Centreforce* being at Pixel helped kick the station on. Teaming up with the likes of Clockwork Orange is great synergy for us. Centreforce has grown into a powerhouse of a brand and its popularity continues to grow and appeal to all ages.

Allister Whitehead: In the three or four years leading up to *Centreforce* coming on air as a pirate, someone could make a really good track for peanuts, nobody knew what they looked like, and they could earn decent money. Like Marshall Jefferson, they could leave their job the next day and make great money without even troubling the charts.

Now producers are virtually dependant on income from live work. A lot of people who went into music back then, and went on to be so influential, may not have bothered under today's circumstances. We would have been lost without people like Marshall, because it's hard to get past their raw influence on the house scene.

Mervyn Victor: There just isn't the quality control that there was back in the day. Now someone can make a track on their laptop, mix it down themselves, which will probably make it sound worse. Back in the day, at least it had to be listened to by a record label or a distributor because it cost money to press the vinyl. So things have changed completely.

When we came back on air for the *Facebook Live* sessions and the DAB, we did what we did first time around...mixed live on air. And that was still quite unique, even in 2018,'19. It's what made us who we were back then, and what makes us what we are today. *Kiss* and *Radio 1* are still trying to copy what Andy created back then, and doing it badly.

I remember saying to my mates, 'When I'm 30, I won't be a DJ, I'll have settled down, be married with kids,' and here I am at 54, still DJing.

The older lot will keeping partying into their 60s, 70s and 80s, if they're allowed to.

Dean Lambert: Back in the day, I'd go to work on a Thursday and then wouldn't get home until Tuesday morning. My last gig was at Stringfellows on a Monday night. Without a doubt, what we had as DJs and punters back then, nobody will ever get close to experiencing again.

Roger The Doctor: I don't do *Centreforce* to further my DJ career — I do it because I love it and for the station. I feel privileged to be one of only a handful of originals with a weekly show still on *Centreforce*, along with Keith Mac, Danielle Montana, DJ One and Andy. I'm not surprised at the success of *Centreforce*, because the music over the years has been so good. *Centreforce* has taken the different styles of dance music and almost created its own genre, being an old school station with new values. At *Centreforce* events I see 15-20% of the people are aged 25 and under and that's huge.

The first time my daughter Tiger Lily saw my decks when I set them back up before I started on *Centreforce*, I'll never forget the confusion on her face. She was ten at the time and couldn't comprehend how the music went from the vinyl to the stylus, down a wire, into the mixer, then the amplifier, and from the amp to the speakers, because someone of her age just touches their phone and the music comes out. Despite technology I like the idea that kids like her might still dig back into their parents vinyl collections, like we did.

Danielle Montana: Andy taught me early on that if it's not happening for you, do it yourself. If nobody will release your tune, set up your own record label. If you're not getting that record reviewed, then start your own magazine. And I've spent most of my life doing my own thing.

When I heard *Centreforce* was coming back, I just knew it would be massive. House music has been around for five decades now, whereas rock and roll is just synonymous with the '60s and punk with the '70s. There are so many house records from the '80s or early-'90s you could play a tech or minimal house kid today, and they'd think it was a new record.

Yes, house splintered off into various sub-genres, but house has always been house. I do like other types of music if I'm chilling, but otherwise it will always be house. I was going through my vinyl the other day, and some of it was still sealed, which is wonderful, because I've got new old records to play on the radio.

Martin Cee: Let alone relaunching my radio career, *Centreforce* reignited my love of music again. I love that all our presenters are completely different and have their own take on our scene, something the *Kisses* and the *Capitals* will never be able to emulate. Yes, it's about the nostalgia, but that will only go so far. If it was a pile of old shit I would have said, 'Okay, good luck, great to hear the old name out there again,' and then I'd tune straight back to *Talksport*, because I wasn't even listening to music radio stations.

It was great to be asked to be 'ringmaster' at the Step Back To Back *Centreforce* party in November 2021, ironically at a time I'd just finished playing a similar role in a new Ray Winstone film, *Prize Fighter.* I was asked to put up some Strongman contacts for parts, and ended up getting one myself.

Sarah LP: The owner of our sponsors Thamesway Transport wanted our *Centreforce* promo artwork on the side of his lorries, and as I'm a signwriter he asked me to come and do it. Martin and I were in a club in that photo, and had loads to drink that night, so putting a photo of myself, drunk, on the side of a lorry is probably one of the weirdest and creepiest things I've ever done. One drove past my house the other day. So awkward.

Jim The Music Man: I'm a property developer now, but still love my music. I was asked via Johnny Eames to do a guest show at The Pixel Building and I went on and played some original old schools, alongside new soulful and progressive house. Bad Boy West came in and Richie Fingers played too, so it was amazing to catch up with everyone like that.

I was only a couple of years younger than the *Centreforce* management in 1989, and compared to them I was just a young ginger boy. I wasn't even into football, they were serious guys, out of my league, but I'll always have a soft spot for them, all amazing people.

Rodge The Dodge: It's amazing what the guys have done with *Centreforce*. Danny wasn't born when we first started, and now he's running the new station. I'm still based in Bethnal Green, and drive arctics out of Tilbury Docks, often tuned into *Centreforce* when I'm on the road. I also still run *Freek FM* online. It would be great to go back on 88.3 at some point and do a little guest show with Jim.

Andy Swallow: I play a lot of ska, mod and punk on my *Centreforce* shows, so I'm playing the music I used to hear at gigs — like The Chords, Secret Affair, Glory Boys, The Stranglers, The Clash, Siouxsie & The Banshees, Purple Halves, The Jolt and all the 2 Tone bands. And in that moment, I'm back on my scooter with my porkie pie hat on. I wasn't a DJ from that era, but I lived it and I'm a fan of it. I always make sure I have some of the guys from that scene on my show too.

Gary Dickel: We acted like we were the nuts because people treated us that way, almost like we were like royalty at the raves at times, to the side of stage, bottles of champagne. Amazing times that can't be beaten. I actually get very emotional talking about it. I'm not surprised at the success Andy and Danny have had because *Centreforce* today is something for the whole family to enjoy. Parents can reminisce and their kids can join in and get into the music too.

Paul Dorsett: We started something, and we didn't have a clue how big it would become. The authorities did all they could to get rid of us. Back then the smiley face was taboo, now it's an emoji on your phone.

Andy asked me in Ibiza in 2018 if I wanted to get involved in the DAB version, and I said, 'Andy, no, I'm fine, it's your thing now.' It's through Andy's perseverance that we have something we're so proud of now. Somehow he got *Centreforce* legal, and I take my hat off to him.

Johnny Eames: Andy asked if I wanted to go get involved when he relaunched *Centreforce*, but it wasn't for me. What he's done with it is unrivalled. It's just nice to be part of *Centreforce*'s history. I can't complain, I've had a great life in boxing and been have a pro coach for 23 years.

Seeker: I'd had nine major operations on my knee in the last 23 years, so have been through some tough times, but it's amazing to be part of *Centreforce* still, second time around.

I've done one-offs like a set for the *Centreforce* 32nd birthday in May 2020 and even appeared as Centre-bot, a mystery robotic DJ, on Danny and Rooney's Super Smiley Show. I haven't been able to settle on a regular slot, but it's great to know the door is still open to me. I can't fault the management, old and new.

Danny Swallow has been amazing in the way that he's taken his dad's radio station forward leaps and bounds. When I met him, I shook his hand and said, 'Well, at least I don't have to teach you how to mix.'

I can't thank Andy, Paul, Micky and everyone involved for what they did back in 1989. They put us Corporation boys on the map.

Rooney: I gotta say, I always thought it was 1988.

Laurence Bagnall: Andy and the boys have smashed it. I've been in the business ever since and much of what I do today is because of the foot-up Andy gave me in 1989, so I have a lot to thank him for. I was lucky I grew up on a slightly suspect estate in Stratford where the radio station was a lot of the time, and managed to get involved.

DJ One: I am amazed about the station's success now but I think after 32 years its fully deserved. I love still being involved in *Centreforce* — it's something in my life I am really proud of.

Steve ESP: We were so lucky to have lived through the last proper cultural explosion to give youth an identity. Looking back now, we feel a massive part of what happened, but back then we were just living our lives. I'm not surprised that *Centreforce* has come back so successfully, because if anyone could pull it off, it would be Andy Swallow. To be on *Centreforce* as both a pirate and now a legal DAB? Well, I could now walk away from radio and say I achieved everything I wanted to.

Paul Larner: I'm an air conditioning engineer who puts his tools down at 5pm, and heads home to work on music, the radio and promos, all for the love of it.

I was in the pub in Perth the other week with an ex-pat friend, originally from East Ham, and he said, 'Paul, fuck, man, you've made it, it's fucking *Centreforce*.' And he's right, I'm an old school raver. If it wasn't for *Centreforce,* I wouldn't have found Lee Valley Industrial Estate and I wouldn't have shaken Evenson Allen's hand as he went on stage that night.

These people are my fucking heroes. I'm involved with a radio station that has Chris Paul on it...and there aren't many people in our scene more influential than Chris with the platform that he gave Fabio and Grooverider through his Orange movement.

I'm just interested in playing music that gives me goosebumps...and *Centreforce* did that to me back in the day. I love to represent them in Australia. What a fucking privilege.

Jonny C: Eventually, pirate radio became stale, saturated and diluted. Every Tom, Dick and Harry had a go. *Radio 1* started playing dance music, because we were so good at it. But we've never really trusted the *BBC*. We knew the mics weren't plugged in on *Top Of The Pops*. Then Kiss became much more commercial, and your average nightclub became much more mainstream, with the birth of those awful Bas-Vegas-type clubs.

Our scene has always been so diverse. All this racist stuff, the accusations, that get thrown about today. I don't remember any of that in the scene that I grew up in. As I battled with cerebral palsy, I never felt discriminated. A lot of us came from the school of hard knocks. We were all Bash Street Kids, really, but entrepreneurial too. Layers make the man. Different combinations get different results.

My dad always said I'd never get anywhere with pirate radio. Now he couldn't be prouder. Back then, when I was putting on parties as a kid or starting my first pirate station, I didn't know what I was doing, and now we're putting on raves for thousands of people, and our radio station is global, listened to in 180 countries. It's incredible, but we must never forget our roots.

When I drive round the 406 towards Barking, London on my right hand side, Essex on the left...and Kent in front of me. There's a bit when I'm on the flyover, if I catch it at the right point of the night, that dusky time, itjust it's amazing to think we're smashing it out all over the area.

Master Pasha: We're not here to tell you what's going on in the world. We're here to take you away from it. If you're on your own, with family or friends, in a bad mood or a good one. You're going out, you're staying in...or you're feeling lonely. We're here, 24-7.

The app is essential because people expect everything at their fingertips these days. There's pretty much no device that can escape us now.

When we began to do 10,000 new listeners a day, people were like, 'Really?', but that soon became everyday numbers. Sometimes I have to step away from it, to realise just how far we've come.

Despite all that technology, I love that much of our success still comes down to what the station was about back in the day...word of mouth.

Now I'm a father too I appreciate even more the trust that my dad had in me, with the relaunch of the station. I just hope I'll be able to give my son, Beau, the same kind of opportunity when he's older.

The station is always improving. It still feels like a pirate, but it's a clean pirate now. The minute we lose that, we lose everything. We're real, and you won't get any more real than this.

Andy Swallow: There was never anyone bigger from our part of east London, whether it was being a mod, on the football terraces, as casuals, or with acid house, pirate radio or UK garage. We've been at the fore-front of so many movements and anything we did get involved in, we did to the best of our abilities. We were party people and we played our part. Carl Cox, the Oakenfolds, the Holloways, they all knew us, whether they liked what we were doing or not.

The main thing that I think makes *Centreforce* unique is our history, but at the time we didn't realise the legacy we were leaving behind. We're not saying we invented this or we did that. We're not bragging, all we're saying is, 'We were there.'

(top) An early Centreforce team meeting at the Pixel Building in 2019.

(above) Catching up in the office, including (second left) DJ One, (centre) Psychedelic Eric and (front) Kelly G.

(right) Andy Swallow and DJ One.

Wayne Soul Avengerz: How we doing Monday morning crew? You are aboard the 10:05 from east London, heading to Love Town. C'mon, guys, it's almost the weekend.

Kenny Ken: Big shout out to Grooverider for putting me on to this track back in the day, I don't forget. Shout out to Fabio too.

Mr Pasha: Big shout out to Andrea. Sorry, I think that's someone from Andover. My handwriting just gets worse. Shout out to Donna, doing the housework...and that's can't be my Donna, I've just seen her in the garden with a Pina Colada.

Danny Lines: Love my Kickers, bruv. In fact, if you're near Whalebone Lane in Dagenham, next to McDonalds, there's a shop there that still sells all the colours, all the sizes.

Rooney: I loved my Wexmans, Dan. It was that little W.

Evenson Allen (Ratpack): Andy in Crawley says, 'Ev, do you remember The Pleasure Rooms in Tottenham in the early days, when you stepped on my foot and put a big dirty print on my brand new Reebok Classics?' Mate, I don't remember that, I'm sorry, but it wouldn't be the first pair of shoes I've christened.

Peter P: That was *I Wish I Didn't Miss You Anymore* - Angie Stone and before that *Missing You* - Artful & Ridney featuring Terri Walker. The Pink Ladies have chosen those, I wish they'd make their minds up!

Sarah LP: Oh no, my sock's come off in my boot. There's nothing worse. I always have a bad day when that happens.

Bubbler: Big up the 321 number...who's that, Ted Rodgers?

Mr Pasha: Alex P is covering for my second hour today, because I need to slip off to the beach at 11, it's scorchio in Tenerife today.

ESP: I'm covering for Matt this week, he's on another modelling job. He's the new face of Millets' eight-birth tents.

Matt Emulsion: That Steve ESP is so nosey, but then he has got such a big nose. (*Later sings 'Gotta be fat and ugly' over Outrage's Tall & Handsome*).

Jeremy Healy: Into the second hour we've got more David Bowie remixes than you can shake a stick at it...but why would we shake a stick at them? That's the sort of thing Judge Jules would say...

Kenny Ken: A lot of people are asking me where they can see me play house out...I don't play house out, it's a hobby, just on the radio. I'm a drum and bass man.

Max Fernandez: Thanks for listening, if you've enjoyed the show, I've been Max Fernandez. If you haven't, I've been Dean Lambert.

Master Pasha: Ah yeah!

Max Isaac: Out to Dad...locked in...yes please, a lift would be great.

Max Fernandez: *(*track playing, *Now That We've Found Love).* How does it make you feel, Pasha, when someone messages in like that, and says, 'Now that we've found *Centreforce*, we're not going anywhere.'

Mr Pasha: It makes me feel proud, mate, that people bought into it then and still do now.

Max Fernandez: And once again, thanks for the opportunity Andy, three years ago.

Mr Pasha: No worries, Steve, you've done a great job...

Peter P: Out to the virtual Viking for pretending he's locked in again.

Dean Lambert: Jeff C, good afternooooon! Message reads, 'Deano, as down as I get, you always make me laugh. Top set.' Jeff, we are honoured to have messages like that. As much as we help you, you help us. It's a two-way thing. We're in this together. We love what we do, and we love you lot listening...

SHOUT TO THE TOP

Sam Supplier: I love the *Centreforce*, 'Oi, let's fucking have it, big up my missus' old school vibe, and I think listening to all those classic house tracks all day gives the listeners a constant feeling of euphoria.

Kiss or *1Xtra* do a few shout-outs but not to extent that *Centreforce* do, and that's what has turned *Centreforce* into the family it is. I've experienced the shout-out mentality on pirates since I was 14 years old. Listeners love that status and going to the parties meeting up with the people behind the names.

Our listeners have never forgotten that core pirate essence and it's played a huge part in *Centreforce*'s resurgence.

Jonny C: The station has helped so many people, and our *Facebook* is alive with it. I could be steaming smoke after a really stressful day, and then the next minute I get a message from someone and my heart melts. I turn the app on, and it's usually a tune I love, then I hear a name that I recognise asking for a shout-out, and I instantly feel part of the community.

I have to tell the DJs off for using the shout-outs as an excuse for forgetting to do something in their show. I say to them, 'But the messages are always busy...'

We were offered the same messaging platform *The X Factor* had, to keep up with our demand. That shows just how far we've come, from one pager to a national prime-time TV voting system.

Master Pasha: The shout-outs are the best thing about the station. Some of the messages we get, well, we wouldn't be human if they didn't touch us. People saying that the station saved their life. Or they were in a really dark place, but *Centreforce* helped them feel like they were connected to something.

It's a cliche, but if the station helped or saved just one person, that's an amazing thing. You can't put a price on that.

I am so thankful to each and every listener, from the bottom of my heart. I could have the best DJs in the world, but without the listeners, the station is nothing. The listeners have helped me get over a lot of hurdles in my life, and I'm so grateful to them.

Wayne Soul Avengerz: The Listeners tune in to get away from all the bad things that are happening in the world, so the last thing they want is for us to be talking about the news or politics. They want to escape, so hopefully we can take them back to a time when we were all kissing and cuddling each other and we had our hands in the air.

Danny Lines: Ours is a very busy show and we have a huge amount of shout-outs to get through. *Centreforce* is pure interaction, but that's what the listeners all over the world want. It's all about their memories.

Bubbler: I listen to the station all the time and you can hear the sheer love from the listeners, day-in, day-out. It really is one big family and I have nothing but love for those people too.

Martin Cee: The names are crazy, like CB handles back in the day. The Handsome Cabbie is quite handsome actually.

Peter Faires: Loyal fans are the cornerstone of so many successful things, be it a pop band, a TV series or a football team. I feel like a diehard *Centreforc*e fan would be in the trenches with me.

Sarah LP: When they start sending shouts in for each other, I draw the line, especially if they've just had their own one read out. Other listeners come in waves. You'll hear from one person loads and then not for a while, and you wonder what happened to them and if they're okay? Maybe they changed their jobs, or life just got in the way? Then invariably they pop up again and it's lovely when that happens.

& AND A BIG SHOUT OUT TO...

CENTREFORCE

Aaron & Tara, Abraham U5s, Adrian Dante, Aggieman Cornwall, Alan Regetti, Alex Artios, Alex Cook, Alfie Suff In Colchester, Alison Verrent, Amanda & Ralph, Ray Kitcher, Amanda In Herts, Amy Alice, Andrew Barber, Andrew, Ange In Belvedere, Angela Brown, Annie Demnal, Annie In Hackney, Ant Beds Turntable, Ant Dec Doctor, Antonio C, Antony Jones, Arbs In Perth, Arron & Tara, Asbo, Ashley, Bacardi Shirl From Hornchurch, Badger, Bald Badger, Beat Master P, Bernie Martin, Bexleyheath Old School Ravers, Big Al, Big Dave, Bionic Man, Bob Mann, Bob The Gooner, Boring Brian, Brendan Blatcher, Brian Hammer Taylor, Brogan Corderoy, Brosenay, Buckaroo Crew (Karen & Lee), Burgess Hill Gaffer, Calculator Kid, Camelot Crew, Camilla Ulysses, Captain Cook, Caroline Moss, Caroline & Tony From Dartford, Caroline From Galway, Casey In Rochford, Cat Rogers, Catherine & The Ladies From West London, Catherine Mulvihill, Chapman Kay, Chelsea Chuckles, Cheryl From Maidstone, Chorton & The Wheelwrongs, Chris Hirts In Austria, Chris The Truck Driver, Clare Cook, Claire Rowlings, Concrete Ken, Core Ladies, Count Down Clare, Crazyskates, Curly, Damian 'Stan' Staunton, Dancing Jaffa, Dangermouse & Miss Lowe, Daniel Holiday, Dark Side Crew, Darren Allix, Darren Scales, Darren Steeplejack, Darren Sullivan, Darren Willard, Dave In Twickenham, Dave Manning, Dave The Cat, Dave The Rave, Dave Tull, Dave Woolvan, Dave, Katrina & The Billericay Nut Nuts, David & Samantha From West Kingsdown, David Tyler, Dazbo, Dazzer, Deano New Zealand, Deb Dicko, Debra Cadet-Wallace, Delivery Dan, Diddy Dave, Dirty Dino, Disco Dan, Dmax, Doberman Crew, Dollis Hill Dom, Don Donz & Fayzi, Donna Collins, Donna Green, Donna Hume, Dot & Eric, Dougie From Kilburn, Dr WHU, Dubai Donna, Dundee Debbie, Eastbourne Dawn, Elevate Tom, Emma Parr, Emma Phillips, Eternal Nightshirt Ravers, Fat Frank, Fiorini, Flo, Fredrica Martin, Galactic G, Gary New Zealand, Gav In Perth, Gavin Parker, Gel, George Hinds, Gibbo, Gina G, Gingercrew, Giraffe, Giraffe Neck, Giulio, Godstone Crew, Graham & Sue Gennings, The Grays Athletic Girls, Gruffalo, Guilio, Oli & Kat, Handsome Cabbie, Hakan, Harvey G, Helen Fernandez, Hemel J, Honey Monster, Hot House Honey, Huggie Bear, Ian Cabel, Ian O, Ian Tucker, Ingrid, Jack Batemen, Jackie & Dave In Tunisia, James From Maidstone, Jane Vanessa, Jason Lodge, Jay Kay, Jay The Vicar, Jella, Jeff The Boxer, Jennifer J, Jennifer Jerman & The Swanley Crew, Jessica Bell, Jim & Mavis Turner, Jimmy Vivas, JJ, Jo Coppin, Jo In Farnham, Jo Jo The Dancing Queen, Jo Walker, Joanne Bryan, Joanne Dean, Joanne Savage, Joey D, John Cook, John Field, John In Sidcup, John Taylor, Jon Yeams, Johnny Mac, Jonny Cain, Juicy Lucy, Jules, Julia From Warrington, Karen KD (Perth Australia), Karl Whiting, Kate Farrelly, Kay Hayes, Keiftboy, Kelly Gannon, Kenny & Chezza, Kerri R, Kevin Suff, Kezza & Daz, Kim Brown, Kimberly, Kimmy B & Wendy Woo, King Concrete Crew, Kirsty Paige, Kir, Ladies Of West London, Lady Chazza, Brendan & The Brighton Massive, Lane Dog Woofer, Larna B, Leigh In Southend, Leigh Whitby, Lewisham Nicos, Liam Powell, Leo, Lincoln Biggs, Lisa Bishop, Lisa C & The Manchester Crew, Lisa Downunder, Lisa Lopez, Lisa Rolands, Lisa Unique, Little Frank, Little Legs, Liz Cook, Lizzy Green, Lottie Cook, LPC, Lucky Heather, Luis Fernandez, Lynn Jackson,

HOUSE MUSIC ALL NIGHT LONG

Lynne Near Reading, Mad Mark, Mark Dunne, Mark Harper, Marky Boi, Marky Mark, Marky P, Martin & Virginia Offiah, Martin Sturges, Master Shoesy, Matt In Finland, Matty B, Matty P, Mauro & Chrissy Tondina, MC Jen Jen, Mediacoms Chris, Mexican Tim, Mexican Wrestlers, Michael, MC Morran, Michael Myers, Michelle Von Blonk, Michelle & Rick, Micky G, Mickey Moore (& The Cockney Hammers Crew), Micky Mushrooms, Micky Pink Shorts, Mike (Perth Australia), Miles & Jackie, Millwall Mark, Missey Bex, Mo & Jel The Crazy Girls, Momo, Monobrow Bob, Mr Beaver, Mr Candy, Mr DMC, Mr Reid, Mr Shoesy, Nat The Painter, Natalie Steff, Natsy Down The Dave, Neil Rice, Neil Sky, Nicky In Billericay, Nicky Mac, Nicky, Nicole Hayes, Nicole Peters, Nigel & Lorraine Tipping, Nina, Nina The Winner, Nnenna, Nurse Sarah, Ollie Fernandez, Olly Suff, One Metre Peter, Pam Chaney, Passon Fruit, Paul Barret, Paul Boakes, Paul Gardner, Paul Goodey, Paul Harlow, Paul Laws, Paul The Tool, Paula & Paul Oakley, Paul Parker, PC Taylor, Pegleg & Chumper, Penge Eddie, Percy Grower, Perry From Basildon, Persian Rug Social Club, Peter & Tracy Aveling, Peter Skipsey, Phil Higgins, Pillow Licker, Pink Ladies, Pipin, Pompey Daz, Princess Zoe, Psychadelic Eric, QPR Rodders, Rachel Devan, Rachel Melissa, Rachel Suff, Randy Candy, Ray Lock, Ray Parlour, Rebecca Haggerty, Red Delicious, Rhino, Rice & Peace, Ricky Mutley, Rico, Rob 'Jack' Daniels, Rob B, Rob Staples, Rob The Glazier, Robbie The Geordie, Rosco Ross Davis, S Class Les, Sam Beckett, Sam From Australia, Sarah Casey, Sarah Cook, Sarah Dark, Sarah Hunt, Sarah Lousie, Security Paul, SG Plastering, Shaun In Hornchurch, Shaun In Shorts, Shaz Taylor, Shoesy, Silver Surfer, Simon Cook, Skully, Smallsy Twins, Somerset Sweetheart, Sophie Camel Hairy, Southern Hemisphere Crew, Sparky Russ, Spider, Stacey B, Steeplejack, Stephen Holmes & Ange, Steve Davidson, Steve Eyebrows, Steve Hewit, Steve Liverpool, Steve-O, Stevie G, Stick The Green Keeper, Stuart Julie Saward, Sue In E16, Sue In Hornchurch, Suzie Tutt, Suziewoo Davey, Suzy D, Swanley Boys, Tech Soul Crew, Tel Bunter, Teresa Ruel, Terry & Sue In Hong Kong, Terry, Thailand, The Accountant, The Aldridge, The Badger, The Boxmoor Dom, The Bromley Sparky, The Dirty Groundworkers, The Enclosure Crew, The Fat Ferret, The Gluten Free Sausage Crew, The Ladies Of West London, The Maltese Monkey, The Old Bexley Ravers, The Orange Ladies, The Pie Man, The Scouse Bear, The Tall One, The Viking (& The Vikingette), Timmy A, Tina Isaac, Tinkerbell, Tony Barker, Tony Cee, Tony Hayes (RIP), Tony In Spain, Tony Jey & His *Centreforce* Cassettes, Tottenham Tone, Tracey Woolven, Tracy Smith, Trev Aka Beaver, Triple F Kev, Trisha (Crisp Street Market) Turkish Delight, Two Stroke Mike, Tylene Foster, Tyrone Hayward, Uncle Cole, Vic Tavern Crew, Vinnie The Spread, Vinyl Man Stan, Wallace & His Gromits, Warren, Effeny, Wedgy, Wendy Gorman, Wendy Woo, West Ham Dave, West Ham Ned, West Ham Rudy, West London Massive, Westy, Will Down South, William Wilson, Windjammer Mike, Zozo Hanks.

● The *Centreforce* DJs interviewed in this book were asked to name the listeners who sent the most shout-outs during their shows to help compile this list.

ACKNOWLEDGMENTS

Andy Swallow would like to thank...

My family: Mum, Donna, Mandy, Danny, Amelia, Amber, Beau, Kayleigh and Conor, plus all my aunts, uncles and cousins.

The original *Centreforce* owners and management. Without them, this would never have happened. Danny Harrison, John Eames, Paul Dorset, Micky Carr, Jason Mood, Gary D and Keith Mac, plus all the original *Centreforce* DJs, the Echoes crew and everyone who helped us back in the day, including Matthew Thomas, Chris Harris, Gus and Jon O 'Brien. Too many to mention here, but you know who you are.

Also: Jonny C and Jo, Danny Turner, Deanne, Peter Faires, Ed Simpson, Darren Clack, Kern, Jungle Jim, Laura, Mrs D, Gary the postman, Sharon Eames and all the girls from those days. Janine, Sharon, Woody, Trudy, TC, Micky Morgan, Big Nat, Micky Cornwall, Dave Cornwall (RIP), Nancy Acid, Micky Woodward, Vic Dark, Dave Hunt, Dave Davies and Moose. All my football firm, old and young, for keeping our feet firmly on the ground.

And a special thank you to all the amazing *Centreforce* DJs and all the background staff, past and present, who worked and work tirelessly, just for the love of the music. I've said it, so many times, but without any of you, there would be no *Centreforce.*

Finally, Matt Trollope for taking this task on, and giving everyone an insight into *Centreforce*. Thank you.

Matt Trollope would like to thank...

Firstly, Danny Swallow, for being so receptive when I first approached him at the start of 2020 about the idea for this book, and all his help since.

To all the interviewees for their time and cooperation.

Andy Swallow for his huge support, and the sterling work in rallying the original Centreforce troops for interviews...and for the contradicting flyers. Lol.

A big shout-out to everybody at the *Centreforce* office/studio, who have made me feel so welcome during the whole process, and for all the banter, in particular Max Fernandez, Peter P, Roger The Doctor, Alex P, Max Isaac and Dean Lambert.

A special thank you to Darren Clack for always pushing things forward.

Many thanks to Ed Simpson and Peter Faires for all their backing.

To Jonny C for all his time and help, and Keith Mac for his insight too.

Genna Gibson for the fine investigative work, for all her support throughout and the late-night checks. Obi-Wan for keeping guard and being my trusty steed.

Jean and D Trollope for the Zooms and all their help, and Meghan Christie for her diligence.

A special thank you to Neil Shand for all his design work, and for being a total

A special thank you to Neil Shand for all his design work, and for being a total pleasure to deal with. Hamish Maclean for the pukka adverts and Graham Vickers for those essential back-end bits and hectic-ness. Dave PhatMedia...you're a star!

Jaqi Loye-Brown for her troubleshooting and her ears...and Newman for his energy and all the licks...

Tony Nicholls for hooking me up with Richard Goldman, and to Richard for the Kevin Saunderson intro. Jon O'Brien for the photos, flyers and all his input.

Mete for his pub quiz special on the book and all his help.

Kelly Isaacs at Dance Crazy Management. Dave and Angelo at Arcade Talent. Estelle Brown for all her help, and to William Frederick Pate for coming on board.

Andrew Barber and Alan Thomas at Sharpscape Photography for their assistance and efficiency. Ian and Alex Vaughan for all their backing, and Ian Cordingley for his constant support.

And finally, a huge thank you to Alistair Morgan, Helena Duncan and everyone at Bell & Bain for all their help and patience.

Everyone at *Centreforce* would like to thank our amazing sponsors and advertisers, including...

King Concrete, ITS, The Prince Albert, Bexleyheath, Britannia K9 Security, Mr Scalp, UK Signs, ACS Aggregates, JCB Skips, All Kinds Of Blinds, Thamesway Transport, City Flooring, Target Zero Training, Jenflow, Deploy UK, MultiPrint Driveways, Faces nightclub, Green Room, Maidstone, The Placement Group, Joyce Bar and Sugareef Terrace & Club, Tenerife, The Rising Sun, Hornchurch and Serious Nugs.

A special thanks to GSL Hire for the set up of our outdoor broadcasts and decking out our green room, and to Ian and Garry at UK Signs for the signage and panel work in the *Centreforce* foyer and studio.

ALSO FROM MT.INK

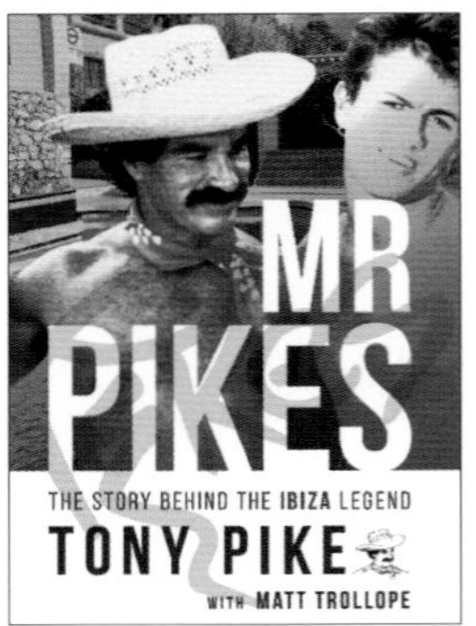

Mr Pikes: The Story Behind The Ibiza Legend — Tony Pike with Matt Trollope The playboy who built himself a playground reveals all in his hard-hitting memoir. The iconic hotelier reflects on a life of hedonism and the globe-trotting backstory that influenced his creation of pioneering Balearic boho bolthole, Pikes. Tony talks candidly about his relationships with hotel guests and friends including George Michael, Freddie Mercury, Julio Iglesias, lover Grace Jones and many more...and also goes exclusively behind the scenes at the Club Tropicana video shoot.

DJ Wags: Housewives of House — Jaqi Loye-Brown (Portobello Novella Series 2) Some yummy mummies are not like the others. What lurks behind the domestic bliss of middle-aged party parents? Piper Blair and Dande Lyon's friendship comes to a head when their loyalties, love and lifestyle are tested under the spot-light of reality TV. Middle-aged, middle class and functioning...just! From Kensal Rise, Queens Park and Westbourne Grove to Ibiza and back again. From disco to discord all the way.

The Life & Lines Of Brandon Block by Matt Trollope Brandon Block strips back his dramatic life as we chart the meteoric rise of a cocky schoolboy from Wembley who became an Ibiza legend along the way. A symbol for an acid house generation of excess, Brandon headlined a clubland era that changed the lives of millions. His spiralling drug habit peaked at an amazing ounce of cocaine a day but somehow he survived to tell the tale. This edition Includes extra chapters published in 2017 as Brandon entered the Celebrity Big Brother house.

Sex $ells — Zaskia Lyndon Life will never be the same again for a group of north London twenty-somethings when renegade housemate Stassy 'Anastasia' Thomas submits a sex survey to a tabloid newspaper in this romp-com set in the mid-Noughties. 'Stage husband' Preston Price feels the full force of Stassy's mischievous meddling and, as her life spirals out of control, she realises that while the rules change, the game remains the same...Sex Sells.

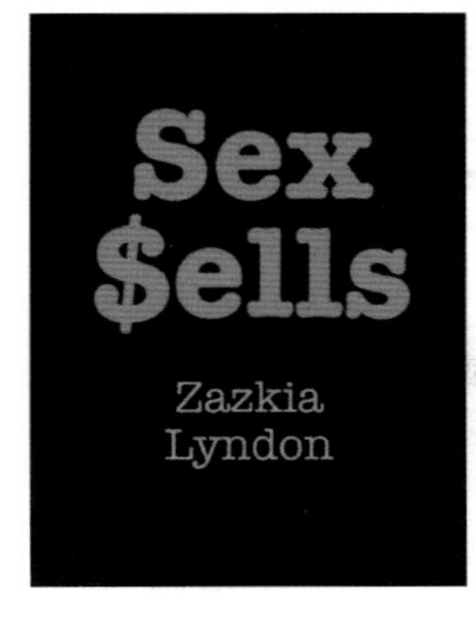

CENTREFORCE 883 LINE-UP 07.12.21

ADE WILLCOX, ALEX LITTLE, ALEX P, ALLISTER WHITEHEAD, ANDY MANSTON, ANTONY P, ASTON, BOYS AT WORK (MASTER PASHA & MAX FERNANDEZ), BUBBLER, CARLY DENHAM, CHRIS DOULOU, CHRIS PAUL, CHRIS PHILLIPS, DANIELLE MONTANA, DANNY CLOCKWORK, DARRELL PRIVETT, DEAN LAMBERT, DJ FRECKLES, DJ FUNKY M, DJ ONE, DJ STERLING, DJ TRE, DJ WOODY, DOLLY ROCKERS, ELYSIA, ESP, FITZY, GINGER ALLIANCE (MARTIN CEE & SARAH LP), GROOVE ALLIANCE, JACK BASS, JAMIE F, JEREMY HEALY, JOE BONNER, JONATHAN ULYSSES, JONNY C, JOSH WATTS, KEITH MAC, KENNY KEN, LENNY FONTANA, LINK LDN, LISA NASH, MATT EMULSION, MAX ISAAC, METE, MICKEY STAR LEWIS, MICKY H, MICKY TURRELL, MR PASHA, NICKY WOODS, NIKI DIMENSIONS, PAUL LARNER, PETER P, PHILO, PINEAPPLE DISCO CLUB (MASTER MAGRI), RAMSEY, RATPACK, RICHIE M, RICKY COOPER, ROGER THE DOCTOR, ROONEY & DANNY LINES, RYAN WILMOTT, SAM SUPPLIER, SCOTT RHYDER, SECRET AGENDA (BECKETT & CASEY), SEEKER, SENSE DA FORCE, SLIPMATT, SONNY KANE, SOUL MASTER T, STEVE KITE, TENACIOUS, TEXSTA, TONY NICHOLLS, TONY PERRY, WATTSIE, WAYNE SOUL AVENGERZ